CASES IN
MANAGEMENT
ACCOUNTING

CASES IN MANAGEMENT ACCOUNTING

RANDOLPH KUDAR

University of Western Ontario

JEFFREY KANTOR

University of Windsor

RICHARD MIMICK

University of Victoria

PRENTICE HALL CANADA INC.

Scarborough, Ontario

Canadian Cataloguing in Publication Data

Kudar, Randolph Parris, 1944 –   .
          Cases in management accounting

ISBN 0-13-320573-8

1. Managerial accounting – Case studies.
2. Cost accounting – Case studies. 3. Cost control –
Case studies. I. Mimick, Richard, 1943 –   .
II. Kantor, Jeffrey, 1951 –   . III. Title.

HF5657.4.K83 1995   658.15'11   C94-931727-6

Prentice-Hall, Inc., Englewood Cliffs, New Jersey
Prentice-Hall International (UK) Limited, London
Prentice-Hall of Australia, Pty. Limited, Sydney
Prentice-Hall Hispanoamericana, S.A., Mexico City
Prentice-Hall of India Private Limited, New Delhi
Prentice-Hall of Japan, Inc., Tokyo
Simon & Schuster Asia Private Limited, Singapore
Editora Prentice-Hall do Brasil, Ltda., Rio de Janeiro

ISBN 0-13-320573-8

Acquisitions Editor: Patrick Ferrier
Production Editor: Kelly Dickson
Copy Editor: Lynne Missen
Production Coordinator: Anita Boyle
Page Layout: Jaytype Inc.
Cover Design: Olena Serbyn

1 2 3 4 5 RRD 99 98 97 96 95

Printed and bound in the USA.

Every reasonable effort has been made to obtain permissions for all articles and data used
in this edition. If errors or omissions have occurred, they will be corrected in future edi-
tions provided written notification has been received by the publisher.

All cases in the book were prepared as a basis for class discussion rather than to illustrate
either effective or ineffective handling of an administrative situation.

*Funded by the Society of Management Accountants of Canada.

To Kathy, Greg, Tyler, and Bradley
Randy Kudar

To Jen, Jonathan, Daniel, and Tamara
Jeffrey Kantor

To Claudia, Kristin, Sara, and Darryl
Richard Mimick

Table of Contents

Preface

Management accounting is an essential input to any management decision that is made within a firm. Management accounting provides management with an analysis of the relevant economic consequences of any decisions management might make. It is important to emphasize that the management accounting input does not dictate or dominate the decision-making process. Management accounting information must be blended with other information and qualitative factors to arrive at a comprehensive analysis to the decision.

Since the range of management decisions in any firm is very wide, the nature of the management accounting information and the format of the data must be equally varied. The design of the information must fit the nature of the decision or problem to which it is being applied. The accounting information must be transformed and classified into the form that is most relevant and suitable to the needs of the decision maker.

In order to do the job properly, the management accountant must understand the nature of the decision being addressed, and then develop the accounting information that will be most relevant to that decision. The ability to define the problems correctly takes practice. The skill to transform the accounting data into useful information for the problem requires management accounting knowledge. This is the basis for this casebook.

Cases in Management Accounting is intended to supplement the concepts and techniques taught in both the first and second level management accounting courses. The cases are arranged into sections corresponding to the topics and concepts presented in most management accounting textbooks. There is a wide array of cases in each section, covering a range of industries, complexities, functions, and issues. These may be used in a variety of ways that suit the instructor and the class of students. They may be used as real-life examples of available accounting information and management problems or as summary vehicles to close out a topic in a course. They may also be used as the fundamental class vehicle to practice the application of management accounting concepts and techniques.

Cases offer a unique opportunity for students to develop the ability to define problems and to apply management accounting knowledge to a situation. Unlike conventional problems, cases provide a setting that requires students to interpret what is relevant and not relevant to the situation. Cases also integrate both the quantitative analysis with qualitative issues that must be examined as part of the relevant information to the problem. In many instances the information is not totally provided or not provided in the proper form. Students must transform the accounting data into a form that is suitable to the situation. Finally, cases can help students develop an internal check on the diagnostic step. If the problem is not defined properly, then the relevant analysis may not be feasible because the necessary accounting data will not be present in the case. However, if the problem has been defined correctly, then the data to undertake the appropriate analysis will be present. All the cases have been tested in classes at both undergraduate and graduate level.

In each section, the cases are arranged from the most simple to the more complex. In most instances, the cases involve real companies and real situations. Often the situation reflected in the case has been disguised to allow release of the case. However, the fundamentals of the issues and the information are similar to what was available at the time that the problem was being addressed. Only the final section of cases, dealing with emerging issues, may not sit in parallel with topics and concepts presented in management accounting textbooks. These cases give students the opportunity to consider how to apply the management accounting concepts that have been taught to situations where there is not prescribed solution.

Frequently, the cases describe the situations from the perspective of the functional manager, as opposed to the accountant. We feel that it is very important that students develop the sense of addressing problems from the perspective of the customer or user of the accounting information. In this way, students can begin to understand how the accounting information must be communicated to the user so that the user will comprehend and be able to interpret the information properly. As well, the perspective of the user should require students to broaden their perspectives to consider the role of the management accounting information in the context of other information, other qualitative factors, and other functional constraints.

It is our hope that the use of cases such as these can become an integral part of the management accounting course for students and allow both future management accountants, and future functional managers, to appreciate the symbiotic relationship that exists between them. The casebook can also be used in conjunction with with a companion book, *Readings in Management Accounting*, compiled by the same authors.

An Instructor's Manual provides extensive teaching notes on each case.

The authors owe a great deal of gratitude to the Society of Management Accountants of Ontario (SMAO). It was through their generous support that many of the cases were written. The continual support of the SMAO to developing management accounting education in Ontario ensures that materials like this will continue to be available to students in the future. We would also like to thank the case writers and authors who are acknowledged in the book. Thanks also to the reviewers of this book: Anthony P. Dimnik, McGill University; Krista Harris, Saint Mary's University; Alan J. Richardson, Queen's University; Grant Russell, University of Waterloo.

We also thank the managers and the companies that gave most generously of their time to allow us to gather information, understand the nature of the issues, and provide us with their perspectives. Their only reward is the contribution that the case may make to the learning of a future management accountant or manager.

Randolph Kudar
Jeffrey Kantor
Richard Mimick

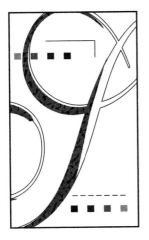

PART **A**

RELEVANT COST
ANALYSIS

PATTI'S PATIO

Lynda E. Whyte and John F. Graham

Patti's Patio was a manufacturer of patio stones and interlocking brick. A variety of styled, coloured, and shaped stones were produced and sold to local wholesalers of landscape materials. Patti had started the business five years ago with a few unique mould designs and manufactured a stronger, more durable stone than her competitors. Patti's Patio was now the largest stone and brick manufacturer in the local area.

The process for patio stone production was almost fully automated. Ingredients of sand, limestone, water, colour, and other binding chemicals were combined in specified proportions in a large mixer. After mixing, the liquid substance was poured into moulds and baked in a large kiln. After cooling, the stone was separated from the mould and the stone was stored outside until shipped. Two workers were employed to add the ingredients, remove the finished stones from the molds, and clean and operate the machines.

During the previous six months, Patti had revised the production process in hopes of reducing production costs. She was anxious to see the results of the change on the firm's financial performance but Patti's accountant drew up the firm's financial statements at the end of each fiscal year only. Six months had elapsed since the last statement date, December 31, 1988, and since the new production process had been implemented. Patti wanted the six-month financial information right away and after pulling out a list of company information (Exhibit 1), began calculating the cost of the stones produced and sold to date (Exhibits 2 and 3). Soon into the project, Patti was shocked to see a gross loss for the six-month period ended. Although she was a good engineer, Patti realized her limitations as an accountant and she knew she would need help to get an objective and accurate measure of the manufacturing financial information to date.

REQUIRED:

You have been asked by Patti to determine the following amounts for the six-month period ending June 30, 1989.

a)   Cost of raw materials used

b)   Cost of work-in-process

c)   Work-in-process inventory, June 30, 1989

d)   Cost of goods available for sale

Exhibit 1

COMPANY INFORMATION

1. Inventory balances indicated on the fiscal 1988 Balance Sheet were as follows:
Raw Materials	$15,450
Work-in-Process	2,800
Finished Goods	540

2. All raw materials were purchased on credit and paid for 10 days after billing, well within the discount period offered. The sand shipment of June 30 had been received but not yet paid for and amounted to $6,111 including the discount, $6,300 without.

3. Patti's Patio operated one truck in order to deliver finished stones and to pick up raw materials. The truck's time and use was divided evenly between the two functions.

4. Salaries included payment to one supervisor and two factory workers. The supervisor received a monthly salary and each of the workers had received $300 per week for the past 25 weeks. One worker spent one-quarter of his time delivering the finished stones to local distributors. No salaries were owing as of June 30, 1989, or as of December 31, 1988.

5. The Patti's Patio building housed the administration offices and production facilities. Approximately 25% and 75% of the floor space was taken up by each of these areas respectively.

6. Utilities for the firm were a major expense due to the washing and baking functions of production; therefore, Patti estimated that only 10% of the total cost was needed for the office area. The $8,650 indicated in Patti's calculations included $250 used to pay utilities charges owing as of December 31, 1988. No utilities charges were owing as of June 30, 1989. The $1,000 of fire insurance was purchased January 2 to provide a full year's coverage on the building.

7. Equipment maintenance included $5,000 interest paid on the promissory notes secured to help purchase $120,000 worth of new equipment on January 2, 1989.

8. Depreciation was calculated at year-end for all assets but Patti knew it was a non-cash item and was unsure whether to include this in the six-month production cost estimate.
   Her projected annual asset depreciation calculations for fiscal 1989 were:

Truck	$ 1,200
Production Equipment	45,900
Office Equipment	1,850

9. Supplies included $200 worth of accounting software for use in keeping Patti's Patio books up-to-date and $200 worth of production supplies.

10. A physical count on June 30, 1989, revealed inventory levels for raw materials to be $10,600 and finished goods to be $2,100. Patti had calculated work-in-process inventory to be $1,975 based on an estimate of $1,750 worth of raw materials; and $225 worth of direct labour included in these unfinished goods. The fiscal 1988 statements indicated machine hours were used as a proxy for determining partial factory overhead. The machine hours accumulated for production to date were 2,025, of which approximately 76 were used in manufacturing the unfinished inventory on hand.

Exhibit 2

PATTI'S CALCULATIONS OF COST OF GOODS PRODUCED
For the six months ending June 30, 1989

Raw materials purchased & paid for	$59,000
Discounts taken on raw materials paid to date	(1,700)
Truck operations	800
Salaries	27,000
Building rent	4,000
Building fire insurance	1,000
Utilities	8,650
New equipment purchases	120,000
Equipment maintenance	5,750
Supplies	400
Total cost of goods produced	$224,830

Exhibit 3

PARTIAL INCOME STATEMENT
For the six months ending June 30, 1989

Sales	$148,870
Cost of goods sold*	$218,085
Six-month gross profit (loss)	$(69,215)

*97% of the goods produced to date had been sold.

KELLERS' FREEHOUSE (A)

Peter A. Goldthorpe, Stephen R. Jakob, and Richard Mimick

In June 1989, Robert and Alex Keller decided to examine the prospect of opening a brew pub. The brothers had always dreamed of being entrepreneurs, but due to financial constraints had given the idea little thought. However, a recent inheritance had changed this situation and prompted them to pursue their dream. Since Robert and Alex had a particular interest in the restaurant industry, it was decided to formally investigate the establishment of a brew pub.

HISTORY OF THE BREW PUB

The production of beer has a rich history dating back to the time of the early Egyptians. Historians believe that it was discovered accidentally when wet barley was left unrefrigerated and subsequently fermented. In Canada, beer holds the highest rate of consumption among alcoholic beverages.

Prior to early 1986, beer production in Ontario had been handled almost exclusively by the "Big Three" — John Labatt Ltd., Molson's, and Carling O'Keefe. In-house brewing had been illegal since prohibition. However, efforts by the provincial government to ease restrictions governing breweries had resulted in the re-introduction of micro-breweries and brew pubs in Ontario. A brew pub is essentially a pub or restaurant which serves specialty beers brewed on the premises. Most brew pubs offer between one and five different house brews including lagers, ales, bitters, and stouts. Since 1986, a number of brew pubs have operated successfully in Southern Ontario.

THE KELLERS

Robert and Alex Keller lived and worked in a large city in Southern Ontario. Robert, the older of the two brothers, had been employed for three years in the soft drink business and Alex had two years' experience as a bookkeeper for a number of small retail outlets. Two months earlier the brothers inherited $180,000 from their grandmother and decided to pursue their dream of starting a business. Combining their inheritance with the money they had managed to save from working, they had almost $200,000 to invest. Robert and Alex knew that before they actually quit their jobs they would have to assess the feasibility of the proposed venture.

OBJECTIVES

To begin their feasibility study, Robert and Alex set objectives for the brew pub venture. They were as follows:

1) Generate enough profit in three years to compensate them with drawings comparable to their current salaries. (Robert — $29,000 and Alex — $25,000).

2) Provide a return comparable to similar risk investments.

3) Break even within the first two years.

Robert and Alex felt that establishing these objectives was a good starting point but were unsure what other information they would require to evaluate the venture's feasibility. They were also uncertain how and where to obtain this information. Anxious to proceed, the brothers met to plan their next step.

REQUIRED:

In groups of four to six:

1) Evaluate the objectives set by Robert and Alex. Why are explicit objectives important in a feasibility study?

2) Generate a list of information required to assess the feasibility of a brew pub. Where can this information be obtained?

KELLERS' FREEHOUSE (B)

Peter A. Goldthorpe, Stephen R. Jakob, and Richard Mimick

After setting the initial objectives for the venture and performing some preliminary groundwork, Robert and Alex Keller thought it would be a good idea to become more familiar with the costs involved in operating a brew pub. Combining Robert's experience with distributors and information gathered from various business contacts and potential suppliers, the brothers were able to estimate a number of start-up and operating costs.

INITIAL COSTS

In order to keep capital requirements to a minimum, the brothers decided to lease rather than purchase a property. Discussions with a real estate company indicated that a suitable location was available at an annual rental fee of $54,000. Extensive renovations would be necessary to prepare the facility for the production of beer and create the appropriate atmosphere. A building contractor estimated that $75,000 would be required. Finally, the brothers budgeted $5,000 of a $10,000 total promotion budget for an initial advertising campaign, $800 for start-up legal fees, $700 for annual licensing and miscellaneous expenses, and $20,000 for start-up inventory.

RESTAURANT

After hearing of the proposed brew pub, Alex's friend Judy Martin approached the brothers. Judy had become dissatisfied with her current job and suggested that the brothers consider letting her manage the kitchen operations. Her duties would include inventory control, kitchen supervision, and staff management. Robert and Alex were receptive to the idea since it would allow them more time to concentrate on the brewing operation, promotion, and financial planning. They agreed that a salary of $25,000 per year with a bonus of 10% of net profit was equitable compensation. The brothers also planned to draw initial salaries of at least $25,000 each.

An equipment dealer indicated that kitchen fixtures and utensils would cost $25,000.[1] Wages for waiters/waitresses and other kitchen and restaurant staff, according to industry averages, were about 18% of total sales. A 2% cushion for theft, credit card charges, etc. was also typical for the industry. In addition, a margin of 60% was expected on food sales. Other restaurant costs are outlined in Exhibit 1.

BREWING OPERATIONS

Establishing an in-house brewery required a substantial investment. Fulstein Brewing Systems indicated that the cost of a suitable system, having a capacity of 40,000 litres/year, would be $115,000 including freight, installation, and training.[1] In addition, an experienced brewmaster requiring an annual salary of $30,000 was necessary to monitor the quality and consistency of the beer. Other direct costs of brewing in-house are shown in Exhibit 1.

BEVERAGE SALES

Beer, wine, and liquor prices were strictly regulated by the Liquor Control Board of Ontario. As a result, consumer prices were similar across the restaurant industry. Research indicated that a price of $2.00 to $2.50 was typical for a 341 mL glass of house-brew. Typical margins for these and other beverages are outlined in Exhibit 2.

---

[1] Depreciation was to be calculated using the straight line method as follows:
Kitchen equipment – 10 years
Brewing equipment – 10 years
Renovations   – 5 years
Intangibles were to be amortized straight line over 5 years.

FINAL THOUGHTS

Robert and Alex were pleased with their initial research but were unsure how to use the information to evaluate the riskiness of the venture. Also, they wondered if they needed any additional information and, if so, where it might be obtained.

REQUIRED:

1. Analyze the behaviour of costs in this venture (i.e., fixed, variable, etc.).
2. What additional information would you like to have in order to evaluate the riskiness of the venture?

Exhibit 1

ANNUAL RESTAURANT COSTS

Chef	$30,000
Utilities	4,200
Insurance	10,000
Telephone	2,000
Property/Business Tax	9,000
Supplies	1,000
Miscellaneous	6,000
(Including Annual Licensing)	
	$62,200

BREWING COSTS

Item	$/hL
Malt Extract	$30.55
Adjunct	1.79
Hops	1.80
Yeast	0.74
Finings	1.31
Sterilants	0.12
Yeast Nutrient	0.04
Filter Medium	0.20
Carbon Dioxide	0.56
Power	1.71
Tax-Provincial	26.60
Tax-Federal	19.33
Tax-Sales	15.90
Total	$100.65

1 hL = 100 litres	1 hL = 300 standard size draughts

Exhibit 2

BEVERAGE MARGINS

	Margin
Bottled Domestic Beer (excludes deposit)	70%
Wine	54%
Spirits	85%
Soft Drinks	93%
Juice and Other	76%

KELLERS' FREEHOUSE (B)-SUPPLEMENT

After discussions with owners of restaurants and existing brew pubs, Robert and Alex managed to compile the following sales information

SALES BREAKDOWN (INDUSTRY AVERAGE)

	% of Sales	Contribution Margin Ratio
Food	60 %	60%
House Brew	12 %	85%
Bottled Beer	10 %	70%
Wine	6 %	54%
Spirits	10.5%	85%
Soft Drinks	1 %	93%
Juice/Other	0.5%	76%

Note: The average customer spends approximately $12 per visit. Other restaurants, with seating capacities similar to the one being proposed for Kellers' Freehouse, had sales ranging from $550,000 to $750,000.

REQUIRED:

1. Calculate the weighted-average contribution for Kellers' Freehouse.

2. Calculate the break-even levels in sales dollars and number of customers.

SEA-LINK VENTURES

Lynda E. Whyte and John F. Graham

While working as a commercial scuba diver during 1985, Steve Read conceived of a product idea that would enable divers to speak to each other underwater. Three years later Steve had invented and tested a prototype of the Sea-Link, a simple yet effective device for communicating verbally underwater. A second year university student, Steve was eager to gain business experience in the scuba diving industry as a possible career start. Sea-Link Ventures (SLV) was formed during 1988 to investigate the feasibility of bringing the Sea-Link to market. With the research complete, Steve had to develop a marketing plan for the firm and implement his decisions in time for the 1989 season. Buyers would be making their purchases in March in order to reach consumer markets for the summer diving season.

SCUBA DIVING

The word scuba was an acronym for "self-contained underwater breathing apparatus". Scuba diving was used extensively for marine research, archaeology, exploration, photography, industrial work, and recreational activity. The largest diving market segment by far was the recreational scuba diver. Instruction leading to certification by professional scuba diving associations such as the National Association for Underwater Instruction (NAUI) had to be undertaken before a diver could dive independently.

Scuba apparatus consisted of a pressurized air tank which was strapped onto the diver's back and a "regulator" which controlled a diver's breathing while underwater. As safety was constantly emphasized, scuba diving instruction included the use of an auxiliary or secondary regulator and actively promoted its inclusion as part of a diver's basic equipment. Consequently, 60% of all divers in 1988 owned an auxiliary regulator and this population was continuing to grow at an annual rate of 10% as the trend toward its use continued.

All divers used the "buddy system" and were never separated by more than six feet during a dive. Verbal communication, however, between two or more divers was severely limited due to the medium in which they operated and the presence of the breathing apparatus within their mouths. The Sea-Link was intended to solve this communication problem while diving.

THE RECREATIONAL SCUBA MARKET

According to the Diving Equipment Manufacturers Association (DEMA), which was considered to be the industry expert on scuba diving, an estimated three million recreational divers resided in Canada and the United States during 1988. Due to increased female participation and an increase in the popularity of the sport in general, the total market was estimated to be growing at a steady annual rate of 15%.

THE SEA-LINK

The Sea-Link design was extremely simple and made of common materials — latex, plastic, and neoprene (a type of rubber). Its purpose was to allow for underwater verbal communication between scuba divers.

The device consisted of an eight-inch plastic tube secured to the auxiliary regulator (see Exhibit 1). At one end of the tube a neoprene mouthpiece was attached and both tube openings were covered by a slit latex sheath with over-lapping folds. Water was cleared from the tube by blowing through it, leaving a section of air available to conduct sound from the lips of one diver to the ear of another — much like the game "telephone." The Sea-Link would be available in a variety of bright colours. No formal approval from a safety standard government body was required.

SLV would co-ordinate the manufacture of the Sea-Link by subcontracting the work to three independent firms, each manufacturing one component. A fourth would be responsible for assembly, packaging, and shipping. All production data is contained in Exhibit 2.

CONSUMER

SLV believed all scuba divers to be potential users of the Sea-Link; however, the recreational diver would be targeted. Consumer demographic information was taken from the 1987 Subscriber Surveys of three popular diving magazines: *Diver, Scuba Times,* and *Skin Diver* (see Exhibit 3). Although this research did not provide direct information regarding the recreational diving population, the demographics of diving magazine subscribers closely resembled that of the diving population as a whole.

Steve's experience in the industry granted further insight into the recreational diver's purchase behaviour. Quality and product safety were most important in the consumer buying decision due to the dangerous repercussions of any diving mishap. Highly technical and engineered equipment satisfied diver safety needs and also helped users be comfortable while diving. Divers tried to maximize comfort at all times by outfitting themselves with light-weight and easy to operate equipment.

Divers wanted products offering quality and comfort at reasonable prices. The recommendation of a notable scuba expert or the diver's instructor was very influential since their opinion helped divers make value oriented and informed purchase decisions. Retail operators were also referred to for product information and recommendations. Even the reputation of a manufacturer or name brand had an impact on the buying decision. Recently fashion had begun to have an increasing influence on diving goods as more equipment became available in bright colours with matching accessories.

MARKET DISTRIBUTION

Penetration of the recreational scuba market could be achieved through a variety of distribution methods. SLV considered three options for selling — directly to the end consumer, or through a scuba products wholesaler directly to individual retail scuba shops.

End Consumer

Mail order, through specialty diving magazines, was a popular means of selling scuba diving products directly to divers, especially in the U.S. Practically any piece of scuba equipment or accessory item could be sold through the mail — from tanks and wet suits to dive lights. All diver magazines carried mail order advertisements that contained a product description and the required process for ordering.

Mail order campaigns were particularly sensitive to the readership of the magazine in which they were displayed. *Skin Diver* and *ScubaTies,* two major diving magazines, had readerships in both Canada and the United States. *Dive Magazine* was sold mainly in Canada. These magazines generally contained information on travel, photography, safety and diving tips, and any other industry news appealing to divers.

Retail

The dive shop was a focal point of a diver's experience. Besides offering a wide variety of scuba products, these retail outlets serviced most other diving needs such as boat rental, diving instruction, travel arrangements, diving clubs, etc. One of the main reasons divers frequented a retail outlet, however, was to fill their air tank(s) by using special filling equipment located on the dive shop premises. Shops were usually owned independently by experienced scuba divers and were concentrated in coastal areas, convenient to the diving population. In 1988 there were 125 dive shops in Canada and between 1,500 and 1,750 in the United States.

Purchases by retail stores were made direct through wholesale or manufacturer sales representatives and through trade magazines. Orders for accessory items were placed monthly as opposed to infrequent ordering of high ticket items. Overall, shops purchased small order quantities due to the wide range of inventory carried and their independent, therefore undercapitalized, nature.

Sales Representative

SLV researched the option of a sales representative to make direct calls on retail dive shops to promote and sell the Sea-Link. Such a person would need to be an experienced diver with direct sales experience. SLV estimated that one sales representative could service the geographical area of Ontario or the equivalent of 75 stores. A salary of $34,000, including benefits, would be paid. Selling costs, including all travelling expenses, were estimated at $3,000 per month per sales representative.

Wholesale

Wholesale distribution allowed for wide access to the retail scuba market. Three companies dominated in North America: U.S. Diver, Oceanic, and Dacor Distributors. All three were American firms with distribution centres located in the United States. Dacor, however, was dominant in the Canadian market and distributed products through operations recently built in Fort Erie, Ontario. It was the third largest North American distributor of scuba goods.

Wholesale distributors either purchased or manufactured scuba equipment and marketed these goods to retail dive shops under their own brand name. All had extensive distribution systems driven by a vast and knowledgeable sales-force, which extended throughout the world. Wholesalers competed with each other based mainly on the selection and quality of products offered.

SLV had approached all three wholesalers mentioned but only Dacor had indicated an interest in the Sea-Link. Dacor would not commit to any order volumes as of yet but if SLV was willing to sell to them, they would agree to take full responsibility for all sales and distribution. Dacor supplied over 1,000 scuba products and accessories to 105 dive shops in Canada and 1,200 in the United States.

COMPETITION

Other means of underwater communication available to the scuba diving market encompassed a wide price and design range; however, there were no discernible products similar in design or in method of use to the Sea-Link.

Sign language was the most obvious and least expensive method of underwater communication. Both divers using sign language had to be well versed in order to communicate to the same degree as regular speech; therefore, most divers used a few basic hand signs to exchange a minimal amount of information.

Grease pens used on a slate were a very popular means of communication in instructional classes and retailed for approximately $20. Two drawbacks of the pen and slate were its limited space for writing and its cumbersome nature when carried on a dive. Radio communicators provided for unlimited verbal communication and retailed between $400 and $2,000. Their use required a bulky transmitter and receiver that attached to the diver's main regulator. These were used almost exclusively by commercial divers.

The most direct competition to the Sea-Link aimed at the recreational diver was determined to be the Aquavox. This verbal underwater communication device currently retailed on the North American market for $99.95 (U.S.). The Aquavox allowed for hands free communication at any depth and from a horizontal distance of 10 to 20 feet. A headpiece replaced the mouthpiece of the regulator and sound was conducted through the bones of the head rather than the ear. The quality of sound was compared to hearing one's own speech while the nose and ears are plugged. The Aquavox was a relatively new product and during 1988, in its first 11 months, 3,000 units were sold with orders for an additional 9,000 in place. The 1989 Aquavox revenue projections were estimated at $1,000,000. Aquavox Inc. had started during 1987 with a capital investment of $200,000. The product was sold independently, mainly through magazine mail orders in *Skin Diver* and *Scuba Times*. The product had been endorsed by a noted scuba expert and a recent feature article in *Venture*, an entrepreneurial magazine, rated the Aquavox as the third top idea of 1988.

PRICE

The Sea-Link was an accessory item competing against such products as snorkels, bags, and watches. At retail, accessory items were priced between $20 and $40. SLV research had shown the Sea-Link to be an "impulse purchase" accessory item but Steve was unsure what effect, if any, this would have on the pricing decision.

Retail shops increased the wholesale price of goods purchased by 100% in order to arrive at a retail selling price. In turn, wholesalers used the same mark-up on goods purchased from the manufacturer.

PROMOTION

Trade Shows

Nine major scuba trade shows were held throughout North America during the spring in time for the summer buying season and during the fall in time for the winter/holiday buying season. Products of both manufacturers and wholesalers were featured. All trade participants attended these shows in order to scout for new products and size up competition. DEMA held a widely attended show each year in Orlando during March. Costs to attend the DEMA trade show are outlined in Exhibit 4. Also outlined in Exhibit 4 are costs to attend a local show in Toronto during September.

Magazine

Diving magazines were used to promote everything within the scuba diving industry and space was available for both black and white or full colour layout advertisements. The number of people exposed to each magazine (readership) was much higher than the number of issues sold since each publication was often passed on and read by at least two or three other divers. Exhibit 5 outlines advertising rates and publishing frequency for three North American diving magazines.

Brochure

The brochure for use by SLV to promote the Sea-Link displayed the device and its use as well as advertising the benefits from using the Sea-Link. Noted after the text was a favourable comment about the product expressed by John Vigars, past president of NAUI (National Association for Underwater Instruction) Canada. Brochures would cost $.10 each to print.

FINANCING AND CORPORATE STRUCTURE

To date, SLV had experienced little business activity. The plastic-tube mould had been purchased for $12,000 and was expected to produce 50,000 units. Only $2,000 had been incurred to date for organizational costs (legal and incorporation). Overhead costs would be low, estimated at $400 per month, as minimal operating space would be required. Steve had personal savings of $18,000 available for investment in SLV and if the Sea-Link showed signs of future success, funds from friends and relatives amounting to $54,000 could be solicited in return for shares in SLV. Although university was Steve's current priority, he would be available for full time participation during the upcoming year.

DECISION

Steve knew he had several decisions to make regarding the marketing plan for the Sea-Link before any action could be taken to put Sea-Link on the market. He was anxious to get his plan finalized, however, in order to participate in the 1989 buying season commencing in the spring. Steve was eager to develop SLV into a viable and profitable business.

Exhibit 1

THE SEA-LINK DEVICE

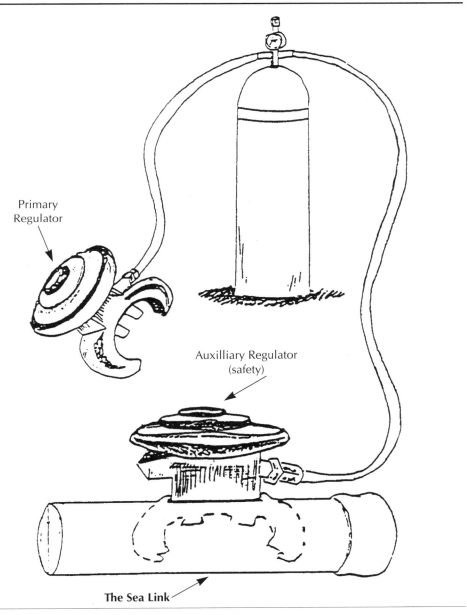

Primary
Regulator

Auxilliary Regulator
(safety)

The Sea Link

Exhibit 2

PRODUCTION COST DATA PER UNIT

Product Cost

Glue	$ .005
Plastic tubes	.59
Neoprene mouthpiece	1.05
Latex coverings	.51

Packaging

Boxes (cut and print)	$0.40
Instruction sheets	.025
Handling fee	1.21

Distribution

Mailing tubes	$0.52
U.S. bulk mail	2.20/shipment
Canadian bulk mail	1.52/shipment

Exhibit 3

MAGAZINE READERSHIP INFORMATION

Diver Magazine

Paid circulation:	20,000
Estimated readership:	70,000
Circulation	
Western Canada	44%
Central Canada	40%
East Coast Canada	6%
United States	10%

Readership profile:	
College or university education	61%
Trade or professional career	84%
Average age	36 years
Average household income	$57,000
Average dive experience	4.9 years

Scuba Times Magazine

Paid circulation:	25,800
Estimated readership:	60,000
Circulation	
South Atlantic	27.5%
Pacific	12.8%

Exhibit 3 (continued)

East North Central	11.0%
West South Central	10.2%
Middle Atlantic	8.5%
Foreign Countries	6.9%
Canada	5.7%
East South Central	4.9%
New England	4.9%
Mountain	4.1%
West North Central	3.5%

Skin Diver Magazine
Readership profile: (the average subscriber)

College education	50 %	
Average income	$53,100	(U.S.)
Average age	34.5	years
Average dive experience	6.7	years

Paid circulation:	216,092
Estimated readership:	1,000,000

Circulation

New England	5.8%
Middle Atlantic	11.6%
East North Central	12.1%
West North Central	4.6%
South Atlantic	26.5%
East South Central	4.4%
West South Central	11.1%
Mountain	5.4%
Pacific	17.8%
Canada	1.6%
Foreign	3.0%

Readership profile:

College attendance or greater	82.7%	
Professional/managerial/technical career	68.4%	
Average age	34.7	years
Male	86%	
Female	14%	
Average household income	$48,500	(U.S.)
Average amount invested in diving equipment	$1,710	(U.S.)
Years diving experience	6.5	years

Other Information

U.S. average household income:	$36,337
U.S. average with college attendance or greater:	35.5%
U.S. average holding professional/managerial/ technical positions:	18.0%

Exhibit 4

PROMOTIONAL TRADE SHOW COST DATA

DEMA Trade Show (Orlando)

Booth rental	$1,350
Video equipment rental	250
Trade samples	840
Travel	1,080

Underwater Canada Tradeshow (Toronto)

Booth rental	$ 525
Video equipment rental	150
Trade samples	218
Travel	200

Exhibit 5

1989 MAGAZINE ADVERTISING RATE INFORMATION

Diver Magazine (Canada)

4 colour	1x	4x	9x
1 page	$2,689	$2,587	$2,317
1/2 page	1,871	1,795	1,713
1/3 page	1,502	1,447	1,386

Black and white			
1 page	$2,040	$1,939	$1,667
1/2 page	1,223	1,145	1,064
1/3 page	853	798	736

Scuba Times (U.S. and Canada)

4 colour	1x	4x	6x
1 page	$2,040	$1,945	$1,820
1/2 page	1,310	1,260	1,165
1/3 page	1,050	1,000	935

Black and white			
1 page	$1,410	$1,350	$1,255
1/2 page	900	870	805
1/3 page	725	690	645
1/6 page	460	400	375

Skin Diver (U.S. and Canada)

4 colour	1x	12x
1 page	$11,440	$10,410
1/2 page	7,345	6,765
1/3 page	6,290	5,725

Black and white		
1 page	$8,940	$8,135
1/2 page	5,545	5,045
1/3 page	4,290	3,905

ELECTRONIC KEY SYSTEMS

Randolph Kudar

Ms. Suroffot, the product manager for electronic key systems, was considering the introduction of a new low-end key system into the local market. Over the past year, the competition had begun selling a new system and had received an enthusiastic response from the customers. To counter this action, Ms. Suroffot felt that it might be necessary to introduce an exclusive competitive product in addition to the ones that were currently offered by 'edmonton telephones'.

LOW-END KEY SYSTEMS

A low-end key system was a business telephone system for small customers. The system took incoming calls on a central office line, through a central answering position and routed them to specific stations or telephone sets in the firm. For outgoing calls, the process was reversed.

Currently 'et' offered the 1A2 key system to its customers. This equipment was based on analogue technology. As such, the 1A2 system provided only the basic services of answer, hold, and hang up. These systems were mostly rented on a month by month basis with no long term contract. The current rate was $150 per month on average.

Electronic key systems provided features such as call pick-up, call forwarding, message waiting, speed calls, and an intercom. Not all electronic key systems offered all the available features.

It was apparent that 'edmonton telephones' competitors were targeting the 1A2 customers with these new systems by selling or leasing electronic key systems to them. Each electronic key system supplied by a competitor eroded the 1A2 rental base for 'et'.

Ms. Suroffot felt that the sale of an electronic key system by 'edmonton telephones' to a 1A2 customer would better secure that customer for 'et'. It was clear that the customers were demanding electronic systems and Ms. Suroffot concluded that an 'edmonton telephones' sale of an electronic key system was obviously preferable to a competitor's sale of a similar product to a customer.

BACKGROUND

'edmonton telephones' was the largest municipally owned independent telephone system in Canada. At the time, it was ranked seventh in overall size. 'et' provided a full range of telecommunication products and services to its residential and business customers. Comprising the service networks were 23 switching centres and associated trunking and distribution cable systems. Repair, installation, and special services were provided through three central production control centres, four primary telephone service centres, and seven phone exchange retail outlets located in major shopping centres and at the head office at 44 Capital Boulevard. 'edmonton telephones' also had a production control centre that controlled outside plant activities. Since 1904, 'et' had grown from 400 telephone lines to 331,698 lines and currently had a staff of 1,870 people. The General Manager of 'edmonton telephones' reported through the City Manager to the City Council of Edmonton.

In the mid eighties, the Edmonton City Council and the Government of Alberta signed a Memorandum of Understanding which, among its provisions, called for the formation of an arbitration committee to determine a toll sharing formula equitable to all Albertans.

Perhaps the greatest impact on 'edmonton telephones' was the decision to permit competition in Edmonton for the sale of telephone terminal equipment. As a result, business customers of 'et' were able to buy telecommunication equipment from whomever they chose after their existing contract ran out. This meant that the sales divisions would have to become market oriented in order to be able to respond to the challenge of this new environment.

THE SELECTED PRODUCT

As an initial stage in the process, Ms. Suroffot had sent out detailed specs to prospective suppliers on the type of product desired. Of the responses received, four were selected for a detailed evaluation. The evaluation criteria included product price to the firm, product features, a features versus price comparison, advertising support, maintenance support, and possible future product developments. Based on the assessment of these criteria, it was decided that the 38 product submitted for consideration would be most suitable to the needs of the firm. The 38 product provided the full complement of features and could be positioned as a premium product.

To convert from a 1A2 system to an electronic system, the customer would likely have to pay for installation (unless these charges were waived such as for a special promotion), and the monthly payments would have to be higher in almost all cases. It was expected that the 38 system would have to be sold or leased to the customer as opposed to rented in order to compete directly with other firms.

Ms. Suroffot was very comfortable with the vendor and the product that had been selected. She anticipated that this contract could be the start of a long and good relationship. However, prior to going ahead and introducing the product, Ms. Suroffot felt that some type of quantitative analysis should be conducted to ensure that this product would be financially sound for the firm.

(a) Revenues

Using her knowledge of the existing key system market, Ms. Suroffot felt that the potential market for such a product as the low-end key system could range from 340 to 425 units in the first year with possible unit sales of 435 to 544 in the second year. The likelihood of sales beyond the two-year horizon would be significantly influenced by technological changes and by growth in the local market.

In assessing the nature of the product, and the existing competition, Ms. Suroffot thought that the price for the product could range anywhere from $2,400 per unit to as high as $3,060 per unit. In the event of a response by the competition to the entry of the 38 model key system into the market, the lower price might have to be all inclusive, meaning that the price would include installation fees. If the competition did not react with price cutting action in this area, the selling price could stabilize at the higher level with additional fees for installation. Currently the price being charged by the competition was in the $2,700 range.

(b) Costs

In the negotiations with the supplier, Ms. Suroffot had been able to arrange to purchase the units at a cost of $1,800 per unit with that price fixed for the first two years of the contract as long as the volume of units purchased ranged between 300 and 600 each year. Sales expense and administration expenses associated with all products handled by 'edmonton telephones' were set at rates of 5% and 7.4% respectively. These rates were percentages of the material cost of the product to 'et'. Both of these items were generally used by the product manager in determining product costs when setting prices for products.

Supplies expense was set at 6.5% of the material cost of the product. This item was used to distribute the costs of warehousing, purchasing, etc. that were incurred when an item was handled through the 'edmonton telephones' warehouse distribution facility. Unlike the sales and administration expense, this supply expense was allocated directly to the products and included in the financial statements.

It was the practice of the company to pay a 1% commission on sales revenue to its agents for all products sold by the firm. At the same time, it was required by statute that the firm had to remit a revenue tax of 1% of sales revenue on competitive products to the local city government and 8% of sales revenue on monopoly products.

Ms. Suroffot consulted with her technical advisors who indicated that the 38 key system would most likely require nine hours to install in the customer's location. Currently the craftspersons responsible for this work received a remuneration of $25.00 per hour. The section in which they operated charged their services out to product sections such as key systems at a rate of $37.50 per hour. The differential cost was the burden and profit associated with that section. The high hourly rate was felt to be necessary because these people were highly trained technicians and the time required to train these personnel was extensive. Thus work was always found for them, even when they could not work at their trade full time.

Currently the advertising budget for terminal products offered by 'edmonton telephones' was $300,000 a year. This was expected to remain the same for at least the next two years. Of this total, it was expected that advertising for all key systems would be $90,000 a year. This would include the new 38 system if it were adopted. Ms. Suroffot planned to spend an additional $22,000 on advertising and promotion specifically for the 38 system in the second year if it was accepted. Finally, as part of the contract, the supplier had agreed to contribute up to $40,000 each of the next two years for co-operative advertising on the 38 system with 'edmonton telephones'.

Currently the key systems marketing personnel, including Ms. Suroffot, occupied an office space in the metropolitan area of the city. The building was leased to the firm and was charged to the marketing group at the rate of $35,000 per year. Ms. Suroffot was presently being paid a salary of $50,000 per year and had received modest pay increases of 2–4% each of the past three years.

She was informed by the data services personnel of 'edmonton telephones' that the introduction of a new product such as the one she was considering at the volume that she proposed would likely require additional programming effort on the accounting system and customer files. The expected cost of this effort was $5,000. She was also informed that there would likely be a need to invest as much as $29,000 at the beginning of the project to acquire display systems and programming sets for internal engineering evaluations. In the start up period, craft and sales personnel would have to be assigned for training on the new product. The expected cost of this effort would be $60,000 in the first year.

CONCLUSIONS

This seemed to be a very critical time for the low-end key systems product lines. The new technology was placing significant pressure in the market place to either change the products or abandon the market segment. In the new competitive environment that was emerging in telecommunications, 'edmonton telephones' was interested in sustaining a position as a full line supplier of telephone services. Ms. Suroffot was now faced with the task of bringing a recommendation forward regarding the status of the 38 system as a viable product for 'edmonton telephones'. She knew that the selling price would have to be competitive and the project would have to be profitable. The firm's policy regarding new products was that any capital investment project would be required to return at least 10.25% after taxes.

THE BEDROCK CORPORATION — AEROSOL DIVISION

Rhonda English, Al Magrath, and Randolph Kudar*

Jason Marsh had an important task ahead. As the marketing manager of Bedrock Corporation's new specialty aerosols group, he was responsible for marketing Seal-a-Wheel sprays, a new line of automotive aerosols, to all outlets in Canada who sold and serviced auto tires. Jason had an $80,000 budget with which to develop a successful introductory marketing strategy for the Seal-a-Wheel product.

THE COMPANY

The Bedrock Corporation was a highly diversified company with operations in Canada, the United States, and Europe. The Canadian operation was located in Montreal, Quebec and was involved in both manufacturing and importing of numerous products. The Canadian company was organized into divisions, with each division responsible for a group of related products. As a full line supplier, the product lines met varying needs within the corporation, some being market leaders and others simply filling out total offering.

Each division was headed by a Division manager, to whom a number of product managers reported. Product managers were responsible for the bottom line operating profit of each product under their umbrella. Marketing managers, who reported to product managers for approval, undertook the promotion, distribution, and advertising activities for various products. Each division had access to the usual support groups, such as marketing research, accounting, legal, etc.

Annual budgets by specific product were developed at the beginning of the year for all divisions. Revenue, cost, and profit figures were set in dollars and percentages using input from all areas of the division (e.g., product managers, marketing managers). This planning dictated how indirect costs would be apportioned to the various products, and were set for the duration of the year. A sample profit and loss budget is outlined in Exhibit 1.

THE PRODUCT

Bedrock had produced and patented a specialty lacquer coating for aluminum cast wheel rims. Aluminum wheel rims oxidized and gathered dirt as a result of expansion and contraction of the rim in hot and cold weather. As well, the seal between the tire and rim tended to leak water and further oxidization occurred. Once a rim was cleaned, Bedrock's lacquer helped to prevent dirt build-up that caused continuing air loss in tires mounted on these rims, and prevented oxidization. Seal-a-Wheel would be sold to tire stores, service stations, car dealers, and other automotive centres (e.g., Canadian Tire, Sears) across Canada through five sales representatives.

THE ALTERNATIVES

Jason had to decide whether to spend his budget on a direct mail campaign, on trade journal ads, or on the tire industry's annual trade show.

Trade Show

Trade shows were a commonly used marketing tool by Bedrock. The tire industry show featured products ranging from changers to balancing equipment as well as air tools, cleaners, etc. Costs of the trade show included construction of a booth ($24,500), space rental and booth transportation ($5,500), literature hand-outs ($4,000), video equipment and a stand-by technician ($2,500), lucky draw tickets and prize ($1,000), and miscellaneous items (i.e., refreshments) ($2,000). As well, the show ran four days, with two shifts per day of four representatives per shift. Hotel, food, and travel costs for each representative amounted to $250 per day.

Trade Journal Ads

Ad inserts had been used periodically by Bedrock to promote products. The journals were received by companies whose business was related to the tire or automotive industry. All ads in the trade magazines were numbered, so that readers could send for further information about specific products, by circling the appropriate number on a reader service card included in the journal. A returned reader service card was considered a lead generated.

The cost of these ads was $5,500 per insert for a contract of 12 insertions. The ads could be purchased on a month-to-month basis; however, the cost of each insert would be 10 percent higher than the 12-month quoted contract price. Artwork for an ad would total $15,000 and lead handling fees to be paid to the magazine would cost $.50 per lead (see Exhibit 2).

Direct Mail

The mailer used to generate leads would be a third party testimonial from a leading tire company on Bedrock's new product. A reply card would be enclosed to write for more information on availability of the product in the prospect's local area. Bedrock had rarely used this type of promotion so did not have a great deal of experience in the area.

List costs for a direct mail campaign amounted to $85 per thousand on the first 35,000 names, $80 per thousand on the next 15,000 names, and $70 per thousand on names over 50,000. The number of mailers sent would depend on the desired number of lead generations (see Exhibit 2). Other expenses per mailing included $1.35 for envelopes, stamps, and label, and $.65 for a cover letter and the literature stuffer.

There was no contractual obligation for mailers so the program could be terminated at any time by Bedrock.

The market research department had provided Jason with estimates of the leads which each media would generate on an optimistic and pessimistic level, based on similar type products sold to such shops. This data is provided in Exhibit 2. In addition, the controller's department had forecasted anticipated sales per customer for three years from any lead converted to a sale, and the contribution margin on such sales (see Exhibit 3).

CONCLUSION

The decision on how the $80,000 budget would be spent now had to be made. Jason wanted to ensure that his strategy would effectively penetrate the market and establish Seal-a-Wheel in a good position. All the alternatives had some potential for success with varying kinds of risk associated. Jason knew he would have to make some trade-offs in determining a marketing strategy for Seal-a-Wheel.

Exhibit 1

PROFIT AND LOSS BUDGET
($000)

PRODUCT CONSUMER AEROSOLS
October 19XX

		This Year	
	Line	**Amount**	**%**
Sales – Domestic	4510	$9,824	100.0
Sales – Export	4511	—	—
Gross Sales	4512	$9,824	100.0
Cash Discounts	4513	—	—
Net Sales	4514	$9,824	100.0
Finished Goods Purch	4515	—	—
Manufacturing Costs	4516	$4,156	42.3
Total Cost Goods Sold	4517	$4,156	42.3
Gross Margin	4518	$5,668	57.7
General Sales Exp	4519	$2,102	21.4
Advert Mdse Purch	4520	$ 825	8.4
Marketing Operations	4521	$ 570	5.8
Total Sales Exps	4522	$3,497	35.6
Administrative Exp	4523	$ 796	8.1
Total Oper Costs	4524	$8,449	86.0
OPERATING PROFIT	4525	$1,375	14.0

Exhibit 2

MARKET RESEARCH ON LEADS GENERATED BY MEDIA

Media	Probable Total Leads Generated	% Conversion Rate of Leads to Customers Who Will Buy	
		Optimistic	Pessimistic
Trade Show	600	90%	75%
Ad Inserts in Trade Journal	4500*	15%	10%
Direct Mailer to Tire Shops	2500** (target)	25%	17%

* Lead generations assuming 12 month contract. Lead generation would be proportionate to inserts run.

**Estimated response rate probabilities of mailer are:
    15% probability of 2% response rate
    75% probability of 5% response rate
    10% probability of 7.5% response rate

Exhibit 3

SALES AND PROFIT RATE PER CUSTOMER

Media	Yr 1	Yr 2	Yr 3	Net Contribution*
Trade Show	$500	$1000	$200	15%
Ad Insert	$750	$350	$100	14%**
Direct Mail	$400	$500	$250	13%**

* Net contribution is before direct media costs on Exhibit 2.

**Ad insert contribution margins were lower due to commission paid to ad agency for ad space purchase.
Direct mail margins were lower because of corporate allocation of overhead from internal advertising group who would assist in the mailing.

EALING PHARMACY (A)

Sue Hanna and Tony Dimnik

Jim Semchism, owner and manager of Ealing Pharmacy in London, Ontario, was faced with one of the toughest decisions in his career. It was July 20, 1986 and for the past four years he had been struggling with the issue of selling tobacco products in his store. He strongly believed that it was contradictory to sell "healing" products alongside tobacco products. However, he realized that the financial rewards of selling tobacco had a significant impact on his bottom line. Semchism felt the time had come to make his final decision on the issue. Should he continue to sell tobacco products through his pharmacy in order to maintain his profits, or should he heed his gut feelings and remove tobacco from his shelves?

ONTARIO PHARMACISTS' ASSOCIATION (OPA)

The OPA was a voluntary association representing some 3,700 retail, hospital and industry pharmacists across the province. More than 95% of the members work in retail pharmacies. The Association represents the profession in negotiations with governments and provides a wide variety of information and benefit services to its members. Over the past few years, the tobacco issue had become a topic of great debate.

In an attempt to gain a united force against tobacco sales in drugstores and pharmacies, Semchism had shared his strong concerns and misgivings with his

OPA colleagues. However, instead of providing support, many OPA members had criticized and attacked Semchism's position on the issue, and some had even stated publicly that Semchism's views did not represent the opinion of the OPA.

PHARMACEUTICAL CODE OF ETHICS

Although pharmacists were not required to take the Hippocratic Oath as were medical practitioners, the Ontario College of Pharmacists expected all practising pharmacists to adhere to a "Code of Ethics." Section 1 of the Code of Ethics stated:

> A pharmacist should hold the health and safety of patients to be of first consideration; he should render to each patient the full measure of his ability as an essential health practitioner.

Section 2 stated:

> A pharmacist should never knowingly condone the dispensing, promoting or distribution of drugs...which lack therapeutic value for the patient.

TOBACCO SALES IN PHARMACIES

Pharmacists and drugstore owners argued that selling tobacco products through drugstores was legal, and therefore acceptable. Many pharmacists believed that tobacco sales were as much a part of their business as were sales of cold medicines. They also thought that providing the public with tobacco products created additional customer traffic. Customers going into a pharmacy to buy a pack of cigarettes might decide to pick up tubes of toothpaste or potato chips, thus creating additional revenue, which would otherwise have been lost.

Furthermore, selling tobacco products offered customers convenience. In a competitive environment, customer satisfaction was increasingly important to pharmacists trying to build a solid customer base.

Tobacco sales were an important source of revenue for pharmacies and drugstores. A small local pharmacy might sell $100,000 worth of tobacco a year, of which approximately $15,000 was profit. Therefore, the owners of small pharmacies argued that the loss of tobacco revenues could put them out of business. Large pharmacy chains such as Shoppers Drug Mart and Big V also depended on cigarette sales. A single chain outlet could have gross tobacco sales of $500,000 a year, providing significant profits for both the individual pharmacy and its parent. One of the major chains, Shoppers Drug Mart, was owned by Imasco, which also owned Imperial Tobacco Company. There was much speculation within the industry as to whether or not Imperial Tobacco supplied its drugstore counterpart with discounted tobacco products, thus forcing prices to be lower than normal market pressures would have dictated.

On the whole, profit margins for tobacco products were relatively small in comparison to other products carried in drug stores. On average, a package of cigarettes had a profit margin of 10–15%. Cartons of cigarettes were often sold at cost because drugstore owners used the low prices on cartons to draw in customers. Typical profit margins for "front store" sales (including tobacco) were approximately 20%, while dispensary profit margins averaged 35–40%.

The strategy of drugstore owners was to attract customers to their front store in the hope that they would patronize the store's dispensary services. To attract dispensing customers, many drugstore owners shaved the profit margins on front store items.

EALING PHARMACY

Ealing Pharmacy, founded in 1952, operated as a full-service drug store. Initially, prescription sales were the primary focus of the business, while front store sales (i.e., health and beauty aids, confectionery, tobacco) played a secondary role. Semchism, a recently graduated pharmacist, took over Ealing Pharmacy upon his father's retirement in 1982. By this time the product mix for the drug store had changed dramatically, with front store sales contributing much more significantly to the store's overall sales and profitability.

Ealing Pharmacy was located in a working-class neighbourhood in London. Studies showed that working-class people were heavier users of tobacco products than were professionals and, thus, a higher-than-average percentage of Ealing's sales were attributable to tobacco. In the 1985–86 fiscal year, Ealing's tobacco sales were approximately $100,000.

Even before he had taken on the store, Semchism had not felt comfortable selling tobacco products because selling "weeds" went against everything that he, as a pharmacist, stood for and believed in. He cited the Pharmaceutical Code of Ethics to demonstrate the inherent contradiction in providing healing medicines to the public, while at the same time selling a known killer. "Profiting from the addiction of smokers to the number one cause of preventable mortality and morbidity is most unprofessional."

The main factor preventing Semchism from immediately pulling the "weeds" from his shelves was the realization of the financial implications. He wondered if he would have to reduce his sales staff and how he might make up sales by promoting alternative products.

There were other implications that concerned Semchism. He realized that if he were to take tobacco products off his shelves, there would be some publicity since he would be the first pharmacist in the London area to take such a measure. Positive or negative public reaction could have a strong impact on his business and personal life.

Ealing Pharmacy was currently in direct competition with a large "super-store" drugstore/pharmacy in the same geographic area. Ealing customers were not limited in their choice of drugstores and would not be inconvenienced if they took their regular business elsewhere.

Semchism looked over some financial data to try to quantify some of the financial risks of his pending decision (see Exhibit 1). One way or the other, he would decide what to do about selling tobacco in his drugstore.

Exhibit 1

EALING STATISTICS
(for the year ended April 30)

	1984	1985	1986
RX* inventory	$ 44,000	$ 43,000	$ 65,000
FS** inventory	39,000	44,000	57,000
Store inventory	$ 83,000	$ 87,000	$122,000
RX sales	519,000	573,000	629,000
FS sales	222,000	245,000	278,000
Store sales	$ 741,000	$ 818,000	$ 907,000
RX cost of sales	259,000	298,000	353,000
FS cost of sales	174,000	199,000	240,000
Store cost of sales	$433,000	$497,000	$593,000
RX turns	5.89	6.93	5.43
FS turns	4.46	4.52	4.21
Store turns	5.22	5.71	4.86
RX gross margin	$260,000	$275,000	$276,000
FS gross margin	48,000	46,000	38,000
Store gross margin	$308,000	$321,000	$314,000
RX gross margin %	50.1	47.99	43.88
FS gross margin %	21.62	18.78	13.67
Store gross margin %	41.57	39.24	34.62

*RX denotes prescription or dispensary data.
**FS denotes front store data.

EALING PHARMACY (B)

Sue Hanna and Tony Dimnik

Pharmacist Jim Semchism, owner and operator of Ealing Pharmacy in London, Ontario, had just sat down at his office desk in order to assess the events of the past year. In August 1986, Semchism had removed all tobacco products from his store. It was now May 4, 1988, and the store had just gone through its first complete fiscal year of "tobaccoless" sales. Since his decision, Semchism had felt much better about his business and was pleased with the outcomes of the change. Semchism hoped that his financial results would provide him with the ammunition he needed to convince other drugstore owners to eliminate tobacco sales from their stores.

THE DECISION TO "BUTT OUT"

Semchism, who firmly believed that selling "killer weeds" was unprofessional for a pharmacist, had announced on July 11, 1986, after much thought and deliberation, that Ealing Pharmacy was pulling all tobacco products from its shelves. As a result of this action, Ealing had become the first pharmacy in the London area to discontinue the sale of tobacco products (see Exhibit 1).

THE OUTCOME

Semchism's decision had been greeted with much media attention. During the past two years, his views had been represented in many articles and papers (see Exhibit 2).[1]

---

[1] This article was reproduced with the expressed consent of *Drug Merchandising Magazine* (vol. 69, No. 2, Feb. 1988).

A few regular Ealing customers had stopped shopping at the pharmacy, but on the whole, Semchism's actions had been met with good publicity and customer support. In fact, some opponents of smoking began to frequent Ealing Pharmacy in order to display their support for the tobacco "ban," and to encourage other pharmacists to follow suit.

Semchism believed that initially the sales of many impulse and confectionery items had decreased with the removal of tobacco products. However, sales of over-the-counter nonprescription drugs and greeting cards had not changed. Even before the figures were available, he suspected that the store's prescription business had increased as a result of the change (see Exhibit 3).

There had been some unexpected benefits of the decision to drop tobacco products. Tobacco sales had required a significant investment in working capital — an estimated $9,000. This money was now available for the purchase of more ethical and higher profit items, such as health and beauty aids.

Semchism also believed that the removal of tobacco products had decreased theft and damage losses from both the general public and his own sales staff.

A final result of his decision was more personal, "I feel more professional and ethical." Semchism no longer felt he was ignoring or contradicting the Pharmaceutical Code of Ethics because he was looking out for the best interests of his customers and supplying them with safe, therapeutic drugs and medicines.

Semchism continued to vocalize his opinions and misgivings regarding the sale of tobacco in drugstores. He stated that, "Profiting from the addiction of smokers to the No. 1 cause of preventable mortality and morbidity is most unprofessional." He wanted other pharmacists to realize the stupidity and detriments of supplying the public with the hazardous "weeds."

However, the OPA still did not agree with or support Semchism's "crusade." Members made it clear that the vocal opinions of Jim Semchism did not represent the views of the OPA.

Exhibit 1

Press Release

—for immediate release

July 22/86

From: Ealing Pharmacy   Contact: Jim Semchism
       873 Hamilton Rd.
       London, Ont.

After thirty-five years of being a full-service drug store, Ealing Pharmacy has stopped selling tobacco products. Pharmacist-owner Jim Semchism is following his conscience. "When my father opened the pharmacy in the 1950s, the health standards of smoking were not obvious. Today they are, and for this reason, my drug store will no longer handle tobacco."

Annually, Ealing Pharmacy has sold over $100,000 in tobacco. Mr. Semchism feels that as a health care provider, he should not be selling a product responsible for killing 30,000 Canadians each year. Smoking is now recognized as being the single most preventable cause of death and disability.

Pharmacists are caught in the classical dilemma, the choice between ethics and economics. Approximately 25% of all tobacco sales are made in pharmacies. The revenue from the sale of this product could make the difference between a struggling business and a successful one. Many pharmacies discount tobacco and use it as a draw to attract customers.

Mr. Semchism feels prevention of the addiction is the key. "It is difficult for smokers to quit. If young people see that their drug store has discontinued or refused to sell tobacco products, then they may be influenced not to start. We are setting a good example for them."

As a pharmacist, Mr. Semchism's chief concerns are the high risks being taken by women on birth control pills who continue to smoke. "The saddest sights are the pregnant mothers who smoke and those patients already suffering from lung and heart disease who cannot stop."

Two years ago the Canadian Pharmaceutical Association asked all pharmacists to take a stand against smoking. To date, very few stores have discontinued the sale of tobacco, and Canada's largest pharmacy chain continues to advertise the product. Ealing Pharmacy is the first drug store in the London area to discontinue the sale of tobacco, although several pharmacies locally have never sold the product.

So far, customer reaction has been quite favourable. Both smokers and non-smokers have praised the decision as being appropriate for a pharmacy. Some have been critical, but most people have been very supportive.

Exhibit 2

You CAN do without discounting, tobacco

I am certain that many pharmacy owners ask themselves, "Why do I own a pharmacy?"

They must wrestle with all of the problems of a small business. They must wear many hats — pharmacist, operations manager, personnel manager, merchandising manager, promotion manager, financial manager and, in many cases, caretaker. As well, they find themselves in two businesses — the dispensary and the front shop. Many feel very comfortable in the dispensary and generally leave the front shop headache to the head sales clerk making half the salary of a staff pharmacist.

So why do pharmacists want to be store owners? Probably for one of two reasons:
1. You wish independence and don't want to work for anybody else at all costs.
2. You have discovered that you can make more money owning your pharmacy than working as a staff pharmacist for somebody else.

I'm going to assume that you have given No. 2 as the reason for being in your own business. So how do you go about earning a good profit? Well, the return on assets used in the pharmacy operation is the best criteria to measure if you are earning a reasonable profit.

Statistics accumulated by Harold Segal of the University of Toronto and published in the Sixth Annual Survey of Community Pharmacy Operations indicate that the operating assets for 1985 for the average pharmacy in Canada were $312,000 (accounts receivable $42,000, inventory $194,000, and fixtures and equipment $76,000). The net profit before income taxes is $69,000. The return on assets was 22% ($69,000 divided by $312,000 times 100). A reasonable target for return on assets in a pharmacy operation is 30%. However, I have seen operations that were in the 50% plus range.

As you can see, the major investment is inventory — 62% of total operating assets. The GPROI (gross profit return on investment) for the average pharmacy in 1985 was 186%. A reasonable target today is 300%, which suggests that the inventory is in excess of the target figure by about $75,000.

Many pharmacy owners are quick to reply that you cannot sell from empty shelves. I agree. However, many of these same pharmacy owners do not realize the activity of the various product groups that they are trying to sell. Examples are toys, stationery products, food products and many other inventory items that are not normally associated with a pharmacy operation.

It's about time that the pharmacy owners recognized what business they are really in. In other words, what is the target market and who are your real competitors? Some pharmacy owners are competing with chain grocery stores and Becker-type convenience stores.

You have an edge on most other retailers. No one but a qualified pharmacist can operate a pharmacy.

In my mind, there are four types of pharmacy operations. First is the dispensary in a medical clinic. Second is the independent community pharmacy. Third are the regional and national chains and fourth is the super discount operation. All are different.

It is important that you realize which one you are. For example, if you are a community pharmacy with the average 2,500-to-3,000-sq.-ft. operation, then there is no way that you can consider yourself a super discounter. You have much more to offer your clientele — personal service, neighbourhood location and convenience.

A super discount store cannot necessarily provide the personal service or be in the neighbourhood or be convenient. What it can offer, of course, is super discount prices (usually 20% gross profit). This is something that the traditional community pharmacy should not offer if a reasonable profit level is to be maintained. The super discount stores operate from 20,000-sq.-ft. (plus) and rely on high turnovers of the low margin products. It is not possible for a 2,500-to-3,000-sq.-ft. pharmacy to turn over enough product in the front shop in order to make deep discounting profitable.

I would now like to debunk some of the old-fashioned theories about marketing in the dispensary.

Over the years, I have been told that you must have an active front shop in order to attract business to the dispensary, which operates at a higher gross profit level. Many independents attempt to attract the customers with super discount sales and variety of product that do not necessarily conform to the target market. I have noticed over the past few years the addition of food items, toys and other products that are not consistent with the image of a pharmacy operation. I am told this is done in order to compete with the "big guys." Effectively, what this does is increase the investment in the pharmacy, requires additional personnel (or increased wages) and in many cases results in a loss in the front shop operation.

Over the years, I have been told by many pharmacy owners that it is important to sell tobacco products in the front shop in order to attract customers to the pharmacy to use the dispensary services. Pharmacy owners are concerned about losing dispensary customers if they don't carry tobacco products. In other words, they feel tobacco is a must.

Let's look at the facts. In the September 1987 issue of *Drug Merchandising*, Tina Kyriakos reported on a study conducted about chain drugstores in the United States. "The average customer is attracted to a particular chain drugstore mainly by convenience of location (64%), followed by the ease of shopping the store (39%), prices (23%), assortment of merchandise (17%) and service (8%)...." Two surveys conducted by the York Enterprise Development Centre of York University confirmed that convenience was the main reason customers were attracted to the dispensary.

Here is another example to prove that you don't need cigarettes to attract customers to the dispensary.

In August 1986, Jim Semchism, owner of Ealing Pharmacy in London, Ont., decided to delete tobacco products from his pharmacy. This was a two-prong decision. First, he did not feel he was making a reasonable return on the investment. Second, he felt this was contrary to the image that a pharmacy should project to the community.

Semchism prepared some careful statistics to evaluate the effect of this decision. The impact of eliminating tobacco products showed an increase in dispensary sales of 17% for the period August to December 1986 versus August to December 1985. The front shop sales were lower by 9% and the overall sales were up by about $500. The tobacco sales for August to December 1985 were $40,300.

Semchism says that it was "definitely" a smart move. "First, I feel more professional and ethical. Second, there was good publicity and customer support and last but not least it was more profitable. In addition, the $9,000 tied up in tobacco products was eliminated." He concludes it was "a brilliant move resulting in less inventory, less theft and damages, and more profit."

The main purpose of this article is to get pharmacy owners thinking more clearly on "What business am I really in?" If you own a community pharmacy with 2,500 to 3,000 square feet of space, then you are not in deep discount business. You can, however, make a reasonable profit selling traditional items in the front shop — provided, of course, you manage the inventory properly.

To quote one of the points in the book *In Search of Excellence* — "Stick to your knitting."

Graham Cunningham, a Toronto chartered accountant, specializes in pharmacy financial operations. If you'd like Cunningham to discuss a specific topic here, please write to the editor. If you have confidential matters you'd like to discuss, call him directly at Cunningham Associates, 200 Consumers Rd., Suite 105, North York M2J 4R4, (416) 496-1051.

Strategies

80 sign PACT$

More than 700 pharmacies now "tobacco-free"

"This is a Health Care Centre....We Don't Sell Tobacco Products." More and more pharmacists are sending that message to the public as they join the Pharmacists Against Cigarette and Tobacco Sales (PACT$) and remove all tobacco products and smoking supplies.

Sponsored by the Canadian Pharmaceutical Association under the chairmanship of Ernest Stefanson, PACT$ reached a high point during National Non-Smoking Week in early January. Some 80 pharmacists pledged support in the first two weeks of the "positive action" against tobacco, the leading cause of preventable death in Canada.

"By removing the products from their shelves, pharmacists reinforce their commitment to good health and encourage their customers to reconsider their smoking habits," says CPhA, which is sending promotional and support materials to all pharmacists who sign up to ensure their transition to a "tobacco-free pharmacy" does not affect their overall economic performance. (By the way, the economics of such a move are discussed by Graham Cunningham in his column.)

There are now more than 700 pharmacies not selling tobacco products. The earlier CPhA/Health and Welfare program called Stand Up and Be Counted won the commitment of the owners of 618 pharmacies.

Participating PACT$ members include:

ONTARIO—Jean-Paul Desjardins, Ottawa; Joe Strofder, Forest Hill Pharmacy, Kitchener; W. Negrave, Spalding Pharmacy Inc., Wallaceburg; David E. Pellow, Hobley Pharmacy Ltd., Walkerton; R.T. Jokinen, Village Pharmacy (Bobcaygeon) Ltd., Bobcaygeon; Aldo Anzil, Courtesy Drug Mart, Oakville; Brown's Guardian Pharmacy, Walkerton; Barry Holliday, Holliday's IDA Pharmacy, Durham; Azilda Pharmacy, Azilda; J.H.M. Shaw Pharmacy Ltd., Sudbury; Port Dover IDA, Port Dover; Scales Big V Pharma-Centre, Stoney Creek....

Exhibit 3

EALING STATISTICS
(for the year ended April 30)

	1984	1985	1986	1987	1988
RX* inventory	$44,000	$43,000	$65,000	$61,000	$75,700
FS** inventory	39,000	44,000	57,000	47,000	40,600
Store inventory	$83,000	$87,000	$122,000	$108,000	$116,300
RX sales	$519,000	$573,000	$629,000	$740,000	$900,000
FS sales	222,000	245,000	278,000	178,000	139,000
Store sales	$741,000	$818,000	$907,000	$918,000	$1,039,000
RX cost of sales	$259,000	$298,000	$353,000	$412,000	$501,000
FS cost of sales	174,000	199,000	240,000	144,000	109,000
Store cost of sales	$433,000	$497,000	$593,000	$556,000	$610,000
RX turns	5.89	6.93	5.43	6.75	6.62
FS turns	4.46	4.52	4.21	3.06	2.68
Store turns	5.22	5.71	4.86	5.15	5.25
RX gross margin	$260,000	$275,000	$276,000	$328,000	$399,000
FS gross margin	48,000	46,000	38,000	34,000	30,000
Store gross margin	$308,000	$321,000	$314,000	$362,000	$429,000
RX gross margin %	50.1	47.99	43.88	44.32	44.33
FS gross margin %	21.62	18.78	13.67	19.1	21.58
Store gross margin %	41.57	39.24	34.62	39.43	41.19

*RX denotes prescription or dispensary data.
**FS denotes front store data.

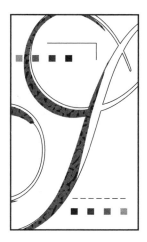

PART **B**

PRODUCT COSTING
SYSTEMS

S. C. JOHNSON AND SON, LIMITED — THE COSTING SYSTEM

Rhonda English and Randolph Kudar*

As Penny McIntyre, Product Manager at S.C. Johnson and Son, Limited in Brantford, Ontario, left the Manufacturing Financial Support department, her thoughts lingered on the discussion she had had with the department's manager, Kim Gillin. Penny had recently heard that the cost of Active A, a raw material used in one of her well-established home care products, was doubling. She was quite concerned about the effect of this increase on her final case cost since she already felt the overall cost of the product was becoming too high to be competitive. Sales volume had begun to suffer as the selling price per case of the popular product was increased to offset rising case costs. Penny wondered if a better understanding of the company's product costing system might help her address this issue before it became an unsolvable problem.

COMPANY BACKGROUND

S.C. Johnson and Son, Limited was founded by Samuel Curtis Johnson in Racine, Wisconsin, in 1886. Initially a manufacturer of parquet flooring, the company soon realized there was an opportunity to make products to maintain and protect their floors. Thus Johnson Wax was created. S.C. Johnson, still a privately owned company, had operations in 41 countries and had 110 distribution centres around the world. The world-wide company was divided into three entities of which the largest was the Consumer Products Division (see Exhibit 1).

The Canadian subsidiary in Brantford was created in 1920 as a maker of floor waxes and had since expanded into furniture polishes (Pledge), domestic insecticides (Raid, Off!), air fresheners (Glade), personal care products (Agree Shampoo and Conditioner, Curel Body Lotion), and cleaning products (industrial and domestic). The sales of Canadian Johnson were approximately $50 million per year, with employment of around 400 full-time employees. About 25% of the workforce was in sales, 25% in the non-unionized plant, and the remaining in head office. The Canadian operation had its own management structure and research facilities, which enabled it to operate fairly autonomously.

Manufacturing

The manufacture of all S.C. Johnson (SCJ) products began with a formula or recipe. Each raw material necessary for production underwent quality control checks when it arrived at SCJ. Upon beginning the production cycle, these raw materials were drawn from the raw material inventory and sent to their designated location. A separate building housed a polymer processing operation, which made the base fluids or polymers as outlined by many of the formulas. These polymers were then piped to the making area, where various polymers would be combined and additional raw materials (liquids and powders) mixed together in large steel kettles. The end result of the making operation was the final bulk to be used in filling the packaging units. Quality control checks were conducted at various stages of bulk making to ensure the meeting of standards and non-contamination.

The manufacturing facility contained a separate fill and pack line for each of: liquid products, aerosol (pressure) products, and personal care products; as well as a drum filling line and paste line. The Canadian subsidiary also manufactured about 70% of its own bottle requirements in its moulding operation. This operation gave SCJ the flexibility to assess priorities and demands, to accommodate their "just in time" inventory system, and to directly control the quality of bottles being used.

A Home Care Product

The manufacturing process for Penny's home care product began with the making of Intermediate 1 and Intermediate 2. These two intermediates were combined with additional raw materials, resulting in a blended intermediate, which was ready to be piped to the liquid fill and pack line. The bottle hopper, which was a large bin where the bottles were temporarily stored, was the starting point for the fill and pack line. The bottles were taken from the hopper and, as they were manually placed on the line, were visually inspected for quality. The bottles were automatically spaced as they travelled down the line on a conveyor belt to the rotary filler, which was connected by plumbing to the appropriate storage tank in the making area. The bottles were filled to a predetermined height (cosmetic fill) by way of two hoses — a filling hose and an overflow hose. The screw-on dispensing caps, sitting in another hopper, were directed into an automatic cap sorter which fed them into a capper machine. The chucker on the capper machine spun the cap onto the bottles before the bottles proceeded to the labeller. Bottles were randomly picked off the line between the capper and labelling operations. An inspector would weigh and visually assess the quality of the product and the container.

The labeller applied glue to the labels and then pressed them onto the bottle. A batch number was put on the bottles as they passed an ink jet on the line. A final visual quality control check for label positioning and cosmetic uniformity was performed as the bottles moved to the case packing machine.

The automatic case packer arranged the bottles into the required carton configuration, while at the end of the line, the cartons and carton dividers were manually erected and fed back underneath the automatic case packer. The process concluded with the bottles being dropped into the carton.

The last stage of the fill and pack was the gluing of the carton flaps and the placing of the batch number, by ink jet, onto the carton. The cases then travelled by conveyor to the palletizing area of the finished goods area to await shipment to the customer.

MANUFACTURING FINANCIAL SUPPORT

Manufacturing Financial Support at SCJ was a relatively new department, set up to document and analyze data that manufacturing could use to improve operations and decision-making, and to offer information and explanations concerning product costs to those departments needing such information. For example, the Support Department may suggest reducing product costs by replacing certain raw materials or packaging components with ones that are already in use in other products, thereby reducing the number of inventory items and increasing volume discounts. A second example might encompass explaining that a certain small volume product is costed so high because unfamiliarity with machine setup specifications results in high labour costs and subsequently high fixed indirect costs. Typically, the greater the volume of a product, the more efficient the set-ups and production runs.

In general, the support department focused on service, in the form of identifying actionable problems and helping people to understand why things were the way they were.

The Budgeting Process

The budgeting process for SCJ began in December, with the preparation of Corplan. Corplan was a formal financial plan that was submitted to Racine head office annually in March. To start, unit sales volumes by brand were forecasted by marketing and sales personnel. These volumes were forwarded to the production planning department which extended the volumes (via computer) using product formulas to develop such data as raw material usage, packaging component usage, and manpower requirements on the production line.

That information was passed on to the individual production department managers and/or supervisors, who generated operating budgets for their areas. These operating budgets were then forwarded to the Cost Department who used the operating budgets and volume information to develop the standard overhead, direct labour, and raw material rates which would be employed in the upcoming fiscal year beginning July 1.

STANDARD COST SYSTEM

On average, the cost of a product was composed of 35% raw materials, 5% direct labour, 15% overhead, and 45% packaging components. The low direct labour cost was the result of a highly automated manufacturing process from raw material to finished packaged product.

Each intermediate, as well as each size of a final product, was regarded as a separate product by the cost system. This meant that each separate product had its own cost card that captured the costs associated with manufacturing and packaging of that product in a run. For example, Exhibits 2 to 5 represented the cost cards for one size of Penny's home care product.

All costs on the cost sheets were expressed at standard rates. The raw material standard cost, based on actual price at standard volume, was changed monthly to correspond to actual prices paid to suppliers, with consideration given to typical volumes purchased and anticipated prices. As a result, there were no material price variances for the period. A standard direct labour cost (standard rate times standard hours) was determined at the beginning of each fiscal year and remained unchanged unless the manufacturing process was altered such that a change in the labour configuration occurred. Overhead costs were allocated to products through the use of five "burden pools": Fringe Benefits, Quality Control, Receiving and Storage, Cost Centre Charges, and Fixed Indirect. As outlined below, each burden pool was the accumulation of a number of specific overhead costs. The standard rates were established for each pool and applied to the products.

1) Fringe Benefits

Fringe Benefits represented 2.4% of the cost of sales. This included night shift and overtime premiums, termination pay, vacation pay, employee benefits, paid absenteeism, and educational aid, from all making (processing), fill and pack, and bottle moulding operating units.

An estimate of the total fringe benefits for the year was divided by an estimate of the total direct hourly wages for the complete manufacturing activity. This ratio currently averaged about 49% of the direct labour costs. This was the rate at which the fringe benefit pool was applied to the various products.

2) Quality Control

Quality Control (QC) charges were approximately 1.4% of the cost of sales. These represented the budgeted expenses of the Quality Control Department within the plant. The total budget expenses of the quality control department were then distributed to the various operating units listed in Exhibit 6. Each operating unit was assigned a proportion of the total QC department budget based upon an assessment, by the quality control manager, of the time spent by quality control on the activities of that specific department.

These quality control costs were then attached to the products that passed through the specific department. In the departments associated with the "making" process, the quality control costs were allocated per kilogram of product processed. For the "fill and pack" departments, the costs were allocated on the basis of cases of product passing through the department. In each situation, it was necessary to estimate the volume of activity that was expected to occur in the specific department during the period.

3) Receiving and Storage

The expenses of the Receiving and Storage department totalled 1.7% of the cost of sales. These expenses included wages and salaries for all personnel working in the receiving bays and warehouse, all materials used in the department, as well as the cost of the facilities. This department primarily handled the raw materials used in the making of the products and the packaging components used to contain the products.

The wages and salary component of this cost pool was split between the raw materials and the packaging components on the basis of the estimated time used to handle each group. All the other expenses in this cost pool were distributed between raw materials and packaging components on the basis of a percentage of average inventory for the firm.

Consider the following illustration. During the period, the firm purchases $13,346,952 in raw materials. This inventory turns over 7.7 times during the period. Thus, the average raw material inventory is $1,733,721. In the case of packaging components, the firm purchases $9,699,980 and this turns over 5.8 times. The average packaging components inventory is $1,672,410. The total average inventory for the period is $1,733,721 plus $1,672,410 or $3,406,131 of which 50.9% is composed of raw materials and the balance of packaging components. This, then, was the proportion upon which the remaining expenses of the receiving and storage department were allocated between raw materials and packaging components.

The next step was to assign the allocated costs for raw materials to specific materials. This was done on the basis of the expected kilograms of each raw material to be obtained during the period. Therefore, each kilogram of raw material acquired during the period would be assigned the same amount of costs for receiving and storage.

To assign the allocated costs for packaging components to specific items, it was necessary to subdivide all packaging components into one of four categories: drums, pails, cans and bottles, and all others. The dollar value of all purchases in a category for the period was compared to the total dollar value for all purchases of packaging components in the period. For example, in the latest period, the dollar value of purchases for cans and bottles represented 42% of the $9,699,980 purchases of packaging components. The receiving and storage costs allocated to packaging goods would be distributed such that 42% of those costs were assigned to the cans and bottles category. This would be done for each of the four categories.

The final step in this allocation process was to incorporate the unit volume to be purchased in each subcategory of components. This resulted in a rate per drum, per pail, per can or bottle, and per other component.

4) Cost Centres

The costs to purchase, run, and maintain the production facilities represented 5.6% of the cost of sales. These costs included items such as repairs and maintenance, factory supplies, water, building depreciation, equipment and fixture depreciation, contract cleaning, building occupancy, steam, power, and heat, liquid waste removal, and fixed service charges. All of these were collected into a cost pool called Cost Centres. This pool was distributed among the production departments on the basis of budgeted amounts of use.

For each of the making departments, it was necessary to estimate the number of kilograms of product that would be processed in that department during the period. The cost centre charges assigned to that department would be divided by the estimated number of kilograms, to generate a cost per kilogram allocation for each material processed in the department.

In the fill and pack departments, an estimate was made of the number of production labour hours that would occur in each department during the period. In this way, a cost per hour was developed for each fill and pack department. This cost was then attached to the final product on the basis of the amount of production time required to process a case of output through a department.

5) FIXED INDIRECT

The fixed indirect cost pool represented 5.6% of cost of sales. Included in the pool were the following items: engineering department, purchasing department, production planning department, manufacturing administration, supervisory salaries, wages, and fringe benefits, and information systems expenses. The total in this cost pool was distributed among the Consumer Product line, Innochem product line, and Purchased Finished Goods product line, on the basis of the estimated time spent by individuals and departments on the products associated with the lines.

The fixed indirect costs assigned to a product line were then divided by the estimated total standard cost accumulated for all products in that line for the period. This percentage was then charged to the standard cost for each product in the line during the period.

PRODUCT COSTING — INTERMEDIATE PRODUCTS

Exhibits 2 to 5 were the standard cost summary cards for all steps in the process of making and packaging the home care product for which Penny McIntyre was responsible. Exhibits 2 and 3 related to specific intermediate products. Exhibit 4 related to the development of a blended intermediate product, and Exhibit 5 reflected the packaging of the final product. For all work in process, the standard cost summary sheets reflected the cost to produce one kilogram of the product. For all final products, the standard cost summary sheet documented the cost to produce one case of product.

Each of the standard cost summary sheets had a column marked Current Month Amount. This column was used to report the most recently used costs for each cost category. In most cases, the only difference between cost reported in this column and that reported in the Next Month column was for raw materials. Since the costs for raw materials tended to change regularly, it was company practice to alter, at the end of each month, the cost per inventory unit of raw materials to reflect any changes for the upcoming month. The information in the Next Month column was the cost data that would become standard for that product or category in the upcoming month. In the case of most of the other cost categories, the rates or overhead applications were set for specific periods of times ranging from three months to one year.

Exhibits 2 and 3 indicated that several different types of raw materials were required to produce each of these products. The quantity of each raw material used was expressed in kilograms. The cost of each raw material used reflected the most recent cost available from the end of the previous month. The total material cost for one kilogram of the product was reported as a variable cost. The direct labour needed to produce one kilogram of the product was also recorded as a variable cost. As described in the previous section, the costs associated with fringe benefits were assigned to all intermediate and finished products on the basis of direct labour dollars. This amount was reported on the cost sheet as a variable cost per kilogram of the product.

The semi-variable costs on the cost summary sheets included quality control, and receiving and storage. As the cost sheets (Exhibits 2 and 3) indicate, these charges were calculated per kilogram of product.

The fixed costs related to the manufacturing cost centre charges. This cost was determined for one kilogram of product based upon the allocation procedure described earlier.

In the case of the work in process products, there were no costs associated with packaging materials. None of these products, at this stage of the process, were being put into packages. The standard cost summary sheets for the two intermediate products indicated the raw material cost per kilogram, the total labour and burden cost per kilogram, and the total cost per kilogram.

PRODUCT COSTING — BLENDED PRODUCT

Exhibit 4 was the standard cost summary for the intermediate product that was generated when the previous two intermediate products were mixed. The exhibit shows the amount of each intermediate needed to produce one kilogram of the blended product. In addition, some other raw materials, including Active A, were required.

On this cost sheet, the costs of the other intermediate products were reported under the column of previous process. The costs associated with the additional blending raw materials, and the labour needed to conduct the blending were reported in the column for this process. Again, the costs associated with the various overhead pools (Fringe, QC, Receiving and Storage, Manufacturing Cost Centres) were also assigned to this blended product in accordance with the allocation procedures previously described.

The direct labour costs and the various burden costs associated with the previous intermediate products were reported as if the two intermediates were now a single blended product. To illustrate the process, see the following table associated with the data on Exhibit 4.

NEXT MONTH

Category	Current Month Amount	This Process Amount	Previous Process Amount	Total
Raw Matls	.35640	.03274	.32259(a)	.35533
Mfg Labor	.01069	.00263	.00806(b)	.01069
Quality Control	.01198	.00635	.00563(c)	.01198
Mfg C.C. Charge	.07442	.03019	.04423(d)	.07442

(a) As indicated on top of Exhibit 4.

(b) (from Exhibit 2)   (from Exhibit 3)
     (Qty Int.1 × Mfg Lab Int. 1) + (Qty Int. 2 × Mfg Lab Int. 2)
     (.62740 × .01067)   + (.10500 × .01305) = $.00806

(c) (Qty Int.1 × QC Int.1)   + (Qty Int. 2 × QC Int. 2)
     (.62740 × .00769)   + (.10500 × .00769) = $.00563

(d   (Qty Int.1 × Mfg C.C. Int.1) + (Qty Int. 2 × Mfg C.C. Int. 2)
     (.62740 × .06040)   + (.10500 × .06040) = $.04423

PRODUCT COSTING — FINAL PRODUCT

Exhibit 5 was the standard cost summary sheet for one case of the final product. The sheet indicated that one case of final product required 9.312 kilograms of the blended product developed in Exhibit 4. In addition, this final process required several different packaging components. These components were detailed on the cost sheet in terms of quantity, unit cost, and total packaging cost.

Examining the data reported in the column for the previous process, the extended costs of the blended product, based upon the quantity required for one case, were reported. This column indicated that 9.312 kilograms of the blended product cost $4.33501. This included all materials, labour, and allocated burden charges as assigned to the previous production stages.

The costs for the final packaging were reported in the column for "this process". Note that there were no raw materials since this process was only for packaging the final product. The components used were classified as packaging materials. The direct labour cost referred to the labour needed on the line to pack one case of product.

The fringe benefits for packaging were attached to the case of final product on the basis of the direct labour cost. The quality control costs, packaging receiving and storage costs, and filling cost centre charges were allocated on the basis of the procedures described earlier.

This standard cost summary sheet reported that the total raw material cost for one case of this product was $3.30883. The total packaging component cost for one case of this product was $4.30105. The total labour and burden for one case of this product was $2.65724. Including manufacturing loss, the total cost to produce one case of this product was $10.47246.

PRODUCT PRICING

One of Penny's responsibilities as a Product Manager was to set selling prices for her brands. Projected sales volume and product cost were primary considerations when establishing selling prices since each brand was expected to contribute a designated amount to the corporate profitability goal. The amount designated would, of course, reflect such things as: competition, product positioning (i.e., premium, middle, low quality), and specific product intentions (e.g., some products were added to complete a line, for instance, rather than to be a big money-maker). Penny knew that if volume fell or product costs increased, an adjustment to her selling price per case would undoubtedly be necessary to maintain her brand's contribution to the company's profit goal. Since her home care product was a large volume product and a significant profit contributor, Penny was quite anxious to have her concerns addressed.

Exhibit 1

S.C. JOHNSON AND SON, INC.
Worldwide Organization

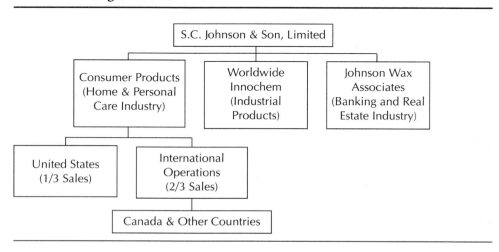

Exhibit 2

S.C. JOHNSON AND SON, LTD.—Intermediate Product A

Standard Cost Summary — Confidential

REPORT NUMBER	COUNTRY	FINISHED GOODS SHIPPING WT	FREIGHT	ITEM CATEGORY WORK IN PROGRESS	PRODUCT DESCRIPTION	EFFECTIVE DATE MO DAY YR	SERIAL NUMBER	CODE
	CANADA							

WORK IN PROGRESS

CODE	DESCRIPTION	QUANTITY	RAW MATERIAL COST PER INVENTORY UNIT	AMOUNT	PACKAGING MATERIAL COST PER INVENTORY UNIT	AMOUNT	LABOUR AND BURDEN COST PER INVENTORY UNIT	AMOUNT	LOSS COST PER INVENTORY UNIT	AMOUNT	TOTAL

RAW AND PACKAGING MATERIALS

CODE	DESCRIPTION	QUANTITY	RAW MATERIAL COST PER INVENTORY UNIT	RAW MATERIAL AMOUNT	PACKAGING MATERIAL COST PER INVENTORY UNIT	PACKAGING MATERIAL AMOUNT
	ACTIVE A	.01751	.17500	.00306		
	ACTIVE B	.00080	1.43500	.00115		
	ACTIVE C	.00080	1.27000	.00102		
	ACTIVE D	.07705	1.48001	.11403		
	ACTIVE E	.02802	2.32562	.06516		
	ACTIVE F	.01751	1.27000	.02227		
	ACTIVE G	.05253	1.43165	.07520		
	ACTIVE H	.00248	5.13750	.01274		
	ACTIVE I	.01488	3.75000	.05580		
	ACTIVE J	.06503	1.30835	.08508		
	WATER	.72339				
				.43551		

BULK 3 – OTHER MAKING 2 – PERS CARE MAKING 1 – MOLDING
WIP 5 – SET-UP A – #NON OPERATORS B – #OPERATORS
F. G. 5 – #NON OPERATORS 4 – #OPERATORS 3 – #SET-UP

COST CTR	FIX DIR CAT	CREW SIZE BY PAY GROUP					VARIABLE DIRECT	VARIABLE INDIRECT	FIXED DIRECT	LABOUR & FRG PER COST CTR
		5	4	3	2	1				
						A	B			
001	13			80				.01067	.00524	.06040	.07631
										.07631

QUANTITY PER SHIPT
9384

SERIAL NUMBER		
PREVIOUS MONTH	CURRENT MONTH	NEXT MONTH
001	001	001

SUMMARY OF COST COMPONENTS FOR THIS ITEM

CATEGORY	PREVIOUS MONTH TOTAL STD	CURRENT MONTH TTL STD	THIS PROCESS AMOUNT	PREVIOUS PROCESS AMOUNT	TOTAL
		CURRENT MONTH AMOUNT	NEXT MONTH THIS PROCESS AMOUNT – OVERDUE	PREVIOUS PROCESS AMOUNT	TOTAL
VARIABLE					
RAW MATERIALS		.43730	.43551		.43551
PKG MATERIALS					
MFG LABOUR		.01067	.01067		.01067
MFG LABOURFRINGE		.00524	.00524		.00524
FILL LABOUR					
FILL LABORFRINGE					
CONTRACT LABOUR					
PURCH F. G. FREIGHT					
PURCH F. G. PRICE					
VAR COST SUB TOTAL		.45321	.45142		.45142
SEMI VARIABLE					
QUALITY CONTROL		.00769	.00769		.00769
RAW MATL REC & STORE		.00969	.00969		.00969
PKG MATL REC & STORES					
F G SHIP & STORES					
SEMI VAR SUB TOTAL		.01738	.01738		.01738
FIXED					
MFG C C CHARGE		.06040	.06040		.06040
FILL C C CHARGE					
TOOL & DIE AMOUNT					
PURCH F G BURDEN					
FIXED DIRECT					
FIXED SUB TOTAL		.06040	.06040		.06040
LOSS%	%				

PREVIOUS MONTH TOTAL STD	CURRENT MONTH TTL STD	TOTAL THIS PROCESS	TOTAL PREVIOUS PROCESS	TOTAL NXT MO STD CST
.53517	.53099	.52920		.52920

TOTAL LABOUR AND BURDEN THIS PROCESS	TOTAL LABOUR AND BURDEN PREV PROC	DEFERRED PROMOTION EXPENSE
.09369	.09369	

TOTAL RAW MATERIAL	TOTAL PKG MATERIAL	TOTAL LAB & BURDEN	TOTAL MFG LOSS	TOTAL STD COST
.43551		.09369		.52920

Exhibit 3

S.C. JOHNSON AND SON, LTD.—Intermediate Product B

Standard Cost Summary — Confidential

REPORT NUMBER	COUNTRY		ITEM CATEGORY	PRODUCT DESCRIPTION		EFFECTIVE DATE			SERIAL NUMBER		CODE
M-XE559	CANADA		WORK IN PROGRESS			MO	DAY	YR	001		225210

WORK IN PROGRESS / FINISHED GOODS / FREIGHT / SHIPPING WT

	LABOUR AND BURDEN				
	COST PER INVENTORY UNIT	AMOUNT	COST PER INVENTORY UNIT	LOSS	
				AMOUNT	TOTAL

RAW AND PACKAGING MATERIALS

CODE	DESCRIPTION	QUANTITY	COST PER INVENTORY UNIT	RAW MATERIAL AMOUNT	PACKAGING MATERIAL AMOUNT
	ACTIVE A	.04580	.17500	.00802	
	ACTIVE B	.00640	1.43500	.00918	
	ACTIVE C	.00512	1.27000	.00650	
	ACTIVE F	.12496	1.27200	.15895	
	ACTIVE K	.06023	1.37000	.08252	
	ACTIVE H	.00895	5.13750	.04598	
	ACTIVE L	.12138	1.30835	.15881	
	WATER	.62716			
				.46996	

BULK 3 – OTHER MAKING 2 – PERS CARE MAKING 1 – MOLDING
WIP 5 – SET-UP A – #NON OPERATORS B – #OPERATORS
F. G. 5 – #NON OPERATORS 4 – #OPERATORS 3 – #SET-UP

COST CTR	FIX DIR CAT	CREW SIZE BY PAY GROUP								VARIABLE DIRECT	VARIABLE INDIRECT	FIXED DIRECT	LABOUR & FRG PER COST CTR
		5	4	3	2	1	A	B				
001	13			104					.01305	.00641	.06040	.07986
												.07986

SERIAL NUMBER		
PREVIOUS MONTH	CURRENT MONTH	NEXT MONTH
001	001	001

QUANTITY PER SHIPT
9976

SUMMARY OF COST COMPONENTS FOR THIS ITEM

CATEGORY	CURRENT MONTH AMOUNT	THIS PROCESS AMOUNT	NEXT MONTH PREVIOUS PROCESS AMOUNT	TOTAL
VARIABLE				
RAW MATERIALS	.46839	.46996		.46996
PKG MATERIALS				
MFG LABOUR	.01305	.01305		.01305
MFG LABOURFRINGE	.00641	.00641		.00641
FILL LABOUR				
FILL LABOURFRINGE				
CONTRACT LABOUR				
PURCH F.G. FREIGHT				
PURCH F.G. PRICE				
VAR COST SUB TOTAL	.48785	.48942		.48942
SEMI VARIABLE				
QUALITY CONTROL	.00769	.00769		.00769
RAW MATL REC & STORE	.01306	.01306		.01306
PKG MATL REC & STORES				
F G SHIP & STORES				
SEMI VAR SUB TOTAL	.02075	.02075		.02075
FIXED				
MFG C C CHARGE	.06040	.06040		.06040
FILL C C CHARGE				
TOOL & DIE AMOUNT				
PURCH F G BURDEN				
FIXED DIRECT				
FIXED SUB TOTAL	.06040	.06040		.06040
LOSS%				

% PREVIOUS MONTH TOTAL STD	TOTAL THIS PROCESS	TOTAL PREVIOUS PROCESS	TOTAL NXT MO STD CST
.55028	.57057		.57057

PREVIOUS MONTH TTL STD	CURRENT MONTH TTL STD
.56900	

TOTAL LABOUR AND BURDEN THIS PROCESS	TOTAL LABOUR AND BURDEN PREV PROC	DEFERRED PROMOTION EXPENSE
.10061		

TOTAL LAB & BURDEN	TOTAL MFG LOSS	TOTAL STD COST
.10061		.57057

TOTAL RAW MATERIAL	TOTAL PKG MATERIAL
.46996	

Exhibit 4

S.C. JOHNSON AND SON, LTD.—Blended Intermediate Product

Standard Cost Summary — Confidential

REPORT NUMBER	COUNTRY	FINISHED GOODS	ITEM CATEGORY	PRODUCT DESCRIPTION	EFFECTIVE DATE	SERIAL NUMBER	CODE
M-XE559	CANADA	SHIPPING WT. / FREIGHT	WORK IN PROGRESS		MO / DAY / YR		

WORK IN PROGRESS

CODE	DESCRIPTION	QUANTITY	RAW MATERIAL COST PER INVENTORY	AMOUNT	PACKAGING MATERIAL COST PER INVENT UNIT	LABOUR AND BURDEN COST PER INVENT UNIT	AMOUNT	LOSS	TOTAL
		.10500	.46996	.04935		.10061	.01056		.05991
		.62740	.43551	.27324		.19369	.05878		.33202
				.32259			.06934		.39193

RAW AND PACKAGING MATERIALS

CODE	DESCRIPTION	QUANTITY	COST PER INVENTORY UNIT	RAW MATERIAL AMOUNT	PACKAGING MATERIAL AMOUNT
	ACTIVE A	.00200	.17500	.00035	
	FORMALDEHYDE	.00200	.38000	.00076	
	ACTIVE M	.00020	42.21900	.00844	
	ACTIVE I	.00100	3.75000	.00375	
	ACTIVE J	.00572	1.30835	.00748	
	WATER	.25618			
	ACTIVE N	.00050	23.91948	.01196	
					.03274

BULK 3 – OTHER MAKING 2 – PERS CARE MAKING 1 – MOLDING
WIP 5 – SET-UP A – #NON OPERATORS B – #OPERATORS
F.G. 5 – #NON OPERATORS 4 – #OPERATORS 3 – #SET-UP

CREW SIZE BY PAY GROUP

COST CTR	FIX DIR CAT	5	4	3	2	1	A	B	VARIABLE DIRECT	VARIABLE INDIRECT	FIXED DIRECT	LABOUR & FRG PER COST CTR
103	12			80					.00263	.00129	.03019	.03411
												.03411

SERIAL NUMBER

	PREVIOUS MONTH	CURRENT MONTH	NEXT MONTH
	015	015	015

QUANTITY PER SHIPT
3800

SUMMARY OF COST COMPONENTS FOR THIS ITEM

CATEGORY	CURRENT MONTH AMOUNT	THIS PROCESS	NEXT MONTH — OVERDUE AMOUNT	PREVIOUS PROCESS AMOUNT	TOTAL
VARIABLE					
RAW MATERIALS	.35640	.03274		.32259	.35533
PKG MATERIALS	.01069	.00263		.00806	.01069
MFG LABOUR	.00525	.00129		.00396	.00525
MFG LABOURFRINGE					
FILL LABOUR					
FILL LABOUR FRINGE			*		
CONTRACT LABOUR			*		
PURCH F.G. FREIGHT			*		
PURCH F.G. PRICE					
VAR COST SUB TOTAL	.37234	.03666		.33461	.37127
SEMI VARIABLE					
QUALITY CONTROL	.01198	.00635	*	.00563	.01198
RAW MATL REC & STORE	.00786	.00041	*	.00745	.00786
PKG MATL REC & STORES					
F G SHIP & STORES					
SEMI VAR SUB TOTAL	.01984	.00676		.01308	.01984
FIXED					
MFG C C CHARGE	.07442	.03019	*	.04423	.07442
FILL C C CHARGE					
TOOL & DIE AMOUNT					
PURCH F G BURDEN					
FIXED DIRECT	.07442	.03019		.04423	.07442
FIXED SUB TOTAL					
LOSS%					

	CURRENT MONTH TTL STD	TOTAL THIS PROCESS	TOTAL PREVIOUS PROCESS	TOTAL NXT MO STD CST
	.46660	.07361	.39192	.46553
PREVIOUS MONTH TOTAL STD %				
.46726				

TOTAL LABOUR AND BURDEN THIS PROCESS	TOTAL LABOUR AND BURDEN PREV PROC
	.06933
.04087	

TOTAL RAW MATERIAL	TOTAL PKG MATERIAL	TOTAL LAB & BURDEN	TOTAL MFG LOSS	TOTAL STD COST
.35533		.11020		.46553

DEFERRED PROMOTION EXPENSE

Exhibit 5

S.C. JOHNSON AND SON, LTD.—Finished Good

Standard Cost Summary — Confidential

REPORT NUMBER	COUNTRY		FINISHED GOODS		ITEM CATEGORY	PRODUCT DESCRIPTION	EFFECTIVE DATE			SERIAL	CODE
M-XE559	CANADA		SHIPPING WT.	FREIGHT	FINISHED GOOD		MO	DAY	YR	NUMBER	
			11.00	1.10							

WORK IN PROGRESS

			RAW MATERIAL		PACKAGING MATERIAL		LABOUR AND BURDEN		LOSS		
CODE	DESCRIPTION	QUANTITY	COST PER INVENT UNIT	AMOUNT	COST PER INVENT UNIT	AMOUNT	COST PER INVENT UNIT	AMOUNT	COST PER INVENT UNIT	AMOUNT	TOTAL
		9.31200	.35533	3.30883			.11020	1.02618			4.33501
				3.30883				1.02618			4.33501

RAW AND PACKAGING MATERIALS

CODE	DESCRIPTION	QUANTITY	COST PER INVENTORY UNIT	RAW MATERIAL AMOUNT	PACKAGING MATERIAL AMOUNT
	BOTTLES	12.00000	.21916		2.62992
	CAPS	12.00000	.07298		.87576
	LABELS	12.00000	.02427		.29124
	CASE	1.00000	.30767		.30767
	CASE DIVIDERS	1.00000	.19646		.19646
					4.30105

BULK 3 – OTHER MAKING 2 – PERS CARE MAKING 1 – MOLDING
WIP 5 – SET-UP A – #NON OPERATORS B – #OPERATORS
F.G. 5 – #NON OPERATORS 4 – #OPERATORS 3 – #SET-UP

COST CTR	FIX DIR CAT	CREW SIZE BY PAY GROUP							VARIABLE DIRECT	VARIABLE INDIRECT	FIXED DIRECT	LABOUR & FRG PER COST CTR
		5	4	3	2	1	A	B				
202	02	63	36	11					.34545	.16965	.18271	.69781
												.69781

SUMMARY OF COST COMPONENTS FOR THIS ITEM

CATEGORY	CURRENT MONTH AMOUNT	THIS PROCESS	PREVIOUS PROCESS	NEXT MONTH AMOUNT	TOTAL
			* – OVERDUE		
VARIABLE					
RAW MATERIALS	3.31880				3.30883
PKG MATERIALS	4.30105	4.30105		3.30883	4.30105
MFG LABOUR	.09955			.09955	.09955
MFG LABOURFRINGE	.04889			.04889	.04889
FILL LABOUR	.34545	.34545		.34545	.34545
FILL LABOURFRINGE	.16965	.16965		.16965	.16965
CONTRACT LABOUR					
PURCH F. G. FREIGHT					
PURCH F. G. PRICE		*			
VAR COST SUB TOTAL	8.28339	4.81615		3.45727	8.27342
SEMI VARIABLE					
QUALITY CONTROL	.15155	.03999	*	.11156	.15155
RAW MATL REC & STORE	.07319	.04706		.07319	.07319
PKG MATL REC & STORES	.04706		*		.04706
F G SHIP & STORES					
SEMI VAR SUB TOTAL	.27180	.08705		.18475	.27180
FIXED					
MFG C C CHARGE	.69300	.18271		.69300	.69300
FILL C C CHARGE	.18271		*		.18271
TOOL & DIE AMOUNT					
PURCH F G BURDEN					
FIXED DIRECT	.84708	.84619		.84619	.84619
FIXED SUB TOTAL	1.72279	1.02890		1.72190	1.72190
LOSS%	.20556	.20534		.69300	.20534
2.000%					

	PREVIOUS MONTH TOTAL STD	CURRENT MONTH TTL STD	TOTAL THIS PROCESS	TOTAL PREVIOUS PROCESS	TOTAL NXT MO STD CST
LOSS%	10.46422	10.48354	6.13744	4.33502	10.47246
2.000%					

TOTAL LABOUR AND BURDEN THIS PROCESS	TOTAL LABOUR AND BURDEN PREV PROC
1.63105	1.02619

TOTAL RAW MATERIAL	TOTAL PKG MATERIAL
3.30883	4.30105

TOTAL LAB & BURDEN
2.65724

TOTAL MFG LOSS	DEFERRED PROMOTION EXPENSE
.20534	

TOTAL STD COST
10.47246

	SERIAL NUMBER	
PREVIOUS MONTH	CURRENT MONTH	NEXT MONTH
009	009	009

QUANTITY PER SHIPT
2800

Exhibit 6

MANUFACTURING OPERATING UNITS

1. Polymer Processing
2. Wax Processing
3. Pressure (Aerosol) Processing
4. Wax Fill and Pack
5. Pressure Fill and Pack
6. Plastic Moulding
7. Personal Care Processing
8. Personal Care Fill and Pack
9. Flo-Thru, Langen Lines (Air Fresheners)
10. Contract Fillers
11. Brantford Receiving (Raw Material and Packaging)
12. Steam, Power, Heat
13. Maintenance
14. Administration
15. General Production
16. Production Planning
17. Engineering
18. Purchasing
19. Building Occupancy — Total Company
20. Quality Assurance — Main Lab

TREMCO PRODUCTION COSTS

Randolph Kudar

"This appears to be a good time to get an objective assessment of our cost system. We are in the process of automating our cost system onto computers. Up to now, almost all of the activities associated with setting standards and budgets for the upcoming year have been done manually. We have spent a lot of time developing our standard cost system and we think that it works pretty well. Still, if there are places where we can make improvements and corrections, we should look at them now before we incur the cost of putting our systems onto the computer.

"At the same time, it would be useful to have you explain, to our sales division managers, how our cost system works. They really do not understand it, and they certainly do not have the time to learn about cost accounting in a manufacturing operation."

With those words, I was given the opportunity to look at the cost system used at Tremco Canada. Bill Essex, the corporate controller, agreed to provide me with whatever information I needed to understand and assess the system being used. He expected a report that would assist him in determining whether the system, as it presently stood, should be automated or whether there should be changes made.

INTRODUCTION

Tremco Canada is a wholly owned subsidiary of a United States major corporation. It is engaged in the manufacture, distribution, and selling of roofing materials, sealants, and paints. Its products are sold nationally across Canada. The firm is organized functionally into three areas, administration, marketing, and production (see Exhibit 1).

Production

The production activities consist of 15 different production departments. The configuration of the departments and the number of departments is not constant. As new products are developed and old products are terminated, some of the production departments are eliminated and new ones are set up. While this does not happen every year, it does happen with some degree of regularity.

The production departments are of various size. The size of the department is a function of the volume and type of products that are generated in the department. In addition, the skill level of the workers and the necessary equipment are different among the departments.

Not all products pass through all production departments. There are many products that only pass through one production department. However there are many products that also pass through several production departments. In those departments, where mixing equipment is used, there are often different capacity mixers which are tended by the same personnel. It is a common practice to have intermediate products produced in different departments and combined into the end product in another department.

The company produces thousands of different products each year. Some of the products are dramatically different from any other type of product made by the firm. Some products are only variations of basic products. For example, each colour of paint produced by the firm is classified as a separate product with a separate product number.

Almost all of the products are produced in batches. For each product there is a standard recipe, developed by the production engineering department, that specifies the ingredients, mixing procedure, and production departments that the product must pass through in order to be completed. In addition, the recipe also specifies the mixing equipment that should be used as well as the yield that should result from the batch.

To produce the wide range of products offered by Tremco, it is necessary for the firm to utilize a large number of different raw materials. Several hundred raw materials are stored and used by the firm in its production process. The materials are purchased in varying quantities depending upon the usage, and availability of supply. In the case of bulk materials, the inventories are stored wherever space is available in the plant. In some instances materials are purchased for special products or one time production runs. In some cases, due to minimum purchase order quantities, the quantity of material purchased far exceeds the amount needed for the batch. In those instances, the remaining material may sit around the plant for a prolonged period of time and may never be used again. This only happens on rare special orders and is not considered to be a major problem.

The production departments are not dedicated to specific sales divisions. Thus it is possible for the output from one production department to be sold to several sales divisions. In order to utilize the capacity of the production departments more effectively, many batches of products are manufactured for inventory. Usually, these products have very high volumes and some seasonality to their sales pattern. This practice enables the firm to keep its work force busy throughout the year and avoids the need to incur excessive amounts of overtime in the peak periods or to lay personnel off during the slack periods. Despite this practice, there is still need at certain times of the year to incur overtime in order to meet sales demand for some products.

Sales/Marketing

The sales and marketing activities consist of nine sales divisions based upon different market segments. The sales divisions are of different sizes in terms of sales. There is a significant difference in the scope of operations among the different divisions.

In some markets, the firm is recognized as the market leader. The products of the firm command a dominant share of the market. Often in these markets, Tremco is also the price setter. For example, the firm is renowned for its rust resistant paint, Tremclad, which is dominant in the market. In other markets, Tremco is just one of many firms. It does not set the price but may have to compete on price. In other cases, the nature of the competition is on quality.

The sales divisions acquire almost all of their products from the production departments of Tremco. However, there are a very few products that are imported from the parent company in the United States and sold in Canada through the sales divisions.

In some instances there are products that are inter-related in terms of sales. Either the products constitute a complete product line for the customer or the product is manufactured and sold only because the firm also sells a complimentary product. One example of this is the wide variety of colours that might be offered for specialized paints. In some cases, the volume of the pigment is not economical. However, the sale of the complimentary product, base paint, is of significant size and may depend upon the availability of the pigment.

Some divisions do not sell products so much as they sell services that ultimately use the products manufactured by the firm. This is the case in the roofing division. Here the division concentrates on selling the customer the need for a roofing system for his buildings. As part of the process, the products manufactured by

Tremco are specified as the standard for the job. Thus, the products are simply a part of the entire package offered by the firm.

Demand for some products is seasonal while demand for others is very stable. In some divisions, the volume of demand can be estimated with a high degree of accuracy while, for other products, the demand is highly uncertain and dependent upon a multitude of factors. Again, roofing is a prime example of a product line that is very hard to estimate sales volume, because the selling process is very long term.

Part of the sales and marketing function involves the identification and sales of new products. There is a constant need to develop new products to compete in many of the markets serviced by Tremco. Often this process entails trying to meet a customer's need by developing a product specifically for his application. To do this, it is necessary for the sales division to indicate to the production operations what it is they want the product to do.

When operations identifies what is needed to produce such a product, sales is informed by accounting what the estimated standard cost of such a product would be for a specific batch size. It now becomes the task of the sales division to determine whether it is possible to sell the product at a price that will be high enough to cover the standard cost estimated for the product. In some cases, pilot batches of new products are produced and the output sold by the sales division. Often the cost for these pilot batches does not include any overhead costs. Instead they are costed at estimated standard material and labour cost only.

THE COST ACCOUNTING SYSTEM

The cost accounting system used at Tremco is a standard cost system. Every product manufactured in the firm is costed at standard. All material, direct labour, variable overhead, and fixed overhead costs are taken into work in process at standard cost. Standard costs are used to value the finished goods inventory of the firm. Standard production costs are used to transfer the production costs of the good to the sales divisions. All variances associated with materials and production costs are closed off to the sales divisions either monthly or annually. Thus the cost of goods sold as reported on the year end divisional income statements are actual production costs for the goods.

Material

Since every product manufactured by Tremco is based upon specified recipes, the standard material cost is not a major problem. The standard cost for materials is based upon the average material cost that the company expects to pay during the year. Thus, at the start of the year, it is to be expected that there will be favourable material price variance. However, by the end of the year, the material price variance should be almost totally eliminated.

Material usage variance is calculated by taking a physical count of raw material inventory in the plant at regular intervals. All shortages, shrinkages, obsolescence, and other factors affecting material usage are assigned to the sales divisions on the basis of the proportion of the materials used in the products that they have sold (see Exhibit 2).

Labour

Standard labour rates are calculated for each production department. This process begins with the determination of the average hourly rate actually paid to all hourly workers in the individual production department during June of the year. This figure is then adjusted to reflect anticipated pay increases for the upcoming year. In addition, the calculated average hourly rate in the specific department is then adjusted for planned productivity increases by labour during the upcoming year. At the end of this process, there is a standard hourly wage rate determined for each production department.

The standard labour hours that each batch of product spends in the various production departments are specified by the recipe for producing a batch of the product. Using these standard labour hours, the standard labour cost is attached to each batch of product produced during the period. At year end, the total labour variance between actual labour cost incurred and standard labour cost attached to the products produced is allocated to the sales divisions in proportion to the volume of product ordered by the sales divisions during the year.

Overhead

The overhead costs of the production departments constitute a more complex problem for the accounting system. Many of the overhead costs are associated with all or some of the production departments. For example, repairs and maintenance for the building would apply to all production departments. However, some of these overhead costs are clearly associated with specific production departments. The repairs and maintenance for equipment would apply only to the departments that utilized equipment.

Few, if any, of the overhead costs are directly related to specific products manufactured by the firm. Some of the overheads are related to various types of activities that occur in the production process. For example, overtime premiums are related to the volume of products generated in some production departments. Other overhead costs appear to be independent of any activity. The dues and subscriptions have no relation to any type of production activity.

Cost Behaviour

The records of Tremco are such that the actual overhead costs incurred in the previous year are known. These actual costs have been classified into 63 different accounts based upon the purpose for which the overhead has been incurred. In addition, it is possible for the system to identify overhead costs that have been incurred in specific production departments. For example, the overtime premiums paid to direct labour in the past year in each production department can be identified.

One of the first steps in treating the overhead costs is to ascertain what proportion of each of the 63 accounts is fixed and variable. For each overhead account, a percentage of the account is determined to be variable and the balance fixed. This judgement is undertaken by personnel in the accounting department. This determination is presented in Exhibit 3.

Estimated Total Cost

The next step is to determine to what extent the total cost for each of the 63 different accounts might change in the upcoming period. This involves understanding how activity might alter, or how cost drivers associated with the accounts might change. For example, the utility rates for water and natural gas might be expected to alter during the year. This analysis allows the accounting department to estimate the total cost that could be expected to be associated with each of the accounts in the coming year.

Department Allocation

The allocation process used by the firm involves assigning all the overhead costs associated with the 63 different accounts to the 15 production departments. The initial part of the process involves identifying what factor makes the most sense in relating the specific overhead cost account to the set of production departments. For example, in assigning the estimated overtime premiums among the production departments, the process began by identifying how much overtime premium was incurred by each of the production departments in the current year. This distribution was defined to be the basis upon which the total estimated overtime premiums budgeted for the upcoming year would be allocated to the production departments. Thus, the total estimated overtime premium for the upcoming year would be multiplied by the distribution of actual overtime premium in the current year to determine how much overtime premium would be allocated to each individual production department.

A similar process is followed for each of the 63 different overhead accounts. In conducting this analysis it is found that the accounting department used 36 different bases for allocating the overhead production costs among the fifteen production departments. In many instances, the determination of the appropriate allocation factor is based upon common sense. The distribution of the allocation factor among the production departments is often based upon the distribution of the same overhead account to the production departments in the previous year. In other instances, the distribution of the allocation factor is based upon managerial judgement. A list of the factors used to allocate the overhead accounts among the production departments is listed in Exhibit 4.

One other step in the allocation of overhead costs to the production departments is undertaken. Some of the production departments have no direct association with the manufacturing of products. Departments such as watchmen, maintenance, and plant cleaners have some overhead costs assigned to them but none of these departments is directly involved in the manufacture of products for sale. These costs are re-allocated to the production departments that do have direct involvement in production of products on selected bases.

This allocation process is conducted for both the fixed and variable components of the overhead accounts. At the conclusion of this analysis, the estimated value for each of the production overhead accounts has been allocated among the 15 production departments. Thus each production department has both a fixed overhead and a variable overhead cost allocated to it for the year.

Product Allocation

The final stage in the process is to develop a method of attaching the production overhead costs to the products that were manufactured by Tremco during the year. It now becomes necessary to allocate the production overheads from the production departments to the products. This involves identifying some activity base upon which to base the allocation and an estimate to the total amount of the activity so that an allocation rate can be established.

After examination of the system, it was concluded that the only activity basis that was common to all production departments was direct labour. Therefore the production overhead costs are allocated to the products on the basis of direct labour hours. For each production department, the total number of direct labour hours expected to be incurred is estimated. This involves estimating the standard number of direct labour hours for the planned production.

The total variable overhead cost assigned to a production department for the coming year is divided by the estimated total direct labour hours to be used in that department. The result is a standard variable overhead cost absorption rate for the individual production department. A similar process is carried out for each of the production departments that are directly involved in the manufacture of products. At the end of this process there is a standard variable overhead absorption rate for each production department.

In a similar manner, the total fixed overhead cost assigned to the production department for the coming year is divided by the estimated total direct labour hours to be spent in the department. The result is a standard fixed overhead cost absorption rate for each of the production departments.

As the data in Exhibit 5 indicates, the magnitude of the overhead costs is large relative to the magnitude of the direct labour cost. While the average standard direct labour cost per hour ranges from $14.40 to $18.60, the variable overhead rate ranges from $28.13 to $58.25 for each hour of direct labour. Similarly, the fixed overhead rate ranges from $29.25 to $102.05 for each hour of direct labour.

Cost Attachment to Products

As each product is put into production, the recipe identifies the standard materials required to complete the specified batch. The recipe also identifies the production departments where the work is to be done as well as the standard labour times required for the batch. Using this information, the accounting system can identify the standard direct labour cost, by production department, for each batch of product produced. The standard direct labour time is multiplied by the standard direct labour cost for the appropriate production department. At the same time, the accounting system also attaches to the batch of product the standard variable and fixed overhead cost associated with the direct labour cost incurred on the batch in each production department. Thus, the total standard cost for each batch of product is determined (see Exhibits 6 and 7).

Cost Transfer to Sales Divisions

When a batch of product is shipped to a customer, the revenue associated with the sale is identified with the sales division who made the sale. At the same time, the standard cost associated with the batch is transferred from the production departments to the sales division. Thus, the cost of goods sold figure reported on the sales division income statement is composed of the total standard cost of all the products sold by the division in the period.

In addition, the sales divisions also receive the material usage variances that occurred during the period. At the end of the period, it is likely that there will be variances associated with the labour inputs and the overheads. These variances will be distributed among the sales divisions according to various criteria.

In this way, all the production costs eventually get transferred to the sales divisions and are included in the calculation of sales division profit for the period.

CONCLUDING COSTS AND COMMENTS

Bill Essex indicated that the biggest problem facing the accounting system was the handling of the overhead variances.

"The difficulty with the overhead variance is the level of frustration that the sales division managers express when they receive it at the end of the period. If the firm has not achieved its sales and production targets for the period, then the overheads have not been fully absorbed by the products that have been sold. Thus it is necessary to assign these costs to the sales divisions. It may be that the sales division managers simply do not understand the concept of underabsorbed variance.

"I appreciate their frustration. There are times when the assigned underabsorbed overhead can wipe out good results for the year. Unfortunately, we cannot identify the magnitude of the overhead variance until it is practically too late for the sales divisions to do anything about it. When your bonus is based on profitability, the overhead variance can take money right out of your pocket.

"But, the only way that we can recover these overhead costs is through sales. If we do not assign them to the sales divisions, the pricing of our products will not reflect the entire costs that are incurred to produce the product. Thus, it is necessary to allocate all the production costs to the sales divisions."

I wondered where I should start this analysis and what impact any changes I might suggest would have on the firm, its products, and the evaluation of its personnel.

Exhibit 1

TREMCO CANADA

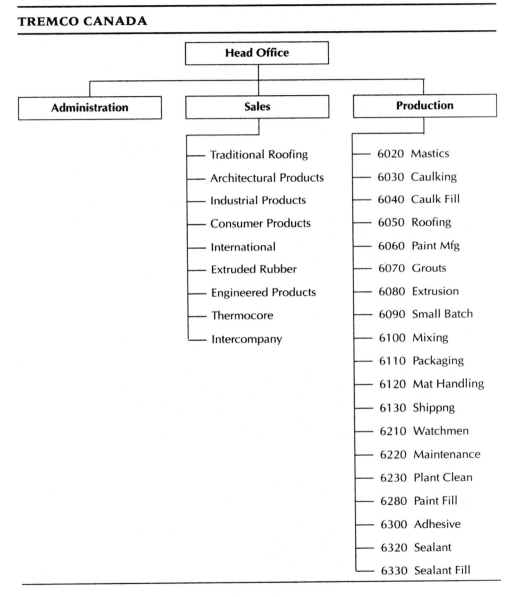

Exhibit 2

MATERIAL COST VARIANCES—Assigned to Sales Divisions

Raw Material Cost Sales Summary — For the Month Ended Sept. 30, 1987

Canada   Page 4 of ___

Acct. No.	Description	CURRENT MONTH						YEAR TO DATE					
		Actual	%	Budget	%	Last Year	%	Actual	%	Budget	%	Last Year	%
	Extruded Rubber Products												
3300	Standard Cost	155,348		207,360		161,412		1,355,320		1,587,600		1,437,153	
	% to Net Sales before												
	allowances, discounts, freight	34.2	35.3		38.6		39.7	33.1	34.2		38.6		35.8
3310	Material Price Variance	(14,881)	(34)	(5,000)	(.9)	(18,825)	(4.6)	(115,063)	(2.9)	(85,500)	(2.1)	(103,224)	(2.6)
3320	Cushion	3,000	.7	2,880	.5	3,000	.7	22,000	.5	22,050	.5	40,194	1.0
3330	Discrepancy Reports	(5,624)	(1.3)	2,000	.4	(3,969)	(1.0)	114,198	2.4	18,000	.4	28,539	.7
3331	Inventory Revaluation	1,500	.3					3,000	.1			19,868	.5
3340	Warehouse Reserve Expense												
3341	Distressed Reserve Expense	2,000	.5			3,669	.9	10,831	.3			18,951	.5
3342	Obsolescence Scrap	6,018	1.4	576	.1	28,964	7.1	36,843	.9	4,410	.1	74,325	1.9
	Total RMC	147,361	33.5	207,816	38.7	274,251	42.8	1,427,129	36.0	1,546,560	37.6	1,515,836	38.6
	ENGINEERED PRODUCTS												
3300	Standard Cost	120,278		129,165		75,156		554,544		865,050		301,570	
	% to Net Sales before												
	allowances, discounts, freight	62.7	63.5		56.4		58.6	57.1	59.2		56.4		58.9
3310	Material Price Variance	9						(39,652)	(4.2)				
3320	Cushion	1,154	.6					4,839	.5				
3330	Discrepancy Reports	4,660	2.5					20,117	2.2				
3331	Inventory Revaluation	1,500	.8					3,000	.3				
3340	Warehouse Reserve Expense												
3341	Distressed Reserve Expense	(7,600)	(4.0)					31,800	3.4				
3342	Obsolescence Scrap	4,616	2.5					19,884	2.1				
	Total RMC	124,617	65.9	129,165	56.4	75,156	58.6	594,532	63.5	865,050	56.4	301,570	58.7

Exhibit 3

PRODUCTION OVERHEAD COSTS

Acct. No.	Cost Item	% Variable	% Fixed
1002	Salaries	0	100
1003	Clerical Salaries	0	100
1006	Overtime Premium	0	100
1101	Hourly Supervision	0	100
1121	Set-up, Clean-up	100	0
1122	Rework	100	0
1124	Indirect Labour General	60	40
1125	Breaks	100	0
1128	Material Handling	100	0
1141	Holidays & Vacations	100	0
1142	Meetings	0	100
1143	Overtime Premium	100	0
1152	Paid Absence	100	0
1154	Night Shift Premium	100	0
2501	Benefits Hourly	100	0
2502	Benefits Salaried & Clerical	0	100
3101	Building Rental	0	100
3102	Equipment Rental	0	100
3201	Gas	80	20
3202	Electricity	80	20
3203	Water	80	20
3204	Nitrogen	100	0
3303	Cleaning	0	100
3304	Guard	0	100
3305	Landscaping	0	100
3306	Rubbish Removal	20	80
3309	Telephone	0	100
3400		0	100
3401	Furniture & Equipment	0	100
3402	Production Supplies	100	0
3403	Supplies	20	80
3405	Dues & Subscriptions	0	100
3406	Garments & Safety Shoes	20	80
3410	Miscellaneous	0	100
3411	Pallets	100	0
3412	Propane	100	0
3501	Repairs & Maintenance (Bldg)	0	100
3502	Repairs & Maintenance (Bldg)	0	100
3503	Repairs & Maintenance (Equip)	10	90
3504	Repairs & Maintenance (Lab)	10	90

Exhibit 3 (continued)

Acct. No.	Cost Item	% Variable	% Fixed
3505	Repairs & Maintenance (Bldg)	0	100
3506	Repairs & Maintenance (Mat'l)	10	90
3610	Moving	0	100
3617	Seminars	0	100
3650	Recruit Fees	0	100
3704	Consulting Fees	0	100
3712	Safety	0	100
4000	Quality Control	20	80
4001	Travel	0	100
4009	Leased Car	0	100
5101	Real Estate Tax	0	100
5202	Insurance	0	100
5301	Building Depreciation	0	100
5302	Building Improvement Dep'n	0	100
5309	Machinery Depreciation	0	100
6010	Manufacturing Manager		
6120	Material Handling		
6220	Maintenance		
	Contingency	100	0
	Watchmen Expense	0	100
	Shipping Watchmen Expense	0	100
	Cleaners	0	100
	Transfer from Variable OH	0	100

Exhibit 4

PRODUCTION OVERHEAD COST ALLOCATION FACTORS

Factor	Name	Basis
a	Overtime	Previous year costs
b	Normal Standard Hours	Previous year hours
c	Number of Men	Previous year manpower
d	Men Adjusted for Rate	Factor c x projected rate
e	Rubbish Removal	
f	Cleaning Adjustment	Square footage of dept.
g	Gas	Previous year cost
h	Electricity	Previous year cost
i	Water	Previous year cost
j	Square Footage	Department area
k	Direct Department Sq. Ft.	Department area
l	Inventory Control & Purch.	Alloc. by P & IC Mgr.
m	Quality Control	Alloc. by QE Mgr.
n	Building Rental	
o	Material Handling	Alloc. by Receiving Mgr.
p	Repair & Maint. Equip.	Previous year costs
q	Repair & Maint. Direct Dep.	Factor p—select depts.
r	Nitrogen	Dept. usage
s	Salary	Alloc. by Mfg. Mgr.
t	Machinery Depreciation	Previous year cost
u	Supplies	Mfg. expense statement
v	Miscellaneous Expense	Mfg. expense statement
w	Real Estate Tax	
x	Fire & Liab. Insur.	
y	Building Depreciation	
z	Building Improvement Depn.	
aa	Material Handling	Prev. hrs. x current rates
ab	Rework	Previous year cost
ac	Indirect General	Previous year cost
ad	Hourly Supervision	Previous year cost
ae	Breaks	Previous year cost
af	Meetings	Previous year cost
ag	Set-up, Clean-up	Previous year cost
ah	Without Extrusions	Previous year cost
ai	Direct Actual Lab. Hrs.	Previous year cost
aj	Direct Labour Incl. Ship.	Previous year cost

Exhibit 5

DEPARTMENT LABOUR AND OVERHEAD RATES

Centre	Name	D.L. Rate	Var. OH	Fix.OH
6020	Mastics	$16.60	$32.08	$50.28
6030	Caulking	17.11	56.81	102.15
6040	Caulk Fill.	14.96	27.15	36.40
6050	Roofing	16.14	39.73	70.99
6060	Paint Mfg.	14.51	36.47	62.62
6070	Grouts	16.90	42.79	102.35
6080	Extrusions	16.76	26.90	29.08
6090	Small Batch	14.76	50.54	90.68
6100	Mixing	17.11	40.30	50.47
6110	Packaging	16.87	32.14	39.33
6120	Mat. Handling	0.00	0.00	0.00
6130	Shipping	17.62	27.03	57.21
6210	Watchmen	0.00	0.00	0.00
6220	Maintenance	0.00	0.00	0.00
6230	Plant Clean.	0.00	0.00	0.00
6280	Paint Fill.	14.41	36.05	41.79
6300	Adhesive	0.00	0.00	0.00
6320	Sealant	0.00	0.00	0.00
6330	Sealant Fill.	0.00	0.00	0.00

Exhibit 6

STANDARD COST FOR INTERMEDIATE PRODUCT WHITE EPOXY

WHITE BS/W3 EPOXY BATCH SIZE 1281

Operation No.	Raw-Material	Usage	SCP%	Std. Cost	Unit	Raw-Matl.	Packaging	Dir-Labor	Var-Ovhd.	Fix-Ovhd.
00000	6060 Paint Dept	270.00			STD			65.2999	164.1160	281.7916
00001	6060 Paint Dept	105.99			STD			25.6355	64.4289	110.6261
050-0447	Titanium Oxide	338.00	2.00	1.1500	Pound	396.4795				
057-0011	Water	546.99	3.00	.0001	Pound	.0563				
057-0034	Isopropyl Alcohol	31.13	3.00	.3723	Pound	11.9367				
066-0202	5 Gal Pail Nested	19.99		3.1330	Each	62.6488	62.6488			
099-1677	Casamid 360	359.99	2.00	3.0200	Pound	1108.9422				
099-1712	BYK Deformer 033	1.11	2.00	1.1990	Pound	1.3630				
099-1714	Triton N-101	2.92	2.00	1.8997	Pound	5.6594				

	Raw-Matl.	Packaging	Dir-Labor	Var-Ovhd.	Fix-Ovhd.
Product Totals	1587.0859	62.6488	90.9354	228.5449	392.4177
Cost/Batch					2298.9839
Shipping Incremen.			.0000	.0000	.0000
Cost/Batch					2298.9839

Type	Mfg-Cost	RM-Cost	Pack-Cost	Dir-Labor	Var-Ovhd.	Fix-Ovhd.
	.5557	1.2389	62.6488	.0709	.1784	.3063

Exhibit 6 (continued)

NEUT. BS/WB EPOXY   BATCH SIZE 1560

Operation No.	Raw-Material	Usage	SCP%	Std. Cost	Unit	Raw-Matl.	Packaging	Dir-Labor	Var-Ovhd.	Fix-Ovhd.
00000	6060 Paint Dept	126.99			STD			30.7141	77.1927	132.5420
00001	6060 Paint Dept	299.99			STD			72.5544	182.3484	313.0973
050-0204	Snowflake Whiting	322.99	2.00	.0694	Pound	22.8644				
060-0345	#1112 Suprex Clay	322.99		.0952	Pound	30.7494				
057-0011	Water	529.99	3.00	.0001	Pound	.0546				
057-0034	Isopropyl Alcohol	30.18	3.00	.3723	Pound	11.5754				
066-0202	5 Gal Pail Nested	23.99		3.1330	Each	75.1694	75.1694			
099-1677	Casamid 360	349.00	2.00	3.0200	Pound	1075.0695				
099-1712	BYK Deformer 033	1.07	2.00	1.1992	Pound	1.3166				
099-1714	Triton N-101	2.82	2.00	1.8996	Pound	5.4710				
	Product Totals					1222.2703	75.1694	103.2685	259.5411	445.6393
								Cost/Batch		2030.7192
				Shipping Increment				.0000	.0000	.0000
								Cost/Batch		2030.7192

Type	Mfg-Cost	RM-Cost	Pack-Cost	Dir-Labor	Var-Ovhd.	Fix-Ovhd.
	.5182	.7835	75.1694	.0661	.1663	.2856

Exhibit 6 (continued)

EPOXY LT. GREY   BATCH SIZE 3065

Operation No.	Raw-Material	Usage	SCP%	Std. Cost	Unit STD	Raw-Matl.	Packaging	Dir-Labor	Var-Ovhd.	Fix-Ovhd.
000000	6060 Paint Dept	164.99						39.9042	100.2896	172.2000
DEV-011-996	Neut BS/WB Epoxy	1400.00		.7835	Pound	1096.9000		92.6764	232.9185	399.9306
055-5109	Lamp Blk GPD 8807B	78.00	2.00	1.6900	Pound	134.4637				
057-0011	Water	400.01	3.00	.0001	Pound	.0412				
057-0093	Arcosolv PM	95.99	3.00	.7654	Pound	75.6794				
099-1711	BYK-321	4.99	2.00	5.8499	Pound	29.8103				
DEV-010-996	White BS/WB Epoxy	1085.99	2.00	1.2389	Pound	1345.4340		77.0878	193.7478	332.6751
	Product Totals					2682.3286		209.6684	526.9559	904.8055
								Cost/Batch		
								.0000	.0000	4323.7584
	Shipping Increment							Cost/Batch		
										4323.7584

Type	Mfg-Cost	RM-Cost	Pack-Cost	Dir-Labor	Var-Ovhd.	Fix-Ovhd.
	.5355	.8751		.0684	.1719	.2952

Exhibit 7

STANDARD COST FOR FINAL PRODUCT LT GREY EPOXY

LT. GREY EPOXY

BATCH SIZE 1

Operation No.	Raw-Material	Usage	SCP%	Std. Cost	Unit	Raw-Matl.	Packaging	Dir-Labor	Var-Ovhd.	Fix-Ovhd.
00000	6280 Paint Fill	.008			STD			.1153	.2884	.3343
DEV-013P-996	Epoxy Lt. Grey	8.7400		.8752	Pound	7.6492		.5979	1.5027	2.5801
064-0662	4 Litre Can E5	1.000		1.0382	Each	1.0382	1.0382			
064-2135	Lined Lid 4LT	1.0000		.2381	Each	.2381	.2381			
	Product Totals					8.9255	1.2763	.7132	1.7911	2.9144
								Cost/Batch		14.3442
	Shipping Increment							.0000	.0000	.0000
								Cost/Batch		14.3442

Type	Mfg-Cost	RM-Cost	Pack-Cost	Dir-Labor	Var-Ovhd.	Fix-Ovhd.
	5.4187	8.9255	1.2763	.7132	1.7911	2.9144

MCKINLEY HATCHERY (ST. MARYS) LTD.

Ian Feltmate and Randolph Kudar

Catherine McKinley, the secretary-treasurer of McKinley Hatchery (St. Marys) Ltd. in St. Marys, Ontario, was considering what changes should be made to the company's accounting system to allow for the most effective management. The former general manager, Berne McKinley, had been able to manage the hatchery without detailed financial records due to his in-depth knowledge of the business. However, with Berne's recent departure, management found they lacked the expertise to manage the hatchery without more information from the accounting system. Catherine described the need for changes as urgent:

"We're losing money and we don't know why. Land values are falling. We have a million dollars in operating line with the bank and they don't have a list of inventory, a list of accounts receivable, not a thing. They are insisting we get things organized in a hurry."

THE HATCHERY BUSINESS

The McKinley family had been farming in Zurich, Ontario, since 1848 and had operated a hatchery there since 1923. Three years ago, the hatchery portion of the business was physically separated from Zurich with the purchase of a hatchery 45 miles away in St. Marys. A new subsidiary of McKinley Farms was formed, called McKinley Hatchery (St. Marys) Ltd., with Berne McKinley as the general manager. Berne's older brother, Anson, was in charge of the farm operations in Zurich.

McKinley Hatchery grew rapidly, reaching over $2 million in sales in the most recent fiscal year (see Exhibit l, Statement of Gross Profit). Approximately 70% of sales were attributed to 20 week old pullets. These birds were sold to producers to lay eggs for human consumption. The hatchery was not involved in the broiler industry, which required a completely different operation. Other major sources of revenue of the hatchery included selling eggs from breeders for human consumption, selling eggs from breeders for hatching, and selling day-old chicks. McKinley's was the third or fourth largest business of its kind in Ontario. It focused its marketing effort on the smaller producers. An average sale for 20 week old pullets would be for 5,000 to 10,000 birds.

The production process (see Exhibit 2) of the hatchery began with the ordering of day-old breeder chicks from the United States for $6 to $8 each. McKinley's placed two orders for breeder chicks a year. These chicks were specially bred to produce offspring that would lay both high quality and large quantities of eggs for human consumption. A minimum of six weeks would elapse before the order arrived. The day-old chicks were delivered to breeder pullet barns owned by McKinley Farms, or by independent farms. In both cases, the hatchery owned the birds. The birds were kept in the breeder pullet barns for 20 weeks, until they reached sexual maturity. Expenses during that time included feed (the largest expense), vaccine, medication, and a grower fee. The grower fee was an amount paid to the farm owner for raising the birds in his barn, and was so much (approximately $.85) per bird that survived the 20 week period. McKinley Farms and independent farms were paid the same grower fee. Hatchery personnel were also involved with the care of the birds during this and other stages, performing such tasks as vaccination, administering medication, and servicing.

At 20 weeks of age the birds were moved to breeder layer houses owned either by McKinley Farms or independent farms. Over the next 48 weeks, each hen would lay approximately 18 dozen eggs, after which time the "spent fowl" were sold to the killing plant. Expenses during this period included feed, vaccine, medication, and a layer fee to the farm owner. The layer fee was for caring for the birds, and amounted to about $.21 per dozen eggs. The eggs laid by the pullets in the first 6 weeks of the 48 week stay in the layer barns (about 3 dozen eggs per hen) were too small to be sent to the hatchery, so they were sent to the grading station and sold as commercial eggs for approximately $.75 a dozen. There was a limit, however, to the number of eggs that could be disposed of this way; legislation allowed McKinley's to sell 7.2 dozen breeder eggs to the commercial market for every breeder hen. Any eggs above that total attracted a severe penalty. From weeks 26 to 68, the eggs were trucked to the hatchery in St. Marys. If McKinley's could not supply enough of its own hatching eggs to meet demand, it could also purchase hatching eggs on the open market for about $1.70 per dozen. It could also sell hatching eggs to other hatcheries for about $1.70 per dozen.

When the eggs arrived at the hatchery, they were loaded into a temperature- and humidity-controlled storage room called the egg cooler. The eggs could be stored here safely for up to 14 days.

From the egg cooler the eggs were moved to the egg traying room where they were placed in large plastic flats. The flats were then placed in machines called setters where once again the temperature and humidity were strictly controlled. Every hour for the next 18 days the flats would be tilted backwards and then forwards to allow for proper development of the chick.

After setting, the eggs were removed from the flats and placed loosely into flat trays. A wire-mesh bottom in the trays facilitated air circulation. The trays were placed in machines called hatchers. Inside the hatchers the humidity was increased and the temperature reduced.

After three days the hatched chicks were removed from the hatchers to the chick processing area. Here they were sexed (male chicks were sold to mink farmers) and given a day-old injection for Marek's disease. The chicks were counted, boxed, and trucked to customers. Each dozen eggs that were set produced approximately 4.8 saleable chicks, for which McKinley's would receive about $.89 each if sold. McKinley salesmen received a commission on each sale of $.06 per chick.

Instead of selling the day-old chicks, McKinley's had two alternatives. First, the chicks could be raised to 20 weeks of age and then sold to producers ready to lay. If McKinley's chose this option, the day-old chicks were trucked from the hatchery to McKinley Farms' pullet barns in Zurich or to barns of independent farms. Expenses during the 20 week period were similar to those for the breeder pullets, i.e., feed, vaccines, medications, and a grower fee. Feed was somewhat less expensive than for the breeder pullets. The grower fee, an amount per saleable pullet, was also less. Without the presence of cockerels, which took up a lot of space, more birds could be housed in a given area. Both McKinley Farms and the independent farms received the same grower fee. The hatchery salesmen received a commission for pullet sales of about $.18 per pullet. Trucking expense was about $.15 per pullet. The selling price per pullet was approximately $3.80. This price could fluctuate greatly, however, since the price offered to producers was actually a certain amount (about $2.35) plus the cost of feed. The latter could vary greatly from load to load and company to company. Since feed formed part of the price calculation, the hatchery kept track of feed cost for the different orders, albeit separate from the accounting system described below. After Berne left, feed was basically the only cost monitored outside the accounting system.

Another alternative for the day-old chicks was known as a buy-back sale. McKinley's would sell the day-old chicks to an independent farm at $.89 per chick. The independent would then raise the pullets to 20 weeks. At 20 weeks McKinley's would repurchase the pullets for the stated fee and feed cost and then sell them to a different producer. These arrangements would allow a farmer to maximize use of his farm's capacity, as well as to earn the mark-up from the pullet raising process.

Regardless of the alternative chosen, at 20 weeks of age McKinley's had to sell the pullets or destroy them. Unlike their competition who had egg quotas, McKinley's did not have the option of putting the pullets into their own layer barns.

Markets for the hatchery's products were extremely competitive and potentially very volatile for a number of reasons. First, there was very little customer loyalty. Second, there was very little difference in the quality of bird produced by the two leading breeder types, H&N (one of two franchises held by McKinley's) and Dekalb. Third, it was common for producers to change the length of time they would keep a flock, from 12 months to 13 months and back again. Shifts of this sort might leave a hatchery without the supply of hatching eggs necessary to meet the egg producer's timing requirements. The combined effect of these factors seemed to balance out over a year. In other words, McKinley's could fairly accurately predict its sales for a given 12 month period, but could not accurately predict the timing of sales from month to month.

As a rule, McKinley's did not set the hatching eggs unless either the day-old chick or the 20 week old pullet was ordered by an egg producer. In the case of buy-backs both the chick and pullet had to be ordered in advance. Effectively then, McKinley's demanded a minimum six month lead time from its customers for sales of 20 week old pullets. The planning range for ordering breeders was approximately a year and a half. McKinley's had to forecast which of their two types of birds would be most popular, what the demand would be for chicks and pullets, and in which two months of the year would demand be the greatest. The latter consideration was important due to the egg laying rate of the breeders. The birds reached maximum production after a few weeks and then tapered off gradually. To have maximum utilization of the eggs, it was necessary that the birds reached their peak coincident with market demand.

THE ACCOUNTING SYSTEM

Prior to the formation of McKinley Hatchery, one bookkeeper maintained the records for both the farming and hatchery operations. Catherine felt this individual was "totally inflexible and wouldn't make a decision if you paid him a million dollars". He left the organization in the year the hatchery subsidiary was established. Catherine was left to her own devices in maintaining the hatchery's books: "He [the former bookkeeper] kept a simple double-entry bookkeeping system but I couldn't find a description anywhere as to where to record transactions or why. To learn accounting I read a grade 13 accounting textbook. Then I have just tried to use logic. I used his list of accounts (see Exhibit 3) and asked myself where should such and such logically go. When I get really stuck I phone our accountant. Well, he usually doesn't have a clue where something should go. Most often he says to put it in miscellaneous and we'll catch it later."

Statements were prepared every six months by an outside accounting firm. Normally it was three months after the close of the period before the statements were ready. At times the accountant indicated that he experienced difficulty interpreting the bookkeeping records. In those instances the accountant combined and presented accounts as he felt appropriate. The result was the set of statements in Exhibit 1.

The lack of detail in the financial statements made communications between Anson and Berne difficult. According to Catherine, "By looking at the financial statements nobody knew if the hatchery was making any money or not. Anson would ask questions of Berne, and he wouldn't use the financial statements to substantiate his answers. And the same thing was happening in reverse. You see we had exactly the same problem on the farm."

In addition to the hatchery in St. Marys, Anson and Berne also owned another hatchery in Truro, Nova Scotia. By mutual agreement between the two brothers, Berne left McKinley Hatchery and formed a separate business from the N.S. operation. After Berne's departure, top management of the hatchery was effectively divided between three persons: Doug McKenzie, who was hatchery manager under Berne; Al Corneir, the newly hired sales manager; and Catherine, who was in charge of accounting, payroll, and "just everything". Catherine felt that the accounting system needed a complete overhaul. Specifically, she wanted information to assist the management team in making a wide range of operating decisions.

One basic decision focused on the number of breeders. Should they buy fewer breeder chicks than they needed and supplement their egg requirement by purchasing eggs from outside producers? Or should they raise more breeders than they needed and minimize the outside purchases?

When McKinley's was approached to custom hatch eggs, they would look up the invoice of the last time a hatchery had custom hatched for McKinley's and charge the customer the same price. Management wanted to know what price would give a reasonable profit. What was a fair price to pay someone else for custom hatching eggs for McKinley's?

In the area of raising chicks to 20 weeks and then selling them, was the hatchery making any money? Could the hatchery afford to raise the amount it paid to the farm for growing?

How could the hatchery practically measure inventory? Catherine described current numbers as coming "out of a hat". There was a natural inclination to pad the inventory figure since the maximum balance in the hatchery's operating loan was 75% of accounts receivable under 90 days plus 75% of inventory. Pullets, the largest component of inventory (see Schedule of Inventory, Exhibit 1), were calculated as follows:

A.   Subtract the market price of the day-old chick from the market price of the 20 week old pullet.

B.   Multiply the result from A by the fraction of the age of the pullets in weeks divided by 20.

C.   Add the result from B to the market price for day-old chicks.

D.   Multiply the result from C by the number of birds in inventory.

There was increasing pressure from the bank for documentation verifying that inventory was being calculated at actual cost. If the documentation was not soon forthcoming, the bank threatened to greatly reduce the percentage of inventory allowed in the calculation of the maximum operating loan.

Exhibit 1

McKINLEY HATCHERY (ST. MARYS) LTD.
Balance Sheet as at April 30, 198x

ASSETS

Current Assets	
Cash on hand	$ 2,456
Accounts receivable	427,589
Inventory - per Schedule of Inventory	355,470
Due from Shareholders	40
	785,555
Fixed Assets – at cost	
Land	10,000
Burlington Farm	64,450
Building	93,500
Equipment	24,665
	192,615
less: accumulated depreciation	14,299
	178,316
	$963,871

LIABILITIES AND SHAREHOLDERS' EQUITY

Current Liabilities	
Bank overdraft	101,357
Bank loan - current	460,000
Accounts payable	184,255
Due to McKinley Farms	121,132
Current portion of long term debt	1,000
	867,744
Long Term Liabilities	
Note payable - bank	48,131
Mortgage — 11¼%, maturing October, 198x	104,312
	152,443
Less: current portion	1,000
	151,443
Shareholders's Equity	
Share Capital	4,041
Retained Earnings	(59,357)
	(55,316)
	$ 963,871

Exhibit 1 (continued)

Statement of Gross Profit

For the Period Ended April 30, 198x

REVENUE

Chickens

Pullets	$1,503,157
Chicks	159,982
Feed	44,710
Eggs	327,658
Hatching	82,781
Custom Hatching	4,283
Boxes and Shaving	7,925
Sale of Remedies	11,992
	2,142,488
COST OF SALES - per Schedule of Cost of Sales	1,805,676
GROSS PROFIT - Chickens	$ 336,812

Schedule of Cost of Sales

For the Period Ended April 30, 198x

Chickens

Inventory		$ 418,278
Purchases		
Eggs - hatching	38,538	
Chickens - Pullets	148,237	
H & N, Hyline breeders	62,370	
Chicks	22,017	
Feed, pullets	994,842	
Feeding	315,568	
Remedies	46,363	
Fuel for heating	11,738	
Blood-testing, sexing and debeaking	10,487	
Supplies, box and shavings	17,502	
Trucking paid	75,206	
		1,742,868
		2,161,146
Less: inventory at end of year		355,470
COST OF SALES - Chickens		$1,805,676

Exhibit 1 (continued)

Statement of Operations		
For the Period Ended April 30, 198x		
Gross Profit – per Statement of Gross Profit		$ 336,812
Operating Expenses		
Accounting and legal	1,600	
Advertising	2,001	
Association fees	625	
Bad debts	12,594	
Bank charges and interest	97,496	
Brokerage and custom sales	1,114	
Building repairs	818	
Equipment repairs	8,815	
Hydro and telephone	15,782	
Insurance	1,160	
Management services	205,968	
Miscellaneous	2,404	
Mortgage interest	11,412	
Office supplies	3,093	
Rent	14,000	
Taxes	1,063	
Travelling	15,545	$395,490
Net Income (Loss)		$ (58,678)

Schedule of Inventoɪ,		
Chickens		
Pullets		$ 253,870
Breeders		78,944
Eggs on hand		4,515
Eggs in incubators		18,141
		$ 355,470

Exhibit 2

MCKINLEY HATCHERY (ST. MARYS) LTD.

Process Flow Diagram

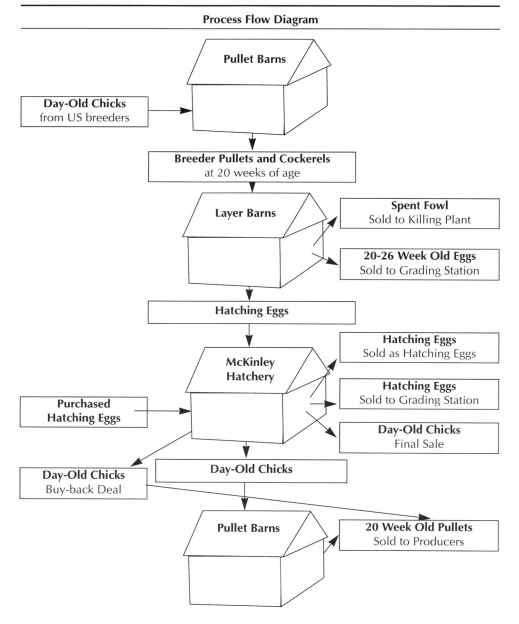

Exhibit 3

McKINLEY HATCHERY (ST. MARYS) LTD.
Journal Accounts

Account Number	Account Description	Account Number	Account Description
1	Cash	2	Bank
2A	Bank-US Funds	3	Accounts Receivable
3A	Due from Shareholders	3B	Inventory
4	Accounts Payable	4A	Due to McKinley Farms
5	Common Shares	6	Notes Receivable
7A	Operating Loan	7B	Notes Payable
7C	Notes Payable to Farms	9	Equipment
9A	Accumulated Depreciation-Equipment	10	Automobiles
11	Trucks	12	New Buildings
14	Bad Debts	15	Corporation Taxes
17	Legal Fees		
19	Office Supplies	20	Boxes and Shavings
21	Pullets	21A	Breeders
22	Chicks	23	Eggs
24	Hatching Eggs	25	Custom Hatching
26	Remedies	27	Miscellaneous
28	Hydro, Telephone and Water	29	Sexing, Bloodtesting and Debeaking
30	Fuel	31	Feed
32	Gas and Oil	33	Taxes
35	Travelling Expenses	36	Management Services
37	Custom Brokers	38	Feeding
39	Advertising	41	Bank Charges
42	Association Fees	43	Equipment Repairs
44	Rent	46	Richardson Securities
47	Mortgage	47A	Mortgage Interest
48	Land	49	Buildings
49A	Accumulated Depreciation-Buildings	50	Depreciation Expenses
51	Retained Earnings	60	Canada Pension
61	Employee Tax Deductions	62	U.I.C.
63	Trucking and Delivery Expense		

Appendix to Exhibit 3

McKINLEY HATCHERY (ST. MARYS) LTD.

In most instances the accounts were self-explanatory. However, the following accounts were interpreted as follows:

4A Due to McKinley Farms
The hatchery was originally financed solely with debt. Since the hatchery was unable to borrow the whole amount the farm borrowed funds on its behalf. This account represented the principal of those funds still outstanding, plus accrued interest.

21 Pullets
This account recorded sales and purchases of 20 week old pullets. Basically, the credits were summed to arrive at revenues and the debits to arrive at purchases. Purchases were comprised primarily of buy-backs, although there were small purchases of pullets to supplement the hatchery's own supplies in meeting a producer's order.

21A Breeders
This account recorded purchases of the day-old breeder chicks.

22 Chicks
This account recorded sales of day-old chicks, both final and buy-back, as well as purchases. Again the totals were derived by separately summing debits and credits. Purchases of chicks would be necessary to supplement the hatchery's supplies in meeting an order. Slight overages or underages would often arise since the precise amount of saleable chicks from a hatch was always uncertain.

23 Eggs
This account recorded the sales of all eggs sold to the grading station for human consumption.

24 Hatching Eggs
This account represented sales of hatching eggs as hatching eggs and purchases of outside hatching eggs.

25 Custom Hatching
If the hatchery had insufficient capacity to meet an order, an option for McKinley's was to have their eggs custom hatched by another hatchery, for which they would be charged a fee. Similarly, hatcheries would approach McKinley's to custom hatch for them. This account recorded the fees received by McKinley's for custom hatching as well as fees paid to other hatcheries.

31 Feed
This account represented feed consumed by the birds at all stages. McKinley's purchased their feed in bulk and resold some to small farming operations at approximately a 10% mark-up. This price was significantly cheaper than the farmer could obtain from the nearest feed mill.

36 Management Services
Everything the hatchery owed to McKinley Farms was recorded in management services.

Appendix to Exhibit 3 (continued)

38 Feeding

This account recorded growing and laying fees, other than those that were included in management services.

20 Boxes and Shavings

Shavings were used in the farms as bedding for day-old chicks. Boxes were the cardboard boxes to put day-old chicks in. Also included in this account were feeder trays, i.e., cardboard trays used in feeding chicks in the early stages of growth. Boxes and shavings were purchased in bulk and some were resold to smaller hatcheries and individual farmers for a small profit.

26 Remedies

Remedies (i.e. vaccination, medication) for the birds were both an expense and a source of revenue. The hatchery sold remedies to preferred customers at a 10% mark-up, and to regular customers at a 25% mark-up.

IN-TOUCH PLACEMENT COMPANY

Rhonda English and Randolph Kudar*

In late June, Judy Danroth, President of In-Touch Placement Company, was preparing for a contract renewal meeting with Rayner Ltd., one of In-Touch's major accounts. After analyzing the financial reports on the contract, she was quite concerned with her findings. The gross profit margin, at 12%, was significantly lower than the company average. Moreover, after all other costs were considered, the contract was generating a lower return than what the company could earn from bank interest. She felt that prices would have to be raised on this account to bring the gross profit margin more in line with the other contracts. Judy was concerned that the renegotiation for higher prices could result in In-Touch losing the contract to a competitor. Having spent several weeks analyzing the Rayner situation, Judy remained unsure of the financial impact of the contract on the company's operating results.

COMPANY BACKGROUND

In-Touch began operations in Ontario in October of 1979. Since that time, the company had opened branches in four major centres in Ontario. In 1988, the original operation was split into two separate branches, dividing the permanent (Branch 1) and temporary (Branch 2) placement services. Thus, as of 1989, In-Touch had six operating branches, employing from four to sixteen persons per branch. Each branch was run by a branch manager who reported directly to a regional manager. Exhibit 1 outlines the organizational structure of the firm.

In addition to expanding geographically, In-Touch had broadened its product line offering. Originally only a permanent placement agency in the technical, office support, and administrative areas, the temporary placement division was developed in 1983. In 1984, specialization in the areas of computer personnel, human resource recruitment, and executive placement were introduced by the company. Since then, sales and marketing, materials (purchasing), contract engineering, training, and out-placement services[1] had also been added.

In-Touch had annual gross revenues of approximately $7 million, and employed 41 regular staff (consultants, secretaries, etc.) and about 2,000 temporary and contract workers. Revenues were forecasted at $10 million for the upcoming year.

THE INDUSTRY

Personnel service was a multi-billion-dollar industry and reported as the second fastest growing industry in North America. The earliest form of the business was the contracting out of domestic help (maids, etc.) in the early 1900s. Throughout the fifties and sixties, temporary and permanent placement services were formally introduced, becoming a viable and prominent business in the seventies.

Permanent placements involved a request by a client to find an employee to fill a full-time position within the client's firm. The personnel agency would be hired to pre-screen prospective candidates, often from the agency's "pool" of available people. A specified number of qualified candidates would be sent to the client for a job interview. The client would make the final hiring decision. For this service, the client would pay the agency a fee, usually the equivalent of one month's salary of the filled position.

Temporary placements could involve short-term or long-term contracts, to fill full-time or part-time positions. Temporary assignments addressed a variety of needs, such as nurses, accountants, warehouse workers, packers, engineers, executive secretaries, etc. The candidates worked at the client's place of business, but were employees of the personnel firm. They were counselled by, paid by, and promoted/demoted by the personnel agency.

The temporary placement process was similar to permanent placements. The personnel firm pre-screened candidates by resume, interviewed pre-screened potential candidates, and subsequently referred a specified number to the client for final interviewing and hiring. The price charged to clients for temporaries was a set hourly wage, based on skill and job category involved. The personnel

---

[1] Out-placement assists companies who are downsizing by counselling and helping in the job search for displaced employees.

agency paid the candidate an hourly wage lower than that charged to the client. The differential between the amount paid to the candidate and the amount charged to the client represented gross margin to the placement firm.

The demand for temporary employment services arose in a number of situations. For instance, if a client was working on a limited-term contract basis for a third party, they would often use temporaries to avoid the tasks of recruiting, personnel documentation, benefit plan arrangements, and laying off of the workers. Another situation occurred when the Head Office of a company mandated a limited, full-time employee head count. If additional human resources were needed, the company used temporary employees to meet demand, thereby not violating the head office mandate. The most common situations for the use of temporary help were pregnancy and vacation leaves.

Industry payment terms for clients using temporaries were 30 days from when the employees were paid. In reality, however, receivables averaged 40 to 50 days since there were lags in obtaining payroll data, generating payroll, and subsequent invoicing of the client.

Competition in the placement industry varied by product line and geographical location. For example, in large urban centres, there were several thousand personnel firms, while in smaller urban centres, less than 50 firms might compete. Key success factors also varied by client type and product line. Some clients were less concerned with price and more concerned with service (reputation), while others made decisions based solely on lowest price. Price was usually a more important factor in temporary placement than in permanent placement since the temporary assignments were shorter term and the candidates were not the clients' employees. Reputation was earned through excellent service. This involved efficient systems (computer, payroll, benefits, reporting), experienced and well-knowledged staff, and a large supply of diverse candidates. Also important to success in the industry was a strong networking system (high visibility, community involvement, etc.).

Placement staff were extremely important to a personnel service and required diverse skills. Dealing with people on a continual basis demanded strong interpersonal skills, while actively pursuing placement business required good sales skills.

In-Touch Placement Company — Branches 1 and 2 Operations

The temporary service at In-Touch was organized by job type. Each desk (consultant) was an entity in itself, serving the needs of a particular employment area (e.g., secretarial, office/administration, accounting, etc.). In this way, each consultant developed familiarity and expertise in a specialized area. In June, there were four temporary consultants employed in Branch 2.

Monthly and annual budgets were prepared with direct participation from the consultants. Target figures for sales (number of placements and sales dollars), advertising costs, marketing expenditures, etc., were developed by the consultants, who had final authority over their own budgets. A formal appraisal, conducted quarterly, compared actual results to budget. If performance was less than satisfactory, consultants were given a written warning and placed on probation for one quarter. During the probationary period, any needed assistance/advice was given to the consultant and a monthly review was conducted. At the end of the quarter, if performance had not improved, a second written warning was issued and the consultant was given one month to make the necessary improvements in performance, at which time the consultant would be released if performance remained uncorrected. This final action rarely had to be exercised. If the initial quarterly review was exeptionally good, the possibility of promotion or salary increase beyond the regular, annual salary review would be considered for the consultant.

Branch meetings were held weekly by the temporary supervisor and attended by all temporary consultants. The meeting served to update the group on each other's activities and generate new ideas. In addition, each consultant was required to submit their daily planner every evening to the supervisor for review.

On the first working day of each month, the temporary supervisor met on an informal one-to-one basis with the consultants. Areas discussed included: percentage changes in sales by account for month to date and year to date data, accounts receivable aging reports for clients, consultants' standing within the company in terms of sales, actual results compared to forecasts, percentage profit produced, average rate charged per client, average rate paid to temporaries, and expectations for the upcoming month.

Bonuses were awarded according to individual as well as overall company performance. The individual bonus was based on actual versus forecasted performance, either quarterly or monthly depending on the consultant's preference. If the company reached a targetted quarterly level of sales, a corporate bonus was distributed to all employees. As well, ongoing throughout the year were incentive contests with trip prizes, and branch challenges.

Information Flow

In addition to the preparation of annual financial statements, monthly income statements and bi-weekly gross profit reports were generated. For Branches 1 and 2 the monthly statements showed aggregate revenues and expenses for temporary and permanent operations, as well as a breakdown of each area. The division of operating expenses between the temporary and permanent branches (1 and 2) was based on a 50-50 split, with the exception of a few directly traceable expenses such as office salaries and bonuses. Exhibit 2 details the monthly statements for May as well as presents year to date data. The bi-weekly statements were by client, also including year to date information which summarized total business of the particular "desk" involved (see Exhibit 3).

When a financial analysis of a specific account was undertaken, a further allocation of operating expenses was necessary. In this situation, the total expenses assigned to a branch were divided by the number of consultants in the branch to produce an overhead dollar amount per consultant. This cost was then allocated to an individual account in accordance with the approximate time spent on the account by the consultant.

THE RAYNER SITUATION

The Rayner contract had been won through a bid process in late 1987. Initially about 50 firms competed for the contract, with 12 companies requested to submit formal bids. Although In-Touch was not the lowest bidder, they were able to offer the best service for the lowest price.

The contract called for the set-up of an assessment centre to fill the production worker requirements of Rayner, a large manufacturing plant locating in the geographical area of Branches 1 and 2. It was analogous to the creation of a mini personnel department for the initial recruitment period of a start-up operation. Rayner expected to need the assessment centre for up to two and a half years, with the labour complement gradually decreasing over that time as production worker requirements at the plant were filled.

Responsibility for the contract was assigned to Diane Collins, the temporary consultant for office/administration positions. The job called for a long-term placement of about 50 or 60 temporaries.

The first contract had been for a six month period ending June 1988, after which time it had been renewed. The terms of the initial contract stipulated the following:

a)   In-Touch would be the exclusive placement agent,

b)   the temporaries would be placed for a minimum of six months,

c)   the price would be set at 26% markup over actual wages paid to the temporaries,

d)   that 30-day credit terms were to be given.

The only contract changes at the first renewal were in the fees and credit terms. Since Rayner had been paying in 60 days rather than the stipulated 30, the terms were altered as follows:

26% markup if paid within 7 days

28% markup if paid within 15 days

31% markup if paid within 30 days

The new contract was set for a period of one year, and was now up for renewal.

The bulk of the work by In-Touch occurred in the first year, recruiting the temporaries and getting the department operational. Three or four candidates per available position at the Rayner assessment centre were sent to be interviewed by Rayner management, who made the final hiring decision. To generate these candidates, it had been necessary for Diane and her colleagues to conduct personal interviews with about ten potential candidates. To generate these ten, anywhere from 50 to 60 applications/resumes were screened. The process had involved significant up-front costs; for example, in marketing expenses to secure an adequate supply of candidates from which to choose. Costs of maintaining the account, however, were now minimal.

A bi-weekly summary of the Rayner account for the pay period ending June 17, 1989, is presented in Exhibit 3. Gross profit margin represented the fees charged to a client less actual wages paid and the related employer payroll taxes (Unemployment Insurance and Canada Pension Plan). The year to date information on the bi-weekly summary encompassed all temporary placement business at Diane's office/administration desk. This report was representative of the average bi-weekly gross profit earned from the current contract with Rayner.

CONCLUSION

With renegotiations fast approaching, Judy wanted to determine why the Rayner account was showing such a low percentage return. Based on this return, Judy questioned whether Diane was performing her job efficiently. Perhaps she was sending out senior candidates (higher paid) but charging junior rates on the positions. These concerns had been raised at Diane's informal monthly review meeting. To get the assessment centre staffed and operational, Diane had spent about three-quarters of her time on the Rayner job. Since it was only returning about 12% gross profit, Judy wondered whether it might be better for In-Touch if Diane put more time into the other accounts with higher gross profit margins, rather than keep the Rayner contract.

Exhibit 1

ORGANIZATIONAL CHART

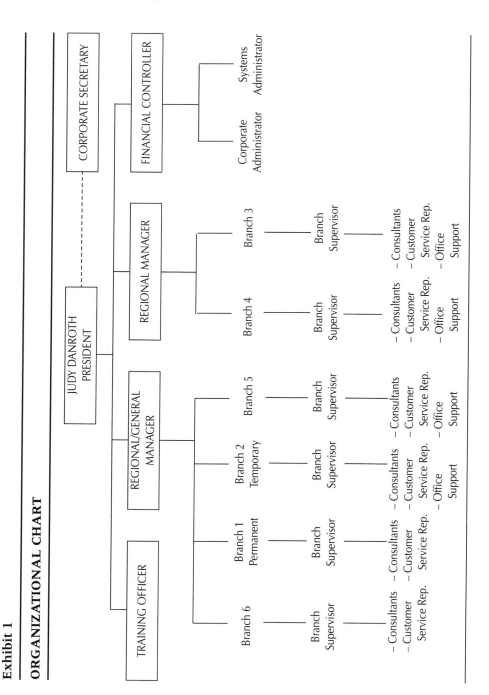

Exhibit 2

STATEMENT OF INCOME
For 5 Months Ending May 31, 1989

	May 1989	%	Year to Date	%
REVENUE				
Temporary placement income	$221,612	424.78	$1,143,149	482.57
Temporary gross salaries	(162,812)	(312.07)	(879,790)	367.59)
Employee benefits - temporaries	(6,629)	(12.71)	(35,470)	(14.97)
NET REVENUES	**$52,171**	**100.00**	**$236,889**	**100.00**
EXPENSES				
Legal & accounting			1,669	0.70
Advertising & promotion	809	1.55	2,337	0.99
Advertising - newspaper	2,757	5.28	8,674	3.66
Auto expense	175	0.34	625	0.26
Bank charges	739	1.42	4,207	1.78
Business tax			300	0.13
Courier	157	0.30	708	0.30
Dues, memberships, subscriptions	197	0.38	881	0.37
Donations			122	0.05
Equipment lease	818	1.57	2,526	1.07
Furniture lease	912	1.75	5,396	2.28
Food & meals			5	0.00
Insurance	117	0.22	142	0.06
Insurance - group	397	0.76	1,857	0.78
Head office expense	6,039	11.58	28,447	12.01
Office expense	1,494	2.86	6,909	2.92
Moving expenses	1,050	2.01	1,513	0.64
Parking	92	0.18	1,003	0.42
Printing	497	0.95	884	0.37
Rent	2,831	5.43	10,919	4.60
Repairs & maintenance	670	1.28	2,269	0.96
Salaries - office	6,039	11.58	36,191	15.28
Salaries - bonuses	4,141	7.94	11,049	4.66
Telephone	1,296	2.48	5,568	2.35
Training expenses			118	0.05
Travel & entertainment	160	0.31	1,261	0.53
Workers' compensation	2,679	5.14	3,992	1.69
TOTAL EXPENSES	**$34,066**	**65.30**	**$139,572**	**58.92**
NET INCOME BEFORE INCOME TAXES	**$18,105**	**34.70**	**$97,317**	**41.08**
NET INCOME FOR THE PERIOD	**$18,105**	**34.70**	**$97,317**	**41.08**

Exhibit 2 (continued)

	May 1989	%	Year to Date	%
REVENUE				
Permanent placement income	$64,884	100.00	$207,651	100.00
NET REVENUES	**$64,884**	**100.00**	**$207,651**	**100.00**
EXPENSES				
Legal & accounting			1,669	0.80
Advertising & promotion	809	1.25	2,337	1.13
Advertising - newspaper	2,757	4.25	8,674	4.18
Auto expense	175	0.27	625	0.30
Bank charges & interest	739	1.14	4,207	2.03
Business tax			300	0.14
Courier	157	0.24	708	0.34
Depreciation	78	0.12	390	0.19
Dues, memberships, subscriptions	197	0.30	881	0.42
Donations			122	0.06
Employee benefits - office	1,169	1.80	6,178	2.98
Equipment lease	818	1.26	2,526	1.22
Furniture lease	913	1.41	5,397	2.60
Food & meals			5	0.00
Insurance	117	0.18	142	0.07
Insurance - group	397	0.61	1,857	0.89
Head office expense	6,040	9.31	28,448	13.70
Office expense	1,494	2.30	6,909	3.33
Moving expenses	1,050	1.62	1,513	0.73
Parking	245	0.38	1,003	0.48
Printing	344	0.53	884	0.43
Rent	2,831	4.36	10,919	5.26
Repairs & maintenance	670	1.03	2,269	1.09
Salaries - office	14,189	21.87	74,509	35.88
Salaries - bonuses	5,025	7.74	24,991	12.04
Telephone	1,296	2.00	5,568	2.68
Training expenses			118	0.06
Travel & entertainment	160	0.25	1,261	0.61
Workers' compensation	2,678	4.13	3,991	1.92
TOTAL EXPENSES	**$44,347**	**68.35**	**$198,370**	**95.53**
NET INCOME BEFORE INCOME TAXES	**$20,537**	**31.65**	**$9,281**	**4.47**
NET INCOME FOR THE PERIOD	**$20,537**	**31.65**	**$9,281**	**4.47**

Exhibit 2 (continued)

REVENUE	May 1989	%	Year to Date	%
Permanent placement income	$64,884	55.43	$207,651	46.71
Temporary placement income	221,612	189.32	1,143,149	257.13
Temporary gross salaries	(162,812)	(139.09)	(870,790)	(195.87)
Employee benefits - temporaries	(6,629)	(5.66)	(35,470)	(7.98)
Other Income - interest earned			41	0.01
NET REVENUES	**$117,055**	**100.00**	**$444,581**	**100.00**
EXPENSES				
Legal & accounting			3,338	0.75
Advertising & promotion	1,618	1.38	4,674	1.05
Advertising - newspaper	5,514	4.71	17,348	3.90
Auto expense	350	0.30	1,250	0.28
Bad Debts			(40,004)	(9.00)
Bank charges & interest	1,478	1.26	8,414	1.89
Business & property tax			600	0.14
Courier	314	0.27	1,416	0.32
Depreciation & amortization	78	0.07	390	0.09
Dues, memberships, subscriptions	394	0.34	1,762	0.40
Donations			244	0.05
Employee benefits - office	1,169	1.00	6,178	1.39
Equipment lease	1,636	1.40	5,052	1.14
Furniture lease	1,825	1.56	10,793	2.43
Food & meals			10	0.00
Insurance	234	0.20	284	0.06
Insurance - group	794	0.68	3,714	0.84
Head office expense	12,079	10.32	56,895	12.80
Office expense	2,988	2.55	13,818	3.11
Moving expenses	2,100	1.79	3,026	0.68
Parking	337	0.29	2,006	0.45
Printing	841	0.72	1,768	0.40
Rent	5,662	4.84	21,838	4.91
Repairs & maintenance	1,340	1.14	4,538	1.02
Salaries - office	20,228	17.28	110,700	24.90
Salaries - bonuses	9,166	7.83	36,040	8.11
Telephone	2,592	2.21	11,136	2.50
Training expenses			236	0.05
Travel & entertainment	320	0.27	2,522	0.57
Workers' compensation	5,357	4.58	7,983	1.80
TOTAL EXPENSES	**$78,414**	**67.00**	**$297,969**	**67.02**
NET INCOME BEFORE INCOME TAXES	**$38,641**	**33.01**	**$146,612**	**32.98**
NET INCOME FOR THE PERIOD	**$38,641**	**33.01**	**$146,612**	**32.98**

Exhibit 3

BI-WEEKLY GROSS PROFIT REPORT

		PAY DAY:	06/23/89
		PERIOD ENDING:	06/17/89
		PAY NO:	#13

Diane (Rayner)	This Payroll	Y.T.D. 1989	Y.T.D. 1988
Fees	$38,269.23	$584,841.72	$570,442.39
Gross Pay	32,140.79	475,242.17	431,304.95
U.I.C.	854.60	$12,635.85	9,211.18
C.P.P.	567.74	8,251.08	6,733.69
Gross Profit	**$4,706.10**	**$88,712.62**	**$123,192.57**
Total Hours	3,168.00	49,637.75	57,351.59
O.T.	34.00	527.25	507.82
Stat	0.00	1,041.75	374.41
Net Pay	$16,582.00	$383,538.88	$364,711.93

ANALYSIS	THIS PAYROLL
% Gross Profit to Fees (Profit/Fees)	12.30%
Gross Profit per Hour (Profit/Hour)	$1.49
Average Fee Billed (Fee/Hours)	$12.08
Average Hourly Rate (Gross Pay/Hours)	$10.14
Average Hourly Rate Less Vaction Pay	$9.74

STUART DAW

Randolph Kudar*

Stuart Daw, the president of Stuart's Branded Foods, put down the book he was reading and thought, "Is Drucker right, that most companies do not know the true unit costs of their business?" It had been two years since his firm entered the food service industry in Toronto. Stuart now wondered what he might do to make his new division competitive with the giants, and yet generate the kind of returns he felt were necessary and appropriate for his investment.

Stuart Daw had spent most of his working career in the coffee business. He had worked in all aspects, from roasting the beans to selling the finished product both wholesale and retail. Over the years he had worked in both large and small firms. When the opportunity arose, he invested money and effort into building his own business, Stuart's Branded Foods, and focused on the roasting and selling of packaged coffee to the "Away from Home" coffee market.

AWAY FROM HOME COFFEE MARKET

The "Away from Home" coffee market designation included all coffee consumed outside of the retail market. Conventional customers in this market included restaurants, hospitals, stadiums, catering trucks, and the like. Because of the volume of coffee purchased, these customers found it advantageous to deal directly with roasters, as opposed to purchasing their needs through the retail channel. The roasters generally sold the coffee to these customers priced by the pound.

Over time, a segment of this market emerged called coffee service. It consisted primarily of very small customers such as business offices. Unfortunately, these customers required frequent purchases of small quantities of coffee. Traditionally, roasters avoided this segment because the cost of serving such small customers was greater than the gross profit generated from the sales transaction of the coffee. If the roaster raised the price to cover this shortfall in margin from selling coffee by the pound, the increased price per pound compared unfavourably with the amount that the customer could pay a general wholesaler or even a retail store.

To address this need in the segment, entrepreneurs formed businesses. Often they operated out of their garage with the family station wagon. These coffee service operators acted as middlemen between the roasters and the small customers. The operator purchased significant volumes of packaged coffee from the roaster. This coffee was then re-packaged into "kits", a kit being equivalent to 500 cups of coffee. As part of the service the operator would also provide the customer with:

1 kit = 500 cups

- rented coffee brewing equipment

- free maintenance of the equipment

- packaged coffee ready for use

- delivery to the customer's location

- allied products such as tea, hot chocolate, cups, etc.

To simplify the process, the coffee service operator would offer the complete package of service to the customer at "so much per cup" or per kit. This avoided the pound price comparison. As well, the quoted price included charges for the equipment, the supplies such as filters, and the coffee.

Gradually, as more Away from Home customers began using the smaller and more flexible coffee machines, the industry began to specialize. The customers wanted pot-sized packages, filters, and more frequent delivery services. Some of the larger roasters created distribution operations to serve this market. These distribution services adopted the practice of selling the coffee to the customers in this market "by the cup" or by the kit.

STUART'S BRANDED FOODS

At its inception, Stuart's Branded Foods faced a broad range of competitors. Aside from the giant roasters such as Maxwell House and Club Foods of Canada, there were national coffee service firms such as Canteen of Canada and Diplomat Coffee Service. Other companies operated within a particular geographic region, for example, Ontario. Finally, there were the local competitors who handled the coffee service segment of the market.

Initially, Stuart's Branded Foods was only a roasting operation selling to distributors. Two years ago, Stuart's Branded Foods began operating a food service division in the Toronto region. Mr. Daw felt that the market was large enough to allow a new firm to enter the business successfully. This division also gave him the opportunity to try out some of his ideas on how such a business might be run.

Roasting Operations

Stuart's Branded Foods operated its own roasting plant. The company purchased and stored green coffee beans. Given the volume of the company's business, Stuart Foods could not afford to buy a full shipload of green coffee. Instead, it purchased its green coffee needs through a local broker. There was a wide variety of green coffee beans available in the world from some 45 exporting countries. The quality and price levels for these beans were spread over a fairly wide spectrum. By carefully blending less expensive beans in the roasting process with higher grade coffees, it was possible to reduce the material cost of some blends of coffee.

The green coffee beans were delivered in 60 or 70 kg bags from places such as Africa, India, Mexico, and South America. In this green state, the beans could be stored for relatively long periods of time. Once roasted and ready for brewing, coffee would become stale very quickly. The use of high grade, expensive packaging would keep coffee fresh for perhaps six months. This allowed food service operators the chance to deliver their product less frequently than in the past.

The first stage of the roasting process involved loading a charge of green coffee beans into a roaster. The mix of beans used in the charge was based upon the recipe for a specific blend of coffee ordered by the customer. Depending on the size of the roaster, a charge of beans could be as small as one or as large as four of the 60 to 70 kg bags. This operation involved blowing hot air through the beans until they were heated to approximately 400°F.

In this heating stage, the beans burst open, and discarded a shell called the chaff. The flow of hot air carried the very light chaff to a separator. The roasted beans, when cooled, were transported mechanically to a grinder, where they were ground into finer particles. To keep the flavour of the roasting process, it was necessary to package the coffee quickly. The ground roasted coffee was taken to an automated packaging machine which loaded the coffee into sealed packages for the customer.

Most of the roasting and grinding equipment had been functioning for more than 30 years. Although the equipment was not new in terms of design, the process was not labour intensive to convert the beans from their green state into packaged coffee. Nevertheless, the cumulative cost of the direct and indirect labour was significantly more than the cost for the energy to roast the beans.

The roasting and grinding process involved a significant amount of shrinkage of green coffee beans. Approximately 12% of the weight disappeared in the roasting process due to moisture loss. A further 4% of the weight disappeared due to combustible material loss. Some beans were lost in the process of separating the chaff. On rare occasions a malfunction in the roaster would burn the beans, making the charge useless for commercial purposes. Finally, some beans simply turned into powder during the grinding stage and could not be packaged.

To accommodate this loss of materials by shrinkage, the cost of green coffee was expressed in terms of the yield of roasted product. Stuart Foods estimated a cost of $2.15 in green beans for each pound of roasted coffee produced. The additional production costs, including direct and indirect production labour, packaging materials, depreciation on the equipment, and general production overhead for the roasting plant, were estimated at $.35 per pound of roasted coffee.

Some of the regional firms and all of the local competitors had to purchase their coffee from roasters before selling it to customers. Several coffee service distributors purchased coffee from Stuart's Branded Foods roasting division in kits. A kit of coffee consisted of 42 packages, each weighing 1.75 ounces. The cost of the kit varied depending upon the blend of coffee involved. The kits also included filters for the brewing operation. Currently, the roasting division priced the kit at the cost of the roasted coffee, the cost of the filters, and a margin to cover administrative costs and profit. Last year, the average market price of a kit to coffee service operators was $18.00.

In order to properly evaluate the different operations within Stuart's Branded Foods, each unit functioned at arm's length from each other. This meant that the roasted coffee was sold to the Coffee Service Division at the same prices that it was sold to competing distributors. This policy avoided the problem of cross-subsidization between functions.

Coffee Service Division

In the food service division, the task involved salespeople contacting potential customers, assessing their needs, and quoting them a price for the service. This process involved a visit to the customer's site to evaluate the operation. On this visit, the salesperson determined the type and quantity of equipment needed for an efficient coffee service in the location. The salesperson also estimated the annual volume and blend of coffee that the customer wanted. This included the frequency with which the customer expected to be resupplied. Using this information, the salesperson quoted one all-inclusive price for the service to the customer. This was expressed as the price per kit of coffee ordered or the cost per brewed cup.

After the contract was signed, the distribution operation of the division became involved. The customer phoned in an order indicating how much coffee was desired, as well as any allied products. The clerk, upon receiving the call, filled out an invoice for the order and gave it to the dispatcher. The dispatcher arranged to have the contents of the invoice gathered from the division's warehouse, loaded on the delivery vehicle, and taken to the customer. The driver who delivered the order dropped off the invoice and either collected for the order or had it signed for by the customer.

The usual administrative overhead of telephones, clerks, files and records, accounting services, and dispatch was needed. These items generally appeared to grow in chunks as the number of customers increased and the volume of order transactions grew. Last year, the annual cost of operating the administration, marketing and sales, and distribution activities was $450,000 (see Exhibit 1).

Division Results

Within two years, the Coffee Services Division of Stuart's Branded Foods had grown to the point where it had a relatively stable customer base in the Toronto area. Last year, it had sold approximately $1,000,000 worth of coffee to some 1,000 customers and had handled in the range of 18,000 invoices.

Given the competitive nature of the business, and the newness of Stuart's Branded Foods division into the industry, the profit margin targeted from sales had been 15% of the sales dollar.

Mr. Daw felt that this represented a fair return for the assets employed. Last year, the average selling price of a "kit" of roasted coffee by the division had been well in line with the industry average. Unfortunately, the desired profit margin of 15% of sales had not been attained. Instead, as Exhibit 2 shows, the profit margin had been lower than 10% of sales. A National Coffee Service Association survey had reported that the average industry earnings had been even lower.

Pricing

The traditional pricing approach by the industry ensured that all costs of the operation were recovered in the selling price of the service. The operating costs charged to the customer were based upon the allocation of the sales and administration costs in relation to the kits of coffee that were sold the previous year. In the case of Stuart's Branded Foods, this amounted to $16.20 per kit for the 27,777 kits sold. The equipment cost involved charges for the brewing equipment used by the customers as well as maintenance. Based on last year's costs and sales volume, this cost was $3.24 per kit, and was included as part of the above $16.20. Finally, the price was marked up to reflect the desired profit margin to the company.

Customers ordered coffee in multiples of kits. The salesperson tried to arrange the size of order for the customer so that it was only necessary to make a delivery to the customer once a month. One of the key competitive dimensions in the food service industry was price. Customers paid from $25.00 to $45.00 per kit for coffee service from most distributors. Each of the distributors offered the same array of service in terms of equipment, coffee, and allied products. The differences between suppliers were reflected in the price charged. It was not uncommon for a competitor to offer a volume discount on the price per kit to a customer as an incentive for the customer to change suppliers for his or her coffee needs.

Recognizing that the larger customers required some price break to attract them to Stuart's Branded Foods service, or to keep such customers, Daw had his salespeople build a somewhat larger net profit margin into their pricing estimates for smaller customers, and a lower margin for larger customers. The intent was to have the total operation average out to a 15% profit margin on sales.

TWO CUSTOMERS

Stuart felt that something was wrong in the whole approach to costing and pricing in this industry. Using the comments he had read in Drucker's book, Stuart Daw began reviewing the manner in which his division, and indeed the whole industry, priced its coffee service. Using two typical customers, Stuart considered the implications of the existing procedure.

The first customer was a small office complex in Rosedale. The customer generally ordered five kits of coffee every month. The office used a single brewing machine. Deliveries could only be made during regular working hours. The salesperson had quoted the price of the service at $44.42 per kit, to reflect the fact that the delivery was somewhat inconvenient and to incorporate a 23% net profit margin on the business. This had been determined as follows:

Cost of Coffee 5 × $18.00 =	$ 90.00
Operating Cost 5 × $16.20 =	81.00
Total Cost	171.00
Selling Price with 23% Profit	222.08
Selling Price per kit	44.42
Customer Cost per cup $44.42/500	$ .088

The second customer was much larger. It was a restaurant operation in downtown Toronto. This client generally ordered 20 kits of roasted coffee per month. This customer operated a single brewing machine in the restaurant. The delivery was very easy because the restaurant was accustomed, and designed, to handle visits from suppliers. The pricing for this customer was as follows, with a net profit margin of 12% in recognition of the higher volume purchased:

Cost of Coffee 20 × $18.00 =	$ 360.00
Operating Costs 20 × 16.20 =	324.00
Total Cost	684.00
Selling Price with 12% Profit	777.28
Customer Price per kit	$ 38.86
Customer Cost per cup $38.86/500	$ .078

The discount had been necessary to get this customer from a competitor. Unfortunately, the offering of the discount meant that this contract could not generate 15% profit on sales. Stuart was concerned that if his salespeople had to offer these discounts to get large order business, and perhaps offer greater discounts to keep large order business, the coffee service division of Stuart's Branded Foods could end up failing to achieve the needed profit to remain viable and grow.

Obviously, the existing pricing approach was not generating the results that were sought. Could it be possible that there was something wrong in the entire approach to costing and pricing in this industry? Stuart wondered what he might do to make his firm competitive and still earn the desired profit levels in this business.

Exhibit 1

STUART DAW

Stuart's Branded Foods Cost Structure
for the Coffee Service Division

Kits of Roasted Coffee 27,777 kits × $18.00	$ 500,000
Personnel Costs This covered the costs of salaries for all personnel (8 people).	$ 220,000
Equipment Costs This covered the cost of coffee brewing equipment and maintenance on the equipment.	$ 90,000
Vehicle Costs This covered the depreciation and operating costs of all division vehicles.	$ 70,000
Other Overhead Costs This covered all other divisional expenses not included in the above categories.	$ 70,000
TOTAL COSTS	$ 950,000

* NOTE: These data have been disguised to preserve confidentiality.

Exhibit 2

STUART DAW

Income Statement for Previous Year for Stuart's Branded Foods
Coffee Service Division

	Revenue	$1,000,000
Less:	Cost of Goods Sold	500,000
	Gross Margin	$ 500,000
Less:	Selling and Administration	$ 450,000
	Net Profit	$ 50,000
	Return on Sales	5%
	Target Return on Sales	15%

S. C. JOHNSON AND SON, LIMITED — A NEW APPROACH TO PRODUCT COSTING

Rhonda English and Randolph Kudar*

Janet Clark, a product manager at S.C. Johnson and Son, was in the final stages of planning a special promotion pack for Sparkle Floor Finish, her high-volume consumer product. Marketing research had reported that a "bonus add-on pack" could increase sales of Sparkle. This promotion would offer a 900 mL bottle of the product for the same price as the regular 750 mL bottle. The promotion was set to run for a limited time only.

Recently, changes in the product costing system had been implemented at S.C. Johnson.[1] Janet was unsure of what impact this might have on the cost of the special promotion pack. For assistance, she decided to consult Dave Ford, a Financial Analyst in the Manufacturing Financial Support Department.

MANUFACTURING FINANCIAL SUPPORT

Manufacturing Financial Support was a relatively new department at SCJ. It collected and analyzed data to improve manufacturing operations and decision-making. It also offered information and explanations concerning product costs to other departments. For example, if a product manager asked how the cost of a

---

[1] For a description of the original costing system S. C. Johnson, refer to "S. C. Johnson and Son, Limited—The Costing System," page 49.

product could be reduced, Manufacturing Support might suggest replacing unique raw materials or packaging components with similar items being used by other products. This would reduce the number of inventory items held by the firm and allow for the possibility of greater quantity discounts from suppliers. The support department focused on service, in identifying actionable problems and helping people to understand how and why costs were assigned to products.

COMPANY BACKGROUND

S.C. Johnson and Son, Limited was founded by Samuel Curtis Johnson in Racine, Wisconsin in 1886. Initially a manufacturer of parquet flooring, the company soon realized there was an opportunity to make products to maintain and protect their floors. Thus Johnson Wax was created. S.C. Johnson, still a privately owned company, has operations in 41 countries and has 110 distribution centres around the world. The world-wide company was divided into three entities of which the largest was the Consumer Products Division (see Exhibit 1).

The Canadian subsidiary in Brantford, Ontario, was created in 1920 as a maker of floor waxes and had since expanded into furniture polishes (Pledge), domestic insecticides (Raid, Off!), air fresheners (Glade), personal care products (Agree Shampoo and Conditioner, Curel Body Lotion), and cleaning products (industrial and domestic). The sales of Canadian Johnson were approximately $100 million per year, with employment of around 300 full-time employees. About 25% of the workforce was in sales, 25% in the non-unionized plant, and the remaining in head office. The Canadian operation had its own management structure and research facilities, which enabled it to operate fairly autonomously.

MANUFACTURING

The manufacture of all S.C. Johnson (SCJ) products began with a formula or recipe. Each raw material necessary for production underwent quality control checks when arriving at SCJ. Upon beginning the production cycle, these raw materials were drawn from the raw material inventory and sent to their designated location. A separate building housed a polymer processing operation, which made the base fluids or polymers as outlined by many of the formulas. These polymers were then piped to the making area, where various polymers would be combined and additional raw materials (liquids and powders) mixed together in large steel kettles. The end result of the making operation was the final bulk to be used in filling the packaging units. Quality control checks were conducted at various stages of bulk making to ensure the meeting of standards and non-contamination.

The manufacturing facility contained a separate fill and pack line for each of: liquid products, aerosol (pressure) products, and personal care products; as well as a drum filling line and paste line. The Canadian subsidiary also manufactured about 70% of its own bottle requirements in its moulding operation. This operation gave SCJ the flexibility to assess priorities and demands, to accommodate their "just in time" inventory system, and to directly control the quality of bottles being used.

STANDARD COST SYSTEMS[2]

On average, the cost of a product was composed of 35% raw materials, 5% direct labour, 15% overhead, and 45% packaging components. For individual product costing, all costs were expressed at standard.

The raw material and component standard costs were based on standard purchase price times standard usage. Standard purchase price was an estimate of the mid-period (three months out) purchase price of the ingredients and components. The revision cycle for raw material and component standard costs occurred every six months, when price increases could be passed on to the customer. This was an industry practice.

Exhibit 2 illustrates a sample Bill of Materials (BOM) for one size of one product. The BOM specified the raw materials/components and amounts (quantity and dollar) of each, required to produce one case of finished product. The type and amount of ingredients for a product was dictated by a formula file, originally developed by the R&D department. The product manager had some input regarding which materials or components were used for his or her product.

The standard direct labour cost per case of finished product was calculated as follows. Engineering estimated the number of labour hours normally required to process and package a run of product. This standard time included the set-up time for the production and filling lines. The standard labour rate was based on the hourly pay rate of the production employees. There were only two labour categories in this non-unionized plant, operators and non-operators. To determine the standard direct labour cost per case, the following calculation was made.

$$\frac{\text{standard labour hours for the product run} \times \text{standard labour rate per hour}}{\text{engineered production rate in cases per run}}$$

This standard labour cost per case was revised annually when new labour rates were set for the employees, or when significant changes were made to the production process.

Overhead costs were allocated to products through the use of four "burden pools": Fringe Benefits, Quality Assurance, Cost Centre Charges, and

---

2 Selected numbers throughout the case have changed to maintain confidentiality.

Manufacturing Support. It was in the area of overhead costs that SCJ's system made its changes. The total costs that had to be absorbed by the products remained the same; however, the allocation methods used to attach the costs to the various products were altered. Exhibit 3 details the major elements in the Overhead Pools.

1) Fringe Benefits

Fringe Benefits represented 2.4% of the cost of sales and were directly associated with SCJ labour usage. An estimate of the total fringe benefits for the year was divided by an estimate of the total direct hourly wages for the complete manufacturing activity. Currently, fringe benefits were assigned to a case of finished product on the basis of 49% of the direct labour cost of case of finished product.

2) Quality Assurance

Quality Assurance (QA) charges were approximately 1.4% of the cost of sales. These charges represented the budgeted expenses of the Quality Assurance Department within the plant. This budget was distributed across seven quality codes, based upon time splits for those codes, as provided by the QA department. Each finished product was assigned to one of the seven quality codes by the QA department, based upon the required procedures needed for the product. The quality assurance cost per case for a specific product in a specific code was determined as follows.

$$\frac{\text{Estimated QA expenses assigned to the Quality Code Estimated}}{\text{Estimated Total Cases of Finished Product in Quality Code}}$$

Therefore all finished products in a particular quality code had the same QA charge per case.

3) Cost Centre Charges

Approximately 5.6% of the cost of sales was made up of cost centre charges. Total costs of operating each production department were determined using budgeted expenses, records of fixed assets, and allocations such as floor area for items like occupancy and utilities.

For each of the making departments, it was necessary to estimate the number of kilograms of product that would be processed in that department during the period. The cost centre charges assigned to that department would be divided by the estimated number of kilograms, to generate a cost per kilogram allocated to each material processed in the department.

In the fill and pack departments, an estimate was made of the number of production labour hours that would occur in each department during the period. A cost per hour was developed for each fill and pack department. This cost was attached to the final product on the basis of the amount of production time required to process a case of final product through a department.

4) Manufacturing Support

The largest element of overhead, manufacturing support accounted for 7.3% of the cost of sales. Allocation of this cost pool began with an estimate by support group personnel of time spent on: raw materials, packaging components, finished goods, and general business (time spent on such areas as budgeting, performance reviews, meetings, etc.). The chart below illustrates this step.

Department	RM	Comp	FG	General	Total
Purchasing	63.0	112.0	36.0	29.0	240
Planning	52.0	52.0	51.0	5.0	160
Engineering	40.5	132.5	92.0	15.0	280
Rec. & Storage	99.5	151.5	14.0	5.0	270
Mftg. Admin./Supv.	46.0	90.0	81.0	23.0	240
Total Hours/Week	301.0	538.0	274.0	77.0	1190
PERCENTAGES	25.3%	45.2%	23.0%	6.5%	100%

These percentages were then applied to the estimated overhead cost pool for the year to determine dollar allocations for the four groups.

Allocation	$714K	$1274K	$650K	$184K	$2822K

Finished products were classified as A through E according to expected production volumes for the period, A being the largest volume products and E being the smallest. The classification of finished products on this basis arose when management realized that 80% of S.C. Johnson's sales volume was generated by only 30% of their products (see Exhibit 4). There were many small-volume products which management suspected were creating a significant portion of overhead costs. The percentage cutoff point was fixed for each category (i.e., top 10% were As, next 15% were Bs, etc.).Volume classifications for each product were redetermined at the beginning of each fiscal year.

Each volume category was assigned a weighting in the form of points, as follows:

A 1 point

B 3 points

C 5 points

D 7 points

E 11 points

This weighting system, when used in conjunction with a dollar value per point (explained below), would assign more manufacturing support overhead to lower volume products, reflecting the perceived cost drivers of this overhead pool.

Using the formula files for each final product, all raw materials and components were also classified according to the best finished product end use classification. Thus, a raw material or component used in an "A" final product was always classified as an "A", even if used in an "E" final product.

Total points for each of raw materials, components, and finished goods were generated by multiplying code counts (# of different RMs, Components, and FGs) by the respective weighting factor and by estimated total volume of the unit (e.g., RM kilograms, Packaging units, FG cases). For general business, total code counts of raw materials, components, and finished goods were multiplied by volumes, with no weightings assigned to the codes. By dividing the total points into the dollar pools for each of the four groups, values per point were arrived at, as indicated below.

	RM	*Comp*	*FG*	*General*
Total Points	57,360,786	39,164,675	10,443,203	58,524,012
Value / Point	$0.01245	$0.03252	$0.06226	$0.00314

These rates were revised annually by the cost department, using information from the Forecasting and Manufacturing departments.

To establish the manufacturing support overhead allocation for a particular end product, total raw material points, component points, and finished good points were multiplied by their respective values per point in each group. The general value per point was multiplied by the total number of unweighted codes from the three other groups. The sum of these was the manufacturing support overhead charge per case of finished product.

To illustrate the allocation of manufacturing financial support, assume the finished product is a "C" classification. The finished good uses five raw materials and four packaging components. There are three "A" raw materials, two "C" raw materials, one "A" component, and four "C" components. The calculation of overhead is as follows:

Raw Materials	3 As × 1 point	=	3 points
	2 Cs × 5 points	=	10 points
			13 points
			× $0.01245

Overhead allocation for RMs	$0.16185

Components	1 A × 1 point	=	1 point
	4 Cs × 5 points	=	20 points
			21 points
			× $0.03252

Overhead allocation for Comps	$0.68292

Finished Goods 1 C × 5 points =   5 points
                                     × $0.06226

Overhead allocation for FG $0.31130

General   11 codes
                                   × $0.00314

Overhead allocation for General $0.03454

Total Mftg Support Overhead/Case $1.19689

PRODUCT COSTING

A standard cost summary card for S.C. Johnson is illustrated in Exhibit 5. This card reports a standard cost per case of finished product, outlining the bill of materials for raw materials and packaging components, details of production costs, and a summary of production costs. Selected terminology used on the cost card is explained below.

BOM — Bill of Material

Data From Previous Processes — These are the costs associated with the making of the intermediate and final bulks (essentially the contents for the package).

Set OP Hrs — set-up hours by operating labour
Set NOP Hrs — set-up hours by non-operating labour

DLAB-OPR — direct labour cost of operating employees
DLAB-NOP — direct labour cost of non-operating personnel

PMF Data — this is engineering information regarding the production run. Such things as production line used, run size, # of cases per hour that can be produced, time in hours for various tasks, and fringe and loss percentages are detailed.

DEF PROMO — the incremental cost of producing a promotional product is charged to marketing expense rather than recorded as cost of goods sold.

Each product manager was responsible for a target gross margin percentage, as well as a dollar contribution towards corporate profitability based on sales estimates. These amounts were determined in the budgeting process, considering product placement, market environment, competition, etc.

The budgeting process began with sales estimates by the product managers for the upcoming year. These estimates were reviewed by the Sales Forecasting Representative of the Finance department. The sales projection figures were negotiated by the finance and marketing personnel to arrive at the final estimates to be used in the budget. These figures were subsequently forwarded to the Production Planning area where consideration was given to current level of inventory, before determination of actual production volume for the year. The finished good "ABC" classification was then based on this production figure.

If actual sales of a particular product did not meet forecasted volumes during a period, there was no incremental cost consequences in that period. Volume classifications were recalculated only once at the beginning of each year.

THE SITUATION

Sparkle Floor Finish had annual sales of 38,000 cases, making it an "A" volume product. Exhibit 6 outlines the current volume classification cutoff points. Sparkle had a selling price of $24.48 per case before any trade deals, and a standard case cost of $9.79187 (see Exhibit 5 for the Sparkle cost card).

The promotion pack Janet was considering was a 20% volume bonus sold for the regular 750 mL bottle price. The promotion would be offered twice throughout the year, with a total production of 5,000 promotional cases. The new size would require a different bottle, label, and carton from the standard Sparkle components. Dave informed Janet that these special components would fall into the "D" volume classification, as would the finished product itself (see Exhibit 6). The effect of these classifications would, of course, be seen in the manufacturing support charges per case of product.

Dave also reported that although the number of workers would remain the same, the larger bottle size would result in a slower production rate per hour on the manufacturing line. Instead of 350 cases per hour, only 300 cases of the special product could be produced each hour. This would cause an increase in the direct labour cost per case and, consequently, increases in both fringe benefits and cost centre charges per case. Dave had generated a cost card for Janet, for the promotional pack, detailed in Exhibit 7.

Janet expected to capture additional sales volume through the special promotion. However, she was aware that a portion of the 5,000 additional cases would probably be sold at the expense of Sparkle's regular sales. The amount could be as high as 2,500 to 3,000 cases. With this information, Dave noted that Sparkle's "A" ranking on the 750 mL product could fall to an overall "B" ranking when the product classifications were redetermined at the beginning of the next fiscal year. If this happened, Dave determined the following resultant volume classifications:

Raw Materials —16 As 12 Bs

Components —1 A 3 Bs

Finished Good —B

CONCLUSION

Janet had received a lot of information from Dave and knew that with it, she had to make a decision on the 900 mL promotion pack. Since Janet was uncertain about the resultant volume classification for Sparkle next year, she wanted to consider the financial consequences under both scenarios — Sparkle remaining an "A" product, and Sparkle becoming a "B" product.

Exhibit 1

S. C. JOHNSON AND SON, LIMITED—World Wide Organization

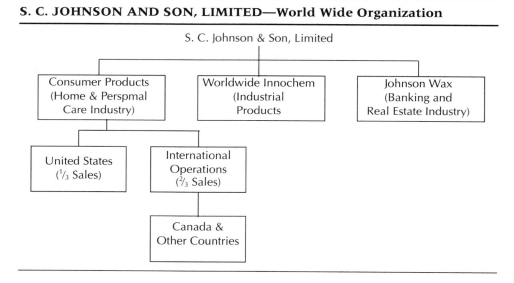

Exhibit 2

S. C. JOHNSON AND SON, LIMITED—Sample Bill of Materials

PRODUCT: SPARKLE FLOOR FINISH

Code	Description	ABC	Inv Unit	Last Period Unit Cost	Last Period BOM Cost	Current Period Unit Cost	Current Period BOM Cost
comp1	Bottle	A	EA			0.18011	2.16132
comp2	Cap	A	EA			0.06137	0.73644
comp3	Label	A	EA			0.02417	0.29004
comp4	Carton	A	EA			0.34982	0.34982
rm1	Active 1	A	KG			0.19890	0.02743
rm10	Active 10	A	KG			5.42538	0.09185
rm11	Active 11	A	KG			43.11948	0.08020
rm12	Active 12	A	KG			3.30000	0.36521
rm13	Active 13	A	KG			1.45152	0.72019
rm15	Soft Water	A	KG			0.00000	0.00000
rm16	Fragrance	A	KG			28.11650	0.19625
rm2	Active 2	A	KG			1.46370	0.02722
rm3	Active 2	A	KG			1.46370	0.00789
rm4	Active 4	A	KG			1.29540	0.00698
rm5	Active 5	A	KG			1.43910	0.75524
rm6	Active 6	A	KG			2.35241	0.44893
rm7	Active 7	A	KG			1.53882	0.18361
rm9	Active 9	A	KG			1.67535	0.59954
336701	Deionized Water	A	KG			0.00000	0.00000

Exhibit 3

S.C. JOHNSON & SON, LIMITED—Major Elements of Overhead Pools

FRINGE BENEFITS
   Employee Benefits
   Vacation Pay
   Paid Leave of Absence Overtime
   Shift Premiums

QUALITY ASSURANCE
   Entire Quality Assurance Department Budget

COST CENTRES
   Factory Depreciation Repairs and Maintenance Building Occupancy
   Factory Supplies
   Utilities

MANUFACTURING SUPPORT
   Planning (includes Manufacturing Information System Allocation) Purchasing
   Engineering
   Manufacturing Administration and Supervision
   Receiving and Storage
   Sundry Labour (includes cleaning, supervision, meetings) Under/Over Manufacturing
      Allocations
   Allocations

Exhibit 4

S.C. JOHNSON AND SON, LIMITED—Volume Classification

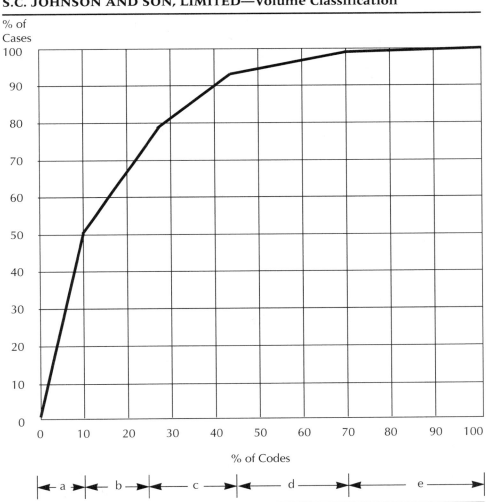

Exhibit 5

S.C. JOHNSON & SON, LIMITED

Sparkle Cost Card — Regular Pack

Bill of Materials — Last Period / Current Period

CODE	DESCRIPTION	A B C	I N V U E N I T T	UNIT COST	BOM COST	GEN PNTS	GLOBAL %ALLOW	UNIT COST	BOM COST
COMP1	BOTTLE	A	EA					0.18011	2.16132
COMP2	CAP	A	EA					0.06137	0.73644
COMP3	LABEL	A	EA					0.02417	0.29004
COMP4	CARTON	A	EA					0.34982	0.34982
RM1	ACTIVE 1	A	KG					0.19890	0.02743
RM10	ACTIVE 10	A	KG					5.42538	0.09185
RM11	ACTIVE 11	A	KG					43.11948	0.08020
RM12	ACTIVE 12	A	KG					3.30000	0.36521
RM13	ACTIVE 13	A	KG					1.45152	0.72019
RM15	SOFT WATER	A	KG					0.00000	0.00000
RM16	FRAGRANCE	A	KG					28.11650	0.19625
RM2	ACTIVE 2	A	KG					1.46370	0.02722
RM3	ACTIVE 3	A	KG					1.29540	0.00698
RM4	ACTIVE 4	A	KG					1.46370	0.00789
RM5	ACTIVE 5	A	KG					1.43910	0.75524
RM6	ACTIVE 6	A	KG					2.35241	0.44893
RM7	ACTIVE 7	A	KG					1.53882	0.18361
RM9	ACTIVE 9	A	KG					1.67535	0.59954
336701	DEIONIZED WATER	A	KG					0.00000	0.00000

	R M PNTS	COMP PNTS	F/G PNTS	GEN PNTS		TOTALS			7.04763
	28	4	1	33					

Data From Previous Processes

				S T A T	SER NO	RAW MAT	COMP	DIR LAB	O/H	TOTAL
CODE	DESCRIPTION				005	3.51	0.00	0.11	0.95	4.57
000550	SPARKLE FLOOR FINISH									
					TOTALS	3.51	0.00	0.11	0.95	4.57

Details of Production — Current Period Ser No. 004

DETAILS OF PROD COSTS	S T A T	PMF DATA	PREV PROC	THIS PROC	TOTAL	PMF DATA	PREV PROC	THIS PROC	TOTAL	CHNG PCT
PURCH FG										
RAW MAT							3.51		3.51	
COMP								3.54	3.54	
PROD LINE						49				
RATE/HR						350				
RUN SIZE						3410				
SET OP HRS						9.0				
SET NOP HRS								0.04	0.04	
DLAB OPR										
DLAB NOP							0.11			
DLAB1 NOFR						3.6		0.15	0.26	
DLAB2 NOFR						5.9		0.21	0.21	
TOT DIR LAB										
COST CTR HR							0.11	0.40	0.51	
FRINGE %						5	0.89	0.19	1.08	
O/H							0.05	0.18	0.23	
REC & MFG SUP								0.13	0.13	
TOTAL O/H								0.64	0.64	
SUB TOTAL							0.94	1.14	2.08	
TOTAL LOSS						1.5%	4.56	5.08	9.64	
DEF PROMO								0.15	0.15	
STD COST									9.79	

Summary of Product Costs

SUMMARY OF PRODUCT COSTS		LAST PERIOD	CURRENT PERIOD	CHANGE	PERCENT CHANGE
PURCHASED FG	V		0.00000		
RAW MATERIALS	V		3.51001		
COMPONENTS	V		3.53762		
DIRECT LABOUR	F		0.50542		
OVERHEAD			2.09411		
SUB TOTALS			9.64716		
MFG LOSS + GLOBAL ALLOW	V		0.14471		
DEF PROMO			0.00000		
STANDARD COST			9.79187		
FIXED COST TOTAL			2.09411		
VARIABLE COSTS TOTAL			7.69776		

	A B C	CURR SER#
	A B A	004

INV UNIT	DESCRIPTION	SHIPPING DATA WEIGHT	RATE	STANDARD COST
CA	SPARKLE	750 ml 12		9.79187

STATS CASES			

REPORT NUMBER	DATA DATE YYYY MM DD			CODE
CST002				000550

Exhibit 6

S.C. JOHNSON & SON, LIMITED—Volume Classification Levels

A	> 37,901 cases	
B	> 14,200 cases	< 37,901 cases
C	>7,150 cases	< 14,200 cases
D	> 2,000 cases	< 7,150 cases
E	< 2,000 cases	

Exhibit 7

S.C. JOHNSON & SON, LIMITED

Sparkle Cost Card – Bonus Pack

BILL OF MATERIALS

CODE	DESCRIPTION	A B C	INVENT UNIT	LAST PERIOD UNIT COST	LAST PERIOD BOM COST	CURRENT PERIOD UNIT COST	CURRENT PERIOD BOM COST
COMP5	BOTTLE (BONUS)	D	EA			0.25000	3.00000
COMP2	CAP	A	EA			0.06137	0.73644
COMP6	LABEL (BONUS)	D	EA			0.04000	0.48000
COMP7	CARTON (BONUS)	D	EA			0.40000	0.40000
RM1	ACTIVE 1	A	KG			0.19890	0.03292
RM10	ACTIVE 10	A	KG			5.42538	0.11019
RM11	ACTIVE 11	A	KG			43.11948	0.09616
RM12	ACTIVE 12	A	KG			3.30000	0.43824
RM13	ACTIVE 13	A	KG			1.45152	0.86422
RM15	SOFT WATER	A	KG			0.00000	0.00000
RM16	FRAGRANCE	A	KG			28.11650	0.23534
RM2	ACTIVE 2	A	KG			1.46370	0.03267
RM3	ACTIVE 3	A	KG			1.46370	0.00947
RM4	ACTIVE 4	A	KG			1.29540	0.00838
RM5	ACTIVE 5	A	KG			1.43910	0.90629
RM6	ACTIVE 6	A	KG			2.35241	0.53870
RM7	ACTIVE 7	A	KG			1.53882	0.22033
RM9	ACTIVE 9	A	KG			1.67535	0.71946
336701	DEIONIZED WATER	A	KG			0.00000	0.00000
	TOTALS						8.82881

REPORT NUMBER	DATA DATE YYYY MM DD	RM PNTS	COMP PNTS	F/G PNTS	GEN PNTS	GLOBAL %ALLOW	SHIPPING DATA WEIGHT	RATE	STATS CASES
CST002		28	22	7	33				

DATA FROM PREVIOUS PROCESSES

CODE	DESCRIPTION	STAT	SER NO	RAW MAT	COMP	DIR LAB	O/H	TOTAL
000550	SPARKLE FLOOR FINISH		005	4.21	0.00	0.14	1.14	5.49
	TOTALS			4.21	0.00	0.14	1.14	5.49

LAST PERIOD SER NO. 004

DETAILS OF PROD COSTS	STAT	PMF DATA	PREV PROC	THIS PROC	TOTAL

CURRENT PERIOD SER NO. 004

DETAILS OF PROD COSTS	PMF DATA	PREV PROC	THIS PROC	TOTAL	CHNG PCT
PURCH FG					
RAW MAT		4.21		4.21	
COMP			4.62	4.62	
PROD LINE	49				
RATE/HR	300				
RUN SIZE	2500				
SET OP HRS	9.0				
SET NOP HRS					
DLAB OPR			0.05	0.05	
DLAB NOP					
DLAB1 NOFR	3.6	0.14	0.17	0.31	
DLAB2 NOFR	5.9		0.24	0.24	
TOT DIR LAB					
COST CTR HR			0.46	0.60	
FRINGE %		0.14	0.23	1.30	
OA	5	1.07	0.22	0.28	
REC & MFG SUP		0.06	0.13	0.13	
SUB TOTAL	1.5%	1.13	1.60	3.31	
TOTAL OH			2.18		
TOTAL LOSS		5.48	7.26		
DEF PROMO				0.19	
STD COST				12.74	12.93

SUMMARY OF PRODUCT COSTS

	LAST PERIOD	CURRENT PERIOD	CHANGE	PERCENT CHANGE
PURCHASED FG		0.00000		
RAW MATERIALS		4.21201		
COMPONENTS		4.61644		
DIRECT LABOUR		0.60084		
OVERHEAD		3.30853		
SUB TOTALS		12.73782		
MFG LOSS + GLOBAL ALLOW		0.19107		
DEF PROMO		0.00000		
STANDARD COST		12.92889		
FIXED COST TOTAL		3.30853		
VARIABLE COSTS TOTAL		9.62036		

INV UNIT	A B C	CURR SER#
CA	A / A	004

DESCRIPTION			STANDARD COST	CODE
SPARKLE	900 ml	12	12.92889	000550

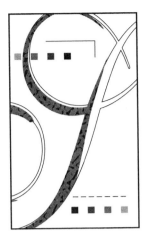

PART **C**

OPERATIONAL BUDGETING

MIDTOWN HOSPITAL

John Cummings, Sonya Head, and John F. Graham

In March 1990, Mr. Martin sat down to ponder his recommendations to the board of Midtown Hospital. Fiscal year end was rapidly approaching and each department had presented its needs to the executive director for the next year. With the recent public scrutiny of the health care system and the pressures rampant on hospitals, Mr. Martin knew that he would have to choose wisely the proposals that he would present to the district health council (after they had been approved by the Board of Governors).

The Board of Governors for Midtown Hospital was representative of the community. There were members from all walks of life and representatives of the hospital staff. The physician representative on the board seemed to sway opinion popularly.

THE HOSPITAL

Midtown Hospital was a 200-bed community facility offering medical, surgical, critical, paediatric, obstetrical (child delivery), and chronic care to the population it served. The hospital was located approximately 40 minutes travelling time from a major medical and teaching centre with extensive facilities in all areas of medical service.

Residents around Midtown Hospital preferred to have their families at the local hospital rather than travelling to the larger centre, particularly when there was an extended illness.

With expenses totalling $19.9 million in fiscal 1989, Midtown Hospital was anticipating a freeze on all expenditures. Alternative solutions (like cut-backs in some areas to favour others) would have to be presented if any major changes to the existing system were to take place. A small increase for inflation was anticipated by the Board of Governors (as allowable) from the provincial government.

The decisions that Mr. Martin would make today required some assessment of the kinds of facilities that would be required over the next decade. The mix of chronic and acute beds was currently similar to that in every other hospital in Ontario. At Midtown Hospital, the major patient service used was general medicine (i.e., 65% of all patients excluding newborns were general medicine). General medicine, considered as the treatment of the more common illnesses, describes care given to persons not falling under one of the three groups: surgery, obstetrics and paediatrics.

Ministry of Health bed-to-population guidelines for chronic care were allocated on a county-wide basis. Currently, the ministry projected an increased need of 15% (chronic beds) by 1990. General surgery represented 20% of patient days, obstetrics 10%, and paediatrics 5% (65% of patient days represented general medicine).

The majority of physicians who utilized the facilities at the hospital were from family practice (22 family practitioners in total). All of the specialties (excluding Obstetrics/Gynaecology, Ophthalmology, and Otolaryngology) were covered by one specialist each. Consulting and courtesy physicians from neighbouring centres augmented the hospital's physician base.

DECISIONS

Pressures on the Emergency Department had caused the department head to request additional beds for emergency care. There was space available at the existing facility; however, expenditures for staff (especially in the evening hours) would have to be increased, and the "quiet" space allocated for the physician on call would have to be used as an assessment room. This latter fact had caused quite a stir among the local physicians who were required to "man" the emergency department 24 hours per day. The physicians used an "on call" system that was decided among themselves.

Surgery had requested some new equipment which would accommodate ·more ear, nose, and throat (ENT) surgery. The equipment purchase could be accommodated within the existing budget; however, pre- and post-surgical care would require additional staff.

The Nursing director had requested some salary increases above and beyond normal allocations for inflation. She had explained her request on the basis of the difficulty of obtaining qualified help. Most of the Registered Nurses in the area preferred to commute to higher paying positions at the larger centre (40 minutes away). The remaining qualified R.N.s in the area preferred part-time work while they raised families. It was particularly difficult to staff the weekends and evenings.

One of the hospital's board members had suggested the establishment of an outpatient clinic, attached to the hospital and staffed from 8:00 a.m. to midnight. The outpatient clinic would be similar to an emergency facility, but would not include much of the expensive, high technology equipment found in most of the emergency units. Those patients whose injuries did not require the use of the emergency equipment could be treated in this outpatient clinic, thus freeing up the emergency facilities for those truly requiring them.

THE BEDROCK CORPORATION —ELECTRONICS DIVISION

Rhonda English, Al Magrath, and Randolph Kudar*

Cindy Bradley, a marketing manager in Bedrock Corporation's Electronics Division, was studying a field report she had just received from her Division manager. Cindy was responsible for making a recommendation on a support program that would assist distributors in increasing sales of the division's products. Since Bedrock had not had much success in dealing with distributors in the past, Cindy was anxious to develop improved working relationships with them. She had to decide what kind of support would be most effective for the distributors as well as for Bedrock.

THE COMPANY

The Bedrock Corporation was a highly diversified company with operations in Canada, the United States, and Europe. The Canadian operation was located in Montreal, Quebec, and was involved in both manufacturing and importing of numerous products. The Canadian company was organized into divisions, with each division responsible for a group of related products. As a full-line supplier, the product lines met varying needs within the corporation, some being market leaders and others simply filling out total offering.

Each division was headed by a Division manager, to whom a number of product managers reported. Product managers were responsible for the bottom line operating profit of each product under their umbrella. Marketing managers,

who reported to product managers for approval, undertook the promotion, distribution, and advertising activities for various products. Each division had access to the usual support groups, such as marketing research, accounting, legal, etc.

Annual budgets by specific product were developed at the beginning of the year for all divisions. Revenue, cost, and profit figures were set in dollars and percentages using input from all areas of the division (e.g., product managers, marketing managers). This planning dictated how indirect costs would be apportioned to the various products, and were set for the duration of the year. A sample profit and loss budget is outlined in Exhibit 1.

THE SITUATION

The Electronics Division sold over 30 major products to the electronics industry through distributors, with sales to the distributors totalling $12 million per year. Sales growth had averaged about 5 percent annually. Cindy had a limited budget of $100,000 to expend on support programs for her products.

The division manager had coordinated a survey of the eight key regional distributors to determine what kind of support they wanted Bedrock to provide to augment their sales. The distributor responses are summarized in Exhibit 2, indicating which supports were most appealing by using a ten point scale (10 being highest, and 1 being lowest). The distributors were also asked their opinion on how long it would take for the supports to increase their business. The time frames suggested were within three to six months, within a year, or within eighteen months to two years. This information is also presented in Exhibit 2.

THE ALTERNATIVES

After studying the survey results, Cindy decided to further examine only those supports which received a ranking of eight or higher from the distributors, because she felt these would be the most effective alternatives. Additional information concerning these top seven options is detailed below.

Co-op Advertising Plan

Co-op advertising was based on planned sales, by the distributor, for the year. However, if the distributor's sales decreased, so too would the cooperative advertising. The cost was estimated to be three quarters of 1 percent of Bedrock sales to distributors.

Training Clinics

Bedrock would send a sales representative to each of the eight distributors to train their people. Three different clinics would be conducted for each distributor, with each clinic running three days. Bedrock's costs would include three days of a sales representative's time per clinic (salary $1,000/week), plus expenses of $100 per night for hotel, $100 per day for meals, and $250 per clinic for travel. Videos of the three types of clinics would also be produced at a cost of $1,000 per video.

Mailers

Four mailings per year per distributor would be directed at target markets customized by distributor. Each mailing would cost $1,200.

Sales Spiffs

Sales spiffs (special promotional incentive for future sales) had been used by Bedrock in the past with varied results. The idea behind spiffs was to give incentives on certain products, which would lead to heavy promotional efforts by the distributors and therefore increased sales. Once the spiff was over, sales were expected to drop off but remain at a higher plateau than their previous level. The success of this kind of support varied depending on what other activity was going on at the time the spiff was offered.

For example, if competition ran a similar program concurrently, the spiff would be less effective. As well, sometimes customers would stock up during the promotion and then reduce future purchases, with no overall gain received by Bedrock. The costs of this program amounted to 10 percent of every extra dollar of sales generated over the average distributor's normal sales for the period over which the spiff was run. One spiff would be run for each distributor for four months.

Trip Prizes

Bedrock would give the two top representatives from each distributor a free trip. One risk with this type of support was that it could become increasingly more expensive. This would happen if competition followed suit and companies tried to outdo one another with the trips offered. On the other hand, Bedrock might be forced to use this kind of support if the competition started to offer trips. Each trip (per representative with spouse) would cost Bedrock $4,000. Currently, only some of the competitors offered incentive trips.

Catalogue

Catalogues were printed every two years and often considered a very useful document for the distributors. A total of 200 copies would be necessary to supply the existing distributor network. They would be as follows: 80 outside distributor representatives, 84 distributor order desk people, 20 distributor management personnel, and 16 extra copies. Preparation and printing costs amounted to $150 per catalogue. Mailing and distribution costs totalled $10 per catalogue.

Samples and Sales Aids

Bedrock had not previously provided this type of support very often because they found it hard to control and difficult to terminate once the program was started. Samples and sales aids in the amount of $750 and $125 respectively per outside distributor representative would be necessary for this support program.

Cindy had met with the divisional controller to forecast the impact of these major support alternatives on distributor turnover and therefore on Bedrock profits. Their estimates are outlined in Exhibit 3. Cindy was interested in calculating quantitative results of the support options based on at least a two year horizon.

CONCLUSION

One of Cindy's concerns was the nature of the costs of the various supports. Some were reallocations of fixed costs as opposed to extra out-of-pocket costs, some were recurring costs where money had to be spent yearly (eg. samples and sales aids), and others were costs incurred in year one with no need to incur the same costs for at least two years (eg. catalogues, training). She wondered how this information should be incorporated into her analysis. As well, although she knew the distributors' preferences for the different supports, she saw a need to determine criteria to use to rank the available options in order to maximize effectiveness for Bedrock.

Exhibit 1

PROFIT AND LOSS BUDGET ($000)

PRODUCT ELECTRONICS

October 19XX

	Line	Amount	%
		This Year	
Sales – Domestic	4510	$12,000	100.0
Sales – Export	4511	—	–
Gross Sales	4512	$12,000	100.0
Cash Discounts	4513	—	—
Net Sales	4514	12,000	100.0
Finished Goods Purch	4515	–	–
Manufacturing Costs	4516	$5,340	44.5
Total Cost Goods Sold	4517	$5,340	44.5
Gross Margin	4518	$6,660	55.5
General Sales Exp	4519	$2,460	20.5
Advert Mdse Purch	4520	$324	2.7
Marketing Operations	4521	$900	7.5
Total Sales Exps	4522	$3,684	30.7
Administrative Exp	4523	$816	6.8
Total Oper Costs	4524	$9,840	82.0
OPERATING PROFIT	4525	$2,160	18.0

Exhibit 2

FIELD REPORT ON FAVOURED SUPPORTS

SUPPORTS	DISTRIBUTOR RATING 10 = highest 1 = lowest	DISTRIBUTOR EVALUATION OF SALES IMPACTS		
		6 Mos Impact	1 Year Impact	Impact Beyond 1 Year
1) Co-op advertising plan	8	No	Yes	Yes
2) Training clinics for distributor reps	9	No	Yes	Yes
3) Mailers to target markets customized by distributor	9	Yes	Yes	No
4) Distributor sales rep $ spiffs for surpassing goals	9	Yes	Yes	No
5) Distributor trip awards for top selling distributor rep in region	10	Yes	Yes	No
6) Easy to use catalogue designed for distributor reference	8	No	Yes	No
7) More samples, sales aids	8	No	Yes	Yes
8) 24 hour order turnaround	6	No	No	Yes
9) Electronic-Data Interchange	5	No	No	Yes
10) Imprinted distributor literature	6	No	No	No
11) Financial consulting help for distributor	5			
12) 1-800 response line to technical questions of distributor personnel	4			
13) Custom packaging/labelling services for distributors	3	No	Yes	Yes
14) More order expediting services on special requests	2	Yes	Yes	Yes
15) Offer private label programs	1.5			

Exhibit 3

SALES & PROFIT IMPACTS OF SUPPORTS

SUPPORT	INCREMENTAL SALES GROWTH IN YEAR 1*	CONFIDENCE LEVEL IN ESTIMATE	% CONTRIBUTION ON EXTRA SALES	COMMENTS
1) Co-op ads	2½%	75%	15%	low % contribution due to Co-op use mostly on fast moving, low contribution items in flyers etc.
2) Training	1½%	90%	25%	emphasize specialty products in training, higher margin lines
3) Mailers	3%	60%	30%	emphasize only high margin products in mailers
4) Rep spiffs	2%	95%	20%	reps will sell both low and high margin items during promotion
5) Distributor rep trip	1¾%	85%	24%	must give wide latitude to reps to move volumes including all types of products, but stress some higher margin lines
6) Catalogues	1%	80%	20%	division average margin plus 2%
7) Samples /Sales aids	.75%	75%	25%	slanted to higher contribution items

Basic Facts
Total sales = $12 million
# of Distributors = 8
Average sales per distributor = $1,500,000
Distributor's normal average growth expected = 5%

*incremental growth is growth on top of 5% normal

THE BEDROCK CORPORATION —INDUSTRIAL AND SURVEILLANCE DIVISION

Rhonda English, Al Magrath, and Randolph Kudar*

Gloria Gardiner, product manager in Bedrock's newest division handling industrial security and surveillance products, was preparing for an upcoming meeting with the Division Manager, Joe Fleming. Gloria was responsible for deciding whether or not the Montreal-based company would assume marketing and sales of the full line of a recently acquired business. As she opened the file of available information, Gloria was aware of both the urgency and significance of this decision.

THE COMPANY

The Bedrock Corporation was a highly diversified company with operations in Canada, the United States, and Europe. The Canadian operation was located in Montreal, Quebec, and was involved in both manufacturing and importing of numerous products. The Canadian company was organized into divisions, with each division responsible for a group of related products. As a full-line supplier, the product lines met varying needs within the corporation, some being market leaders and others simply filling out total offering.

Each division was headed by a Division manager, to whom a number of product managers reported. Product managers were responsible for the bottom line operating profit of each product under their umbrella. Marketing managers, who reported to product managers for approval, undertook the promotion, distribution, and advertising activities for various products. Each division had access to the usual support groups, such as marketing research, accounting, legal, etc.

Annual budgets by specific product were developed at the beginning of the year for all divisions. Revenue, cost, and profit figures were set in dollars and percentages using input from all areas of the division (e.g., product managers, marketing managers). This planning dictated how indirect costs would be apportioned to the various products, and were set for the duration of the year. A sample profit and loss budget is outlined in Exhibit 1.

THE MARKET

Industrial security and surveillance was an ever-growing industry. The 24 hour world in which companies operated demanded extensive surveillance, and thus security had become a key part of business. Protection of corporate information, people, and property required the use of high-tech electronic security systems. The major components of these systems were state-of-the-art alarms, card access systems, and closed-circuit televisions. Card access control was the fastest growth area with predictions of 35 to 40 percent annual increases over the next five years.

THE SITUATION

Bedrock Corporation had recently purchased an Ohio-based firm involved in the sale of a complementary group of industrial security and surveillance products. The Ohio company had been selling in Canada for a few years through four regional distributors, and had achieved sales last year of $2 million, with an annual growth rate of 15 percent.

The company's product line was arranged into three classifications: A products, B products, and C & D products. Gloria had already decided that Canadian Bedrock should carry the A and B items, which were high-volume, major products, and that selling should continue using the existing distributors, along with the addition of three others to better service the Prairies, Atlantic Canada, and Southwestern Ontario. Existing distributors were located in Vancouver, Toronto, Ottawa, and Montreal. Her dilemma was whether the C & D items should also be handled by the division, or left with the Ohio firm to be sourced directly by the Canadian distributors.

Gloria had collected detailed information on sales by the Ohio firm to its Canadian distributors. Exhibit 2 outlines sales of the company in the last fiscal year, sales dollars, and inventory turns, by line item. Exhibit 3 details typical distributor sales, percentage of distributor inventory, and average mark-ups, by item description.

C & D items consisted mainly of replacement, secondary, and supplemental parts for security and surveillance products. Due to the nature of these items (many small products), distributors acted primarily as order-takers with the selling company shipping the items directly to the customers. Existing distributors had been contacted by Gloria and had made the following observations regarding C & D products:

> "C & D items are relied upon to help keep volume discounts high in calculating discounts."
>
> "C & D items round out the line, and help keep competitors out of the market."
>
> "C & D items are slow movers so we rely on the source vendor to ship orders of these separately and to provide rapid response time on these items."

With the help of her controller, Gloria had made estimates of incremental costs associated with taking on the line in full versus only the A and B items. Exhibit 4 contains her notes. All of these items would be charged against her profit and loss statement for these product lines.

There were several other factors that Gloria was considering that could influence her decision. The first was the fact that in the future it might become necessary to package the line in Canada to keep product costs competitive. If only a portion of the line was being sold by Canadian Bedrock, packaging in Canada might be more manageable and less costly in terms of design work and initial ordering of packaging supplies.

Secondly, in the past, distributors had always had combinability privileges in ordering any of the Ohio firm's line to obtain maximum total order discounts from list. If Gloria decided to involve Canadian Bedrock in the sale of only part of the line, existing distributors would be upset with their loss of margin.

Thirdly, overall dealings for the distributors would become more complicated. For example, returned goods privileges of the two firms might differ, two sets of price lists would be in effect, etc.

Gloria's initial reaction was that C & D items were low in sales volume and high in inventory carrying costs, obsolescence costs, sales training costs, and other overhead transaction costs. Her profitability target after all overhead assessments was 20 percent. She wondered about arranging "indent sales" whereby Bedrock would receive a commission on all sales of C & D items in Canada, leaving all aspects of sales to be handled by the U.S. company. Under this scenario, Bedrock would have no direct involvement with distributors or customers regarding C & D product line items.

CONCLUSION

Mr. Fleming, the Divison manager, was leaving the following week to meet with the various distributors, as he made a trip across Canada, so Gloria did not have

Bdrk traditionally a full line supplier

a lot of time to make a decision on the new line. A further consideration in her decision was the fact that, traditionally, Bedrock had opted to be a full-line supplier to distributors. Consequently, she knew that any deviation from this practice would have to be well-supported.

Exhibit 1

PROFIT AND LOSS BUDGET
($000)

PRODUCT SECURITY SYSTEMS

October 19XX

	Line	This Year Amount	%
Sales – Domestic	4510	$5,958	100.0
Sales – Export	4511	—	—
Gross Sales	4512	$5,958	100.0
Cash Discounts	4513	—	—
Net Sales	4514	$5,958	100.0
Finished Goods Purch	4515	—	—
Manufacturing Costs	4516	$3,054	51.2
Total Cost Goods Sold	4517	$3,054	51.2
Gross Margin	4518	$2,904	48.8
General Sales Exp	4519	$1,225	20.5
Advert Mdse Purch	4520	$ 161	2.7
Marketing Operations	4521	$ 447	7.5
Total Sales Exps	4522	$1833	30.7
Administrative Exp	4523	$ 407	6.8
Total Oper Costs	4524	$5,294	88.7
OPERATING PROFIT	4525	$ 664	11.3

Exhibit 2

OHIO COMPANY'S SALES TO CANADIAN DISTRIBUTORS

	# Items Sold SKUs	% of Items	% of Sales	Avg.# Invent (Annual)	Manuf Gross Margin
A ITEMS	700	35%	65%	12 x	50%
B ITEMS	300	15%	15%	9 x	54%
C & D ITEMS	1,000	50%	20%	3 x	58%
TOTAL	2,000	100%	100%		

Note

S.K.U. = Stock Keeping Unit
TOTAL SALES = $2 million

Exhibit 3

AVERAGE CANADIAN DISTRIBUTORS' SALES OF OHIO COMPANY'S PRODUCTS

	% of Sales	% of Distributors Inventory	Average Mark-Ups (On Cost) Earned
A ITEMS	67%	55%	30%
B ITEMS	13%	40%	35%
C & D ITEMS	20%	5%	40%
	100%	100%	

Note - Distributor average = $650,000 annual sales

Exhibit 4

INCREMENTAL COSTS OF TAKING ON C & D ITEMS

1. Obsolescence of stock
   — 2% on A and B items on average inventory value during the year
   — 5% on C & D items on average inventory value during the year

2. Extra catalogue pages, extra literature for selling (e.g., tech sheets), and samples for C & D items

Catalogue	+ $30,000
Literature	+ $20,000
Samples	+ $ 8,000

3. Extra price pages (more pages, print, and distribution costs) for C & D items
   — $12,000 each time prices are changed

4. Carrying costs of inventory
   — 22% per year flat rate of average inventory value of all S.K.U.s, to cover storage, insurance and interest costs

5. Corporate overheads assessed
   — $15 flat rate per S.K.U. for data processing costs, invoicing transaction costs, and training costs for branch order desk people

6. Extra training time to make 6 sales reps proficient on C & D items (as well as A and B)
   — 10% of reps' time
   — reps average salary is $40,000 per year

7. Extra time spent with new distributors to familiarize them with C & D items
   — 5% of sales reps' time in 3 regions

8. Extra time for special task force personnel in inventory control to integrate C & D items into system (one time cost)
   — 50% of one person for four months duration

9. Cost of returns to division is flat rate of 3% of sales on such items

10. Flat rate administrative corporate charges are assessed at 18% of sales by product

ED TEL—PRIVATE BRANCH EXCHANGE SYSTEMS

Randolph Kudar*

Jeff Orr, the product manager for Private Branch Exchange (PBX) systems at ED TEL, picked up his financial statements for the month of November. This was the first time that he had received the newly formatted statements. He wondered if there would be any discrepancies or anomalies within the accounts of the nine products in his portfolio. He would be required to identify, investigate, analyze, and interpret these items for his monthly variance report to the marketing manager for Business Systems.

BACKGROUND

ED TEL was Canada's largest municipally owned and independent telephone system. Incorporated as the Edmonton District Telephone Company in 1893, the telephone system served nearly 300 Edmontonians and 100 district residents through four exchanges when the City of Edmonton assumed ownership in 1905. At the end of the 1980s ED TEL employed 1,889 permanent employees and serviced 351,000 access lines. Its annual revenue exceeded $245 million, net income was more than $20 million, and total assets amounted to over $440 million.

The network currently operated through 12 switching centres and 10 remote switches, with digital service available to customers throughout 65% of the service area. Fully 75% of the system's interoffice traffic was carried by optical fibre. Repair, installation, and special services were provided through two central production control centres, four primary telephone service centres, six Phone Exchange retail outlets, and the Business Communication Centre.

As a leader in the telecommunications industry, ED TEL has achieved many firsts: the first in Western Canada to introduce touchtone service (1967); the first to introduce the 911 "help" number (1969); the first to operate and install a computerized order system (1973); the first in Canada to introduce a computerized directory assistance system (1977); the first in Western Canada to introduce the CALRS 611 repair system (1979); the first to introduce a fully electronic PBX system integrating radio and telephone communications for police and fire operations (1980); and the first in Alberta to utilize optical fibre facilities for transmission of commercial broadcast video signals (1987). In continuing with these achievements, another first for ED TEL was the Talking Yellow Pages. In March 1989, the Talking Yellow Pages directory crew initiated the first telecommunications audio production house in Canada. The technicians created and produced all talking advertisements on the system and coordinated the production of the updates for "Direct Connect", featuring sports, weather, entertainment, lotteries, culture, horoscopes, financial news, and soap operas.

ED TEL's mission was to understand and fulfil the customers' communications and information needs in a superior and profitable manner. As the result of a customer survey, ED TEL was developing a new corporate campaign and the marketing plan focused on preserving the customer base through excellent customer service. ED TEL promoted itself as a "single source" supplier, supplying the terminal equipment, network and data services required to meet customer needs as well as additional "value added" services. The concept of "one stop shopping" was introduced for business customers, allowing them the convenience of calling one number to receive information on billing enquiries for long distance, cellular and regular service. Catering to the retail customers, the Phone Exchanges had become more customer oriented, with video demonstrations on telecommunications products, and wall displays featuring the latest products and services.

The most significant organizational event of the past year had been the decision to establish ED TEL as a subcorporation of the City of Edmonton. Previously, ED TEL had been owned and operated by the City of Edmonton, with the general manager of ED TEL reporting through the City Manager to City Council. Under the new structure, ED TEL operated under a Board of Directors, with City Council retaining ultimate control as owner and regulator. The Board replaced City Council as the policy setting body. The General Manager of ED TEL became the President and Chief Executive Officer representing ED TEL on the board. He and 10 other prominent members of Edmonton's business community were entrusted with guiding ED TEL in its future operations. An organization chart for ED TEL is presented in Exhibit 1.

MERIDIAN 1 SYSTEMS

Meridian 1 was a product line of electronic Private Branch Exchanges (PBX). These were switchboard systems for medium to large customers and/or specific applications such as Automatic Call Distribution for smaller systems. Designed for economical modular growth from 30 to 10,000 lines, the Meridian 1 system could be configured to suit end user requirements ranging from a small business seeking advanced calling features, to a large corporation in need of more sophisticated options. After having identified the customer's specific goals — improved service, increased staff productivity, better management of communication costs — ED TEL could propose a powerful, adaptable Meridian 1 system that was tailor-made for the job at hand.

Since its introduction in 1975, the Meridian 1 had been unsurpassed in its ability to meet demanding customer requirements. The system had maintained its competitive superiority by evolving to address changing market needs while ensuring that even the earliest Meridian 1 models could continue to take advantage of the latest developments. The key to Meridian 1 versatility was the modular architecture. Every major system component had been designed as a separate unit to allow independent, incremental growth as the customer's needs expanded and the communications requirements changed. The system's unique modular packaging promoted quick, cost-effective evolution to take advantage of the latest technological enhancements with minimal disruptions.

The Meridian 1 offered a whole range of business solutions: customer applications such as Hospitality Voice Services and Messaging; value-added services such as Automatic Call Distribution (ACD), and Voice Processing; and networking with ESN and ISDN to improve multi-location communications. In addition, there were the data connectivity options: personal computers interacting with digital telephones; and multiple access to local area networks, wide area networks, and multi-vendor host computers. Whatever the business environment, Meridian 1 was unmatched in its delivery of clean, reliable, and economical voice/data integration.

Three Classifications

The current line of Meridian 1 systems was classified into three basic configurations which were identified as the following:
- Option 21, the small- to medium-sized business solution;
- Option 61, for large or small companies requiring full redundancies; and
- Option 71, the institutional solution.

The Option 21 was designed specifically to serve the fastest growing segment of the PBX market, that of fewer than 100 lines. At the same time, this system was capable of growing cost effectively to over 1,000 lines. All the applications available across the Meridian 1 systems were available to the Option 21.

The Option 61 was designed to meet the needs of industry leaders from fewer than 200 lines to over 2,000 lines. Fully duplicated central processing units and memory modules provided outstanding reliability and dependability. Selecting from the multitude of software features currently available provided the customers with a custom designed system tailored to meet their unique applications.

The Option 71 was designed to meet the needs of industry leaders from fewer than 1,000 lines to over 10,000 lines. As in the case of Option 61, these systems had fully duplicated central processing units and memory modules. The packaging of the Option 71 provided modularity and flexibility, allowing maximum utilization of product resources without the undue burden of extraneous hardware.

THE PBX MARKET

At ED TEL, there were nine different PBX switchboard products in Orr's portfolio. In addition to the three options of Meridian 1, there were several other older systems sold and serviced by ED TEL. As well, each system used a wide array of components that were products in their own right. (The business segment for PBX systems was unique and very competitive.) ED TEL competed for business in the Edmonton market with AGT Limited, a subsidiary of TELUS Corporation, Canadian Telecom Group (CTG), and TTS.

Because the market in Edmonton for PBX systems was not very large, competition to get and retain customers was fierce. The strategy often entailed bidding for the initial contract for a PBX system at a very low margin. Due to the high price for these systems and their modular construction, it was possible to offer the customer an evergreen policy of regular updates to the system to keep it current and suitable to the needs of the customer. These updates and additional modules could be sold to the customer at the regular margins over time, thus making the overall contract more financially attractive. Another competitive approach was to offer a Service Management Concept where a dedicated service person was assigned to that specific customer to maintain the system. Over the years, the Service Management Concept craftsman had become one of ED TEL's major competitive advantages.

Sales Contracts

The development of a sales contract with a customer generally involved the sales, engineering, and marketing departments at ED TEL. The sales representative initiated the contact with the customer to establish the needs of the customer. This step often involved the input of the engineering department which specifically configured the set of components and modules that would meet the requirements of the customer. Given the number of options and alternatives available, it was not uncommon for ED TEL to develop a set of alternative packages for a customer that involved 20 or 30 different configurations.

In a recent contract with a firm, the proposed contract involved 39 different alternatives from which the customer could choose. These ranged from the basic choice of the PBX system in analogue or digital format, to several different option cards for specific features, as well as maintenance contracts on the system. In this case, the customer elected to select four different alternatives from the 39 presented as the configuration of the PBX system.

Uniquely Designed Systems

Because each system sold to a customer was uniquely designed, there was no standard cost for a system. Also, because of the competitive nature of the market in this area, there was no standard margin on the contract, although there was a range of markups that were targeted for achievement. The price for the system was the responsibility of the marketing product manager. In this area, it was Orr's responsibility to price out the various alternatives that would be presented to the customer. In this step, he determined, based on information from the sales representative and his own knowledge of the market, what size of margin should be assigned to the cost of the components in each alternative in order to attract the customer to select ED TEL as the supplier of the PBX system. In cases of a major discount, he presented the justification for the pricing decision to senior management and developed a detailed contribution analysis for the contract. The sales representative then presented the alternatives to the customer. If the customer decided to purchase a system from ED TEL, the sales representative prepared a customer sales request which he forwarded into the direct sale billing system for implementation.

NEW PRODUCT REPORTS

During the previous three years, the Business Development Department at ED TEL had undertaken a project to promote the understanding and use of contribution analysis among the product managers. The newly formatted reports were the latest step in this project. The design of the statements had involved the participation of many people, including those in marketing, finance, and systems. The new reports were structured so that a parallel reporting format extended from the individual product level right up to the aggregation of all products in Business Systems.

Product Contribution Statements

One of the new reports, at the product level, was called the Product Contribution Statement (see Exhibit 2). This report included all revenues and expenses for the individual product classified in a manner similar to an income statement. However, the report was different from the previous type of financial statement used in two distinct ways. The first way was the manner in which the cost of goods was expressed. In this new format, only the accounts associated with stock issues and returns, and equipment in place, were included in cost of goods sold. Previously, several different expense accounts had been included along with the stock accounts as part of this classification. Now these additional expense accounts were classified as part of the Other Product Costs in the new reports.

The second major difference was the manner in which the year to date information was reported and analyzed. In the new format, all the actual accounts were expressed in both dollars and as a percentage of gross revenues. As well, each specific account was compared to both the corresponding budget and projection figure. The variance in the individual account was expressed in both dollars and as a percentage of the budget or projection. Previously, the actual year to date accounts had only been compared to the budget figure, and the variance expressed in dollars. The projection figures represented subsequent adjustments to the budget in response to new information about the product and market conditions. In this way, the product manager could track performance in relation to the original budget as well as to adjusted figures.

Product Contribution Statement by Revenue Stream

The second specific product report was the Product Contribution Statement by Revenue Stream (see Exhibits 3 to 10). This was a totally new report, unlike anything that had been used previously. It was designed to facilitate the analysis of product performance by the product marketing manager. The report classified all the revenue and expense accounts for the product line into one of four different revenue streams — direct sales, rentals, installation, and maintenance. In this report, the product manager could relate changes in specific expense accounts to specific revenue accounts. As well, the manager could see and trace the manner in which the financial performance of the product was generated.

ACCOUNTING AND INFORMATION SYSTEM

Identification Codes

Like many telecommunications firms, ED TEL sold, serviced, rented, and repaired a wide range of product items. In many cases, such as for PBX switchboard systems, these product items were common to several products, product types, and product lines. To handle this diversity, ED TEL used Universal Service Order Codes (USOC) to specify the individual items of equipment instead of lengthy descriptions. In most cases there was a one-to-one relationship between the USOC and inventory stock codes. Since the business side of ED TEL was organized on the basis of products, product types, and product lines, it was necessary to link the specific items of equipment with this structure through Class of Service Codes (COS). This code specifies the particular product for which the individual item had been used. As a final step, it was necessary to relate the kind of activity performed on the product with the revenue and cost system through a third mechanism called the Revenue Account Code (RAC). This code linked the revenue and cost elements for products for billing purposes through the Business Order Automation system (BOA) and for internal reporting. In the case of labour activities, there was a Labour Account Code (LAC) which, when combined with the COS, allowed the labour charges to be assigned to the specific product and, hence, billed to the right customer and reported for the right product, product type, or product line.

The information process commenced with the generation of a service order, often from a sales representative. Through consultation with the customer and ED TEL engineers, the sales representative drew up a service order specifying the type of system that the customer desired and the equipment needed. In the service order, the USOC for the specific product items was listed. As well, the service order specified the COS so that the RAC could identify how the billing and reporting information should be assigned.

On occasion, a customer might trade in some equipment or system as part of the order for the new system. In this case, it was necessary for the accounting system to track the value of the trade-in for the product that was newly acquired, and to assign the individual product items back to their respective USOCs.

Stages in the Service Order

Once the service order had been initiated, it was forwarded to the warehouse operations where the individual product items were kept. On a parallel course, PBX engineering would order the Meridian 1 switching system through the warehouse operation. If the switching system was not in stock, it was ordered, and shipped directly to the installation site. All equipment USOC codes and system parts were translated manually into inventory codes by the warehouse operations personnel. The individual product items could be issued from either new or refurbished stock depending on the choice made by the customer. New systems were sold unless refurbished systems were specified. Refurbished stock were those items that had been rebuilt, or repaired after previous use. Generally, the individual product items were drawn in bulk on the basis of inventory codes rather than on the basis of service orders. As such, all the needed items of one type of code for the next day were drawn at the same time. After having issued the individual items, the stock personnel were responsible for indicating to which COS the individual items should be assigned. To do this, the personnel consulted a large file that specified all the COS codes.

The individual items were issued to the field service personnel who took the items, and a copy of the service order, and went to the customer's site. There the items were installed according to the service order instructions. Then, field service personnel completed the service order indicating (through a LAC) the amount of labour that had been required. At the same time, the specific COS was indicated.

When maintenance needed to be performed on a system, the field service personnel often had to draw a selection of product items from stores as possible replacements at the site. Usually, as a result of remote diagnostics, the repair personnel could anticipate the types of components that would likely be required to service the system. Since the field service representative would not know exactly what was needed until the system had been examined, several different items were drawn from stores and immediately charged to a specific COS. If the items were returned to stores without being used, they were credited to the specific COS through the returned stores' accounts. The stock personnel had to determine whether the returned stores were new or refurbished equipment. Because the stores' personnel often did not know or could not tell whether the returned items were new or used, the technician had to specify the status of the items. Unfortunately, this was not always done. Consequently, new items might be returned to stores and classified as used returned items.

The accounting procedures resulted in the inclusion, in the cost of goods accounts, of the charges of the materials at the start of the job. Unbilled revenues and revenues for work in progress were not reported until the job was complete and operating.

PBX PORTFOLIO

Given the modular structure of the PBX systems and the use of so many common components among the various systems, it was possible that revenues for one type of PBX system might be misallocated to a different PBX system. Similarly, the costs of components, installation, and maintenance could be assigned incorrectly to the specific PBX product. As well, the focus in budgeting in the past for each product had been on an aggregate basis of all revenue streams, as compared to the accuracy of the specific revenue streams present in the new reporting format. It was possible that some accounts were out of proportion when considered in this disaggregated state. While these issues did not make any major difference in the aggregate results for the total portfolio or product line, they had the potential to create confusion and problems at the individual product level. It was Orr's job each month to examine the product reports (see Exhibits 2 to 10), and to identify and explain any variances that existed on those reports by specific product.

Exhibit 1

ORGANIZATION STRUCTURE

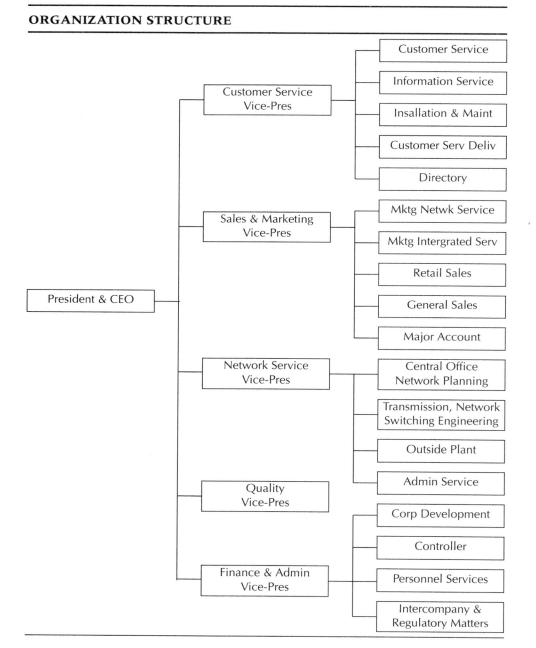

Exhibit 2

ED TEL PBX SYSTEMS—Contribution Statement for Custom PBX

Product Contribution Statement
PC — Custom PBX

Account	Object	MONTH November Actual	Budget	Variance	Y.T.D. Actual	% Sale	Budget	Variance	% Var	Project	Variance	% Var	ANNUAL Budget	Project
REVENUE														
Direct Sale	986	62946	61976	970	2270517	37.28%	681950	1588567	232.94%	2354059	-83542	-3.55%	744000	2568252
DS—Discounts	98D	-3277	-2499	-778	-82704	-1.36%	-27498	-55206	200.76%	-22339	-60365	270.22%	-30000	-24372
Trade Ins	98T	-567	-2499	1932	-6837	-0.11%	-27498	20661	-75.14%	-27498	20661	-75.14%	-30000	-30000
Lease Purchase	987	27541	17077	10464	264515	4.34%	187903	76612	40.77%	22360	242155	1082.98%	205000	24394
Monthly Rental	989	31407	169349	-137942	1547569	25.41%	1863448	-315879	-16.95%	1772903	-225334	-12.71%	2033062	1934216
Revenue Adjustment	981	-15292	-1666	-13626	172780	2.84%	-18332	191112	-1042.50%	-92577	265357	-286.63%	-20000	-101000
Fractional Rental	98F	93368		93368	-647	-0.01%		-647	0.00%	45830	-46477	-101.41%		50000
Install—NRC	985	24623	26073	-1450	341798	5.61%	286896	54902	19.14%	411772	-69974	-16.99%	313000	449238
Tier II	984	49801	62142	-12341	682802	11.21%	683784	-982	-0.14%	780287	-97485	-12.49%	746000	851284
Mtcs—Char Rep	98A	676	1083	-407	22290	0.37%	11916	10374	87.06%	24156	-1866	-7.72%	13000	26354
Mtce Contract	98M	71265	68139	3126	877618	14.41%	749779	127839	17.05%	728110	149508	20.53%	818000	794360
Total Gross Revenue		342491	399175	-56684	6089701	100.00%	4392348	1697353	38.64%	5997063	92638	1.54%	4792000	6542726
COST OF GOODS SOLD (Material)														
Stock Issued-N	114	-26914	-48397	21483	-1302310	-21.39%	-532545	-769765	144.54%	-1165882	-136428	11.70%	-581000	-1271964
Stock Issued-R	115	-27435	-24157	-3278	-293674	-4.82%	-265814	-27860	10.48%	-304695	11021	-3.62%	-290000	-332419
Stock Return-N	124	48137	6414	41723	167523	2.75%	70578	96945	137.36%	129727	37796	29.14%	77000	141531
Stock Return-R	125	11592	11579	13	146758	2.41%	127407	19351	15.19%	149270	-2512	-1.68%	139000	162852
Equipment Place	104		-13328	13328	-848840	-13.94%	-146656	-702184	478.80%	-865662	16822	-1.94%	-160000	-944427
Total Cost of Goods Sold		-237420	-67889	-169531	-2130543	-34.99%	-747030	-1383513	185.20%	-2057242	-73301	3.56%	-815000	-2244427
FIRST LEVEL CONTRIBUTION		105071	331286	-226215	3959158	65.01%	3645318	313840	8.61%	3939821	19337	0.49%	3977000	4298299
OTHER PRODUCT COSTS														
Repair Shop-L	S	-40062	-30938	-9124	-1075672	-17.66%	-340416	-735256	215.99%	-972958	-102714	10.56%	-371391	-1061485
Installation-L	L	-62167	-59548	-2619	-721555	-11.85%	-596198	-125357	21.03%	-596198	-125357	21.03%	-641868	-641868
Installation-P	X	-559	-1045	486	-10383	-0.17%	-8069	-2314	28.68%	-8069	-2314	28.68%	-11667	-11667
Maintenance-P	J	-18345	-20973	2628	-289912	-4.76%	-230781	-59131	25.62%	-231220	-58692	25.38%	-251778	-252259
Maintenance-L	R	-54401	-53358	-1043	-551555	-9.06%	-587134	35579	-6.06%	-587134	35579	-6.06%	-640556	-640556
Labour	4				-134	0.00%		-134	0.00%		-164	0.00%		
Accumulated Depreciation	351	10829	10829		824231	13.53%	119158	705073	591.71%	835838	-11607	-1.39%	130000	911890
Other Costs	569	-389		-389	-998	-0.02%		-998	0.00%	143	-1141	-797.90%		
Material OH	89	-11260	-4400	-6860	-103990	-1.71%	-48420	-55570	114.77%	-112821	8831	-7.83%	-52925	-123087
Engineering	86	-12797	-5331	-7466	-263276	-4.32%	-58663	-204613	348.79%	-272321	9045	-3.32%	-64000	-297099
Revenue Tax		-3425	-3992	567	-60897	-1.00%	-43923	-16974	38.64%	-59971	-926	1.54%	-47920	-65427
Total Other Product Costs		-203405	-168756	-34649	-2254141	-37.02%	-1794446	-459695	25.62%	-2004711	-249460	12.44%	-1952105	-2181558
SECOND LEVEL CONTRIBUTION		-98334	162530	-260864	1705017	28.00%	1850872	-145855	-7.88%	1935110	-230123	-11.89%	2024895	2116741
ASSET RELATED COSTS														
Allocated Debt		-24670	-27380	2710	-274944	-4.51%	-301276	26332	-8.74%	-272078	-2866	1.05%	-328689	-296833
Depreciation		-49934	-59596	9662	-549457	-9.02%	-655768	106311	-16.21%	-549457	0	0.00%	-715435	-599451
Total Asset Related Costs		-74604	-86976	12372	-824401	-13.54%	-957044	132643	-13.86%	-821535	-2866	0.35%	-1044124	-896284
CONTRIBUTION TO PRODUCT TYPE		-172938	75554	-248492	880616	14.46%	893828	-13212	-1.48%	1113575	-232989	-20.92%	980771	1220457
Contribution/$1000 Gross Sales		-505	189	N/A	145		203	N/A	N/A	186	N/A	N/A	205	187

Exhibit 3

ED TEL PBX SYSTEMS—Contribution Statement for Meridian 1 Sets

Product Contribution Statement
By Revenue Stream—
PCP — Meridian 1

		Direct			Rental (YEAR TO DATE)			Install			Maint		
	Object	Actual	Budget	Project	Actual	Budget	Project	Actual	Budget	Project	Actual	Budget	Project
REVENUE													
Direct Sale	986	442762	196152	425441									
Lease	987	44575	10999	145									
Rental	989				262519	274063	284881						
Installation	985							221482	160405	241033			
Maintenance	98A 98M										76806	8249	22915
Miscellaneous	988												
Total Gross Revenue		487337	207151	426856	262519	274063	284881	221482	160405	241033	76806	8249	22915
COST OF GOODS SOLD (Material)													
Stock Issued-N	114	-328654	-100826	-362392									
Stock Issued-R	115	-57751	-28415	-73106									
Stock Return-N	124	10420	2750	12572									
Stock Return-R	125	1366	1833	1857									
Equipment Place	104	-95587	-54996	-175230									
Total Cost of Goods Sold		-470206	-179654	-596299									
ADJUSTMENTS:													
Internal Billing	978				254472	216776	216776						
Internal Equip Use													
Total Adjustments		0	0	0	254472	216776	216776	0	0	0	0	0	0
FIRST LEVEL CONTRIBUTION		17131	27497	-169443	516991	490839	501657	221482	160405	241033	76806	8249	22915
OTHER PRODUCT COSTS													
Maintenance	183J										-96111	-38106	-71710
Installation-L	183L							-343836	-340690	-340690			
Installation-P	183X							-2173	-4083	-4083			
Maintenance-L	183R										-154858	-179280	-179280
Repair Shop	183S										-104647	-62046	-74451
Material OH	89	-21860	-7401	-25467									
Courier Service	404	-46											
Engineering	86	-2079		-2013									
Revenue Tax		-10481	-6499	-9757									
Depreciation—Rent	351				93871	45830	165694						
Total Other Product Costs		-34466	-13900	-37237	93871	45830	165694	-346009	-344733	-344733	-355616	-279432	-325441
SECOND LEVEL CONTRIBUTION		-17335	13597	-206680	610862	536669	667351	-124527	-184368	-103740	-278810	-271183	-302526
ASSET RELATED COSTS													
Allocated Debt					-36313	-39791	-35935						
Depreciation					-96468	-117182	-96468						
Total Asset Related Costs		0	0	0	-132781	-156973	-132403	0	0	0	0	0	0
CONTRIBUTION TO PRODUCT TYPE		-17335	13597	-206680	478081	379696	534948	-124527	-184368	-103740	-278810	-271183	-302526
Contribution/$1000 Gross Rev		-36	66	-484	1821	1385	1878	-562	-1149	-430	-3630	-32875	-13202

Exhibit 4

ED TEL PBX SYSTEMS—Contribution Statement for System 61

Product Contribution Statement
By Revenue Stream—
PC7—Meridian 1 System 61

(All money columns fall under the heading ••••••• YEAR TO DATE •••••••)

REVENUE	Object	Direct Actual	Direct Budget	Direct Project	Rental Actual	Rental Budget	Rental Project	Install Actual	Install Budget	Install Project	Maint Actual	Maint Budget	Maint Project
Direct Sale	986	755062		579581									
Lease	987												
Rental	989												
Installation	985							1106		25502			
Maintenance	98A 98M										7534		
Miscellaneous	988												
Total Gross Revenue		755062	0	579581	0	0	0	1106	0	25502	7534	0	0
COST OF GOODS SOLD (Material)													
Stock Issued-N	114	-9433		-10376									
Stock Issued-R	115	-444		-489									
Stock Return-N	124	11187		8821									
Stock Return-R	125	1373		1511									
Equipment Place	104												
Total Cost of Goods Sold		2683	0	-533	0	0	0	0	0	0	0	0	0
ADJUSTMENTS:													
Internal Billing	978												
Internal Equip Use													
Total Adjustments		0	0	0	0	0	0	0	0	0	0	0	0
FIRST LEVEL CONTRIBUTION		757745	0	579048	0	0	0	1106	0	25502	7534	0	0
OTHER PRODUCT COSTS													
Maintenance	278J							-24082		-24082	-14609		-17950
Installation-L	278L	-3701		-8377									
Installation-P	278X	-26965		-34685									
Maintenance-L	278R										-9905		-9905
Repair Shop	278S										-322434		-458330
Material OH	89												
Engineering	86										497		
Other Costs	569	-7637		-6051									
Revenue Tax	351				422		464						
Depreciation—Rent													
Total Other Product Costs		-38303	0	-49113	422	0	464	-24082	0	-24082	-346451	0	-486185
SECOND LEVEL CONTRIBUTION		719442	0	529935	422	0	464	-22976	0	1420	-338917	0	-486185
ASSET RELATED COSTS													
Allocated Debt													
Depreciation													
Total Asset Related Costs		0	0	0	0	0	0	0	0	0	0	0	0
CONTRIBUTION TO PRODUCT TYPE		719442	0	529935	422	0	464	-22976	0	1420	-338917	0	-486185
Contribution/$1000 Gross Rev		953	N/A	914	0		0	-20774		56	-44985		0

Exhibit 5

ED TEL PBX SYSTEMS—Contribution Statement for System 21

Product Contribution Statement
By Revenue Stream—
PC8—Meridian 1 System 21

		Direct Actual	Direct Budget	Direct Project	Rental Actual	Rental Budget	Rental Project	Install Actual	Install Budget	Install Project	Maint Actual	Maint Budget	Maint Project
REVENUE	Object												
Direct Sale	986	206721		457037									
Lease	987	128134											
Rental	989												
Installation	985							4807		17965			
Maintenance	98A 98M										1532		
Miscellaneous	988												
Total Gross Revenue		334855	0	457037	0	0	0	4807	0	17965	1532	0	0
COST OF GOODS SOLD (Material)													
Stock Issued-N	114	−496232		−312327									
Stock Issued-R	115	−10977											
Stock Return-N	124	74017		51250									
Stock Return-R	125	4536		4536									
Equipment Place	104												
Total Cost of Goods Sold		−428656	0	−256541									
ADJUSTMENTS:													
Internal Billing	978												
Internal Equip Use													
Total Adjustments		0	0	0	0	0	0	0	0	0	0	0	0
FIRST LEVEL CONTRIBUTION		−93801	0	200496	0	0	0	4807	0	17965	1532	0	0
OTHER PRODUCT COSTS													
Maintenance	288J										−17409		−20964
Installation-L	288L							−50035					
Installation-P	288X							−29					
Maintenance-L	288R										−18777		
Repair Shop	288S										−167098		−139179
Material OH	89	−33833		−23712									
Engineering	86	−97756		−98091				−122					
Other Costs	0												
Revenue Tax													
Depreciation—Rent	351	−3412		−4750									
Total Other Product Costs		−135001	0	−126553				−50186	0	0	−203284	0	−160143
SECOND LEVEL CONTRIBUTION		−228802	0	73943				−45379	0	17965	−201752	0	−160143
ASSET RELATED COSTS													
Allocated Debt		0		0				0		0	0		0
Depreciation													
Total Asset Related Costs		0	0	0				0	0	0	0	0	0
CONTRIBUTION TO PRODUCT TYPE		−228802	0	73943				−45379	0	17965	−201752	0	−160143
Contribution/$1000 Gross Rev		−683	0	162				−9440	0	1000	−131692	0	0

Exhibit 6
ED TEL PBX SYSTEMS—Contribution Statement for Meridian 1SN

Product Contribution Statement
By Revenue Stream—
PSC—Meridian 1SN PBX

	Object	YEAR TO DATE Direct Actual	Direct Budget	Direct Project	Rental Actual	Rental Budget	Rental Project	Install Actual	Install Budget	Install Project	Maint Actual	Maint Budget	Maint Project
REVENUE													
Direct Sale	986	590439	60496	731494									
Lease	987	64086	91660	11778									
Rental	981				-4953		3666						
Installation	985							45512	27498	35802			
Tier II	984										32604	12832	32602
Maintenance	98A 98M										112478	87994	96087
Miscellaneous	988												
Total Gross Revenue		654525	152156	743272	-4953	0	3666	45512	27498	35802	145082	100826	128689
COST OF GOODS SOLD (Material)													
Stock Issued-N	114	-415083	-366640	-428780									
Stock Issued-R	115	-157731	-119158	-159115									
Stock Return-N	124	49562	54996	32955									
Stock Return-R	125	132371	109992	138080									
Equipment Place	104												
Total Cost of Goods Sold		-390881	-320810	-416860	0			0			0		0
ADJUSTMENTS:													
Internal Billing	978				75								
Internal Equip Use													
Total Adjustments		0	0	0	75	0	0	0	0	0	0	0	0
FIRST LEVEL CONTRIBUTION		263644	-168654	326412	-4878	0	3666	45512	27498	35802	145082	100826	128689
OTHER PRODUCT COSTS													
Maintenance	638J										-70766	-14113	-77811
Installation-L	638L							-111591	-113013	-113013			
Installation-P	638X							-1335	-1336	-1336			
Maintenance-L	638R										-81276	-45980	-45980
Repair Shop	638S										-23623	-184530	-25133
Material OH	89	-26923	-30724	-38298									
Engineering	86	-60872	-43997	-64559									
Other Costs	046	-8402	-2805	-9114							-483		
Revenue Tax	351												
Depreciation—Rent													
Total Other Product Costs		-96197	-77526	-111971	0	0	0	-112926	-114349	-114349	-176148	-244623	-148924
SECOND LEVEL CONTRIBUTION		167447	-246180	214441	-4878	0	3666	-67414	-86851	-78547	-31066	-143797	-20235
ASSET RELATED COSTS													
Allocated Debt													
Depreciation													
Total Asset Related Costs		0	0	0	0	0	0	0	0	0	0	0	0
CONTRIBUTION TO PRODUCT TYPE		167447	-246180	214441	-4878	0	3666	-67414	-86851	-78547	-31066	-143797	-20235
Contribution/$1000 Gross Rev		256	-1618	289	985	0	1000	1481	-3158	-2194	-214	-1426	-157

Exhibit 7

ED TEL PBX SYSTEMS—Contribution Statement for System 71

Product Contribution Statement

By Revenue Stream—
PC9—Meridian 1 System 71

	Object	Direct Actual	Direct Budget	Direct Project	Rental Actual	Rental Budget	Rental Project	Install Actual	Install Budget	Install Project	Maint Actual	Maint Budget	Maint Project
REVENUE													
Direct Sale	986												
Lease	987												
Rental	989												
Installation	985												
Maintenance	98A 98M												
Miscellaneous	988												
Total Gross Revenue		0	0	0	0	0	0	0	0	0	0	0	0
COST OF GOODS SOLD (Material)													
Stock Issued-N	114												
Stock Issued-R	115	-2137		-1959									
Stock Return-N	124												
Stock Return-R	125												
Equipment Place	104												
Total Cost of Goods Sold		-2137	0	-1959	0	0	0	0	0	0	0	0	0
ADJUSTMENTS:													
Internal Billing	978												
Internal Equip Use													
Total Adjustments		0	0	0	0	0	0	0	0	0	0	0	0
FIRST LEVEL CONTRIBUTION		-2137	0	-1959	0	0	0	0	0	0	0	0	0
OTHER PRODUCT COSTS													
Maintenance	298J												
Installation-L	298L												
Installation-P	298X							-64					
Maintenance-L	298R												
Repair Shop	298S										-78		
Material OH	89	-77		-5520							-80		
Engineering	86												
Revenue Tax													
Depreciation—Rent	351												
Total Other Product Costs		-77	0	-5520	0	0	0	-64	0	0	-158	0	-126491
SECOND LEVEL CONTRIBUTION		-2214	0	-7479	0	0	0	-64	0	0	-158	0	-126491
ASSET RELATED COSTS													
Allocated Debt													
Depreciation													
Total Asset Related Costs		0	0	0	0	0	0	0	0	0	0	0	0
CONTRIBUTION TO PRODUCT TYPE		-2214	0	-7479	0	0	0	-64	0	0	-158	0	-126491
Contribution/$1000 Gross Rev		0	0	0	0	0	0	0	0	0	0	0	0

Exhibit 8

ED TEL PBX SYSTEMS—Contribution Statement for Discontinued Meridian 1

Product Contribution Statement
By Revenue Stream—
PCD Mfr Disconinued Meridian 1 PBX

		Direct			YEAR TO DATE — Rental			Install			Maint		
	Object	Actual	Budget	Project	Actual	Budget	Project	Actual	Budget	Project	Actual	Budget	Project
REVENUE													
Direct Sale	986	107538	339142	30953									
Lease	987	27720	76078										
Rental	989				1170310	1446395	1312951						
Installation	985							58646	69662	60963			
Tier II	984										629638	595790	672524
	98A 98M												
Maintenance	988										561864	572875	550770
Miscellaneous													
Total Gross Revenue		135258	415220	30953	1170310	1446395	1312951	58646	69662	60963	1191502	1168665	1223294
COST OF GOODS SOLD (Material)													
Stock Issued-N	114	-9165	-50413	-9994									
Stock Issued-R	115	-58115	-109992	-62856									
Stock Return-N	124	40	12832	73									
Stock Return-R	125	1711	15582	1882									
Equipment Place	104	-753253	-91660	-661593	0								
Total Cost of Goods Sold		-818782	-223651	-732448	0	0	0	0	0	0	0	0	0
ADJUSTMENTS:													
Internal Billing	978				174982	171404	171404						
Internal Equip Use													
Total Adjustments		0	0	0	174982	171404	171404	0	0	0	0	0	0
FIRST LEVEL CONTRIBUTION		-683524	191569	-701535	1345292	1617799	1484355	58646	69662	60963	1191502	1168665	1223294
OTHER PRODUCT COSTS													
Maintenance	718J										-41391	-171888	
Installation-L	718L							-116395	-84061	-84061			
Installation-P	718X							-2622	-2674	-2674			
Maintenance-L	718R										-218279	-302768	-302768
Repair Shop	718S										-34298	-74298	-38457
Material OH	89	-2939	-8725	-6636							-352		
Engineering	86	-35540		-44455									
Other Costs	456	-25557	-30999	-26282									
Revenue Tax					726564	73328	665969						
Depreciation—Rent	351												
Total Other Product Costs		-64036	-39724	-77373	726564	73328	665969	-119017	-86735	-86735	-294320	-548954	-341225
SECOND LEVEL CONTRIBUTION		-747560	151845	-778908	2071856	1691127	2150324	-60371	-17073	-25772	897182	619711	882069
ASSET RELATED COSTS													
Allocated Debt					-173785	-190429	-171974						
Depreciation					-358814	-405743	-358814						
Total Asset Related Costs		0	0	0	-532599	-596172	-530788	0	0	0	0	0	0
CONTRIBUTION TO PRODUCT TYPE		-747560	151845	-778908	1539257	1094955	1619536	-60371	-17073	-25772	897182	619711	882069
Contribution/$1000 Gross Rev		-5527	366	-25164	1315	757	1234	-1029	-245	-423	753	530	721

Exhibit 9

ED TEL PBX SYSTEMS—Contribution Statement for Meridian 1XT

Product Contribution Statement
By Revenue Stream—
PCX Meridian 1XT PBX

REVENUE	Object	Direct Actual	Direct Budget	Direct Project	Rental Actual	Rental Budget	Rental Project	Install Actual	Install Budget	Install Project	Maint Actual	Maint Budget	Maint Project
Direct Sale	986	35608		48550									
Lease	987												
Rental	989												
Installation	989				−9			1898	2750	3925			
Maintenance	98A 98M												
Miscellaneous	988										−4000	17415	7333
Total Gross Revenue		35608	0	48550	−9			1898	2750	3925	−4000	17415	7333
COST OF GOODS SOLD (Material)													
Stock Issued-N	114	−10466		−11512									
Stock Issued-R	115	−6519		−7171									
Stock Return-N	124												
Stock Return-R	125												
Equipment Place	104												
Total Cost of Goods Sold		−16985	0	−18683									
ADJUSTMENTS:													
Internal Billing	978	0			132067	416595	416595	0	0	0	0	0	0
Internal Equip Use													
Total Adjustments		0	0	0	132067	416595	416595	0	0	0	0	0	0
FIRST LEVEL CONTRIBUTION		18623	0	29867	132058	416595	416595	1898	2750	3925	−4000	17415	7333
OTHER PRODUCT COSTS													
Maintenance	788J										−12224	−1095	−14491
Installation-L	788L							−17369	−24620				
Installation-P	788X									−24620			
Maintenance-L	788R												
Repair Shop	788S										−6708		−7379
Material OH	89	−1013		−1142									
Engineering	86	−16687		−16585									
Revenue Tax		−335	−202	−598	3375		3712						
Depreciation—Rent	351												
Total Other Product Costs		−18035	−202	−18325	3375	0	3712	−17369	−24620	−24620	−18932	−1095	−21870
SECOND LEVEL CONTRIBUTION		588	−202	11542	135433	416595	420307	−15471	−21870	−20695	−22932	16320	−14537
ASSET RELATED COSTS													
Allocated Debt		0			−49282	−54002	−48769	0			0		
Depreciation		0			−73483	−92998	−73483						
Total Asset Related Costs		0			−122765	−147000	−122252	0			0		
CONTRIBUTION TO PRODUCT TYPE		588	−202	11542	12668	269595	298055	−15471	−21870	−20695	−22932	16320	−14537
Contribution/$1000 Gross Rev		17	0	238	−1407556	0	0	−8151	−7953	−5273	5733	937	−1982

Exhibit 10

ED TEL PBX SYSTEMS—Contribution Statement for Meridian 1NT

Product Contribution Statement
By Revenue Stream—
PCN Meridian 1NT PBX

•••••••• YEAR TO DATE ••••••••

	Object	Direct Actual	Direct Budget	Direct Project	Rental Actual	Rental Budget	Rental Project	Install Actual	Install Budget	Install Project	Maint Actual	Maint Budget	Maint Project
REVENUE													
Direct Sale	986	42511	12832	12832									
Lease	987												
Rental	989				-408	0	0						
Installation	985							7427	16499	16499			
Tier II	984										1682	8249	8249
Maintenance	98A 98M										143307	75161	75161
Miscellaneous	988												
Total Gross Revenue		42511	12832	12832	-408	0	0	7427	16499	16499	144989	83410	83410
COST OF GOODS SOLD (Material)													
Stock Issued-N	114	-33277	-14666	-30502									
Stock Issued-R	115		-8249										
Stock Return-N	124	17315		18774									
Stock Return-R	125												
Equipment Place	104												
Total Cost of Goods Sold		-15962	-22915	-11728	0	0	0	0	0	0			
ADJUSTMENTS:													
Internal Billing	978				968	550	550						
Internal Equip Use													
Total Adjustments		0	0	0	968	550	550	0	0	0			
FIRST LEVEL CONTRIBUTION		26549	-10083	1104	560	550	550	7427	16499	16499	144989	83410	83410
OTHER PRODUCT COSTS													
Maintenance	778J	-12862	-1257	-3318	-15563	-17053	-15401	-56131	-28797	-28797	-36629	-5376	-28091
Installation-L	778L	-17896	-917	-2828	-9166	-28069	-9166	-1317					
Installation-P	778X										-42287		-30746
Maintenance-L	778R										-394760	-30746	-85747
Repair Shop	778S												
Material OH	89												
Engineering	86												
Other Costs	569	-1945	-1127	-1127							-622		143
Revenue Tax													
Depreciation—Rent	351												
Total Other Product Costs		-32703	-3301	-7273	-24729	-45122	-24567	-57448	-28797	-28797	-474298	-36122	-144441
SECOND LEVEL CONTRIBUTION		-6154	-13384	-6169	-24169	-44572	-24017	-50021	-12298	-12298	-329309	47288	-61031
ASSET RELATED COSTS													
Allocated Debt													
Depreciation													
Total Asset Related Costs		0	0	0				0	0			0	0
CONTRIBUTION TO PRODUCT TYPE		-6154	-13384	-6169	-24169	-44572	-24017	-50021	-12298	-12298	-329309	47288	-61031

ZIP AUTOMOTIVE LTD.

Mark A. Heisz and Randolph Kudar

Mr. Clarence Boyd, President of Zip Automotive Ltd., was about to enter a meeting with his product and regional marketing managers. The purpose of the meeting was to assess the product and marketing strategies of the firm. As part of the assessment, Mr. Boyd wanted the managers to develop a financial plan for their area of responsibility that would translate the strategies into increased profitability for the firm. To assist the process, Mr. Doug Gilmer, the Vice-President, Finance and Accounting, had developed a spreadsheet file for all company revenues and expenses.

BACKGROUND

Company

Zip Automotive Ltd. had been purchased in December 1981 from Zed International Inc., a U.S. based conglomerate. Following the purchase, several key management personnel left the company including the General Manager, the Vice-President of Marketing and Sales, and the Vice-President of Finance and Accounting. During the past three years, these positions had been filled by those who had remained with the firm.

Zip Automotive Ltd. was one of several manufacturers and distributors of automotive products in Canada. In 1982, the company recorded revenues of

$28.5 million from sales of its full line of mufflers, tail pipes, exhaust pipes, and related products (see Exhibit 1). Zip Automotive's manufacturing facility and head offices were located in Mississauga, Ontario. National distribution of the company's products was facilitated through four warehouses located across Canada.

Product

Auto exhaust systems were mounted underneath all automobiles. These systems served to cool and vent the various gases leaving the engine following combustion. As well, they were designed to reduce engine noise. A typical exhaust system was composed of one or more exhaust pipes, and a muffler. The exhaust pipes carried the engine exhaust from the engine manifold to the muffler at the rear of the vehicle. Inside the muffler, the gases passed through sound deadening materials such as glass wool, where the gases slowly expanded and cooled, eventually exiting under greatly reduced pressure and temperature.

Exhaust systems naturally deteriorated with use, and required replacement, on average, following two to three years of use. Replacement was necessitated by corrosion, mainly from the condensation of water vapour within the muffler and pipes. However, exterior corrosion caused by rain, snow, and road salt also contributed to deterioration of the system. The addition of catalytic converters during the 1970s to reduce the emissions of harmful pollutants caused exhaust systems to have to operate at higher temperatures. This tended to reduce internal condensation and extend the replacement cycle. The replacement cycle in Canada tended to be shorter, due to the more severe winter driving conditions and the greater use of salt on the roads.

Marketing and Distribution

The high incidence of replacements led many manufacturers of exhaust systems to concentrate their selling efforts on the large aftermarket for exhaust products as opposed to servicing the original equipment manufacturers (OEM). Replacement sales in 1982 represented 80–85% of all exhaust products sold in Canada. Retail sales in the aftermarket had been growing at rates of 10–15% during the early years of the decade while unit sales had been growing at 5–10%. Growth levels in dollar sales in the aftermarket were expected to continue at 10–15%, while sales to original equipment manufacturers were expected to be relatively unstable and overall growth was expected to be small.

The distribution of automobile exhaust products to OEMs was fairly simple. The part producer simply dealt with the few large automobile manufacturers who would request competitive price bids and purchase mainly on the basis of price and delivery. Conversely, distribution of exhaust products in the aftermarket was much more complex and fragmented. The level of complexity was the result of the fact that several thousand retail outlets existed in Canada, and several distribution channels were used to reach them.

The retail outlets which replaced exhaust products included new car dealers, franchised service stations, independent service stations, specialty shops, and mass merchandisers. New car dealers normally secured their requirements through the major automotive manufacturer with whom they were allied. However, all other retailers purchased their products through one or more of the available suppliers (see Exhibit 2).

The distribution of exhaust products underwent significant change during the 1970s, predominantly due to increased volume being sold by muffler specialty shops (see Exhibit 3). This shift in retail market share was mainly at the expense of service stations. Consequently, those distributors who supplied service stations with exhaust products suffered a similar decline in volume. The increase in market share of the specialty shops could be related to two factors:

• the marketing ability of the specialty shops

• the forward integration by the manufacturing firm to increase margins.

Speedy and Midas, which together had a market share of 40–45% at retail were fully integrated into manufacturing. The magnitude of the advantage of being fully integrated may best be illustrated by outlining the typical discount structure which existed within the automotive exhaust parts industry:

Manufacturer - direct cost	$0.30

Price to:

Mass Merchandiser	$0.36
Warehouse Distributor	$0.38
Specialty Shop	$0.41
Buying Groups	$0.45
Jobber	$0.54
Service Stations	$0.75
Consumer – list installed	$1.00

The significant increase in volume through specialty shops led to a drastic decline in volume for full-line warehouse distributors. Independent specialty shops continued to purchase some of their parts requirements from the warehouse distributors; however, retailers with high volume requirements tended to deal directly with manufacturers, particularly for faster moving parts. This trend led to a reliance on wholesale distributors for slower moving parts or for emergency supplies.

Another significant volume shift occurred in the "add-on shops" which grew from 0% in 1968 to 18% of the aftermarket in 1981. An add-on shop simply involved an independent service station using one service bay exclusively for muffler and exhaust work. The add-on shops were typically located in smaller towns across Canada which were not served by Speedy or Midas. The associate program for independent add-on shops provided the operator with a recognized name, marketing assistance, and a source of supply through buying groups, which assured lower prices than those available through warehouse distributors.

Canadian Manufacturers

The two major manufacturers of exhaust products in Canada were Walker Manufacturing Company and Midas Canada Inc. These manufacturers tended to sell mainly in the aftermarket because of the size of the market and the presence of Canadian import duties on exhaust products for the aftermarket of 12–15%. In contrast, exhaust products for use by the Canadian automotive manufacturers were predominantly sourced in the United States, since these parts could be imported duty free under the Canada-U.S. Auto Pact.

Walker Manufacturing had a fully integrated operation with retail distribution through Speedy Muffler King. Walker also sold its products to other parts distributors including two of the largest warehouse distributors in Canada. Through Speedy, Walker had 20% of the retail market, but its sales to other distributors gave it the largest combined share of the Canadian aftermarket for exhaust products of approximately 35%.

Midas operated a production facility in Ontario which supplied its franchised and company owned shops throughout Canada. Midas also sold to other auto part distributors but to a lesser extent than did Walker. Midas had a 22% share of the retail market through its shops and, with other sales, had a combined market share of approximately 26%.

Zip Automotive was one of a few smaller manufacturers who sold a full line of exhaust products in the Canadian aftermarket. The company sold to all levels of the distribution system with an emphasis on the traditional warehouse distributors. In response to the retail market success of Speedy and Midas, Zip Automotive began organizing existing independent muffler shops into the Zipway MufflerCentre chain in 1975. These shops remained independently owned and managed but all operated under the Zipway name and purchased their parts requirements from Zip Automotive.

Several other companies manufactured parts for the auto exhaust aftermarket, but most produced a "short line" of products, concentrating on faster moving parts.

MARKETING AT ZIP AUTOMOTIVE

At the time of the takeover, Zip Automotive had been directing all marketing efforts at the Canadian aftermarket. Mr. Boyd and Mr. Gilmer continued this approach but began shifting the company's distribution emphasis away from the traditional warehouse distributor to include more direct dealings with independent muffler shops (including the Zipway chain) and with national retail accounts such as Canadian Tire. Despite this change in distribution emphasis, sales to warehouse distributors continued to represent the vast majority of the company's sales (see Exhibit 3). The company also began selling in the United States with a short line of fast-moving products. These products were sold to aftermarket users at significantly reduced prices. Zip Automotive had also made efforts to enter the OEM market, but had experienced very limited success.

To service its many customers, Zip Automotive maintained three full-line warehouses across Canada, as well as the main warehouse in Mississauga, Ontario. Inventory levels at the various warehouses were set in order to ensure that 92% of all incoming orders could be served from on-hand stock. Mr. Gilmer believed that prompt delivery was critical if Zip Automotive were to retain its independent muffler shop and national retail accounts. Orders were communicated to the warehouses via remote computer terminals.

Zip sold a full line of exhaust products and accessories. This full line consisted of some 1,500 different exhaust and tail pipe parts, and some 600 different mufflers in five different categories. These included the following:

Master Line   the top of the line products essentially equivalent to OEM products.

Muffler Shop Line   specifically for muffler shops. These mufflers had a number of unique features including expandable collars which allowed the products to be adapted to fit various automobiles in order to reduce inventory levels for the muffler shops.

Competitor   low cost products being developed for the small "do-it-yourself" market.

Turbo   high performance products

Foreign   products designed for foreign automobiles.

PRODUCTION AT ZIP AUTOMOTIVE

While Zip sold upwards of 2,100 different products, the company in fact concentrated its production efforts on only the higher volume products, relying on smaller manufacturers for the balance of their products. Nevertheless, Zip produced several hundred parts in the Mississauga plant.

Muffler Production

Raw material consisting mainly of steel tubing and coiled steel were received at one end of the plant and stored until issued into production. For mufflers, the materials were first issued to parts production where parts of the muffler such as nipples, baffles, and covers were cut or stamped from the tubing or coils, and then moved into parts storage. The parts were then moved as required to the sub-assembly area. Once sub-assembled, the parts were loaded onto conveyors or manually transported to the muffler production line. The production line combined the inner components of the muffler, installed the galvanized steel skin, and attached the front and rear nipple assemblies. The production lines were highly automated with the labour involvement limited primarily to some spot welding operations, loading sub-assemblies at various points along the line, and other material handling functions. The completed mufflers were then packaged and transferred to the company's central warehouse.

Since the takeover, the company had made significant strides aimed at reducing the number of muffler products. The company had reduced the number of muffler cross sections from 20 to 5 by standardizing inner components and varying only the length and diameter of the nipples to maintain proper fit. This innovation had increased the plant's flexibility, reduced set-up times, and reduced product costs.

Pipe Production

Pipe production was considerably simpler than muffler production. Tubing was ordered from the manufacturer by the length required to complete specific finished parts. The raw materials proceeded directly to the bending area where the tubes were bent, sized, trimmed, welded, and spun to flare joints. Manual pipe benders were used on longer runs while computerized benders were used on shorter runs, in order to reduce total set-up time. Approximately 15 employees were directly involved in pipe operations, compared to about 100 in muffler operations.

ACCOUNTING AT ZIP AUTOMOTIVE

Zip Automotive used a standard costing system to value its inventories. The costing system was originally developed by the former owners of the firm to be compatible with the system for the rest of the organization. Raw materials were assigned to products at standard values when the products were put into production, as were standard labour costs, and absorbed overheads. Standard costs were not assigned to work-in-process inventory due to the short time period to complete the production cycle.

The standard costs for raw materials were established annually, based on prevailing market prices at the beginning of the period, and on well established standard quantities. The difference between actual and standard cost was recorded as a purchase price variance and included as part of the manufacturing overhead expense. The difference between actual quantities of materials used and standard quantities reflected material waste or scrap. The production process resulted in two types of scrap:

Offal Scrap   the result of the cutting process, and considered unavoidable. It was weighed daily and the total accumulated in a manufacturing scrap report. The cost of the scrap was the product of the actual quantities valued at standard cost less any proceeds from selling the metal. This amount was added to manufacturing overhead.

Avoidable Scrap   the result of errors in the production process. The material cost was determined in the same manner as offal scrap. Labour and overhead portions were estimated and the full cost of the scrap was included in manufacturing overhead.

Standard labour cost was based upon the standard times required to generate the output and the prevailing union labour rates for the period. This amount was exclusive of shift and overtime premiums, and vacation pay. These items were included in manufacturing overhead. Daily payroll reports were used to determine the amount of indirect labour to be charged to manufacturing overhead. The labour variances were separated into rate and usage components and included in the manufacturing overhead account.

Manufacturing overhead costs were allocated to finished goods based upon the direct labour cost component of the finished goods using predetermined overhead application rates. These rates were computed annually for both muffler and pipe production by estimating the level of manufacturing overhead associated with each line and then dividing that amount by the expected number of direct labour dollars. Generally, the manufacturing overhead had been apportioned 85% to mufflers and 15% to pipes based on the number of employees in each department. The manufacturing overhead included the following cost elements:

Indirect labour, supplies, employee benefits, labour variances, scrap expenses, utilities, repairs and maintenance, depreciation, production planning, industrial engineering, product engineering, process engineering, service engineering, quality assurance, and warehousing.

BUDGETING AT ZIP AUTOMOTIVE

Selling prices for budget preparation of product lines and regions were determined by using the average selling price for a representative mix of products in each product group and distribution channel. Proposed price increases were then added to these averages to arrive at expected revenue figures. The selling prices were then used in conjunction with the volume projections of products to develop total budgeted sales revenues. The forecast of unit sales volume for the period was prepared by marketing personnel from existing customer accounts, supplemented with estimates of sales to new customers. The forecasts were prepared on a regional basis as well as on a product basis. These forecasts included units of mufflers, pipes, and various parts.

The forecast of the cost of goods sold involved the use of the forecasted volume and the unit standard cost of the product line. Various other cost elements including distribution costs, general, administrative, and selling costs were also forecast for the period. These costs were allocated to both products and regions in various ways (see Exhibit 5). In this way it was possible to develop a profit and loss statement for each region and for each product line.

Recently, the data for sales volumes of products, prices, and various cost elements had been incorporated into a spreadsheet file for use by the marketing personnel of the firm (see Exhibit 4). The file included profit and loss statements for each of the regions and for each of the product lines. All costs including distribution, overheads, selling, and administrative were allocated among the regions and products to calculate a contribution margin as well as a profit margin.

OBJECTIVES OF THE MEETING

Mr. Boyd was interested in hearing how each of the regional and product managers would assess the forecast for the upcoming year. He felt that there were some real strengths in Zip's strategies, but there were also some real problems. He expected each of the regional and product managers to examine their area of responsibility and report on the strengths and weaknesses in their respective areas.

He was also interested in getting their reaction to a distribution proposal that had been recently received by the firm. The current distribution costs were as follows:

$0.40 per unit to Eastern Canada

$0.20 per unit to Quebec and Ontario

$0.70 per unit to Western Canada

$0.83 per unit to the US and for national accounts

A competitive carrier had offered the firm a different plan. The plan was structured such that if the annual volume of units into a region exceeded 500,000 units, the unit cost for every unit shipped into the region would be reduced by $0.04 from the current rates. However, if the annual volume of units into the region was less than the 500,000 units, the unit cost would be $0.03 per unit above the rate the firm was currently paying. The proposal only applied if all the shipping business was handled by the new carrier. It would not be available to individual regions of the country.

Mr. Boyd wondered if it was time to consider expanding the sales effort. If the strategy warranted it, he was prepared to hire two additional field sales personnel. The marketing research department had estimated that a single person could increase sales volume in different ways, depending upon where the individual was assigned. The potential sales increases for a single person were identified by product and region. The individual could be expected to sell one of the following volumes in the course of a year.

Mufflers:	National accounts	118,000 units
	All other regions	36,000 units
Pipes:	Eastern Canada	67,000 units
	Quebec, Ontario	36,000 units
	Western Canada or	
	National accounts	19,000 units

Company history indicated that it generally cost $87,000 a year to keep a person operating in the field as a sales representative. Mr. Boyd wondered where two such people could best be employed by the firm.

As part of their task, the marketing research department had examined the potential sensitivity of the products and regions to changes in prices. They concluded that for forecasting purposes, it was possible to apply the following sensitivity conditions for a range of 5% price change above or below the current prices listed for the products in a region. The sensitivities were as follows:

Mufflers	If unit price declines 1%, volume increases 1.7%
	If unit price increases 1%, volume declines 1.75%
Pipes	If unit price declines 1%, volume increases 1.7%
	If unit price increases 1%, volume declines 1.5%
Parts	If unit price declines 1%, volume increases 2%
	If unit price increases 1%, volume declines 1.5%

Mr. Boyd expected the regional and product managers to consider the impact that these sensitivities might have on their area of responsibility, and to offer specific recommendations regarding price changes at the meeting.

Exhibit 1

INCOME STATEMENT FOR THE YEAR—Ending December 31, 1982
($ 000)

Gross Sales	$ 28,500
Less: Sales Returns, Discounts, and Allowances	4,600
Net Sales	$ 23,900
Less: Cost of Goods Sold	16,650
Gross Margin	$ 7,250
General and Administrative	2,150
Selling	2,550
Advertising	350
Operating Income	$ 2,200
Interest Expense	1,200
Net Income Before Tax	$ 1,000

BALANCE SHEET as of December 31, 1982
($ 000)

ASSETS		LIABILITIES AND OWNERS' EQUITY	
Current Assets:		Current Liabilities:	
Cash	$ 700	Accounts Payable	$1,900
Net Receivables	3,500	Accrued Expenses	800
Net Inventories	5,400	Current Long Term Debt	720
Prepaids	50		$ 3,420
	$ 9,650		
		Long Term Debt	6,800
Property, Plant &			
Equipment (net)	5,700		
Other Assets	600	Shareholders' Equity	5,730
Total Assets	$15,950	Total Liabilities and Shareholder's Equity	$15,950

EXHIBIT 2

AFTERMARKET DISTRIBUTION NETWORK

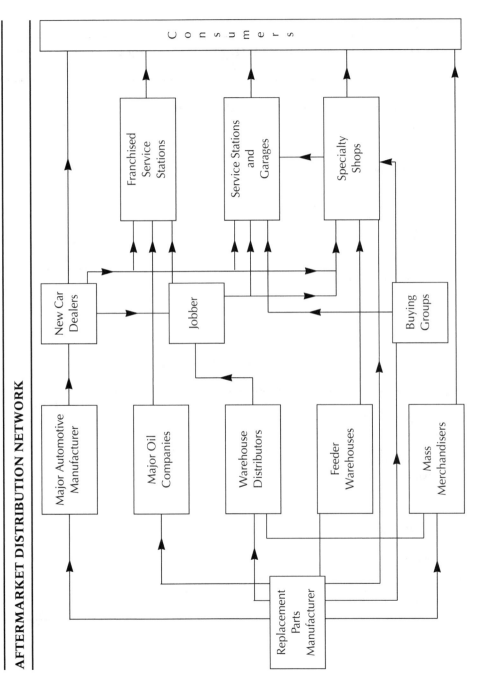

Exhibit 3

DISTRIBUTION ANALYSIS OF AUTOMOTIVE EXHAUST PRODUCTS

	1968	*1981*
Service Stations	54	12
Specialty Shops	28	55
Mass Merchandisers	10	8
New Car Dealers	5	3
Do-It-Yourself	3	4
"Add-On Shops"	0	18
	100%	100%

SALES OF ZIP BY DISTRIBUTION CHANNEL

	1980	*1981*
Warehouse Distributors	44.3	43.3
Independent Muffler Shops	22.6	26.7
Zipway Mufflercentres	11.5	12.9
National Retail Accounts	15.7	13.5
Other (OEM, Export)	6.1	3.6
	100%	100%

Exhibit 4

SPREADSHEET CONTENTS

	East Cda	Quebec	Ontario	West Cda	National	Total
		Revenues (A1..G20)				
Muffler						
Number of Units	60,400	229,500	134,900	91,400	944,900	1,461,100
Average Price	$19.97	$19.75	$18.65	$18.97	$13.54	$15.59
Revenue	1,206,188	4,532,625	2,515,885	1,733,858	12,793,946	22,782,502
Pipe						
Number of Units	64,900	237,000	126,400	69,300	117,650	615,250
Average Price	$13.04	$13.50	$13.16	$13.06	$8.13	$12.31
Revenue	846,296	3,199,500	1,663,424	905,058	956,495	7,570,773
Other						
Parts: # of Units	206,900	255,200	132,000	282,300	168,000	1,044,400
Price	$0.70	$0.70	$0.70	$0.70	$0.70	$0.70
Revenue	144,830	178,640	92,400	197,610	117,600	731,080
Tubing: # of Units	19,200	21,500	7,600	25,000	60,700	134,000
Price	$8.36	$8.36	$8.36	$8.36	$8.36	$8.36
Revenue	160,512	179,740	63,536	209,000	507,452	1,120,240
Shocks: # of Units	1,700	3,930	6,500	1,500	0	13,630
Price	$13.70	$13.70	$13.70	$13.70	$13.70	$13.70
Revenue	23,290	53,841	89,050	20,550	0	186,731

Exhibit 4 (continued)

Variable Costs (A23..D40)—Unit Variable Cost Data		
	Mufflers	*Pipe*
Direct Labour	$0.94	$0.49
Efficiency Var	$0.03	$0.01
Vac Pay @ .06 Comp	$0.06	$0.03
Benefits	$0.24	$0.12
Material @ $4.52	$4.52	$2.52
Offal Scrap	$0.07	$0.04
Avoidable Scrap	$0.05	$0.03
Overhead	$0.18	$0.07
Overtime @ $5.88*1.5	$75,200.00	0.00
Parts	$0.37	
Tubing	$5.34	
Shocks	$9.21	

Exhibit 4 (continued)

Allocated Costs by Region	East Cda	Quebec	Ontario	West Cda	National	Total
		Allocated Costs by Region (I1..O20)				
Total Labour	$118,808	$445,135	$253,185	$160,826	$1,269,941	$2,247,895
Total Units	$353,100	747,130	407,400	469,500	1,291,250	3,268,380
Total Material	$642,714	1,922,770	1,101,849	834,406	5,073,208	9,595,447
Factory Indirect	$43,947	164,656	93,653	59,490	469,753	831,500
Indirect Benefits	$13,184	49,397	28,096	17,847	140,926	249,450
Indirect Vacation	$2,637	9,879	5,619	3,569	28,185	49,890
Staff Overhead	$105,488	360,811	196,005	135,833	636,863	1,435,000
Staff Benefits	$31,646	108,243	58,802	40,750	191,059	430,500
Staff Vacation	$6,329	21,649	11,760	8,150	38,212	86,100
Supplies	$63,632	190,364	109,089	82,611	502,274	950,000
Utilities	$83,134	259,535	148,521	110,969	697,840	1,300,000
Repairs, Maint	$35,172	109,803	62,836	46,949	295,240	550,000
Depreciation	$36,755	125,718	68,294	47,329	221,903	500,000
Warehousing	$165,942	351,119	191,461	220,645	606,833	1,536,000
Distribution	$141,240	149,426	81,480	328,650	1,078,194	1,778,990
Selling Expenses	$156,333	469,000	312,667	312,667	625,333	1,876,000
Gen & Admin	$168,708	577,046	313,471	217,239	1,018,537	2,295,000

Exhibit 4 (continued)

Allocated Costs by Product (I25..N43)				
Allocated Costs by Product	*Muffler*	*Pipes*	*Other*	*Total*
Total Labour	$1,844,404	$403,491	$ 0	$2,247,895
Total Units	1,461,100	615,250	1,192,030	3,268,380
Total Material	6,776,937	1,590,989	1,227,520	9,595,447
Factory Indirect	682,248	149,252	0	831,500
Indirect Benefits	204,674	44,776	0	249,450
Indirect Vacation	40,935	8,955	0	49,890
Staff Overhead	1,009,310	335,400	90,290	1,435,000
Staff Benefits	302,793	100,620	27,087	430,500
Staff Vacation	60,559	20,124	5,417	86,100
Supplies	670,953	157,516	121,531	950,000
Utilities	950,689	217,876	131,435	1,300,000
Repairs, Maint	402,214	92,178	55,607	550,000
Depreciation	351,676	116,864	31,460	500,000
Warehousing	686,655	289,141	560,204	1,536,000
Distribution	950,012	245,388	583,591	1,778,990
Selling Expenses	1,319,488	438,474	118,037	1,876,000
Gen & Admin	1,614,193	536,407	144,401	2,295,000

Exhibit 4 (continued)

Income Statements for Eastern Region (A60..C102) and Mufflers (E60..G102)

Income Statement for Zip Automotive Eastern Region		%	*Income Statement for Zip Automotive Mufflers*		%
REVENUE:			**REVENUE:**		
Mufflers	$1,206,188	51	Eastern	$1,206,188	5
Pipes	846,296	36	Quebec	4,532,625	20
Parts	144,830	6	Ontario	2,515,885	11
Tubing	160,512	7	Western	1,733,858	8
Shocks	23,290	1	National	12,793,946	56
Total Revenue	2,381,116	100	Total Revenue	22,782,502	100
TOTAL VARIABLE COSTS:			**TOTAL VARIABLE COSTS:**		
Mufflers	367,040		Eastern	367,040	
Pipes	214,645		Quebec	1,394,629	
Parts	76,553		Ontario	819,763	
Tubing	102,528		Western	555,421	
Shocks	15,657		National	5,741,984	
TVC	776,423		TVC	8,878,836	
CONTRIBUTIONS:			**CONTRIBUTIONS:**		
Mufflers	839,148	52	Eastern	839,148	6
Pipes	631,651	39	Quebec	3,137,996	23
Parts	68,277	4	Ontario	1,696,122	12
Tubing	57,984	4	Western	1,178,437	8
Shocks	7,633	0	National	7,051,962	51
Total Contribution	1,604,693	100	Total Contribution	13,903,666	100
Cont % of Sales	67		Cont % of Sales	61	
Distribution	141,240	6	Distribution	950,012	4
Selling Costs	156,333	7	Selling Costs	1,319,488	6
Region Contribution	1,307,120		Muffler Cont.	11,634,166	
Unit Distrib. Cost	0.40				
Salesmen	2				
FIXED COSTS:	756,576	32	**FIXED COSTS:**	6,976,898	31
NPBT:	550,544		NPBT:	4,657,268	
NPBT % of Sales	23		NPBT % of Sales	20	

Exhibit 4 (continued)

Income Statements for Quebec Region (A104..C146) and Other Products (E104..G146)

Income Statement for *Zip Automotive Quebec Region*			*Income Statement for* *Zip Automotive Other*		
		%			%
REVENUE:			**REVENUE:**		
Mufflers	4,532,625	56	Eastern	328,632	16
Pipes	3,199,500	39	Quebec	412,221	20
Parts	178,640	2	Ontario	244,986	12
Tubing	179,740	2	Western	427,160	21
Shocks	53,841	1	National	625,052	31
Total Revenue	8,144,346	100	Total Revenue	2,038,051	100
TOTAL VARIABLE COSTS:			**TOTAL VARIABLE COSTS:**		
Mufflers	1,394,629		Eastern	194,738	
Pipes	783,835		Quebec	245,429	
Parts	94,424		Ontario	149,289	
Tubing	114,810		Western	251,766	
Shocks	36,195		National	386,298	
TVC	2,423,894		TVC	1,227,520	
CONTRIBUTIONS:			**CONTRIBUTIONS:**		
Mufflers	3,137,996	55	Eastern	133,894	17
Pipes	2,415,665	42	Quebec	166,792	21
Parts	84,216	1	Ontario	95,697	12
Tubing	64,930	1	Western	175,394	22
Shocks	17,646	0	National	238,754	29
Total Contribution	5,720,452	100	Total Contribution	810,531	100
Cont % of Sales	70		Cont % of Sales	40	
Distribution	149,426	2	Distribution	583,591	29
Selling Costs	469,000	6	Selling Costs	118,037	6
Unit Distrib. Cost	0.20				
Region Contribution	5,102,026		Region Cont.	108,903	
Salesmen	6				
FIXED COSTS:	2,328,221	29	**FIXED COSTS:**	1,167,431	57
NPBT:	2,773,806		NPBT:	(1,058,528)	
NPBT % of Sales	34		NPBT % of Sales	(52)	

Exhibit 4 (continued)

Income Statements for Ontario Region (A149..C191) and Pipes (E149..G191)

Income Statement for Zip Automotive Ontario Region		%	*Income Statement for Zip Automotive Pipes*		%
REVENUE:			**REVENUE:**		
Mufflers	2,515,885	57	Eastern	846,296	11
Pipes	1,663,424	38	Quebec	3,199,500	42
Parts	92,400	2	Ontario	1,663,424	22
Tubing	63,536	1	Western	905,058	12
Shocks	89,050	2	National	956,495	13
Total Revenue	4,424,295	100	Total Revenue	7,570,773	100
TOTAL VARIABLE COSTS:			**TOTAL VARIABLE COSTS:**		
Mufflers	819,763		Eastern	214,645	
Pipes	418,045		Quebec	783,835	
Parts	48,840		Ontario	418,045	
Tubing	40,584		Western	229,197	
Shocks	59,865		National	389,106	
TVC	1,387,097		TVC	2,034,829	
CONTRIBUTIONS:			**CONTRIBUTIONS:**		
Mufflers	1,696,122	56	Eastern	631,651	11
Pipes	1,245,379	41	Quebec	2,415,665	44
Parts	43,560	1	Ontario	1,245,379	22
Tubing	22,952	1	Western	675,861	12
Shocks	29,185	1	National	567,388	10
Total Contribution	3,037,198	100	Total Contribution	5,535,943	100
Cont % of Sales	69		Cont % of Sales	73	
Distribution	81,480	2			
Selling Expenses	312,667	7	Distribution	245,388	3
Unit Distrib. Cost	0.20		Selling Costs	438,474	6
Regional Contribution	2,643,051		Region Cont.	4,852,081	
Salesmen	4				
FIXED COSTS:	1,287,608	29	**FIXED COSTS:**	2,069,111	27
NPBT:	1,355,443		NPBT:	2,782,970	
NPBT % of Sales	31		NPBT % of Sales	37	

Exhibit 4 (continued)

Income Statement for Western Region (A193..C236)

Income Statement for
Zip Automotive Western Region

		%
REVENUE:		
Mufflers	1,733,858	57
Pipes	905,058	30
Parts	197,610	6
Tubing	209,000	7
Shocks	20,550	1
Total Revenue	3,066,076	100
TOTAL VARIABLE COSTS:		
Mufflers	555,421	
Pipes	229,197	
Parts	104,451	
Tubing	133,500	
Shocks	13,815	
TVC	1,036,384	
CONTRIBUTIONS:		
Mufflers	1,178,437	58
Pipes	675,861	33
Parts	93,159	5
Tubing	75,500	4
Shocks	6,735	0
Total Contribution	2,029,692	100
Cont % of Sales	66	
Distribution	328,650	11
Selling Expenses	312,667	10
Unit Distrib. Cost	0.70	
Region Contribution	1,388,375	
Salesmen	4	
FIXED COSTS:	991,380	32
NPBT:	396,995	
NPBT % of Sales	13	

Exhibit 4 (continued)

Income Statement for National Region (A238..C280)

Income Statement for
Zip Automotive National Region

		%
REVENUE:		
Mufflers	12,793,946	89
Pipes	956,495	7
Parts	117,600	1
Tubing	507,452	4
Shocks	0	0
Total Revenue	14,375,493	100
TOTAL VARIABLE COSTS:		
Mufflers	5,741,984	
Pipes	389,106	
Parts	62,160	
Tubing	324,138	
Shocks	0	
TVC	6,517,388	
CONTRIBUTIONS:		
Mufflers	7,051,962	90
Pipes	567,388	7
Parts	55,440	1
Tubing	183,314	2
Shocks	0	0
Total Contribution	7,858,104	100
Cont % of Sales	55	
Distribution	1,078,194	8
Selling Expenses	625,333	4
Unit Distrib. Cost US	0.84	
Region Contribution	6,154,577	
Salesmen	8	
FIXED COSTS:	4,847,625	34

Exhibit 5

BASIS FOR COST ALLOCATIONS

Factory Indirect Cost, Indirect Benefits, Indirect Vacation
These costs have been allocated to regions and product lines on the basis of the proportion of direct labour cost for the region or the product to total direct labour cost.

Staff Overhead, Staff Benefits, Staff Vacation
These costs have been allocated to regions and product lines on the basis of the proportion of sales dollars in the region or product line to total sales dollars.

Supplies
This cost has been allocated to regions and product lines on the basis of the proportion of material costs in the region or product line to the total material costs.

Utilities
This cost has been allocated to regions and product lines on the basis of the proportion of the variable cost in the region or product line to the total variable costs.

Repairs and Maintenance
This cost has been allocated to regions and product lines on the basis of the proportion of the sales dollars in the region or product line to the total sales dollars for the firm.

Depreciation
This cost has been allocated to regions and product lines on the basis of the proportion of sales dollars in the region or product line to total sales dollars for the firm.

Warehouse
This cost has been allocated to regions and product lines on the basis of the proportion of the sold units in the region or product line to total units sold.

Distribution
This cost has been allocated to regions and product lines on the basis of $.40 per unit in Eastern Canada, $.20 per unit in Quebec and Ontario, $.70 per unit in Western Canada, and $.83 per unit for national and US accounts.

Selling Expenses
This cost has been allocated to regions and product lines on the basis of the rate of approximately $78,000 per year to keep a salesperson in the field.

General and Administrative
This cost has been allocated to regions and product lines on the basis of the proportion of sales dollars in the region to total sales dollars for the firm.

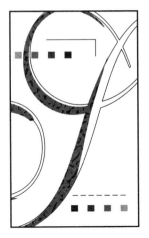

PART **D**

CAPITAL BUDGETING

BEDROCK CORPORATION— OFFICE PRODUCTS DIVISION

Rhonda English, Al Magrath, and Randolph Kudar*

Amanda Morris was under a considerable amount of pressure. As a marketing manager in the Office Products Division of Bedrock Corporation, it was her responsibility to decide whether to begin manufacturing a new style of "desk caddy" or continue manufacturing the old design. Amanda had been considering a new prototype caddy design for some time but had not expected to have to make a decision on the caddy so soon.

THE COMPANY

The Bedrock Corporation was a highly diversified company with operations in Canada, the United States, and Europe. The Canadian operation was located in Montreal, Quebec and was involved in both manufacturing and importing of numerous products. The Canadian company was organized into divisions, with each division responsible for a group of related products. As a full-line supplier, the product lines met varying needs within the corporation, some being market leaders and others simply filling out total offering.

Each division was headed by a Division manager, to whom a number of product managers reported. Product managers were responsible for the bottom line operating profit of each product under their umbrella. Marketing managers,

who reported to product managers for approval, undertook the promotion, distribution, and advertising activities for various products. Each division had access to the usual support groups, such as marketing research, accounting, legal, etc.

Annual budgets by specific product were developed at the beginning of the year for all divisions. Revenue, cost, and profit figures were set in dollars and percentages using input from all areas of the division (e.g., product managers, marketing managers). This planning dictated how indirect costs would be apportioned to the various products, and were then set for the duration of the year. Exhibit 1 outlines a sample profit and loss budget.

THE SITUATION

The caddy decision had become urgent because the mold used to make the caddy had worn out rather unexpectedly. The production supervisor indicated that the mold had only a few weeks of life remaining. To complicate the situation, the division had only enough money to replace one mold ($80,000), so that the option of buying two molds (old and new design) and producing both caddies in-house was not available.

THE PRODUCT AND MARKET

The "desk caddy" was a standard office product made out of molded plastic and used to hold such things as paper clips, pens, elastics, and note paper. The caddy was sold through office product stationers and generated annual revenue of $500,000 for the Office Products Division. It had been designed 15 years earlier and had only had colour changes since its introduction.

Bedrock held the dominant position in the fairly stagnant market with a 75 percent market share (in dollars). The remaining 25 percent of the market was split between clones of the Bedrock caddy imported from offshore stationers. These clones were featured next to Bedrock's caddy in the stationer catalogues and listed at a 25 percent lower price. The overall market was flat in terms of unit growth, with Bedrock experiencing 2 to 3 percent annual unit increases as a result of only minor price increases every two years.

The Bedrock desk caddy was sold by the stationers at a price of $10, which allowed the stationers a margin of 55 percent. Amanda felt that the stationers played a significant role in the purchase decision of the final consumer, with sales often prompted by the stationer's order desk people. Consequently, Amanda wanted to ensure that the stationers were in favor of any changes to the caddy product. She had asked the market research group to obtain feedback on the new caddy and the results are outlined in Exhibit 2. It appeared that the stationers were interested in switching to a new caddy that could be priced at a premium to improve their margins.

Amanda was also interested in the opinion of the end consumers and had received their responses to a survey about the new prototype from the market research group. Their preferences are summarized in Exhibit 3.

One concern about going with the new caddy was a write-off of packaging supplies which would occur. The new caddy would not fit the boxes or labels already in stock from the old design. Boxes worth $35,000 and labels amounting to $7,500 would be useless if the new design was adopted.

A final option Amanda was considering involved outsourcing all caddy purchases. With this option, Amanda could go with the two caddy designs and not have to worry about making a choice between them. However, minimum order quantities of 65,000 units per caddy were required by the outside supplier, since the products would be manufactured in annual one-time, limited production runs. The caddies would also be shipped all at once in a bulk order. Although raw material prices were volatile in this business, with costs of a caddy varying plus or minus 10 to 12 percent, costs from the supplier, as outlined in Exhibit 4, would be fixed for one-year periods. Costs and margins of the new and old caddy if manufactured in-house are also detailed in Exhibit 4.

Currently, the units were manufactured in relatively small lots, several times during the year in response to orders from the stationers. This reduced the level of finished goods inventory held by Bedrock.

CONCLUSION

Amanda knew that regardless of what decision she made, the competition would be quick to fill the market with an offshore clone of the successful caddy at a lower price. She was more concerned, though, with the stationers' preferences for the old versus new caddy, and wondered at what point they would be indifferent to the two designs.

Exhibit 1

PROFIT AND LOSS BUDGET
($000)

OFFICE PRODUCT CADDY

October 19XX

	Line	This Year Amount	%
Sales - Domestic	4510	$500	100.0
Sales - Export	4511	–	–
Gross Sales	4512	$500	00.0
Cash Discounts	4513	–	–
Net Sales	4514	$500	00.0
Finished Goods Purch	4515	–	–
Manufacturing Costs	4516	$250	50.0
Total Cost Goods Sold	4517	$250	50.0
Gross Margin	4518	$250	50.0
General Sales Exp	4519	$88	17.6
Advert Mdse Purch	4520	$11	2.2
Marketing Operations	4521	$17	3.4
Total Sales Exps	4522	$116	23.2
Administrative Exp	4523	$34	6.8
Total Oper Costs	4524	$400	80.0
OPERATING PROFIT	4525	$100	20.0

Exhibit 2

STATIONERS' VIEWS ON NEW VS. OLD DISPENSER
(National Representative Sample)

	%
Like new one a lot better	35%
Like new one a little better	35%
Like the current one a lot more	15%
Like the current one a little more	5%
No preference between the two designs	10%
	100%

Stationer Suggested Pricing of New Caddy - $11.50
Stationer Margin on New Caddy - 55%

Note: — 60% of the stationers stated that they would not stock more than two major caddy brands due to limited catalogue and warehousing space.
— 40% stated they might consider three lines as long as at least one was a low cost line.

Exhibit 3

END USER CUSTOMER OPINIONS OF NEW VS. EXISTING DESIGN

	%
Like new caddy better	20%
Like new caddy a little more	40%
Like current caddy a lot better	15%
Like current caddy a little better	5%
No preference between old and new design	20%
	100%

Note: 250 in-person market surveys where respondents were shown both caddies and asked which they preferred to buy/use. Respondents were all regular users of the caddy.

Exhibit 4

COSTS/MARGINS OF CADDIES IN-HOUSE VS OUTSOURCING

	IN-HOUSE		OUTSIDE SUPPLIER	
	OLD	NEW	OLD	NEW
Selling price to stationers	$4.50	$5.20	$4.50	$5.20
Cost of product	2.25	2.35*	2.95	3.00
Gross Margin	$2.25	$2.85	$1.55	$2.20
Gross Margin %	50%	55%	34%	42%

* Includes mold amortization — cost estimate vary plus or minus 20 cents per caddy

THE BEDROCK CORPORATION —PACKAGING SYSTEMS DIVISION

Rhonda English, Al Magrath, and Randolph Kudar*

Paul Welch, marketing manager of Bedrock Corporation's Packaging Systems Division, was recalling a meeting he had had with his boss, the Divison Product Manager, several weeks ago. Paul's mandate was to generate a plan to revitalize sales in the next three to five years of Wrap N Stick, one of the products under his jurisdiction. The product had only been introduced three years earlier; however, sales had levelled off recently, necessitating some decisions on appropriate marketing action.

THE COMPANY

The Bedrock Corporation was a highly diversified company with operations in Canada, the United States, and Europe. The Canadian operation was located in Montreal, Quebec, and was involved in both manufacturing and importing of numerous products. The Canadian company was organized into divisions, with each division responsible for a group of related products. As a full-line supplier, the product lines met varying needs within the corporation, some being market leaders and others simply filling out total offering.

Each division was headed by a Division manager, to whom a number of product managers reported. Product managers were responsible for the bottom line operating profit of each product under their umbrella. Marketing managers,

who reported to product managers for approval, undertook the promotion, distribution, and advertising activities for various products. Each division had access to the usual support groups, such as marketing research, accounting, legal, etc.

Annual budgets by specific product were developed at the beginning of the year for all divisions. Revenue, cost, and profit figures were set in dollars and percentages using input from all areas of the division (e.g., product managers, marketing managers). This planning dictated how indirect costs would be apportioned to the various products, and were then set for the duration of the year. For example, Paul would indicate how he expected to divide his time between various products and his salary would then be allocated to different products on that time basis, through Account #4523 on the profit and loss budget outlined in Exhibit 1.

THE PRODUCT

Wrap N Stick was a unique decorative gift wrap paper with an adhesive back which enabled gifts to be wrapped without the use of tape. The paper was designed so that it could easily be peeled off without damage to the packaging on the gift item.

The product was manufactured by a sister U.S. company and imported by Bedrock's Packaging Systems Division. It was sold in Canada through the Home Products Division, which was the selling arm for all Bedrock products going to the retail market. The Packaging Systems Division employed the Home Products Division to sell Wrap N Stick and paid them a commission of 10 percent of selling price for their efforts. Although sold by a separate division, the product was carried on the profit and loss statement of the Packaging Systems Division.

The product was sold to the end consumer in individual sheets through retail stores. Currently, Paul's list price to stores was $1.20 per sheet with annual sales of $300,000. Cost of the product was $0.67 per sheet, which was forecasted to be stable for at least one year and subsequently expected to decline 3 percent per year. In addition to the direct cost of the product and the 10 percent fee, Wrap N Stick was promoted by Paul twice annually at a cost of $12,000, was allocated a third of Paul's time (annual salary $35,000), and absorbed a small portion of overhead costs. Operating income after all expenses averaged 20 percent.

THE MARKET

In Canada, the gift wrap market (including all types) had wholesale sales of over $50 million, with the wholesale price per equivalent sheet averaging $0.65. The industry was very seasonal, generating 60 percent of revenues during the two months prior to Christmas.

Marketing Alternatives

A number of options for Wrap N Stick had presented themselves to Paul recently, and each alternative was significantly different. In evaluating the alternatives, besides profit percentage figures, Paul was unsure of what criteria he should use to select among the different strategies.

OPTION 1—PENTECT EXCLUSIVE

Bedrock had been approached by Pentect for an exclusive to sell Wrap N Stick. Exclusivity agreements were not a new concept for Bedrock as this type of deal had been agreed to in the past on various smaller volume, stagnant products. For this option, the Packaging Systems Division would have to cease all selling efforts on Wrap N Stick.

Under the terms of the deal, Pentect would receive a 25 percent discount off current list price and would guarantee purchases of 500,000 sheets annually. If volume exceeded half a million sheets in a year, an additional discount of 3 percent off price at each 200,000 sheet increment, would be effective on the incremental purchases. Pentect believed there was a 75 percent probability that they would sell 1,000,000 sheets of Wrap N Stick.

Pentect agreed to future annual price increases from Bedrock not to exceed the annual consumer price index, which was currently averaging 5 percent. The warehouse had informed Paul that due to Pentect's desire for just in time inventory service from Bedrock, a $25,000 flat rate charge would be added to the Wrap N Stick line, to cover such things as additional frequency of handling orders and rescheduling.

OPTION 2—FUND RAISING

A large wholesaler of fund raising incentives had contacted Paul and was interested in adding Wrap N Stick to his product line. The wholesaler's products were sold to fund raising groups who used them to raise money for schools, sports teams, charities, and other not-for-profit groups.

The wholesaler forecasted sales of 100,000 sheets in the first year with a 20 percent increase each subsequent year. Although the wholesaler agreed to buy at current list price less 10 percent, Paul determined that his cost per sheet would increase by 15 percent as a result of special packs that the wholesaler would require.

Regular retail business with the Home Products Division would continue alongside the fund raising deal; however, there was some concern that the fund raising sales of Wrap N Stick might cannibalize over-the-counter store sales. School children would likely sell the wrap to their parents and grand-parents during the key Christmas buying season when hockey clubs and schools typically chose to raise money for special projects. The Home Products Division estimated that 12 percent of the Packaging Systems Division's annual retail volume from existing markets would be lost due to cannibalization.

OPTION 3—PRIVATE BRANDING

Four large retailers had approached Paul about private branding of Wrap N Stick. Bedrock did not have much experience with this type of arrangement, having only a few products that were currently being privately labelled. Private branding did, however, appear to be a concept increasing in popularity. These four major jewellery and gift shop chains would guarantee minimum aggregate yearly purchases of 142,000 sheets, and anticipated volume growth of 15 percent annually after the first year and a half. Current sales of Wrap N Stick to all four chains totalled approximately $40,000 per year.

In order to sell to these retailers, it was determined that product costs would increase 15 percent for packaging and special imprinting of the corporate chains' colours. The chains agreed to purchase the wrap at 10 percent off list but insisted that list prices remain constant for at least two years.

Although the chains did not want a retail exclusive, they would only sign the deal if fund raising wholesale distribution was not undertaken by Bedrock. This was because their trade categories were so dependent on Christmas gift volumes.

OPTION 4—ENHANCED MARKETING

The Bedrock sales support group in the Home Products Division believed Paul could dramatically improve sales of Wrap N Stick by spending more on advertising. They felt that paying for ad space in the flyers of Canada's five biggest national accounts (currently selling the largest volume of the product) was the key to increasing sales. These five big accounts included two mass merchandisers, a national department store chain, and two giant drug store chains.

The Home Products Division of Bedrock estimated sales of 500,000 sheets within two years if ad features were bought twice per year with each major chain. The cost of each flyer ad insert averaged $5,000, having just increased by $1,000 this year. The Division believed sales of one million sheets could be achieved within five years if, in addition to continuing advertising, Paul improved the product itself, by using licensed cartoon characters from Saturday morning cartoon shows and newspaper comic strips. To license characters for designs, Paul could expect to incur a 4 percent royalty fee payable to licence holders. Extra converting costs in the United States would add another 5 percent to the product cost.

For the successful implementation of this strategy, prices would have to be kept at reasonable levels. To this end, using coupons in the ad features for $.20 off per package was recommended by the Home Products Division. Coupon redemptions from such ads rarely surpassed 2 percent of coupons printed in the ads, with combined insert mailings per feature reaching, on average, 4 million Canadian homes. The chains agreed that coupon handling and printing costs would comprise part of the $5,000 ad feature insert fee.

Bedrock had not previously been involved with such large scale mass advertising programs and Paul wondered if there were underlying factors he should be considering in his analysis of the final option.

CONCLUSION

Paul was somewhat overwhelmed with the options available for the Wrap N Stick line. Bedrock usually used a discounted cashflow analysis approach (15 percent rate) for this type of decision situation, so Paul knew how to quantify the alternatives. The qualitative considerations, however, were going to present a much more difficult task. To further add to the urgency of the situation, Paul had recently seen a sample Taiwanese-sourced, self stick gift paper that had been sent to Carson Greeting Cards Inc. for possible sale into their retail accounts. Although the adhesion was of a poorer quality than that of Bedrock's Wrap N Stick, the threat of offshore competition was clearly becoming a reality.

Exhibit 1

PROFIT AND LOSS BUDGET
($000)

PRODUCT WRAP N STICK

October 19XX

	Line	*This Year*	
		Amount	*%*
Sales – Domestic	4510	$300.00	100.0
Sales – Export	4511	–	–
Gross Sales	4512	$300.00	100.0
Cash Discounts	4513	–	–
Net Sales	4514	$300.00	100.0
Finished Goods Purch	4515	$167.50	55.8
Manufacturing Costs	4516	–	–
Total Cost Goods Sold	4517	$167.50	55.8
Gross Margin	4518	$132.50	44.2
General Sales Exp	4519	$30.0.00	10.0
Advert Mdse Purch	4520	$12.0.00	4.0
Marketing Operations	4521	–	–
Total Sales Exps	4522	$42.00	14.0
Administrative Exp	4523	$30.60	10.2
Total Oper Costs	4524	$72.60	24.2
OPERATING PROFIT	4525	$59.50	20.0

ECLIPSE LUGGAGE CO. LTD.

Society of Management Accountants of Canada

The Eclipse Luggage Company began operations in Canada in 1978 as a branch plant of a Buffalo based luggage manufacturer. Its sales volume had grown steadily but it had never reached the expectations of the U.S. parent company. The manufacturing plant, built in 1978 in London, Ontario, was larger than warranted by Canadian sales and lost money in its early years. However, as sales volume increased, Eclipse began to show a profit and in 1988 earned a 10% net return on equity (see Exhibit 1).

In 1986, Eclipse was incorporated in Canada and one-third of its common voting shares issued to the Canadian public at a price of $20.00 per share. These shares, 200,000 altogether, were widely held by small investors, and early in 1989 were trading at a price of $21.00. The other two-thirds of the voting stock was issued to the parent company in return for the plant and equipment and current assets.

In 1988, Eclipse was marketing only the "Serendipity" line of luggage in Canada, which it manufactured in London. Serendipity had been a huge success and dominated the high-price field in both Canada and the United States. It was sturdily constructed around a metal alloy frame, with recessed locks and hinges and had an enviable reputation in the trade as the best quality, best designed, hard side luggage available. The parent company, which manufactured the Serendipity line for the U.S. market at a plant in Buffalo, had supplied all the needed technical support in product design and production methods for which it charged Eclipse a royalty of 2-1/2% of sales. The parent company also supplied a good deal of assistance in promotion and advertising and generally made itself available for consultation. Charles Jonas, the president of Eclipse, had come to rely very heavily on the advice of the parent company. As he put it, "Many of the problems that confront us have already been solved in Buffalo. For 2-1/2% their advice and patents make it the best buy anywhere."

MANUFACTURING ACTIVITIES

The plant and equipment in London had cost about $10 million in 1978. It had not been necessary to make any changes or additions to the building since then, although a number of new machines had been purchased as activities expanded. With only one line of luggage to cope with, the production processes had long since become standardized and routine. Workers knew their jobs well and many had been with Eclipse since 1978.

The expected costs for the 50 cm Serendipity case for 1989 follow:

Expected Costs for the 50 cm Serendipity Case

Labour	$20.00
Materials	14.40
Variable Overhead	6.40
Fixed Overhead	9.60
Total	$50.40

Although costs naturally varied according to the size of the case involved, the average percentage of variable costs to sales revenue held at about 50%. Fixed manufacturing overhead had held constant at about $800,000 since 1985.

In 1982 the workers at the London plant joined a major international trade union. Relationships between the union representatives and Mr. Jonas had been less than cordial, and a prolonged strike in 1984 had hurt Eclipse's reputation. The central issues were wage rates and bonuses and management's plans to change work standards as a result of improvements in technology. After several weeks Mr. Jonas capitulated to union demands partly as a result of pressure from dealers and distributors who were anxious to get delivery. No strikes had occurred since 1984, but management found it difficult to adopt new process methods or technologies, and wage rates had climbed steeply. The union and some of the workers expressed the opinion that new technologies or processes would result in layoffs. As a result, Eclipse had been unable to match wage increases with equivalent increases in productivity; productivity was almost 20% below that of Buffalo, and Eclipse's total dollar gross margin would have declined had it not been for increased sales.

One difficult problem in the production department was that of inventory control. In the Serendipity line there were eight different sizes of cases and seven different colours. An inventory of 56 units was required just to keep one of each available. The distributors who were supposed to keep an adequate stock to service the dealers in their areas generally attempted to cut inventory requirements to the bone to preserve working capital, so the main pressure was on Eclipse's own finished goods inventory. As a result of these pressures, Eclipse usually carried about ten weeks sales in finished goods in addition to the necessary stocks of raw materials and in-process inventories.

At 1988 sales and production volumes the plant was still only utilized to 60% of its capacity in terms of floor space. The Production Manager felt, in fact, that output of the new Seredipity line could be doubled with the outlay of $1,200,000 to $1,300,000 in new equipment and a few minor changes in production methods. He had repeatedly urged Mr. Jonas to consider a price cut on Serendipity or an increase in advertising to increase sales volume and reduce average production costs. But Mr. Jonas had simply urged him to be patient and told him that sales volume on Serendipity would grow at the present price and would eventually utilize the entire plant.

MARKETING ACTIVITIES

Eclipse sold its Serendipity line through distributors to a total of about 500 jewellery and leather goods stores across Canada. Eclipse also sold direct to department stores and certain large jewellery chains. These direct accounts placed large orders and were always prompt in paying within ten days. They accounted for 40% of all 1988 sales, the other 60% going to distributors. The distributor markup was 20% on the factory price and for this margin, distributors were expected to carry and finance inventories, service all dealers in their territories and collect all dealer accounts.

Eclipse's Sales Manager was growing increasingly dissatisfied with the performance of these distributors. Not only did they keep low inventories, but they also failed to service all the dealer accounts satisfactorily and dealer complaints were frequent. About 100 of the dealers did such marginal business that their sales in total amounted to only 10% of distributor sales. There was a good possibility that these accounts could be cultivated back into activity by conscientious salespeople, but to replace the distributors would take ten full-time Eclipse representatives at $90,000 each (salary and expenses), plus a bad debt expense of around $120,000 a year and $400,000 in increased working capital. Ms. Ferguson, the Sales Manager, felt confident that such an expenditure would generate an additional $400,000 a year in sales at existing factory prices of the Serendipity line, but her recommendations to Mr. Jonas had met with a firm refusal, "until sales volume is considerably higher".

One thing Ms. Ferguson had insisted on at the retail end was a fixed retail price. There was very little price cutting in the Serendipity line and although small dealers paid 20% more (distributor margins) than department stores, both sold at the same prices. To support this price stability policy, Ms. Ferguson refused to do business with discount stores or mail order houses, and refused to manufacture private brands.

The retail price of the Serendipity line was high relative to average Canadian luggage prices. Because a line of luggage consisted of many different sizes of case, each selling at a different price, it had become common practice to compare prices between competing brands by reference to the standard 50 cm overnight case. The retail price of the Serendipity 50 cm case was $152, and the factory price, i.e., to distributors and department stores, was $84. Total Canadian sales of all hand luggage (excluding briefcases) by price category for the years 1984 through 1988 are shown in Exhibit 2.

The 1984 figure in Exhibit 2 reflects the impact of the strike. Note that the figures in Exhibit 2 represent the sales of all sizes of Serendipity cases. The weighted average factory price turned out to be close to $100 a case as compared to $84 for the 50 cm overnight case.

Eclipse expenditures on advertising and promotion were set by company policy at 4% of prior year's sales. Other selling expenses consisted of Ms. Ferguson's salary, several office staff and other fixed costs.

EXECUTIVE OFFICERS

The formal organization at Eclipse followed a simple functional structure with Charles Jonas as president and three executives reporting directly to him. Jane Lemiski, Vice President—Finance, handled all accounting and financial problems and general administration, and acted as president in the absence of Mr. Jonas. Ms. Lemiski had joined Eclipse only two years ago after her predecessor quit for another position. She was in her early thirties and had earned a CMA designation.

Frank Harris, the Production Manager, was in his early forties and had also been with Eclipse for only two years. Mr. Harris was the fifth production manger in the firm's 11 year history and Ms. Lemiski the sixth head of finance. Executive turnover had been a major problem at Eclipse.

Bernadette Ferguson was in her mid-forties and had been with Eclipse for over five years. She travelled extensively and was not therefore close to the other executives, but apart from the request to replace distributors with direct salespeople, she had generally managed to get her own way.

Charles Jonas had been head of Eclipse since it began in 1978. He had an M.B.A. from a recognized U.S. business school and had been working his way up in the parent organization when he was sent "to see what he could with a new branch in Canada". He was hoping for a recall to an executive position in Buffalo, but after 11 years he had begun to think that he was destined to work out his last ten years to retirement in Canada. He was somewhat disillusioned but nevertheless took great pride in his leadership position.

A NEW PROJECT PROPOSAL

In March 1989, shortly after release of the 1988 financial statements (Exhibit 1), a management meeting was called to review 1988 performance and to develop budgets for the remainder of 1989. Mr. Jonas was clearly pleased with the 1988 results.

Jonas: "Well, we have achieved a new milestone this year. Sales have passed the 8 million dollar mark and profits are up substantially. What do you expect sales volume to reach in 1989, Bernadette?"

Ferguson: "I think we'll hit 10 million without much trouble. If only we could get our distributors to hustle a little faster—or replace them with..."

Jonas: "Let's not get into that again today. Tell me, Jane, what kind of profit can we expect from sales of 10 million?"

Lemiski: "Offhand, I'd say about $1,500,000 after taxes."

Jonas: "Things are looking much, much better. Steady solid progress."

Harris: "I have a recommendation to make that could help us to move forward a lot faster. When I was in Germany last month I saw a demonstration of a machine that produces injection-molded luggage direct from pelletized basic plastics. With a little extra design work in the molds, it would be possible to produce a case that would be strong enough without a metal frame; and we could have it imprinted on the inside to simulate a lining. With these savings and the use of a simplified hinge, we could probably produce a 50 cm case that would retail around $100."

Lemiski: "I've been talking to Frank about this and I think we may be onto something big. We could land the necessary equipment here for about $2,500,000 and would need another $1,000,000 for molds of various sizes. We could use a polypropylene blend and easily manufacture a variety of colours. Now the beauty of this process is that it reduces the labour cost component significantly. It would cost us no more than $6.00 in direct labour to produce a 50 cm case and the total cost of materials would be close to $12.00 per unit of which $6.00 would be for the basic plastic. Variable overhead on a new line like this would be less than $2.00 a unit. In short, we could...."

Jonas: "In short, you want us to get into the cheap luggage business with an inferior product. And what do you think that would do to our quality image?"

Ferguson: "If it was in any way related to our Serendipity brand name, it could have a very adverse effect. But if it were given an altogether different brand name and backed by a major national advertising campaign, it might just succeed on its own without affecting Serendipity. In fact, we might be able to open up discount stores and mail order accounts and a host of new outlets. Our distributors would be very pleased."

Mr Jonas: "You're not serious, Bernadette! Surely you, after all these years, know Eclipse's policy on quality. Buffalo would be down our necks in a flash if we moved into discount houses. We just don't compete in the low-priced market with all its kickbacks and special deals. We're better off as we are."

Harris: "I've already talked to the production manager in Buffalo, and it happens they are looking into injection-molded luggage too. As you know, with free trade the 20% tariff on U.S. imports will be gone in three years and Buffalo is talking about supplying Canada too. This is no cheap product we're talking about. It will be as durable as the Serendipity line, if not more so, and I think we could design a very modern appearance into it. What's more, it will take a while for our competitors to copy us because of the high investment required."

Jonas: "You are obviously very serious about this. Let's take a more thorough look at it. You know it will really upset our budget procedures. Things have really moved along smoothly in the past. What will the sales forecast look like if we introduce a whole new line?"

Ferguson: "If this product is as good as Frank says, we will have no trouble moving it in the medium-price field. A lot of luggage in the $80 to $120 range is poor quality stuff. We could move at least 50,000 units in the first year; maybe as high as 100,000."

Jonas: "That kind of estimating doesn't help the budgeting process at all. You'll have to be more specific."

Ferguson: "I don't have a crystal ball, you know. I haven't even seen the product yet. I reckon if we invested $500,000 in national advertising and promotion we should move about 7,500 units a month. Now by units, I mean cases. We are used to talking price on a 50 cm case. Now if the 50 cm case retailed at $85—and that's the price I'm basing my sales estimate on—the average selling price of all the different sizes in the line would probably work out to around $100 at retail or $55 factory price. So I'm really forecasting annual sales of 90,000 times $55 or $5 million. We could double our total sales volume."

Lemiski: "I think the average variable production cost would be about $20 per unit given our normal mix of sizes, and $12 of that would be for materials. This would leave..."

Jonas: "Just a minute! What if we sold the 50 cm case for $120? What would this do to the forecast?"

Ferguson: "This would mean a weighted average retail price of $140 for the entire line, and a factory selling price of about $80. I'd have to think about it."

Jonas: "Well, consider a price of $80 and give us your best and worst estimates on sales. Frank, would you get together with Jane and let me have estimates of the life of the equipment and molds, and the working capital requirements for a new line. Oh and you might let me know where we can get our hands on the capital we'll need."

Lemiski: "That's the least of our worries. I could place a 12-1/2% first mortgage bond for a million dollars with a private institution, and we would enjoy the benefits of some leverage for a change. However, I think we should still use our after-tax hurdle rate of 20%."

Jonas: "Don't forget the risks of leverage. Don't you realize that if this product fails, it would be disastrous for us and all our shareholders? Perhaps it's just too big for us to cope with, with our resources. It will certainly disrupt all our budget procedures. We'll be in a constant state of uncertainty."

Harris: "I think this firm needs a challenge of this magnitude. It would shake us out of our lethargy and inject some excitement into the old place."

A few days after the above meeting, Mr. Jonas received reports from his management team relating to the injection-molded luggage project. These reports appear as Exhibits 3 and 4.

Exhibit 1

FINANCIAL HIGHLIGHTS

Statistical Highlights

	1984	1985	1986	1987	1988
Sales	$4,400,000	6,240,000	7,040,000	7,760,000	8,800,000
Gross Profit	1,599,000	2,519,000	2,919,000	3,279,000	3,799,000
Net Profit/(Loss)	(147,000)	288,002	604,942	1,014,738	1,260,870

Income Statement
Year Ended December 31, 1988

Sales		$8,800,000
Cost of Goods Sold		
Beginning Inventory	$976,000	
Labour	2,192,000	
Materials	1,616,000	
Variable Overhead	656,000	
Fixed Overhead	841,000	
Less Ending Inventory	(1,280,000)	5,001,000
Gross Margin		3,799,000
Royalties and Selling and Administration		1,420,000
Net Profit Before Income Tax		2,379,000
Income Tax		1,118,130
Net Profit After Tax		$1,260,870

Balance Sheet
As at December 31, 1988

Assets		
Current:		
Cash and Securities	$2,240,000	
Accounts Receivable	1,000,000	
Inventories	1,280,000	
Other	200,000	$4,720,000
Fixed:		
Building, net	5,080,000	
Machinery and Equipment, net	3,200,000	8,280,000
Total Assets		$13,000,000
Liabilities		
Current:		
Accounts Payable	320,000	
Other	160,000	480,000
Equity:		
Common Shares	12,000,000	
Retained Earnings	520,000	12,520,000
Total Liabilities and Equity		$13,000,000

Exhibit 2

INDUSTRY SALES

Estimated Number of Units Sold in Canada					
Price (Standard 50 cm case)	*1984*	*1985*	*1986*	*1987*	*1988*
Over $160	24,000	38,000	46,000	60,000	86,000
$140 - $159.99	52,000	73,000	77,000	83,600	91,000
$120 - $139.99	61,000	64,000	66,500	71,000	69,500
$100 - $119.99	173,000	175,000	200,000	240,000	270,000
$80 - $99.99	175,000	210,000	240,000	300,000	370,000
Under $80	200,000	170,000	165,000	140,000	105,000
Total	685,000	730,000	794,500	894,600	991,500
Serendipity Sales	44,100	62,600	70,360	77,650	87,600

Exhibit 3

To: Charles
From: Bernadette
Re: Injection-Molded Luggage Project

I have given a good deal of thought to this project during the past few days. One manufacturer in the U.S. is already producing injection-molded luggage, and I was able to purchase a full set for examination. The product is without a doubt a very significant innovation and will, I feel sure, eventually become very popular.

Using the U.S. product as a sample, I obtained opinions from our distributors and from the buyers of many department stores and discount houses. The response was very enthusiastic and I feel confident that we should go ahead with manufacture here.

As you suggested, I looked at two different price points for the new luggage and I estimated volume levels for each price point. The following sales projections assume an advertising and promotion budget of $400,000 per year. This figure for advertising and promotion has been developed in consultation with our agency and represents a realistic estimate.

Pricing Options	*$47 Price*	*$64 Price*
Retail Price (50 cm)	$ 85	$ 120
Factory Price (50 cm)	47	64
Average Retail Price	$ 100	$ 140
Average Factory Price	55	80
Forecast Monthly Sales		
Most Likely Sales (Units)	7,500	1,500
Optimistic (Units)	9,000	3,500
Pessimistic (Units)	5,000	1,000

You will note that the above estimates are not quite as optimistic as my verbal guess, but I am convinced that they are very realistic. In all probability, sales will continue to grow from year to year as well, but for planning purposes we can conservatively expect to maintain the above sales levels for at least five years, given the same annual advertising expenditure.

Exhibit 4

To: Charles
From: Jane and Frank
Re: Injection-Molded Luggage Project

As per your request, here is more information about the proposed project:

Additional Inventories

Raw materials	two months' supply
Work in process	two week production cycle
Finished goods	two months' sales
Additional accounts receivable	one month's sales
Less additional accounts payable	one month's materials

Work in process includes 100% of raw materials and 50% of labour and overhead.

Further to the working capital requirements, we can expect to incur an additional $120,000 per year in fixed administrative costs to handle all the new accounts and accounting procedures.

The molds can be expected to last two years and will be valueless after that time. Molds for a full range of sizes will cost us approximately $800,000, not $1,000,000 as mentioned in our meeting. For tax purposes, this would constitute an annual expense of $400,000. The injection molding equipment itself will cost $2,500,000 installed.

We would be faced with an annual maintenance charge of $100,000 under a fixed maintenance contract. On this basis the equipment will last at least five years at which time it would have a negligible salvage value. The equipment has a CCA rate of 20%.

Average variable cost of production—considering our normal mix of sizes—should work out to $20 per unit. Of this amount $12 is for materials, $6 labour and $2 variable overhead.

FALCONBRIDGE LIMITED — THE CAPITAL EXPENDITURE POLICY AND ENVIRONMENTAL IMPACT

Nola Buhr and Randolph Kudar*

Bob Michelutti, Superintendent Environmental Services for the Sudbury operations of Falconbridge Limited, was reviewing the Company's capital expenditure policy.

Five years earlier, in 1986, Falconbridge had made significant changes to the capital expenditure policy in order to address the Company's environmental impact. Since then, there had been many changes in environmental legislation and public expectations.

Bob considered a number of the environmental issues that concerned Falconbridge (Exhibit 1) and he wondered if the capital expenditure policy still appropriately addressed environmental concerns or if there was a need for some changes.

THE COMPANY

Falconbridge was an international resource company engaged in the exploration, development, mining, processing and marketing of metals and minerals. The Falconbridge group of companies had operations in Canada, Norway, the Dominican Republic, and Zimbabwe; marketing and sales offices in Toronto, Brussels, Pittsburgh, Tokyo, and Barbados; research laboratories in Canada and Norway; and exploration offices in Canada and abroad. Its products included nickel, ferronickel, copper, zinc, cobalt, cadmium, silver, gold, platinum group metals, various metal concentrates, and sulphuric acid. In September 1989, Noranda and Trelleborg AB became joint owners of Falconbridge, making Falconbridge a privately held company. Consolidated revenue for Falconbridge in 1990 was $2.03 billion dollars (Canadian).

In 1987, top corporate executives developed an environmental policy for Falconbridge which was updated in 1990. The policy (Exhibit 2) explicitly stated that the Company would:

Design, manage and decommission our operations to meet or surpass applicable regulations and laws.

SUDBURY OPERATIONS

Falconbridge started as a company in Sudbury in 1928. Since then, the Sudbury operations (which actually take place in Falconbridge, Ontario, just outside of Sudbury) have focused on the mining, milling, and smelting of nickel-copper ores.

Five underground mines supply the ore. In 1990, 2.8 million tonnes of ore were hoisted out of the ground, resulting in production of 33,600 tonnes of nickel. Ore is taken from the mines and then crushed and processed further in the mill.

In the mill the ore is treated in order to separate the valuable minerals: pentlandite (which contains nickel) and chalcopyrite (which contains copper) from the uneconomic materials: pyrrhotite (which contains iron and sulphur) and silicates. The mill produces a concentrate which then goes to the smelter.

There are several stages of processing in the smelter. First, the concentrate is partially roasted in two slurry-fed fluid bed roasters. This material is then subjected to gas cleaning. A sulphur dioxide gas is released and transferred to the acid plant to be turned into sulphuric acid. The end product from the roaster is conveyed to two electric furnaces for smelting to produce a waste slag and furnace matte. The slag goes to the disposal area and furnace matte containing the metal values is processed in the converters for further removal of iron and sulphur. During the whole process the goal is to minimize the loss of nickel, copper, and cobalt to slag.

The final product of the smelter is nickel matte which is about 75 percent nickel plus copper. This matte is shipped to a Falconbridge company in Norway for refining.

SUDBURY ENVIRONMENTAL SERVICES DEPARTMENT

Bob Michelutti joined Falconbridge in 1970, and after working a few months as a technical assistant in the lab, he started work in the newly created

Environmental Services Department. Over the last two decades Bob had seen a steady increase in environmental awareness and concerns in the mining industry. Mining practices that were seen as acceptable even in recent years were no longer deemed acceptable.

Over the years the Environmental Services Department had grown and now employed a total of five individuals. Each individual was responsible for different aspects of environmental matters.

Key responsibilities of the department included:

- negotiations with the Ministry of the Environment
- obtaining current knowledge of environmental laws
- ensuring employees were aware of environmental laws
- R & D management
- property close-out co-ordination as per the *Mining Act*
- waste rock and tailings management
- spill reduction
- monitoring of sulphur dioxide emission levels
- performing environmental audits
- undertaking biological surveys
- water quality monitoring
- developing reclamation programs
- rectifying unsafe conditions and practices in the field
- development and implementation of waste management systems

CAPITAL EXPENDITURE POLICY

Falconbridge had developed a written manual to outline their Capital Expenditure Policy. The objective of the Policy was stated as follows:

> to enhance control over capital expenditures by ensuring that all capital in vestments are evaluated on an appropriate and consistent basis and that all such expenditures are approved by and reported to Senior Management.

A capital expenditure that fell under this policy was defined as any expenditure over $5,000 whose usefulness is expected to extend over several years.

Although capital requests could be made at any time, it was expected that any capital requirements would be included in the annual plan. The annual plan was formulated every year, in September and October, for the following year. The annual plan identified the magnitude of proposed capital spending for the coming year based on projected projects. Each department would prepare a list of capital requirements. Then these requirements would be reviewed at the smelter, mill, mine, and administration levels. Once a consensus was reached, the final version would go to the Board in November for approval.

This annual plan only specified a general level of capital spending. No specific capital expenditures or commitments were made unless they were first covered by a Capital Appropriation Request (CAR) which required appropriate economic justification and senior management approval.

Some of the items in the capital budget were fixed as far as priority. For example, expenditure required to meet the acid rain legislation was one of these priorities. However, because Falconbridge had been working on technology in advance of legislation, there was some room to manipulate capital expenditures on acid rain reduction between years if funds were needed for other projects.

All CARs were approved by the general manager of the Sudbury operations. However, any items that were covered by the annual budget and were greater than $250,000 were approved by the President who was at corporate headquarters in Toronto. Items that were not covered by the annual budget and were greater than $100,000 would be sent to the President for review. Any expenditures over $3 million would be sent to the Board for approval.

The Capital Expenditure Policy had provisions for overruns and post-completion reviews. Whenever the expenditure on a project exceeded the approved amount by 5% (minimum $5,000), a supplementary request had to be submitted to the VP/General Manager for Sudbury Operations for approval before any further expenditures would be made. All completed capital expenditures were subject to post-completion review to determine if the project was in compliance with the Capital Expenditure Policy and whether the economic benefits identified at the time of approval were achieved.

CAPITAL EXPENDITURE DECISION PROCEDURES

The capital expenditure decision process is outlined in Exhibit 3. Each capital expenditure began with a project initiator who developed an idea for a capital project and discussed the idea with his or her superior. The idea was then discussed with Engineering who offered technical advice. If the project appeared feasible, then a draft proposal was developed and submitted to the Department Head or Manager for approval. If the Manager accepted the preliminary proposal, then a tentative project team was established and a preliminary project plan was written up.

Research and development played a key role in the development of many project plans. Much of the capital expenditure at Falconbridge was committed for the development of new technology. In the case of developing technology to reduce sulphur dioxide emissions, research and development sought to develop technology to reach the desired emissions level at the least cost. Because the government set mandated emission levels, there would likely be some interaction with the government during this process. Research and development typically derived several technologies. Then engineering costed out the different processes and the least-cost process was chosen.

The capital accounting department, if required, was contacted for assistance in preparing preliminary cash flows and a feasibility study or similar economic analysis. If the project met Company objectives and stipulated guidelines for internal rate of return, then a Capital Appropriate Request (CAR) was developed and reviewed by all members of the project team and approved by the manager.

Once the manager approved the CAR it was sent to capital accounting for a review of the documentation and economic evaluation. The justification was thoroughly reviewed and an effort was made to troubleshoot and resolve any questions that might arise before the CAR was submitted to the VP/General Manager at Sudbury.

If the VP/General Manager at Sudbury had any questions, there would be some discussion regarding the CAR. Those CARs requiring head office approval were sent to Toronto for final approval.

Once final approval was received the project could begin.

Capital Appropriation Request Forms

It was the process of completing the CAR that ensured that environmental impacts were considered for each and every capital project. Regardless of the purpose of the capital project, each project had to complete an Environmental Check List (Exhibit 5) in order to determine if it was environmentally sensitive. There were nine questions on the check list that could be answered yes, no or unsure. If any of the questions were answered with a "yes" or "unsure", then the project leader had to contact the Environmental Services Department before submitting the CAR. The Environmental Services Department would perform any necessary environmental assessments and obtain government approval where required. The check list clearly stated that it might take three to nine months to obtain the necessary approval and that the project could not commence until the approval was received.

This check list had been introduced five years ago and at that time was used only on major capital projects. However, after a couple of years it was decided that all projects that were environmentally sensitive, regardless of the amount of capital committed, required an environmental assessment. And so, it became a required practice to complete an Environmental Check List for all CARs.

Directions for completing the CAR included the following item:

Environmental Considerations—If project is expected to be environmentally sensitive in any way, contact the Environmental Group prior to submission of the CAR. An environmental assessment form may be required to be completed.

Each CAR (Exhibit 4) had to be filled out according to the purpose of the request. The choices were:

- Increase Profitability
- Maintain Production
- Exploration/Research
- Environmental
- Safety
- Other

Only one purpose could be chosen even though the benefits of the expenditure might affect more than one area. For example, projects undertaken for environmental reasons such as converter slag cleaning would be classified as environmental projects even though they would help to improve the recovery of nickel and thereby improve profitability. Conversely, sometimes projects that were undertaken for the purpose of increasing profitability also had environmental benefits.

Each category on the CAR had a different review process because each category had its own corporate objectives and stipulated guidelines. For example, items in the environmental category might be necessary because they were mandated by law. Therefore, approval of an environmental CAR would not depend on meeting the corporate hurdle rate for the internal rate of return. This didn't mean, however, that environmental projects had carte blanche to spend money. The policy manual stated the following regarding economic analysis:

Where a proposed expenditure is for environmental, safety, health or other non-economic purpose, it is not necessary to carry out a full economic analysis as described herein. However, to the extent that costs and other items are identifiable, these items must be shown.

Each CAR required at least two appendices: one, a justification, and the other, an economic evaluation. The nature and extent of each justification varied with the size and complexity of the specific project. The policy manual stated the following:

Where a project is likely to have some form of environmental impact, or some doubt exists in this regard, the project should be discussed with appropriate site and/or Corporate officials. This should be identified on the face of the CAR and if needed, detailed further on the justification and estimate sheet.

It was clear that there was an over-arching need to ensure that approval of all projects took sensitive issues like the environment into consideration. The corporate policy manual stipulated the following:

> The person authorizing the project is responsible for ensuring that the project is in accordance with the Company policy from a technical and policy point of view and if the project is sensitive, discuss it/forward it to his superior.

BOB'S DILEMMA

Bob was pretty satisfied that the Capital Expenditure Policy made it clear that environmental impact was to be considered in each and every CAR and it should be brought to the attention of the Environmental Services Department if the CAR involved any environmental issues.

However, there were a few things that concerned him.

Projects that were labelled "sensitive" required approval at a higher level. Bob wondered if "sensitive" was well defined and well understood by those involved in completing CARs.

Bob wondered if the Environmental Check List was taken seriously. It would be easier to check "No" and thereby avoid the delays that would occur while the project leader waited for the Environmental Services Department to do their environmental assessment and get the appropriate government approval.

Also, projects completed under the operating budget, i.e., ongoing maintenance, did not require an Environmental Check List. This might put the company at risk of non-compliance for process changes that may have required certificates of approval.

While Bob was personally pleased that the corporation was committed to not only meeting, but going beyond, environmental laws, Bob wasn't sure how going beyond environmental laws translated into capital expenditure policy.

Bob was also wondering if it would be possible to track the costs and benefits of the environmental impacts of all capital projects so that they could have a better measure of their environmental performance as a corporation. The way that the CAR was designed now, it wasn't possible to track the environmental benefits of all capital projects.

Exhibit 1

ENVIRONMENTAL ISSUES AT FALCONBRIDGE

Sulphur Dioxide Emissions
The biggest environmental challenge that the Sudbury operations faced was the reduction of sulphur dioxide (SO_2) emissions.

Falconbridge had been working to reduce SO_2 emissions even before there were government regulations stipulating allowable levels. Since 1953 the Company had undertaken research and development projects to improve pyrrhotite rejection (which reduces the amount of sulphur per tonne going into the smelter). This research and development had a key economic benefit of improving nickel recovery.

In 1969, the Ontario provincial government issued its first regulation regarding SO_2 emissions. The regulation required a 50% reduction in SO_2 emission from the 1969 rate of 1,028 tons per day to 465 tons per day (154 kilotonnes per year) by December 31, 1975. This order focused on ambient air quality and total tonnes SO_2 emitted per year and was motivated by a public desire to improve the local air quality around Sudbury.

At this time the super stack approach to pollution control was encouraged because it improved local air quality by dispersing the pollution to a location out-side of Sudbury. However, the super stack concept was not an option for Falconbridge. The Falconbridge site is located three to four kilometres away from the airport and any super stack would be extremely hazardous for air travel. So, rather than disperse the pollution, Falconbridge had to take a process approach in the 1970s which focused on prevention.

In response to the regulation, Falconbridge commissioned the Smelter Environmental Improvement Project (SEIP) in 1969. It was recognized that the cur-rent technological limits had been reached on the rejection of pyrrhotite and that it would be necessary to focus on the smelting process. Although SEIP was consid-ered one big capital project, it was actually a collection of many smaller projects.

Under the most recent Ontario government regulation, the Countdown Acid Rain Program, the Falconbridge smelter was required to reduce emissions from 154 kilotonnes per year in 1985 to 100 kilotonnes per year by 1994. This legislation resulted from Federal-Provincial agreements to reduce sulphur dioxide emissions in Canada for the area east of the Manitoba-Saskatchewan border and from Canada-U.S. discussions on acid rain abatement.

The process developments undertaken by Falconbridge in response to the Countdown Acid Rain Program required a capital expenditure of $38 million. Again, this was not treated as one big project but rather as a series of smaller capital projects.

In 1991 Falconbridge announced that it was able to achieve the 1994 limit of 100 kilotonnes/per year while operating at full capacity. Falconbridge publicly stat-ed in its reports to the provincial government that it planned to lower SO_2 emissions to 75 kilotonnes per year on a voluntary basis prior to 1998.

Other Environmental Concerns
There were several other areas of the operations that had environmental implications.

Exhibit 1 (continued)

Water Usage

Large amounts of water were used in mining and milling processes. It was necessary to treat the water before it was returned to local water systems. The treatment was required to remove the small concentrations of metal that build up over time and could eventually affect aquatic life.

Water discharges are regulated by federal, provincial and municipal laws.

Spills

Spills are regulated under federal, provincial and municipal laws.

Spills can occur as a result of transportation accidents involving the railcars that transport slurry to the mill or failures in the pipelines that carry tailings and water to holding ponds.

Acid Mine Drainage

Acid mine drainage occurs when the sulphur in exposed tailings reacts with oxygen to form an acid. If the seepage is not contained it can find its way into local surface and ground water systems.

At present there are no direct governmental regulations. However, there are indirect regulations which set minimum standards for pH and metal levels in water.

Land Restoration

Mining does not take place without disturbing the surrounding land. Tailings, roads, railways, power lines, pipelines and water supply reservoirs all disturb the land.

Up until 1991, mining companies were required to provide the government with plans for mine closure and site restoration several years in advance of the actual closure date.

However, in June 1991, the Ontario *Mining Act* was changed to provide new regulations requiring closure plans and financial assurance for the decommissioning of mine sites. It was now necessary to provide the government with closure plans before the mine even opened. Detailed Environmental Impact Assessments had to be undertaken. And, the government now required that financial assurance (e.g., cash or letter of credit) be provided to the government before production even started on a new mine.

This was just one example of how environmental laws were getting tougher.

Metal recycling

Although there were no regulations regarding metal recycling, Falconbridge had established custom feed operations to recycle metals from outside sources. They accepted three types of material: (i) distressed material that would otherwise go to landfill; (ii) marginal material such as miscast pieces; and (iii) material containing cobalt.

Exhibit 2

ENVIRONMENTAL POLICY

FALCONBRIDGE IS COMMITTED TO THE PROTECTION OF LIFE, HEALTH AND THE ENVIRONMENT FOR PRESENT AND FUTURE GENERATIONS

ALL EMPLOYEES ARE RESPONSIBLE FOR INCORPORATING INTO THEIR PLANNING AND WORK THE ACTIONS NECESSARY TO FULFIL THIS COMMITMENT

FALCONBRIDGE WILL MEET THESE RESPONSIBILITIES BY PROVIDING THE RESOURCES NECESSARY TO:

- DESIGN, MANAGE AND DECOMMISSION OUR OPERATIONS TO MEET OR SURPASS APPLICABLE REGULATIONS AND LAWS
- WORK IN PARTNERSHIP WITH CUSTOMERS, SUPPLIERS, TRADE ASSOCIATIONS, AND GOVERNMENT AGENCIES TO ENSURE THE SAFE HANDLING AND DISPOSITION OF ALL MATERIALS AND PRODUCTS
- ACQUIRE SCIENTIFIC KNOWLEDGE AND TECHNOLOGIES THAT CONTINUOUSLY IMPROVE THE SAFE, EFFICIENT USE OF OUR PROCESSES AND PRODUCTS
- FORMULATE AND IMPLEMENT EFFECTIVE EMERGENCY RESPONSE SYSTEMS
- INVOLVE OUR EMPLOYEES IN AND KEEP THE PUBLIC INFORMED OF OUR PLANS, PROGRAMS AND PERFORMANCE
- PROMOTE EMPLOYEE AWARENESS OF THIS POLICY AND ENHANCE THEIR CAPABILITIES TO IMPLEMENT THIS POLICY

Exhibit 3

CAPITAL EXPENDITURES DECISION

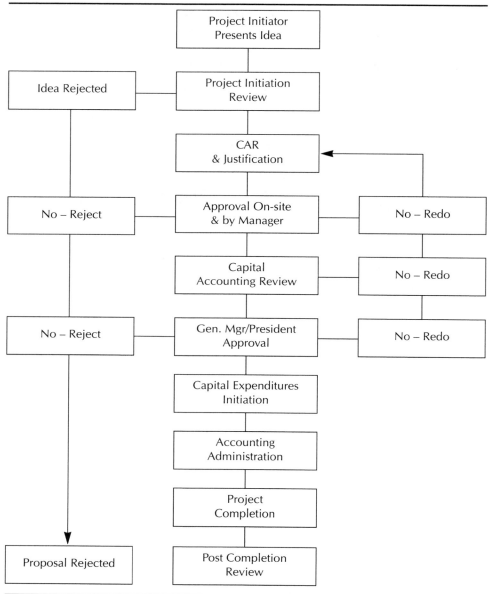

Note: Smaller or routine capital expenditures are not subject to the entire process described above.

Exhibit 4

CAPITAL APPROPRIATION REQUEST

FALCONBRIDGE

Capital Appropriation Request

(1) C.A.R. # ___50-070___

Date: ___December 20, 1990___

(2) Total: ___$780.000.00___

Amount in Plan: (1991 Budget:)

(3) ___$780.000.00___

Company Location:	Sudbury Operations
Department:	Mines: Lockerby Mine
Project Title:	LHD EQUIPMENT
Sub-Project Title:	
Request By:	M. J. PARNELL

(4) Previous Approvals: ___

(5) Total Capital for Project: ___$780.000.00___

Purpose:

(10)

	Increase Profitability
X	Maintain Production
	Exploration/Research
	Environmental
	Safety
	Other

Payment Profile (9)

Actual $ 1990 $_____

$ 1991 $___780, 000___

$ 199_ $_____

$ 199_ $_____

(6) IRR: 53

(7) Payback: 1.4 yrs.

(8) Supplementary Request:

$_____

(13) Environmental Impact Assessment Req'd   Yes ___ No ___   Done Yes ___ No ___
Hazop Req'd   Yes ___ No ___   Done Yes ___ No ___
(14) Energy Management Considerations   Yes ___ No ___   Done Yes ___ No ___

Description:

(11)
Two (2) 6 yd remote LHD units are required to replace four (4) high maintenance cost LHD machines.

Justification

Based on the present projected mine life of Lockerby (4 years) the incremental maintenance cost savings incurred

with the removal of those four LHD's gives the following results:

Capital Cost (2 X 6 yd remote LHD's)	$780.00
1991 Incremental Maintenance Cost Save (Old vs New)	$556,000

Payback   – 1.4 years
NPV(15%)   – $588,000
1RR   – 53X

Review: (12)   Date: Approval: Date:

Prepared By:
Engineering:
Purchasing:
Department Head:
Manager:
Capital Accountant:

J.E.B.
F.G.T.P.
B OF D

In order to comply with the Capital Expenditure Policy, an economic justification must be included with this request

FALCONBRIDGE LIMITED Sudbury Operations
Falconbridge , Ontario P0M 1S0, Cable *Falconfrij* Telex 067-7194 Telephone705/693-2761

Exhibit 4 (continued)

Falconbridge Limited—Capital Appropriation Request Form

To ensure that we are all consistent in applying for capital, the following guideline is intended to clarify what is expected from you in submitting your Capital Appropriation Request Forms.

Examine the Capital Appropriation Request Form provided with this memo. The important items have been numbered and an explanation as to the required documentation is provided as follows:

1) C.A.R.— the CAR # is to be provided by Capital Accounting when you submit your CAR with the appropriate justification.

2) Total (this request)—the total is the amount that you will be applying for on this request.

3) Amount in Plan—the amount in plan is the amount that has been provided for in the current year's budget. Therefore, to determine this amount, you must refer to the current year capital (PPE) budget.

4) Previous approvals—previous approvals will be those amounts that have been approved previous to the current request whlch pertains to the same capital project.

5) Total capital for Project—this amount is the total amount of capital required to complete the entire project including capital already spent. This figure will be the number you are required to use in your justification of capital (i.e., to calculate the IRR, Payback and NPV of the capital project).

6) IRR—Internal rate of retum is the required rate of return calculation for submission. It is derived by setting the Net Present Value of future cash flows equal to 0 and interpolating the rate. Capital Accounting will provide you with a lotus-based program that will generate both the net present value of cash flows and the IRR of the investment in capital. If you have any questions regarding this calculation, please contact Capital Accounting for assistance in order to minimize the chances of having CARs retumed due to improper information being submitted.

7) Payback—it is the length of time required to recoup the initial investment. This calculation, too, is performed for you using the software that will be provided to you.

8) Supplementary Requests—supplementary requests for capital are to be applied for at the time when it is apparent that you will exceed your original estimate of capital requirements. The amount to be used in your justification of supplementary capital will be the "total" capital required for the entire project and not just the incremental supplementary capital required. This implies that these requests will require revised calculations for IRR, NPV and Payback on the total amount. In addition, no spending or commitments will be allowed on a project that will put it into an overrun position beyond the acceptable limits until an approved supplementary request has been received.

9) Payment Profile—this simply indicates in what year you plan to spend the authorized dollars.

10) Purpose—you must indicate what the purpose of the expenditure is to be; this will reflect what you have indicated in your justification that is to be included in this package. Note that only "one" purpose is to be selected.

Exhibit 4 (continued)

11) Description—the description here is meant to be a synopsis of your justification; describe in precise detail what you are applying for.

12) Signatures—the signatures to be obtained include the following:
    - Preparer/Initiator
    - Engineering Dep't (or Master Mech./Chief Electrn)
    - Purchasing
    - Department Head
    - Manager
    - Capital Accountant

13) Environmental Considerations—if project is expected to be environmentally sensitive in any way, contact the Environmental group prior to submission of the CAR. An environmental assessment form may be required to be completed.

14) Energy Management Considerations—consultation should be made with the appropriate services group to assess energy impact if applicable.

Please remember to include an appropriate justification along with the CAR. It is imperative that all CARs be submitted to capital accounting before they are presented to the VP/General Manager for approval in order that they not be lost in the system.

Exhibit 5

CAPITAL APPROPRIATION ENVIRONMENTAL CHECK LIST

If any of the following questions are answered as "YES " or "UNSURE," then the capital appropriation request must be reviewed by the Environmental Services Department for issuance of an application to obtain the necessary government approvals prior to construction. Please note that three to nine months are required to obtain an approval, and that construction and operation cannot commence prior to receiving the approval.

		Yes	No	Unsure
1.	Will a waste management system, waste disposal site, transfer site, sewage system or storage area be used, operated, established, altered, enlarged or extended?			
2.	Will any liquid, gas or solid be deposited, added to, stored or discharged to the natural environment?			
3.	Will any plant, structure, equipment, apparatus or mechanism be constructed, altered, extended or replaced which may discharge a contaminant (liquid, solid or gas)?			
4.	Will the process or rate of production be altered which would result in an altered rate or manner of emission?			
5.	Will there be any changes pertaining to storage location, storage duration, hauling, collecting or transferring of materials or wastes?			
6.	Will there be any utilization or removal of natural resources (water, gravel, timber)?			
7.	Does the fuel burning equipment (natural gas or No. 2 oil) produce more than 1.5 million B.T.U.s per hour?			
8.	Will the emission cause discomfort to persons, loss of enjoyment of normal use of property, damage to property or interfere with normal conduct of business?			
9.	Will there be heat, sound, vibrations, radiations or visible emissions produced? (vehicles with approved air emissions standards are exempt)			

MINNOVA INC.— LAC SHORTT MINE

Rhonda English and Claude Lanfranconi*

In early June 1988, John Carrington, Senior Vice President at Minnova Inc., was preparing a presentation for the Minnova Board of Directors. He had just received, from the Lac Shortt Mine manager, the preliminary data necessary for him to decide whether to recommend an extension of the Lac Shortt gold mine from its present 500 metre depth to 830 metres. With this information John wanted to determine if the estimated $19.425 million investment met the company's proposed rate of return and, at the same time, consider any other business factors relevant to the decision.

THE MINING INDUSTRY

Mining was a highly capital-intensive business with a cost structure made up mainly of fixed components. In establishing a mine, significant up-front exploration costs, preproduction and development expenditures, and large investments in fixed assets were necessary. Because most mines were located in fairly remote areas, preparation for production was often a long and expensive process (for example, roads to the site might have to be built, large equipment would have to be transported in, etc.). As well, hiring the necessary labour force was usually a time-consuming task.

Selected mining terminology is defined in Exhibit 1, while Appendix A briefly describes the gold mining process.

MINNOVA INC.

The history of Minnova Inc. dated back to 1928 when Ventures Limited and Falconbridge Nickel were established. These two companies conducted mine exploration and development around the world through an organization of associated companies. The merger of Opemiska Copper Mines (Quebec) and Lake Dufault Mines in 1971 created Falconbridge Copper which later became Corporation Falconbridge Copper (CFC). In August 1986, Kerr Addison Mines Limited, which was controlled by Noranda Mines, acquired just over 50% interest in CFC and changed the name to Minnova Inc.

Minnova is a natural resource company involved in the exploration, development, and mining of copper, zinc, gold, and silver. Exhibit 2 highlights Minnova's financial position for fiscal 1987 and the first three months of 1988. Although the company reported a positive net income for financial purposes, accumulated writeoffs in the form of CCA provisions and deferred exploration expenditures resulted in Minnova not being taxable currently, nor was it expected to be in the near future. In 1988, the company had a statutory tax rate of 47%.

While a mine was producing, Minnova would conduct exploration within a large radius around the site. The objective was to find another ore body which could be brought on stream by the time the original was exhausted. If a nearby ore deposit was discovered, costs could be greatly reduced since existing mine facilities and labour could then be utilized. As a result of this strategy, much time and money were dedicated to ongoing exploration and, as long as a mine was producing, the search would continue. Maximizing returns from mining and processing, and locating new ore deposits to replace exhausted ones, were essential factors to the continued profitability of a mining company.

THE LAC SHORTT MINE

Located in Gand township, Quebec, the Lac Shortt Mine cost roughly $51 million, including exploration, to bring into production. It began operations in December 1984. Ore reserves between the surface and the 500 metre level, including a 15% dilution factor, were estimated at 2,239,596 tonnes with a head grade of 5.30 grams of gold per metric tonne. Annual production capacity was 400,000 tonnes per year, resulting in a mine life of about 5.6 years. By June 1, 1988, 1,338,198 tonnes of ore at 4.99 grams per tonne had been mined, producing 198,773 ounces of gold. Exhibit 3 summarizes historical production data at Lac Shortt.

To extend the life of the mine and replace the depleted ore, exploration of the area surrounding the mine site was ongoing. Although to date no other major ore reserve deposits had been located, important showings had been found and there remained significant opportunity for discovery in the unexplored areas.

Once mining from the 500 metre level in the original mine began in January 1988, extension of the ore limits below that level was possible and, therefore explored. A vertical longitudinal section of the mine is illustrated in Exhibit 4. As outlined, exploration drilling from a northwest crosscut was undertaken, intersecting the ore zone as deep as the 800 level. The series of numbers beneath each exploratory drill point (circles on exhibit) indicated the grams of gold per ore tonne and the width in metres of the ore body at that point. Since the drill intersections cut the ore zone diagonally, the metre figures were converted to a horizontal distance, indicated in brackets, across the ore body. Minimum requirements of 3 grams of gold per tonne with a horizontal width of at least 2 metres (3.0/(2.0)m) were being sought.

From the drilling results, it appeared that the reserves below 500 metres were open to the east and beneath, although the width of the ore body seemed to be decreasing with depth. Diluted ore reserve estimates between 500 and 800 metres were 885,000 tonnes with a head grade of 4.6 grams per metric tonne. This head grade was equivalent to 0.148 ounces of gold per tonne of ore. A 93% recovery rate from the milling process was expected.

THE PROPOSED DEVELOPMENT

Following analysis of several alternative methods of deepening the mine, conventional shaft sinking and simultaneous ramping down were decided upon, mainly due to shorter and more flexible scheduling. As indicated on Exhibit 4, the project involved:

– driving a decline from 500 metres to 830 metres

– developing the 800, 750, and 700 levels and facilities

– deepening the shaft to the 830 metre point, installing loading facilities, and developing two stations at the 800 and 700 levels

– installing a crusher on the 800 level and a conveyor to transfer ore to the shaft

– increasing the capacity of the existing tailings pond and developing an appropriate effluent treatment system.

Lac Shortt personnel would complete the ramping and lateral development, while the shaft deepening was to be subcontracted out to the lowest tender.

The $19.425 million investment consisted of preproduction costs and fixed asset costs. The former, amounting to $14,467,000, were composed primarily of shaft deepening, ramping, and developing the underground levels/facilities. For tax purposes, these capital expenditures fell into CCA Class 12 which had a 100% CCA rate. The fixed assets included both surface ($2,250,000) and underground ($2,708,000) equipment, all of which could be written off under CCA class 41 at 25% per year. Exhibit 5 details the breakdown of expenditures between the two classes for 1988, 1989, and 1990, at which time the extension would be complete.

Mining would begin in 1990 with expected production that year of 330,000 tonnes of ore. Production of 360,000 and 195,000 tonnes was forecast for 1991 and 1992, respectively, at which time the estimated reserves would be exhausted.

The market price of gold was expected to average $450 U.S. per ounce with an exchange rate of $1 U.S. equal to $1.22 Canadian. Historical gold prices and exchange rates are documented in Exhibit 6. Operating costs were calculated on a per tonne of ore mined basis and were expected to decrease as follows, over the three years of production:

1990 – $50.05 / tonne

1991 – $48.05 / tonne

1992 – $40.74 / tonne.

CONCLUSION

Minnova Inc. used a range of hurdle rates in assessing investment proposals. These rates were set at 12% for no risk projects (e.g., equipment replacements), 15% for marginal risk projects, and 20% for highly risky investments. John felt the Lac Shortt proposal fell into the 15% category. Given the uncertainty involved in a number of the factors used in the analysis, John wanted to ensure that he would be prepared to answer any questions the Board might have regarding the sensitivity of the projected return. If the Board rejected the investment proposal, John would be faced with deciding whether to keep the Lac Shortt mine open to continue further exploration projects in the area.

Exhibit 1

GLOSSARY OF MINING TERMS

Grades
Ore Reserve Grade — the estimated amount of gold, in grams per tonne of ore, derived from calculations based on geological interpretation and drill intersection results.

Estimated Head Grade — the estimated amount of gold, in grams per tonne of ore, which will enter the mill for processing. Generally, this will be lower than the ore reserve grade due to dilution and other mining losses.

Head Grade — the actual amount of gold in grams per tonne of ore which enters the mill, based on detailed sampling of the mill feed.

Dilution — refers to the reduction in the ore reserve grade caused by waste or low grade ore outside the reserve being incorporated into the actual mining method and therefore, included in processing.

Recover—the percentage of gold actually retrieved from processing the ore.
    —as described in Appendix A, the gold must be on the surface of the crushed particle to be retrievable.
Tailings Pond — repository for all liquid and solid wastes from the milling process.

Mill — where the ore is ground to a slurry and mixed with cyanide to dissolve the gold. Subsequently, the gold is recovered from the cyanide solution as bullion.

Exhibit 2

FINANCIAL HIGHLIGHTS
(000)

	1987	3 months ending March 31, 1988
Net Sales	$ 55,030	$ 14,729
Cost of Production	37,349	10,626
Net Income	3,257	415
Earnings Per Share	$0.24	$0.03
Current Assets	$ 107,754	$ 82,041
Net Plant and Equipment	13,085	42,935
Net Preproduction and Dev't Costs	6,477	42,826
Properties Under Dev't	98,674	63,080
Current Liabilities	16,227	14,330
Retained Earnings	116,958	115,068

Exhibit 3

LAC SHORTT HISTORICAL PRODUCTION DATA

	1984*	1985	1986	1987	1988**
Tonnes milled	61431	315565	399647	395747	165808
Grade (g/t)	4.03	5.62	5.32	4.53	4.48
Recovery (%)	90.6	90.0	93.7	93.2	93.4
Total ounces†	7215	51300	64031	53889	22338
Direct Operating Costs ($/t)	–	53.01	46.57	48.26	52.42
Operating Costs Incl. Exploration	–	53.78	49.65	53.99	57.08

  * Pre-production
** To June 1, 1988
† Total ounces = (tonnes milled x grade x recovery) ÷ 31.1
   (difference in actual ounces and formula result is due to rounding)

Exhibit 4

VERTICAL MINE SECTION VIEW

Minnova Inc. – Div. Lac Shortt

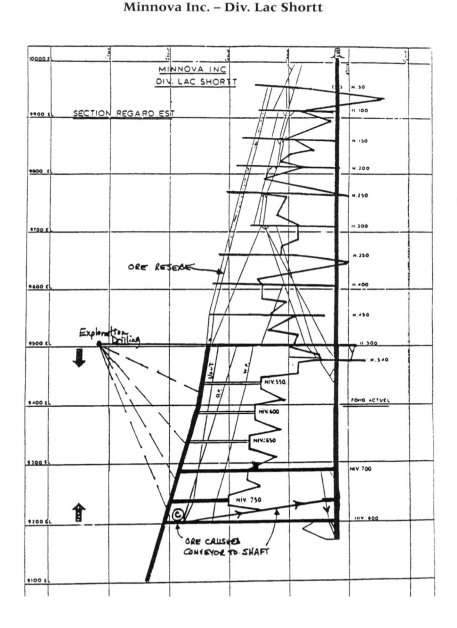

Exhibit 5

INVESTMENTS BY CCA CLASS

	1988	*1989*	*1990*	*Total*
Preproduction Costs (CCA 12)	$2,674,100	$11,599,500	$193,800	$14,467,400
Fixed Assets (CCA 41)	1,377,900	2,950,900	629,000	4,957,800
Total	$4,052,000	$14,550,400	$822,800	$19,425,200

Exhibit 6

HISTORICAL GOLD PRICES AND EXCHANGE RATES

Year	Gold US $/oz.	Exchange	Gold Cdn $/oz.
1980	$612.56	$1.1968	$733.11
1981	459.71	1.1989	551.15
1982	375.79	1.2338	463.65
1983	424.18	1.2324	522.76
1984	360.44	1.2951	466.81
1985	317.26	1.3655	433.22
1986	367.51	1.3895	510.65
1987	446.47	1.3260	592.02

Appendix A

THE MINING OF GOLD

Once an orebody has been located and the mine prepared for production, the mining and processing of the ore containing the gold can be initiated. The ore is drilled, blasted and transported to an underground crusher where it is crushed to approximately 6 inches in size. Once hoisted to the surface, it undergoes further crushing and grinding in water, to the consistency of a very fine slurry. To this slurry is added cyanide which attacks and dissolves any exposed gold on the surfaces of the ground ore particles. The recovery rate in the milling process reflects the efficiency of the dissolving capacity of the cyanide as well as the fineness of grind — the finer the grind, the greater the amount of gold that appears on the surface of an individual ore particle. The gold in the cyanide solution is separated from the ground ore slurry which goes to a tailings pond for final deposition. The cyanide/gold solution is subsequently sent through large steel cylinders which contain numerous racks of activated carbon. The gold in the solution is attracted to and deposits itself on the carbon as it passes over the racks. The final process is the burning off of the carbon, leaving the pure gold bullion.

WOLVERINE TUBE (CANADA) INC.— THE NORANDA ACQUISITION

Rhonda English, Randolph Kudar, and Richard Mimick*

Bob Worthy, Executive Vice President and Chief Financial Officer of Wolverine Tube (Canada) Inc., was reviewing the information that had been collected on Noranda Metal Industries Limited. Wolverine and Noranda were direct competitors in the Canadian seamless copper and copper alloy tubing industry. Wolverine was considering the acquisition of Noranda's brass mills, strip mill, rod mill, and warehouse facility. Since 1980, Noranda had been incurring major losses (see Exhibit 2) primarily as a result of a very high cost structure (about 25% higher than Wolverine). This fact had contributed to the decision by Noranda Mines Inc., the parent company, to sell the copper operation. As well, Noranda Mines wanted to concentrate on its primary businesses of mining. Wolverine felt there was an opportunity to achieve significant efficiency gains that would enable them to compete more effectively against imported products.

From a quantitative perspective, Bob was interested in determining whether the acquisition would meet the company's 20% after-tax (tax rate 48%) required rate of return, within a five year period. He wondered if the financing of such a deal would have any negative effects on the company's future strategies. As well, approval under the *Competition Act* would be necessary so Bob needed to put together a strong proposal for the benefits of the merger of the only two Canadian competitors in the seamless tubing industry.

THE INDUSTRY

The seamless copper, alloy, and aluminum tubing industry had 1988 sales of $2 billion in the United States and $150 million in Canada. The five major subcategories in the industry, from most sales to least were:

1. *Commodity* This is primarily copper water tube used in plumbing and refrigeration. The tube is manufactured to standard specifications. Commodity tubing has the highest sales of all the subcategories but the lowest margins.

2. *Industrial* This is a smaller tube used by commercial air conditioning and refrigeration manufacturers. It commands higher margins due to greater technical specifications required by the user.

3. *Technical Applications (Fin Tube)* This particular application of copper tube was first introduced to the market by Wolverine and is used for increased heat transfer and condensing. It is the only noticeable area in which research and development are still occurring to improve the product.

4. *Alloy Tube* This product is made of copper, zinc, and/or nickel and is primarily used in power and processing for condenser tubes.

5. *Aluminum Tube* Aluminum tube is used mainly in the cooling and automotive industries for specialized products and uses. It has the least sales of the five groups.

The Purchasing of Copper

Primary copper was refined directly from mines, whereas scrap copper consisted of used radiators, wire, and manufacturing scrap. Kidd Creek Mines Ltd., Inco Limited, and Noranda Mines were major suppliers of prime copper, while major scrap dealers included United Smelting and Refining, and London Salvage and Trading Company Ltd. Scrap copper could be purchased for about $.06 per pound cheaper than primary copper but was less readily available.

The copper tubing industry was set up such that the price of copper, for the most part, was passed through to the tubing customers. Customer orders were priced based on primary copper prices at the time of ordering, plus a handling charge ($.05 per pound). If the price of primary copper dropped, however, customers often called to request a lower price and received it; otherwise they could just cancel their original order and reorder.

Since customer invoices were based on primary copper prices at the time of order, further profits were made as a result of using lower-priced scrap copper in production. Depending on the furnaces used and the availability of scrap copper, large percentages of scrap, generally in the 40% range, could be utilized, increasing the contribution earned by the tubing manufacturers.

Copper was ordered to correspond with customer orders. Payment terms on the copper varied depending on source. Terms for primary copper averaged net 25 days, while for scrap copper, larger customers with established relationships could usually obtain terms of net 20 days. Tubing orders were generally delivered within three weeks, with wholesaler terms averaging 30 days with a 2% cash discount, net 45 days. All other customer terms were net 30 days.

Canadian Market

From the early twenties until 1942, Canada had only one seamless copper and copper alloy tubing mill (Anaconda Brass). As part of the war effort, the government built a second brass mill in Montreal in 1942, staffing it with Anaconda management. After the war, the plant was put up for bids and Noranda's lower bid was accepted over Anaconda's higher bid, in order to prevent a monopoly in the industry.

Wolverine and Western Copper Mills both began operations in 1958 in London, Ontario, and New Westminister, B.C., respectively. Severe price cutting by Anaconda resulted in heavy losses for Western Copper Mills, while Wolverine managed to earn a small profit. Western Copper Mills was eventually purchased by Noranda in 1962 with a significant tax write-off.

In 1978 Anaconda was sold and its name was changed to ArrowHead Metals Ltd. A series of labour disputes and a lengthy strike resulted in the closing of the mill in 1980. ArrowHead today operates mills producing rod, sheet, plate, strip, and architectural shapes, but no tube. The survivors in the Canadian tubing business were Noranda and Wolverine.

Both Noranda and Wolverine were primarily engaged in the manufacture, distribution, and sale of commodity and industrial copper tube products. Alloy tubing was also produced and sold but on a much smaller scale.

Principal commodity products included copper water tube, copper drainage tube, and soft copper general purpose tubing. The main commodity tube customers were the residential and commercial building industry and plumbing wholesalers. Of the total domestic production of copper and copper alloy tubing, 64% represented commodity tubing, with the remaining 36% of industrial tube.

There was no proprietary technology and little distinctive brand differentiation in the commodity tubing business. Imports in this segment of the copper tube business were estimated at 4% of Canadian domestic consumption, with the United States being the primary import competition. 1987 volumes of commodity copper tube delivered to Canadian customers by Noranda, Wolverine, and imports are outlined in Exhibit 1A.

Industrial products comprised tubing used in the manufacture of refrigeration and air conditioning equipment, hydro-electric applications, and a wide variety of other general industrial uses. Industrial tube was made to customer specifications and special requirements. The principal customers included manufacturers of fittings, air conditioning, and household appliances and utilities.

Being a specialty business, the industrial segment potentially involved the manufacture of thousands of products. Imports, coming from Japan, Germany, and the United States, accounted for 15% of total Canadian domestic consumption of industrial tubing. Exhibit 1B outlines 1987 volumes of Canadian domestic consumption of industrial tubing.

WOLVERINE TUBE, INC. & WOLVERINE TUBE (CANADA) INC.

Wolverine Tube Inc. was formed in 1916 and operated as an independent entity until 1968. Through mergers of parent corporations, Wolverine Tube Inc. became a unit of successively: Universal Oil Products (UOP), The Signal Companies Inc., Allied-Signal, and The Henley Group Inc. On May 18, 1987, Wolverine Holding Company acquired the assets of Wolverine Tube Limited in Canada and Wolverine Tube Inc. in the U.S. from the Henley Group Inc. Wolverine Holding Company (a Delaware Corporation) was jointly owned by Wolverine senior management, Morgan Stanley & Co. of New York, and Drake, Goodwin & Co. of London, Ontario. At the time of the buyout, Wolverine had three manufacturing plants, two located in the U.S. and one in Canada.

The Decatur, Alabama, plant was built in 1948 and was capable of producing all five non-ferrous tubing products. Employing over 850 salaried and hourly workers, the plant operated close to full capacity (95 million pounds) running three shifts daily.

Due to a heavy technical product mix, longer production time and high costs, Decatur was the least efficient Wolverine facility. As well, in 1986 an early retirement plan was offered at the plant and one-sixth of the workforce left, resulting in negative impacts on productivity and cost during the subsequent hiring and training period.

The Shawnee, Oklahoma, facility, built in 1973, manufactured all forms of exclusively copper tubing (plumbing, industrial, fin). Functioning as a stand-alone operation, it too was operating at full capacity (50 million pounds) employing over 300 employees.

A warehouse in Dallas, Texas, and a conversion plant in Ardmore Tennessee acted as sub-facilities to Decatur. The Ardmore plant converted tubing drawn in Decatur, to higher margin tubing and fabricated components.

The Canadian plant, located in London, Ontario, operated independently from the U.S. organization. It manufactured plumbing and industrial tubing and was recognized as a top quality producer of seamless copper tube products. Full capacity of 43 million pounds was achieved with a workforce of 285 people. The London operation supplied approximately 20% of total Wolverine sales and 40% of total earnings (before interest and tax).

NORANDA METAL INDUSTRIES LIMITED

Noranda Metal Industries Limited (NMI) was a wholly owned subsidiary of Noranda Mine Inc., producing copper and copper alloy products at three plants. The manufacturing facilities were located in Fergus, Ontario, Montreal East, Quebec, and New Westminster, British Columbia.

The Fergus operation employed about 140 people and produced copper, brass, and refractory alloy rolled products (strip) for use by original equipment manufacturers in the automotive, construction, electrical, and electronic industries, and by warehouse distributors in the resale market. Of the plant's total 1987 shipments (21,449,000 pounds), 53% were domestic and 47% were to the U.S. market. NMI's domestic competitors were ArrowHead Metals in New Toronto, Ontario, and Ratcliff's in Richmond Hill, Ontario. NMI had 23.7% share of domestic mill shipments, while imports accounted for 30.8% of Canadian consumption.

Employing approximately 310 people, the Montreal East facility produced both copper and copper alloy rod and tubes. Rod customers were primarily in the aluminum, construction, electrical, and warehouse distribution areas. Domestic customers consumed 49% of 1987 rod shipments, while 51% went to the U.S. market. ArrowHead Metals was NMI's domestic competition. NMI held a 26.6% market share of domestic consumption; however, imports dominated the rod market with a 55% share.

Copper and copper alloy tube customers were mainly in the plumbing, air conditioning, and refrigeration industries (commodity and industrial). In addition to being produced at the Montreal East facility, tubing was manufactured at the New Westminster plant (170 employees). Domestic consumption accounted for 72% of NMI sales, the U.S. 27%, and other exports consumed about 1%. Wolverine Tube Canada represented the only domestic competitor of NMI in the tubing industry. Imports for all five tubing subcategories represented 18% of the Canadian tubing market.

In addition to the three plants discussed above, NMI had a warehouse facility in Rexdale, Ontario, which housed finished inventory and the company's marketing department.

A summary of Noranda's financial history since 1980 is documented in Exhibit 2. Exhibit 3 presents Noranda's financial position at September 30, 1988.

ACQUISITION DETAILS

Wolverine Tube, for many years, had a desire to acquire the Western operations of Noranda Metals, seeing a great opportunity to make and sell water tube in Western Canada. Noranda Mines had approached Wolverine in the past about selling Noranda Metals; however, nothing materialized. When Noranda recently approached Wolverine, Wolverine decided to give the deal serious attention. Although Wolverine's original intent was to acquire only the New Westminster brass mill of Noranda Metals, Noranda insisted that the sale package include the Montreal East rod and tube mill, the Fergus strip mill, and the Rexdale warehouse.

Presently, Wolverine London was running at capacity (three shifts per day) with no extra space to place more equipment. Since their business strategy included expanding the industrial and commercial product areas where there were higher margins, to avoid disrupting the water tube business, their only option was to increase capacity. There were three alternatives reviewed by Wolverine to increase product availability — 1) build additional plant space at the London facility, 2) bring product to Canada from their U.S. plants, or 3) acquire Noranda Metals.

Since Wolverine was leasing the land and building in London, it was felt that constructing a new building would not be in their best interests. Due to the locations of their U.S. plants (Oklahoma and Alabama), bringing product up from the States also did not seem very feasible. Consequently, the Noranda acquisition became the primary consideration for Wolverine's solution to their capacity problem.

FINANCING THE ACQUISITION

The suggested price for the Noranda acquisition was $50 million. This included all fixed assets and working capital items (net accounts receivable plus inventory less accounts payable) at the New Westminster, Montreal, Fergus, and Rexdale locations. Total fixed assets had a book value of about $12 million, of which land accounted for approximately $400,000, buildings $6,950,000, and manufacturing equipment $4,650,000. The buildings had a Capital Cost Allowance rate of 4% declining balance, while for manufacturing equipment, the government had introduced a modified declining balance rate effective in 1988. The rate was as follows: 40% in 1988, 35% in 1989, 30% in 1990, and 25% in 1991 and each subsequent year thereafter (the half-year rule applied in the year of acquisition). The working capital was valued at $38 million.

Wolverine Canada was currently in a healthy financial situation. With $10 million in the bank and no outstanding term loan or revolver credit line, they enjoyed an excellent rapport with the Bank of Nova Scotia. The bank agreed to lend Wolverine all necessary money on a revolving basis at prime (10%) plus a quarter percent, secured against Wolverine London's book receivables and inventory.

Bob decided that excluding the accounts receivable from the purchase would result in less money being needed as at October 31, 1988, the potential acquisition date. Noranda receivables were running at about 60 days and $30 million, and therefore, by not buying the existing receivables, instead of Wolverine having to borrow $30 million up front, this part of the debt would be incurred gradually as the new receivables accumulated (i.e., about $15 million in November and another $15 million in December). Inventory was valued at $20 million and accounts payable at $12 million. Using their cash of $10 million, Wolverine would need to borrow $10 million on October 31, 1988, $15 million in November, and $15 million in December 1988. It was anticipated that the loan would be paid back by 1991.

Wolverine continually had offers of business opportunities presented to them; however, Bob felt that if Noranda Metals was acquired, all other potential deals would have to be disregarded. In addition to the financial implications of a large-scale acquisition, a tremendous amount of time and effort would be required to turn the Noranda operations around and consolidate the two companies.

ORGANIZATION OF MERGED OPERATIONS

Production processes of the three copper tube manufacturing plants (New Westminster, Montreal, London) would have to be reorganized to maximize production runs for common items and to eliminate extra transportation costs. As well, manufacturing procedures and production techniques used by Wolverine would have to be applied to the Noranda operations to create additional volume and cost savings. The following realignment of production was foreseen.

–   Production of all alloy products in the Montreal plant, except where delivery was to a Western Canadian or U.S. destination in which case New Westminster would be assigned.

–   Production of all industrial (original equipment manufacturer) tubing in the London plant except where low technology and point of delivery suggested otherwise.

–   Commodity items (copper water tube, refrigeration, general purpose tube) produced in all three plants, depending upon regional and export demand, and plant capacity.

–   The country would be divided into three geographical regions (Eastern, Central, Western).

–   The Eastern area (Quebec, New Brunswick, Nova Scotia, Newfoundland, P.E.I.) would be primarily serviced by the Montreal facility (approx. 30 million lbs.).

- The Central area (Ontario and Manitoba) would be serviced out of London (approx. 43 million lbs.).

- The Western area (British Columbia, Alberta, Saskatchewan) would be supplied by the New Westminster plant (approx. 13 million lbs.). Additional capacity at New Westminster would be exported to Northwestern U.S., or Manitoba if the London plant could not meet demand.

Expected cost savings from the Noranda acquisition could be broken down into three areas — 1) primary efficiency gains, 2) secondary efficiency gains, and 3) other cost savings. Within each area were a number of specific items expected to produce these savings.

1) Primary Efficiency Gains

a) Facilities—by eliminating redundant facilities, Wolverine would be able to reduce costs. The Rexdale facility would be sold in 1989 for a one-time gain of approximately $3 million, while the proceeds would give Wolverine a 10% annual return amounting to increased yearly flows, beginning in 1990, of about $350,000. As well, a Vancouver warehouse could be eliminated immediately, resulting in annual cost savings of $55,000.

b) Marketing—through consolidation of the two companies' marketing functions, Wolverine could eliminate the need for commissioned sales agents (currently used by Wolverine), and thereby save $500,000 per year in commissions. As well, an estimated $100,000 would be avoided annually, through reorganization and rationalization of travel, communications, and related expenses. These savings were expected to materialize in 1990.

c) General and Administration—savings in the areas of travel, communications, postage and mail services, and outside professional services would amount to $275,000 annually beginning in 1989.

d) Freight—savings would be achieved by manufacturing products closer to the markets in which those products were likely to be sold, and by shipping a higher percentage of full truck load shipments. Cost reductions were expected to amount to $0.015 per pound by 1989, on domestic shipments of 76 million pounds per annum.

2) Secondary Efficiency Gains

These efficiency gains were expected to result from anticipated economies of scale and scope, subsequent to rationalization of production.

a) Production Tools and Supplies—through decreased inventory levels and reduced purchases, savings would amount to $160,000 per year as of 1989.

b) Maintenance Material and Labour Costs—yearly cost reductions of $850,000 were expected by 1990 in this area.

c) Utilities—as a result of increased volume gas purchases and improved utilization of annealer furnaces, savings were estimated at $211,000 annually to be realized starting in 1989.

d) Labour and Overhead—the major saving would come from reduced shut-down times in the various operations due to longer production runs of fewer products at the plants. Annual cost reductions would amount to $343,000 by 1990.

e) Increased Volume—overall production increases of 1,784,640 pounds by 1991 would create additional gross margins. Wolverine's standard gross margin averaged $0.32 per pound, while freight, duty, marketing, and general and administration expenses would average $0.054 per additional pound produced.

3) Other Cost Savings

The 1987 production levels at Noranda's New Westminster and Montreal facilities were roughly equal to Wolverine's output from its London plant. A comparison of projected 1988 variable and period expenses between Wolverine and Noranda resulted in a variable expense variance of $5,800,000 and a period expense variance of $1,200,000. These yearly savings were based on the assumption that Wolverine could achieve a noticeable reduction of Noranda's production costs so that they would be roughly equivalent to Wolverine's costs, given similar output levels. These benefits would not be realized until 1991.

THE COMPETITION ACT

Under the *Competition Act*, a merger was defined as a direct or indirect acquisition or establishment, by one or more persons, of control over or significant interest in the whole or a part of the business of a competitor, supplier, customer, or other person. Under the Act, a merger was examined by the Director to determine if it prevented or lessened, or was likely to prevent or lessen competition substantially in a relevant market. Some of the factors considered included:

a)   effectiveness of foreign competition

b)   failing business

c)   availability of acceptable substitutes

d)   barriers to entry

e)   extent of effective competition remaining

f)   removal of a vigourous and effective competitor

g)   change and innovation in a relevant market

The Act stated that determining that a merger or proposed merger prevented or lessened competition substantially could not be made solely on the basis of market share or concentration. While these were important, they had to be considered along with the qualitative factors listed above.

The merger provisions provided an exception where the parties could establish that the actual or likely gains in efficiency would be greater than and would offset the effects of reduced competition.

Wolverine knew that receiving approval for the merger from the *Competition Act* would be a major issue. The company felt, however, that strong arguments could be made concerning both the qualitative and quantitative criteria outlined by the Act. Appendix 1 gives a description of the U.S. market, describes how the Canadian and U.S. markets for copper and copper alloy tubing have interacted in the past, and outlines future implications for the North American market.

Wolverine also suspected that some of the larger customers would have concern regarding available alternate sources of supply, and therefore wanted to address this issue in their presentation to the *Competition Act*.

CONCLUSION

As Bob contemplated his task at hand, he recognized a need to assess not only the direct quantitative aspects of the acquisition, but also the implications of the resultant financial structure of Wolverine, and the overall strategic implications for Wolverine. Furthermore, he would have to be prepared for both the favourable and unfavourable factors that would influence acceptance or rejection of the deal by the *Competition Act*. Bob felt that as long as the quantitative analysis looked positive, Wolverine would have a strong incentive for putting together a proposal for the *Competition Act*.

Exhibit 1A

COMMODITY COPPER TUBE VOLUMES

Supplier	Pounds Supplied	% of Total
Noranda	32.1 million	49.7%
Wolverine	30.0 million	46.4%
Imports	2.5 million	3.9%

Note: During this period Wolverine exported 953,000 pounds of commodity copper tube, mostly to Europe.

Exhibit 1B

INDUSTRIAL TUBE VOLUMES

Supplier	Pounds Supplied	% of Total
Wolverine	13.4 million	58%
Noranda	6.1 million	27%
Imports	3.5 million	15%

Note: Export sales were 3 million pounds by Wolverine in 1987. Export markets served were Europe, U.S., and Israel.

Exhibit 2

NORANDA METAL INDUSTRIES — FINANCIAL HISTORY

	1986	1985	1984	1983	1982
Sales (million $)	110.3	118.6	120.7	103.2	87.4
Sales (million lbs.)	75.0	80.0	83.1	69.0	60.9
Net Earnings (000s)	$(3,278)	$(344)	$179	$(1,800)	$(3,261)
Ratios & Statistics					
Return on Net Operating Capital %	-ve	9.0	5.4	1.8	-ve
Working Capital Ratio	2.16	2.50	1.87	1.90	1.58
Avg Collection Period	56 days	53 days	52 days	57 days	58 days
Inventory Turnover	4.62	4.55	4.72	4.68	3.79
Employee Statistics					
Hourly	499	548	530	536	467
Salaried	181	180	194	202	201
Avg Hourly Wages (excl. overtime)	$12.75	$12.78	$12.23	$11.99	$11.39
Property, Plant, Equip. (000s)					
Cost	$56,556	$54,585	$54,550	$53,979	$54,139
Net Book Value	$11,993	$11,379	$12,559	$14,211	$16,401

Exhibit 3

NORANDA FINANCIAL POSITION — September 30, 1988
($000's)

ASSETS

Current	
Cash and Short Term Pool	$82
Accts Receivable & Inc. Tax Recoverable	26,682
Inventories	18,131
Prepaid & Deferred	476
Total Current	$45,371
Fixed	
Property, Plant, Equipment	$58,184
Accumulated Depreciation	46,212
Total Fixed	$11,972
TOTAL ASSETS	$57,343

LIABILITIES & SHAREHOLDERS' EQUITY

Current	
Accts Payable & Accrued Expenses	$24,012
Income Tax Payable	–
Total Current	$24,012
Deferred Taxes	342
Shareholders' Equity	
Common Shares	$32,608
Contributed Surplus	6,000
Retained Earnings	(5,619)
Total Shareholders' Equity	$32,989
TOTAL LIABILITIES & EQUITY	$57,343

Appendix 1

THE U.S. MARKET

The industry consolidation which took place in Canada after the mid-seventies was accompanied by a consolidation in the United States. A decrease in the North American copper tubing market of $100 million, caused by the introduction of plastics as replacements for copper tubing, resulted in the number of major U.S. mills going from 20 in the mid-seventies to six in 1986. These consolidations, combined with increasing continentalization of the industry, prompted copper tubing manufacturers to increase capacity and greatly improve efficiency.

Following is some detail on the major U.S. copper tubing manufacturers.

1. *Cerro Metal Products Ltd.* – Based in East St. Louis, Illinois, Cerro had the largest capacity of all the American producers with an estimated volume of 180 million pounds per year. The focus of their production was on the high volume, low-quality commodity tubing segment. By using higher concentrations of scrap, Cerro had been able to produce tubing for the plumbing and refrigeration sectors of the industry while maintaining high margins. Cerro was the first of the major American producers to set up sales agents in Canada.

2. *Halstead Industries Inc.* – Halstead was structured very similar to Cerro. They had also focused on the huge commodity segment of the tubing industry. With an estimated capacity of 160 million pounds per year, Halstead had managed to secure 31.9% of the North American commodity market. This focus allowed them to produce volumes in excess of theoretical capacity (approximately 175 million pounds per year) and improve their return. It was rumoured that Halstead might purchase Reading Tube Corp., which would increase their capacity by an estimated 75 million pounds. Reading was a high-cost producer (one of the six major mills) that had recently filed for Chapter 11 (protection from creditors to avoid bankruptcy).

3. *Wolverine Tube Inc.* – Wolverine was a leading manufacturer of all forms of seamless copper, alloy, and aluminum tubing. Operations in the U.S. consisted of two major plants. Capacity at the two facilities was approximately 145 million pounds per year. Wolverine held the leading market position in the U.S. in technical (58%), alloy (58%), and industrial tubing (20%).

4. Mueller Brass Co. - Mueller manufactured only commodity tubing. With an estimated production capacity of 120 million pounds per year, they were currently operating with excess capacity. Because of their less than strategic location in the Northeast, they had had to pay higher freight costs and thus had only been able to capture 10.9% of the commodity market.

5. *American Brass Co.* – American Brass was the only large tube manufacturer to produce a welded tube. Since this process was less costly, they had had a cost advantage in the lower margin industrial (commercial) tubing segment. It was

Appendix 1 (continued)

believed that American Brass would be moving to higher quality products in the future. Their estimated capacity was 30 million pounds per year.

THE NORTH AMERICAN MARKET

Traditionally, the U.S. and Canadian markets operated fairly independently of one another. Until recently, capacity limitations and high U.S. domestic demand levels restricted the quantities of product available for shipment out of the U.S. to Canada. As well, an import duty of 4% and a depressed Canadian dollar had, in the past, made exporting to Canada unattractive.

All these factors, however, were changing in favour of the Americans. Under Free Trade, the 4% tariff would gradually be reduced to nil over ten years. Peak demand levels in the U.S. had slackened and a number of major U.S. copper tube manufacturers had undertaken significant capacity increases. Recent adjustments in the currency exchange rates between Canada and the United States had made U.S. imports more competitive.

It was estimated that pre-tariff U.S. copper tube manufacturers had on average about a 15% cost advantage over Canadian manufacturers. Freight and duty advantages of Canadian manufacturers (average $.11 per pound) currently neutralized the cost advantage, but the changing environment would clearly put the cost advantage in favour of the U.S. suppliers. In what was essentially a homogeneous product market, as the price position of foreign products improved, their share of the Canadian market was expected to increase.

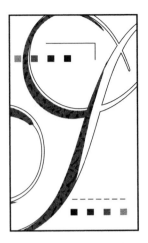

 PART **E**

MANAGEMENT CONTROL SYSTEMS

CONTEMPRA AND SOLO

Randolph Kudar

Until yesterday, Mr. Bill Price, the residential product merchandising manager for 'edmonton telephones' felt that he had a potential solution to a major problem that had arisen in the local market for residential rental units. Recently, the rental customers had begun turning in the Contempra phones that they had been renting. These 17 year old dial-in handset phones were perceived to be old fashioned. Instead, the customers were purchasing touchtone units that were currently available from a number of sources. Unless some action could be taken, the residential rental operation would likely experience a decline in revenues and profits.

Currently 'et' handled a broad product line of telephones for the rental and retail market. The units were classified into two groups — touchtone and rotary. In each group was a basic unit that represented the largest volume of units rented or sold by 'et'. There were also Contempra units in both groups. The Contempra units were positioned as the premium products in both groups.

BACKGROUND

'edmonton telephones' was the largest municipally owned independent telephone system in Canada. At this time it was ranked seventh in overall size. 'et' provided a full range of telecommunication products and services to its residential and business customers. Comprising the service networks were 23 switching centres, and associated trunking and distribution cable systems. Repair, installation, and special services were provided through three central production control centres, four primary telephone service centres, and seven Phone Exchange retail outlets located in major shopping centres and at the head office at 44 Capital Boulevard. 'edmonton telephones' also had a production control centre that controlled outside plant activities. Since 1904, 'et' had grown from 400 telephone lines to 331,698 lines and currently had a staff of 1,870 people. The General Manager of 'edmonton telephones' reported through the City Manager to City Council.

Competition in the sale of residential telephone sets has been permitted in Edmonton for over a decade. 'edmonton telephones' has been active in both the rental and retail markets.

Bill Price's Plan

Mr. Price had developed a two-phased approach toward addressing the issue. One part of the plan called for a campaign to try and encourage the customers to consider purchasing their existing Contempra units at a reduced price from 'et'. Currently there were 57,882 rental Contempra units in service.

(a) Disposing of Contempra

It was expected that not all the Contempra units would be suitable for resale to the customer. The plan called for only 50% of the units to be purchased by the rental customer on an "as is" basis at a price of $10 per unit. Of the remaining units it was thought that 20% of the units turned back in to 'edmonton telephones' could be refurbished and sold in the phone exchanges at a price of $20 per unit. The remaining 80% of the units returned could be sold for scrap to a wholesaler at a price of $1 per unit.

The refurbishing operation for the Contempra units was costed out at $8.42 per unit. This consisted of $3.75 for materials, $2.67 for supply expense, and $2.00 for overhead. The supply expense was used to distribute the costs of warehousing, purchasing, etc. that were incurred when an item was handled through the 'edmonton telephones' warehouse distribution facility. All revenues generated from the sale and disposal of Contempra units were subject to a revenue tax of 1% payable to the city government. In addition, the firm had a policy of paying a 1% commission to its agents on all revenues generated in their departments.

An analysis of the current pattern of returns of the Contempra units suggested that without a replacement product, it would take six years for all the units to be turned in. In this period the revenues associated with the Contempra units would gradually decline in the following manner.

Exhibit 1

Year	Units Turned In	Rental Revenue Earned
1	8,263	2,584,157
2	13,598	1,949,457
3	4,649	1,840,282
4	12,872	1,204,350
5	7,500	858,660
6	11,000	286,220

The program to encourage the customers to purchase the Contempra units involved an advertising campaign that was expected to cost $2,000 per year for each of the six years needed to phase the units out.

(b) Introduction of Solo

As the second part of the plan, Mr. Price had identified a replacement unit called Solo. This unit was manufactured in Canada and designed specifically for the rental market. It was a touchtone handset unit and belonged to the same family of units as the Harmony and Signature units that were currently being offered by 'et'. One of its prime features was reduced maintenance costs. Experience with the unit had indicated that the warranty returns on these units was less than 2% of volume.

The introduction of the Solo unit was expected to have a significant impact on this pattern of returns. It was thought that the Contempra units would be turned in much quicker, as per the following pattern.

Exhibit 1

Year	Units Turned In	Rental Revenue Earned
1	21,861	2,127,760
2	17,521	1,315,350
3	18,500	438,450

If the Solo unit was introduced now, the campaign was expected to cost $4,000 but would only operate for the three years needed to recover all the Contempra units still in service.

The Solo units were expected to capture the customers who turned in their Contempra units but did not want to purchase them. It was expected that the Solo units would be put into service at the rate as shown in Exhibit 3 at the end of the case.

In developing his plan, Bill Price had anticipated that the rental rates for the Solo units would increase by 15% at the end of year 2 and again at the end of year 4. The contract with the supplier stated that the units could be purchased by 'edmonton telephones' at a cost of $73.00 per unit if purchased in multiples of 24 sets per colour per order. The manufacturer recommended a specific mix of colours for the Solo sets based upon their experience with sales for the other products in the same family of handsets. There would be no discount for volume.

In addition to the purchase price of the units from the supplier, Bill Price was aware that there were supply and administrative expenses associated with all products handled by 'edmonton telephones'. The expenses associated with Solo would include the standard rates of 6.5% of the material cost for supply expense, and 7.4% of material cost for administrative expenses. The supply expense was used to distribute the costs of warehousing, purchasing, and other activities. The supply expense was allocated directly to products and included in the financial statements. The administrative expense existed for the purpose of allocating administrative costs to the products. These costs were not included in the financial statements. His plan also called for a modest advertising campaign to promote the Solo units.

The plan seemed very logical and feasible until Price met with the controller's office of 'edmonton telephones'.

CONCERN ABOUT THE PLAN

Bill Price asked the controller's office to explain what the impact of his plan for disposing of the Contempra units would be upon the financial statements for his product line. A sample of the financial report for a product line is shown in Exhibit 5. The controller's office indicated that the revenues associated with the disposal of the Contempra units would be recorded in account #998 (miscellaneous revenue). The costs associated with refurbishing the Contempra units that would be sold in the Phone Exchange retail outlets would be reported in account #283R (500 &2500 sets - repairs). The net book value for all Contempra sets disposed of would be charged to the product line in the depreciation charges account. At this time, the average net book value of the Contempra units was $13.58 each.

Bill became concerned that his plan to dispose of the Contempra units might cost 'et' a significant amount of money. To clarify his understanding, he prepared an analysis of what the impact of disposing of the units by the various methods that he had identified would be. This is shown as Exhibit 4 at the end of the case. According to his calculations, every time he sold a Contempra unit "as is" to a customer for $10.00 he would incur a cost to the company of $13.58. When he refurbished a unit and sold it for $20.00, he would incur a cost to the company of $22.00. Worst of all, when he disposed of a unit to the wholesaler for $1.00, he would be incurring a cost of $13.58.

"Maybe I should just put all the Contempra units that are returned into the warehouse and forget all about trying to dispose of them."

With respect to his plan for introducing Solo as a new product to be offered by 'edmonton telephones', the controller's office informed Bill that such a project would have to generate a return of 13% over the life of the project in order to qualify for consideration as an investment at this time.

Bill Price sat back in his office considering his problem. The Solo product seemed to be such a natural success. It had many of the features desired by the customer today (Exhibit 6). Prior to his meeting with the controller's office he thought that he had a great solution to a difficult problem. Now he wondered what he should do.

Exhibit 3

REVENUES AND COSTS FOR SOLO

	Year 1	Year 2	Year 3
Units	21,500	42,316	47,020
Revenue	$1,251,300	$2,462,791	$3,142,817
Expenses			
Capital	1,569,500	1,519,568	343,392
Revenue Tax	12,513	24,628	31,428
Commission	12,513	24,628	31,428
Supply Expense	102,017	98,772	22,320
Advertising	34,000	40,000	26,000
Contract Cost	5,000	3,000	2,000
Administration	116,143	112,448	25,411
Maintenance	42,000	42,000	25,000
TOTAL COST	$1,893,686	$1,865,044	$506,979
Profit	(642,386)	597,747	2,635,838

	Year 4	Year 5	Year 6
Units	54,200	51,300	48,800
Revenues	$3,622,728	$3,945,996	$3,753,696
Expenses			
Capital	524,140	0	0
Revenue Tax	36,277	39,460	37,537
Commission	36,277	39,460	37,537
Supply Expense	34,069	0	0
Advertising	0	0	0
Contract Cost	1,000	1,000	1,000
Administration	38,786	0	0
Maintenance	25,000	35,000	45,000
TOTAL COST	$695,449	$114,920	$121,074
Profit	2,927,279	3,831,076	3,632,622

Exhibit 4

DISPOSAL WITHOUT SOLO

UNITS	Year 1	Year 2	Year 3	Year 4	Year 5	Year 6
Refurbish	826	1,360	464	1,287	750	1,100
Wholesale	3,305	5,439	1,860	5,149	3,000	4,400
Customer	4,132	6,799	2,325	6,436	3,750	5,500
TOTAL	8,263	13,598	4,649	12,872	7,500	11,000
REVENUE						
Refurbish	16,520	27,200	9,280	25,740	15,000	22,000
Wholesale	3,305	5,439	1,860	5,149	3,000	4,400
Customer	41,320	67,990	23,250	64,360	37,500	55,000
TOTAL	61,145	100,629	34,390	95,249	55,500	81,400
EXPENSES						
Refurbish	18,172	29,920	10,208	28,314	16,500	24,200
Wholesale	44,882	73,862	25,259	69,923	40,740	59,752
Customer	56,113	92,330	31,573	87,401	50,925	74,690
Rev Tax	611	1,006	344	952	555	814
Commission	611	1,006	344	952	555	814
TOTAL	120,389	198,124	67,728	187,542	109,275	160,270
LOSS	(59,244)	(97,495)	(33,338)	(92,293)	(53,775)	(78,870)

Exhibit 4 (continued)

DISPOSAL WITH SOLO

UNITS	Year 1	Year 2	Year 3
Refurbish	2,186	1,752	1,850
Wholesale	8,744	7,008	7,400
Customer	10,931	8,761	9,250
TOTAL	21,861	17,521	18,500
REVENUE			
Refurbish	43,720	35,040	37,000
Wholesale	8,744	7,008	7,400
Customer	109,310	87,610	92,500
TOTAL	161,774	129,658	136,900
EXPENSES			
Refurbish	48,092	38,544	40,700
Wholesale	118,749	95,174	100,492
Customer	148,443	118,968	125,615
Rev Tax	1,616	1,297	1,369
Commission	1,618	1,297	1,369
TOTAL	318,520	255,280	269,545
LOSS	(156,746)	(125,622)	(132,645)

Exhibit 5

EDMONTON TELEPHONES—Product Type Financial Statement

Business Unit: L — Residence Term. Equip Product Type: LR — Single Line — Res

Period ending ••••••••••••

	Acct	Month Actual	Month Budget	YTD Actual	YTD Budget	YTD Projection	YTD BU Plans	Annual Budget	Annual Projection	Annual BU Plans
Harmony Sets – RE	203L	-2808	-4191	-16450	-38590	-16195	-38590	-51112	-21450	-51112
Harmony Sets – RE	203M			-8111		-9558			-12744	
Harmony Sets – RE	203R	-1086	-5053	-72836	-45438	074294	-45438	-60584	-99059	-60584
Harmony Sets – RE	203S	-7588	-4120	-99	-37051	-727	-37051	-49401	-963	-49401
Harmony Sets – RE	203X		-140	-1957	-1288	-1699	-1288	-1706	-2265	-1706
Signature Sets –	263L	-290		-2270						
Signature Sets –	263M			-14525						
Signature Sets –	263R	-230		-271						
Signature Sets –	263S	-2349		-4094		-13489			-17985	
Non Specific Aux	286L	-53		36						
Non Specific Aux	286R	-248		-103						
Non Specific Aux	286S	72	-1796		-16434	-5740	-16434	-21805	-7653	-21805
Non Specific Aux	286X									
Telephone Answer I	296R	-334		-4167						
Direct Cost Total:		-80608	-81798	-713692	-742697	-731671	-742697	-987564	-973802	-987564
Revenue Tax:		-7815	-7394	-75323	-85381	-86145	-85381	-121283	-120199	-121283
Contribution before Debt and Depreciation:		677594	561953	5866421	6177528	6269957	6177528	8488379	8394844	8488379
Allocated Debt:		-44056	-48805	-411795	-440053	-408654	-408654	-586354	-543976	-543976
Depreciation:		-199552	-180538	-1692741	-1623541	-1678895	-1794964	-2164721	-2238527	-2393286
Contribution:		433986	332610	3761885	4113934	4182408	3973910	5737304	5612341	5551117
Contribution/$1000 of Gross Revenue		555	450	499	482	486	465	473	467	458
Current Year Capital Expenditures:	Acct									
500 & 2500 Sets	283C	68166	24741	146185	185581	748209	185581	222135	897316	222135
Harmony Sets – RE	203C	246744	120559	1042616	893176	485135	893176	1042833	578550	1042833
Signature Sets –	263C	43055		455411						
Sold Sets – Resid	233C		208000		416000		416000	1040000		1040000
Non Specific Aux	286C	12659		102518						
Telephone Answer I	296C	43009		184557						
Total Capital Expenditure		413633	353300	1931287	1494757	1233344	1494757	2304968	1475866	2304968
Return on Investment:										
Net Investment at Beginning of Year:		5599985	5599985	5599985	5599985	5599985	5599985	5599985	5599985	5599985
Net Invest during Year:		466579	472925	732718	2414885	2534366	2414885	3366933	3069187	3666933
Total Net Investment:		6066564	6072910	6332703	8014870	8134351	8014870	9266918	8669172	9266918
Return on Investment %		46.50	35.40	68.62	61.91	64.74	59.90	61.91	64.74	59.90

Exhibit 6

Today's Featured Phone

SOLO* is a state-of-the-art electronic Dial-In-Handset Touch-Tone™** phone. Sleek and compact, it's decorator styled and comes in five high-fashion colours.

SOLO has everything you want in a rental telephone. A variety of time saving features provide quicker and more accurate dialing, as well as instant access to special numbers. A simple touch of a button gets all your Custom Calling Features and you can even adjust the volume of the Tone Alerter for your personal preference.

SOLO. The rental phone that's unique in its class.

SOLO
Today's kind of phone

SOLO. For high performance and the features you want in an elegant rental phone. Consider these:

- Dial-In-Handset makes dialing easy and a Release Button means you can disconnect without replacing the handset to its cradle

- Code Dialing allows quick and easy access to 10 most frequently called numbers

- Colour-Coded Buttons in red, blue and green for instant access to special or emergency numbers

- Last Number Redial for redialing automatically at the touch of a button

- Link button provides immediate access to Custom Calling Features

- Index Card is a mini-directory that records emergency numbers and numbers in memory

- Desk or wall-mountable for your convenience

Available in soft red, almond, blue, grey and taupe, SOLO is fully modular decorator phone.

CEDAR ELECTRONICS LIMITED

Society of Management Accountants of Canada

John Big, the president of Cedar Electronics Limited (CEL), was troubled that the recently acquired Appliance Division had been incurring large losses. CEL was a widely held Canadian corporation that had specialized in the design and manufacture of electronic devices. One particularly successful product developed was the RX-100, an electronic processor, designed to replace mechanical switching devices. The RX-100 was an instant success in the appliance industry, but within a year, competing products were rapidly replacing the RX-100. In response to this competitive pressure, CEL had acquired Domino Appliances Limited (DAL) to give CEL a captive market for the RX-100 and a base for developing new devices.

At the time DAL was acquired, John restructured CEL into three divisions: Electronics, Appliances (formerly DAL), and RD&I (Research, Development, and Inspection) — each of which was designed to be an investment centre. Division managers were free to sell externally, but were expected to supply, source, and service internally. About 12% of the Electronics Division's sales were comprised of RX-100s transferred to the Appliance Division at full cost plus 10%. The RD&I Division sold a production quality control service on contract to the other divisions at variable cost plus 10% and also contracted externally. RD&I was given a budget appropriation for researching new products, which was not included in the calculation of its ROI.

265

[handwritten margin notes: "o/h allocated as % of sales", "5%", "Earn 10% on Blk value on current + fixed assets"]

John Big's objective in decentralizing the corporate structure was to make each division operate and be evaluated as if it were an independent business. Corporate overhead was allocated to the divisions on the basis of a percentage of sales. The division managers were each allowed to make annual investments of not more than 5% of their divisional net assets on their own authority. CEL's after-tax cost of capital was estimated to be 10%. Division managers were expected to earn 10% before taxes on their investment base, calculated on the book value of their current assets plus the net book value of their divisional fixed assets.

In addressing the problem of the low ROI in the Appliance Division, John had called in Rita Smart, an external management consultant, for advice. The discussions in the meeting were as follows:

John   Thank you for coming. There are some developments in our organization which disturb me and need some attention. While our results for this past year show a profit, the Appliance Division shows a loss (Exhibit 1). Bill Jones, the Appliance Division manager, claims that the RX-100s are a major problem and that, if he could source these externally, his division operating results would be greatly improved. As it is, our appliances are over-priced and we are becoming unable to keep our sales outlet managers because they feel the performance targets of achieving a 5% profit on sales is unreasonable (Exhibit 2).

Rita   The concept behind the decentralization structure, which we helped you introduce two years ago, was that each division would operate as an investment centre and so maximize the divisional and corporate profits. Since one of your objectives in purchasing the Appliance Division was to acquire the twenty-odd appliance sales outlets, it was also decided that these outlets should be managed as profit centres.

John   Two problems have arisen here. First, the prime objective in acquiring the Appliance Division was to establish a protected market for the RX-100 and for any subsequently patented in-house developed devices. Bill Jones, the Appliance Division manager, uses every excuse to source RX-100s externally (Exhibit 3). Second, our total appliance sales are just not of sufficient volume to provide enough throughput to make the sales outlets economically viable. We may have to close some or all of them.

Rita   How would you then market the division's product?

John   That is the problem. To add to this problem, Tom Smith, the manager of the Electronics Division, has decided to make a capital investment to increase RX-100 production capacity (Exhibit 4). I may not only have to step in and block this investment, but also enforce the internal sourcing rule.

Rita   Strictly speaking, you should not involve yourself in investment centre decisions as long as the divisional ROI is on target.

John   Well, I would like your advice on these matters. Remember that my prime responsibility to the shareholders is the bottom line of the income statement.

REQUIRED

1.   Identify and analyze all the business decisions relating to:
     a) product RX-100 and
     b) the Appliance Division.

2.   Evaluate the managment control system (including transfer price issues) and make appropriate recommendations.

     Show all calculations and give complete reasoning.

Exhibit 1

CEDAR ELECTRONICS LIMITED—Summarized Operating Statements

$ '000s

	Internal RX-100 included in Electronics Division (1)	Electronics Division	Appliance Division (2)	RD&I Division	CEL Total Including Internal Sales
Sales					
External	N/A	363,000	320,900	26,578	710,478
Internal	49,500	49,500	–	25,422	74,922
Total Sales	49,500	412,500	320,900	52,000	785,400
Cost of Sales					
Material	15,000	143,477	180,600	6,860	330,937
Labour	12,500	87,068	69,370	27,110	183,548
Var OH	5,000	16,360	9,230	1,101	26,691
Var RD&I	2,200	13,982	11,440	–	25,422
Fixed OH	3,000	18,753	15,063	3,350	37,166
Total Cost	37,700	297,640	285,703	38,421	603,764
Operating Profit	11,800	132,860	35,197	13,579	181,636
Administration	825	7,501	4,760	4,500	16,761
Selling					
Variable	2,000	20,753	12,836	150	33,739
Fixed	2,000	15,002	7,506	60	22,568
Corporate Charge	2,475	20,625	16,045	2,600	39,270
Total	7,300	63,881	41,147	7,310	112,338
Divisional Profit	4,500	68,979	(5,950)	6,269	69,298
Manufacturing Variances (4)					7,074
RD&I Allocation					5,000
Income Taxes (5)					18,020
Net Income					39,204
Net Assets		350,000	110,000	55,000	530,000
ROI		19.7%	–	11.4%	7.4%

Exhibit 1 (continued)

(1) The operating results of RX-100 sales to the Appliance Division were included at Mr. Big's request.

(2) Appliance Division sales and selling expenses relate directly to the sales outlets. Cost of sales represents the manufacturing department costs. Administration and corporate over-head represent overall divisional charges.

(3) All inter-divisional sales from the Electronics Division to the Appliance Division were priced at full cost plus 10%. The transfer price of RX-100s to the Appliance Division was $9.90 per unit. Internal sales of the production quality control service from the RD&I Division were priced at variable cost plus 10%.

(4) The operating costs were all at standard cost with the annual aggregate variance expensed at year-end.

(5) The effective tax rate was abnormally low due to RD&I write-offs and loss carry-for-wards. The incremental tax rate is 40%.

Exhibit 2

CEDAR ELECTRONICS LIMITED—Appliance Division Sales Outlets
Summarized Aggregate Operating Statements
(000's)

Sales	$ 320,900
Cost of Sales (1)	314,273
	$ 6,627
Outlet Operating Costs	
Variable	12,836
Fixed	7,506
Outlet profit (loss) before	
Manager's Bonus	$ (13,715)
Manager's Bonus	0
Outlet Profit (Loss)	$ (13,715)

NOTES: (1) The Appliance Division's sales outlets sell only products transferred from the Appliance Division's manufacturing department. *Transfers are made at full manufacturing cost plus 10%.*

Exhibit 3

CEDAR ELECTRONICS DIVISION—Memo from Appliance Division General Manager to President

FROM: Bill Jones
TO: John Big
DATE: January 4, 19xx
SUBJECT: Explanation of External Sourcing of RX-100s

During 19xx, approximately *23% of our annual RX-100 requirements were sourced externally.* The reasons for external sourcing were as follows:

1. *Insufficient* internal production *capacity* to fulfil all our needs.

2. *Inability* of the Electronics Division *to service rush orders on time.*

3. Avoidance of *undue delays* arising from *quality control problems* with internally sourced RX-100s.

   It should also be pointed out that equivalent products can be sourced externally at *considerably lower cost.*

	Source	
	Electronics Division	Externally on the Market
Cost per unit – RX-100 Equivalent	$ 9.90	$9.00

   If I could source all my division's requirements of RX-100s externally, we could eliminate most of our losses.

Bill Jones

Exhibit 3 (continued)

CEDAR ELECTRONICS DIVISION—Memo from Electronic Division Manager to President

FROM:	Tom Smith
TO:	John Big
DATE:	January 8, 19xx
SUBJECT:	Capital Investment

Currently our department has an annual RX-100 production capacity of 5,500,000 units which represents only about 85% of the Appliance Division's annual requirements of RX-100. Because Bill Jones claims that we cannot service his orders on time, he has sourced RX-100s externally. This results in my department having a 500,000 unit surplus of RX-100s which were sold *on the external market at a price of $9.00.*

In order to solve the problem of undercapacity and late delivery, I have decided to purchase a new, specially designed machine which will be able to produce *1,500,000 units of RX-100s, expanding our total capacity to 7,000,000 units.* Units produced by the new machine will not require the quality control services of the RD&I Division. We will be able to fill all of the Appliance Division's requirements on a timely basis and still sell 500,000 units to external customers each year.

The ROI resulting from this $15,000,000 investment will be 19.7% as calculated below:

Unit transfer price		$ 9.90
Unit Production Cost		
Direct Materials	$ 3.00	
Direct Labour	2.50	
Direct Overhead	1.00	
Fixed Factory Overhead *	1.43	7.93
Profit per Unit		$ 1.97

*$15,000,000 / (1,500,000 x 7 years) = $1.43
  Additional Profit = 1,500,000 x $1.97 = $2,955,000
  ROI = $ 2,955,000 / $ 15,000,000 = 19.7%

The new machine should last about 7 years, by which time the RX-100 will be obsolete. (Note: The machine will be subject to a special capital cost allowance treatment, because it can be put into the class 29 category with an allowable CCA rate of 50%.)

ED TEL—NORSTAR KEY SYSTEMS

Randolph Kudar*

In September, Sue Smith and Joel Dean, the ED TEL product managers responsible for selling Norstar key systems to different market segments, decided to meet together to address a common problem. During the summer months, the reported contribution per $1,000 of revenue had fluctuated widely, but in opposite directions for both segments of the market. In July, the reported contribution of the medium segment of the market had been very high; whereas in August, the reported contribution for the small segment had been very high. The marketing manager for key systems had asked both product managers for an explanation of this phenomenon.

BACKGROUND

ED TEL was Canada's largest municipally owned and independent telephone system. Incorporated as the Edmonton District Telephone Company in 1893, the telephone system served nearly 300 Edmontonians and 100 district residents through four exchanges when the City of Edmonton assumed ownership in 1905. At the end of the 1980s ED TEL employed 1,889 permanent employees and serviced 351,000 access lines. Its annual revenue exceeded $245 million, net income was more than $20 million, and total assets amounted to over $440 million.

The network currently operated through 12 switching centres and 10 remote switches, with digital service available to customers throughout 65% of the service area. Fully 75% of the system's interoffice traffic was carried by optical fibre. Repair, installation, and special services were provided through two central production control centres, four primary telephone service centres, six Phone Exchange retail outlets, and the Business Communication Centre.

As a leader in the telecommunications industry, ED TEL had achieved many firsts: the first in Western Canada to introduce touchtone service (1967); the first to introduce the 911 "help" number (1969); the first to operate and install a computerized order system (1973); the first in Canada to introduce a computerized directory assistance system (1977); the first in Western Canada to introduce the CALRS 611 repair system (1979); the first to introduce a fully electronic PBX system integrating radio and telephone communications for police and fire operations (1980); and the first in Alberta to utilize optical fibre facilities for transmission of commercial broadcast video signals (1987). In continuing with these achievements, another first for ED TEL was the Talking Yellow Pages. In March 1989, the Talking Yellow Pages directory crew initiated the first telecommunications audio production house in Canada. The technicians created and produced all talking advertisements on the system and coordinated the production of the updates for "Direct Connect", featuring sports, weather, entertainment, lotteries, culture, horoscopes, financial news, and soap operas.

ED TEL's mission was to understand and fulfil the customers' communications and information needs in a superior and profitable manner. As the result of a customer survey, ED TEL was developing a new corporate campaign and a marketing plan focused on preserving the customer base through excellent customer service. ED TEL was promoting itself as a "single source" supplier, supplying the terminal equipment, network, and data services required to meet customer needs as well as additional "value added" services. The concept of "one stop shopping" was introduced for business customers, allowing them the convenience of calling one number to receive information on billing enquiries for long distance, cellular, and regular service. Catering to the retail customers, the Phone Exchanges had become more customer oriented with video demonstrations on telecommunications products, and wall displays featuring the latest products and services.

The most significant organizational event of the past year had been the decision to establish ED TEL as a subcorporation of the City of Edmonton. Previously, ED TEL had been owned and operated by the City of Edmonton, with the general manager of ED TEL reporting through the City Manager to City Council. Under the new structure, ED TEL operated under a Board of Directors with City Council retaining ultimate control as owner and regulator. The Board replaced City Council as the policy setting body. The General Manager of ED TEL became the President and Chief Executive Officer representing ED TEL on the board. He and 10 other prominent members of Edmonton's business community were entrusted with guiding ED TEL in its future operations. An organization chart for ED TEL is presented in Exhibit 1.

BUSINESS TELEPHONE SYSTEMS

Key Systems

Business telephone systems had undergone tremendous changes during the previous 10 to 15 years. One of the major areas of development had focused on the needs of businesses ranging from small firms to large corporations which used multiple sets. Key systems had initially been developed for small business applications. Since their primary benefit involved simplicity of operations, they were very user friendly. The basic features available on the system were usually operated by the push of one or two buttons, also known as keys, on the telephone set. These key systems were generally configured so that most or all of the lines (telephone numbers) appeared on each set. Thus each set had a series of buttons, each of which corresponded to a specific line. Because most key systems did not have a central answering position, the individual sets had to be relatively sophisticated. Gradually, key systems became capable of reaching larger system size.

Private Automatic Branch Exchange Systems

Private automatic branch exchange systems (PABX), which were more sophisticated than key systems in terms of features and benefits, were used mainly in large businesses. These systems were more complex in their operations. For example, features were accessed by dialling codes. Calls coming into the system were handled by a central answering position and a number was pressed to make an outgoing call ("dial 9..."). A primary advantage of the PABX systems was that they made use of inexpensive telephone sets for the majority of the end users.

Hybrid Systems

Hybrids, and more recently digital hybrids, had been developed to fill the gap between key systems and PABXs. This new type of system provided the ease of use associated with the key system as well as a full complement of features previously available only on PABX systems. Most hybrid systems could be set up to operate as a key system or as a PABX, or even as a combination of both. However, the hybrid was usually more effective when set up to resemble one of the basic configurations. This versatility made the hybrid systems applicable to a very wide range of users.

NORSTAR DIGITAL KEY SYSTEMS

Norstar Digital Key Systems (DKTS), although referred to as a key system, was, in fact, a digital hybrid. The reference to key gives a good indication of where its strengths as a product lay. Norstar was designed and manufactured by Northern Telecom Canada Ltd. The system stressed simplicity of operations. Each telephone set was equipped with a liquid crystal display (LCD) which provided the user with instant feedback on call status (both incoming and outgoing) and ease of feature access. Superior call handling was accomplished through features such as automatic hold, call forward, distinctive ringing, and handsfree. Some additional standard features included automatic set relocation, flexible call restrictions, night service, and adjustable volume control for the handset and ringer. Norstar was flexible enough to allow virtually any combination of line appearances and features at each set location, through the programming process.

The system was substantially protected from obsolescence. As new features and enhancements were made, existing Norstar customers could upgrade their systems with new software cartridges as opposed to a whole new system. Increased system size was accomplished through the addition of trunks (lines) and station (set) modules.

With the popularity of voice mail systems on the rise, Northern Telecom had developed one for the Norstar called Startalk. It was capable of providing voice messaging and automated attendant functions. Much like the Norstar system itself, upgrades to Startalk were accomplished through software.

Finally, Norstar was designed to use applications software: a series of software-based packages that allowed a customer's personal computer (PC) to interact with the Norstar system through a personal computer interface card. Several of these packages were:

- Dial-By-Name, a directory located in the customer's PC that can be accessed by the Norstar system.

- Call Accounting and Call Detail Recording, that enabled the customer to track call activity on the system, provide cost data, and generate a variety of reports;

- Hourglass, that allowed the Norstar user to track and allocate billable time in a convenient, accurate manner; and

- Professional Organizer, that provided a comprehensive time management system.

The Norstar DKTS, developed by Northern Telecom, was made in Calgary, Alberta. It had become a very successful product for several reasons. One was the unique design features and the flexibility of the product. Another was the fact that the product was the result of an excellent response to the results of market research in the needs of the customer. A third reason was the cost efficiency of the plant which incorporated some of the latest approaches to the use of robotic manufacturing and assembly. Approximately 75% of the units produced were exported to countries around the world.

NORSTAR BUSINESS SEGMENTS

Norstar Compact Digital Key System

The Norstar key system which had been first developed for the low end of the market was aimed at very small firms. It could handle a maximum of six lines and sixteen stations. The system, called Norstar Compact, was self-contained and supported a full complement of integrated features. All systems were identical and unalterable. Once the customer went beyond the set capabilities of this system, it was necessary to remove the system and replace it with a completely different system. For many small customers, the design of the Compact system was exactly what they needed. ED TEL commanded 80 to 85% of the small key system market in Edmonton.

Norstar Modular Key Systems

The modular Norstar had been developed to meet the needs of a wider market than the low or small end. Many medium sized-customers were attracted to the Norstar system. These systems used the same equipment as the Compact systems, but they were designed to take advantage of all the versatility and integration intended by the manufacturer. The components of the system were unique to each customer, permitting specific tailoring to each customer's needs. This flexibility allowed a wider range of customers because the system provided variable capacity. The system could be altered at any time without complete removal. Since this was a different segment of the market, ED TEL created a second product manager position to handle the Norstar Modular.

NEW PRODUCT REPORTS

During the previous three years, the Business Development Department at ED TEL had undertaken a project to promote the understanding and use of contribution analysis among the marketing personnel. The newly formatted reports were the latest step in this project. The design of the statements had involved input from marketing, finance, and systems. The new reports were structured so that a parallel reporting format extended from the individual product level right up to the aggregation of all products in Business Systems.

Product Contribution Statement

One of the reports, at the product level, was called the Product Contribution Statement (see Exhibits 2 to 5). This report included all revenues and expenses of the individual product classified in a manner similar to an income statement. However, the report was different from the previous type of financial statements used, in two distinct ways. The first was the manner in which cost of goods sold was expressed. In this new format, only the accounts for stock issues and returns, and equipment in place, were included in the cost of goods sold. Previously, several different expense accounts had been included as part of this calculation. Now, these additional expense accounts were classified as part of the Other Product Costs in the new report.

The second major difference was the manner in which the year to date information was presented and analyzed. In the new format, the actual totals in the year to date column were expressed in both dollars and as a percentage of the gross revenues. As well, the actual total in each specific account was compared to both the corresponding budget and projection figure. The variance for each specific account was expressed both in dollars and as a percentage of the budget or projection figure. Previously, the actual total in the year to date accounts had only been compared to the budget figure, and the variance expressed only in dollars. The projection figures represented subsequent adjustments to the budget in response to new information about the product and market conditions.

Product Contribution Statement by Revenue Stream

The second specific product report was the Product Contribution Statement by Revenue Stream (see Exhibits 6 and 7). This was a totally new report, unlike anything that had been used previously. It was designed to facilitate the analysis of the product by the product marketing manager. The report classified all the revenue and expense accounts for the product into one of four revenue streams — direct sales, rentals, installation, and maintenance. In this report the product manager could relate changes in specific expense accounts to the relevant revenue account. As well, the manager could see and trace the manner in which the financial performance of the product was generated.

ACCOUNTING AND INFORMATION SYSTEM

Identification Codes

Like many telecommunications firms, ED TEL sold, serviced, rented, and repaired a wide range of product items. In many cases, such as for Norstar key systems, these product items were common to several products, product types, and product lines. To handle this diversity, ED TEL used Universal Service Order Codes (USOC) to specify the individual items of equipment instead of lengthy descriptions. In most cases there was a one to one relationship between the USOC and inventory stock codes. Since the business side of ED TEL was organized on the basis of products, product types, and product lines, it was necessary to link the specific items of equipment with this structure through Class of Service Codes (COS). This code specified the particular product for which the individual item had been used. As a final step, it was necessary to relate the kind of activity performed on the product with the revenue and cost system through a third mechanism called the Revenue Account Code (RAC). This code linked the revenue and cost elements for products for billing purposes through the Business Order Automation system (BOA) and for internal reporting. In the case of labour activities, there was a Labour Account Code (LAC) which, when combined with the COS, allowed the labour charges to be assigned to the specific product and, hence, billed to the right customer and reported for the right product, product type, or product line.

The information process commenced with the generation of a service order, often from a sales representative. Through consultation with the customer, the sales representative drew up a service order specifying the type of system that the customer desired and the equipment needed. In the service order, the USOC for the specific product items was listed. As well, the service order specified the COS so that the RAC could identify how the billing and reporting information should be assigned.

On occasion, a customer might trade in some equipment or system as part of the order for the new system. In this case, it was necessary for the accounting system to track the value of the trade-in for the product that was newly acquired, and to assign the individual product items back to their respective USOCs.

Stages in the Service Order

Once the service order had been initiated, it was forwarded to the warehouse operations where the individual product items were kept. There, the stock personnel would have to translate the USOC into inventory codes. The individual product items could be issued from either new or refurbished stock. Refurbished stock were those items that had been rebuilt, or repaired after previous use. Generally, the individual product items were drawn in bulk on the basis of inventory codes rather than on the basis of service orders. As such, all the needed items of one type of code for the next day were drawn at the same time. After having issued the individual items, the stock personnel were responsible for indicating to which product account the individual items should be assigned. To do this, the personnel would consult a large file that specified all the product account codes.

The individual items were issued to the field service personnel who took the items and a copy of the service order, and went to the customer's site. There the items were installed according to the service order instructions. Then field service personnel completed the service order indicating (through a LAC) the amount of labour that had been required. At the same time, the specific COS was indicated.

When maintenance needed to be performed on a system, the field service personnel often had to draw a selection of product items from stores as possible replacements at the site. Since the field service representative would not know exactly what was needed until the system had been examined, several different items would likely be drawn from stores immediately. If the items were returned to stores without being used, they were credited to the specific product account through the returned stores accounts. The stock personnel had to determine whether the returned stores were new or refurbished equipment.

NORSTAR PERFORMANCE

The financial performance of both products had been very erratic over the summer months (see Exhibits 2 through 5). As the summer passed, the problem did not appear to resolve itself. The marketing manager had asked for an explanation of the results at the end of July and now there was a need to make a further explanation at the end of August because of the significant changes in the performance of both products. The cumulative results to date indicated that the Compact product was performing relatively close to budget and slightly better than projection. However, the Modular product was significantly below budget and projection (see Exhibits 6 and 7). This was the first time that either product manager had received the newly formatted reports. The results for the two summer months had been generated in the new format to assist the managers in their investigation.

Exhibit 1

ORGANIZATION STRUCTURE

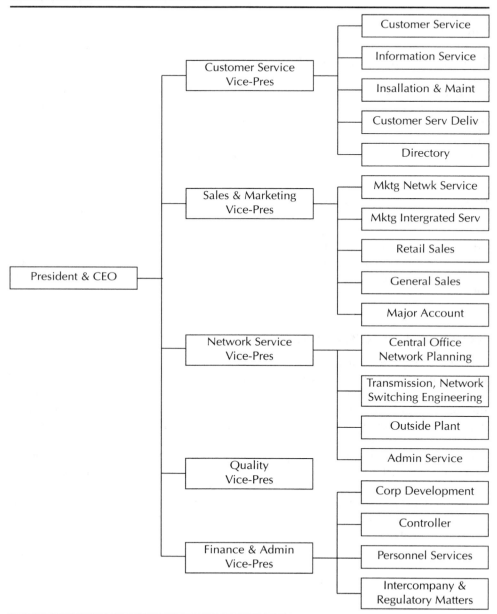

Exhibit 2

ED TEL NORSTAR KEY SYSTEMS—July Contribution for Compact DKS

Product Contribution Statement - Meridian Norstar Compact DKS

		MONTH July			Y.T.D.								ANNUAL	
	Object	Actual	Budget	Variance	Actual	% Sale	Budget	Variance	% Var	Project	Variance	% Var	Budget	Project
REVENUE														
Direct Sale	986	41409	32904	8505	133335	20.61%	230404	-97069	-42.13%	230404	-97069	-42.13%	395000	395000
DS - Discounts	98D	-4712	-3249	-1463	-12009	-1.86%	-22749	10740	-47.21%	-22749	10740	-47.21%	-39000	-39000
Trade Ins	98T	-703		-703	-2505	-0.39%		-2505	0.00%		-2505	0.00%		
Lease Purchase	987	52346	131697	-79351	377719	58.39%	922197	-544478	-59.04%	922197	-544478	-59.04%	1581000	1581000
Monthly Rental	989	40	40		230	0.04%		230	0.00%		230	0.00%		
Revenue Adjustment	981	-4809		-4809	-6054	-0.94%		-6054	0.00%		-6054	0.00%		
Fractional Rental	98F	42		42	3	0.00%		3	0.00%		3	0.00%		
Install - MRC	985	14727	20825	-6098	89464	13.83%	145825	-56361	-38.65%	145825	-56361	-38.65%	250000	250000
Mtcs - Char Rep	98A	165	250	-85	2142	0.33%	1750	392	22.40%	1750	392	22.40%	3000	3000
Mtce Contract	98M	11100	8747	2353	64511	9.97%	61247	3264	5.33%	61247	3264	5.33%	105000	105000
Total Gross Revenue		109605	191174	-81569	646836	100.00%	1338674	-691838	-51.68%	1338674	-683512	-51.06%	2295000	2295000
COST OF GOODS SOLD (Material)														
Stock Issued-N	114	-82752	-83300	548	-316803	-48.98%	-583300	266497	-45.69%	-583300	266497	-45.69%	-1000000	-1000000
Stock Issued-R	115	-13360	-10829	-2531	-64084	-9.91%	-75829	11745	-15.49%	-75829	11745	-15.49%	-130000	-130000
Stock Return-N	124	6923	3332	3591	31725	4.90%	23332	8393	35.97%	23332	8393	35.97%	40000	40000
Stock Return-R	125	22052	417	21635	70144	10.84%	2917	67227	2304.66%	2917	67227	2304.66%	5000	5000
Equipment Place	104			0	-24	0.00%		-24	0.00%		-24	0.00%		
Total Cost of Goods Sold		-67137	-90380	23243	-279042	-43.14%	-632880	353838	-55.91%	-632880	353838	-55.91%	-1085000	-1085000
FIRST LEVEL CONTRIBUTION		42468	100794	-58326	367794	56.86%	705794	-338000	-47.89%	705794	-329674	-46.71%	1210000	1210000
OTHER PRODUCT COSTS														
Repair Shop-L	408S	-1581	-639	-942	-12152	-1.88%	-4471	-7681	171.80%	-11455	-697	6.08%	-7665	-19638
Installation-L	408L	-12609	-20143	7534	-72921	-11.27%	-141048	68127	-48.30%	-141048	68127	-48.30%	-241810	-241810
Installation-P	408X	-129	-121	-8	-1257	-0.19%	-850	-407	47.88%	-850	-407	47.88%	-1458	-1458
Maintenance-P	408J	-5100	-479	-4621	-11112	-1.72%	-3353	-7759	231.40%	-3353	-7759	231.40%	-5749	-5749
Maintenance-L	408R	-4439	-6728	2289	-24027	-3.71%	-47115	23088	-49.00%	-47115	23088	-49.00%	-80773	-80773
Norstar Applic	418L							-429			0			
Norstar Applic	418X													
Material OH	89	-8100	-5558	-2542	-17515	-2.71%	-38918	21403	-55.00%	-38918	21403	-55.00%	-66720	-66720
Engineering	86			0		0.00%		0	0.00%		0	0.00%		
Revenue Tax		-1096	-1912	816	-6468	-1.00%	-13387	6919	-51.68%	-13387	6919	-51.68%	-22950	-22950
Total Other Product Costs		-33054	-35580	2526	-145881	-22.55%	-249142	103261	-41.45%	-256126	110674	-43.21%	-427125	-439098
SECOND LEVEL CONTRIBUTION		9414	65214	-55800	221913	34.31%	456652	-234739	-51.40%	449668	-219000	-48.70%	782875	770902
ASSET RELATED COSTS														
Allocated Debt		-1583	-821	-762	-11085	-1.71%	-5747	-5338	92.88%	-11085	0	0.00%	-9852	-19004
Depreciation														
Total Asset Related Costs		-1583	-821	-762	-11085	-1.71%	-5747	-5338	92.88%	-11085	0	0.00%	-9852	-19004
CONTRIBUTION TO PRODUCT TYPE		7831	64393	-56562	210828	32.59%	450905	-240077	-53.24%	438583	-219000	-49.93%	773023	751898
Contribution/$1000 Gross Sales		71	337	N/A	326		337	N/A	N/A	328	N/A	N/A	337	328

Exhibit 3

ED TEL NORSTAR KEY SYSTEMS—August Contribution for Custom DKS

Product Contribution Statement - Meridian Norstar Compact DKS

		MONTH August					Y.T.D.						ANNUAL	
	Object	Actual	Budget	Variance	% Sale	Actual	Budget	Variance	% Var	Project	Variance	% Var	Budget	Project
REVENUE														
Direct Sale	986	48941	32904	16037	23.18%	182276	263307	-81031	-30.77%	153318	28958	18.89%	395000	230000
DS - Discounts	98D	-8154	-3249	-4905	-2.56%	-20164	-25997	5833	-22.44%	-25997	5833	-22.44%	-39000	-39000
Trade Ins	98T	-144		-144	-0.34%	-2649		-2649	0.00%		-2649	0.00%		
Lease Purchase	987	67448	131697	-64249	56.60%	445167	1053895	-608728	-57.76%	599940	-154773	-25.80%	1581000	900000
Monthly Rental	989	39		39	0.03%	268		268	0.00%		268	0.00%		
Revenue Adjustment	981	33		33	-0.77%	-6021		-6021	0.00%		-6021	0.00%		
Fractional Rental	98F	22		22	0.00%	25		25	0.00%		25	0.00%		
Install - MRC	985	19448	20825	-1377	13.85%	108913	166650	-57737	-34.65%	103323	5590	5.41%	250000	155000
Mtcs - Char Rep	98A	351	250	101	0.32%	2493	2000	493	24.65%	2000	493	24.65%	3000	3000
Mtce Contract	98M	11634	8747	2887	9.68%	76144	69993	6151	8.79%	69993	6151	8.79%	105000	105000
Total Gross Revenue		139618	191174	-51556	100.00%	786452	1529848	-743396	-48.59%	902577	-107748	-11.94%	2295000	1354000
COST OF GOODS SOLD (Material)														
Stock Issued-N	114	-58309	-83300	24991	-47.70%	-375112	-666600	291488	-43.73%	-433290	58178	-13.43%	-1000000	-650000
Stock Issued-R	115	-11735	-10829	-906	-9.64%	-75819	-86658	10839	-12.51%	-73326	-2493	3.40%	-130000	-110000
Stock Return-N	124	3685	3332	353	4.50%	35411	26664	8747	32.80%	26664	8747	32.80%	40000	40000
Stock Return-R	125	13680	417	13263	10.66%	83825	3333	80492	2415.00%	79992	3833	4.79%	5000	5000
Equipment Place	104	-8		0	0.00%	-24		-24	0.00%		-24	0.00%		
Total Cost of Goods Sold		-52679	-90380	37701	-42.18%	-331719	-723261	391542	-54.14%	-399960	68241	-17.06%	-1085000	-715000
FIRST LEVEL CONTRIBUTION		86939	100794	-13855	57.82%	454733	806587	-351854	-43.62%	502617	-39507	-7.86%	1210000	639000
OTHER PRODUCT COSTS														
Repair Shop-L	408S	-1917	-639	-1278	-1.79%	-14069	-5109	-8960	175.38%	-14176	107	-0.75%	-7665	-21266
Installation-L	408L	-14050	-20143	6093	-11.06%	-86971	-161191	74220	-46.04%	-161191	74220	-46.04%	-241810	-241810
Installation-P	408X	-264	-121	-143	-0.19%	-1521	-972	-549	56.48%	-972	-549	56.48%	-1458	-1458
Maintenance-P	408J	-2370	-479	-1891	-1.71%	-13482	-3832	-9650	251.83%	-3832	-9650	251.83%	-5749	-5749
Maintenance-L	408R	-5478	-6728	1250	-3.75%	-29505	-53843	24338	-45.20%	-53843	24338	-45.20%	-80773	-80773
Norstar Applic	418L	-8		-8	0.00%	-437		-437	0					
Norstar Applic	418X													
Material OH	89	-4862	-5558	696	-2.85%	-22377	-44475	22098	-49.69%	-29657	7280	-24.55%	-66720	-44490
Engineering	86			0	0.00%				0.00%	0	0	0.00%		
Revenue Tax		-1396	-1912	516	-1.00%	-7865	-15298	7433	-48.59%	-9026	1161	-12.86%	-22950	-13540
Total Other Product Costs		-30345	-35580	5235	-22.41%	-176227	-284720	108493	-38.11%	-272697	96907	-35.54%	-427125	-409086
SECOND LEVEL CONTRIBUTION		56594	65214	-8620	35.41%	278506	521867	-243361	-46.63%	229920	57400	24.97%	782875	229914
ASSET RELATED COSTS														
Allocated Debt														
Depreciation		-1583	-821	-762	-1.61%	-12668	-6567	-6101	92.90%	-12668	0	0.00%	-9852	-19004
Total Asset Related Costs		-1583	-821	-762	-1.61%	-12668	-6567	-6101	92.90%	-12668	0	0.00%	-9852	-19004
CONTRIBUTION TO PRODUCT TYPE		55011	64393	-9382	33.80%	265838	515300	-249462	-48.41%	217252	57400	26.42%	773023	210910
Contribution/$1000 Gross Sales		394	337	N/A		338	337	N/A	N/A	241	N/A	N/A	337	156

Exhibit 4

ED TEL NORSTAR KEY SYSTEMS—July Contribution for Modular Systems

Product Contribution Statement - Meridian Norstar Modular

	Object	MONTH July Actual	Budget	Variance	% Sale	Y.T.D. Actual	Budget	Variance	% Var	Project	Variance	% Var	ANNUAL Budget	Project
REVENUE														
Direct Sale	986	42592	36652	5940	15.09%	177267	256652	-79385	-30.93%	256652	-79385	-30.93%	440000	440000
DS - Discounts	98D	-16223	-4165	-12058	-4.91%	-57733	-29165	-28568	97.95%	-29165	-28568	97.95%	-50000	-50000
Trade Ins	98T	-2192		-2192	-0.85%	-9955		-9955	0.00%			0.00%		
Sale in Place	980			0	0.00%				0.00%			0.00%		
Lease Purchase	987	148481	84966	63515	68.56%	805423	594966	210457	35.37%	594966	210457	35.37%	1020000	1020000
Monthly Rental	989	1146	1666	-520	7.45%	87518	11666	75852	650.20%	11666	75852	650.20%	20000	20000
Revenue Adjustment	981	-9666		-9666	3.09%	36328		36328	0.00%			0.00%		
Fractional Rental	98F	114		114	-3.54%	-41543		-41543	0.00%			0.00%		
Install - MRC	985	26409	13745	12664	13.48%	158391	96245	62146	64.57%	96245	62146	64.57%	165000	165000
Mtcs - Char Rep	98A	193	417	-224	0.11%	1301	2917	-1616	-55.40%	2917	-1616	-55.40%	5000	5000
Mtce Contract	98M	5864	2499	3365	1.51%	17715	17499	216	1.23%	17499	216	1.23%	30000	30000
Miscellaneous	988			0				0	0.00%			0.00%		
Total Gross Revenue		196718	135780	60938	100.00%	1174712	950780	223932	23.55%	950780	239102	25.15%	1630000	1630000
COST OF GOODS SOLD (Material)														
Stock Issued-N	114	-44543	-77469	32926	-66.83%	-785005	-542469	-242536	44.71%	-542469	-242536	44.71%	-930000	-930000
Stock Issued-R	115	-10808	-10413	-395	-4.14%	-48602	-72913	24311	-33.34%	-72913	24311	-33.34%	-125000	-125000
Stock Return-N	124	210	9996	-9786	5.13%	60124	69996	-9782	-13.98%	69996	-9782	-13.98%	120000	120000
Stock Return-R	125	7445	4165	3280	2.33%	27331	29165	-1834	-6.29%	29165	-1834	-6.29%	50000	50000
Equipment Place	104			0	0.00%			0	0.00%			0.00%		
Total Cost of Goods Sold		-47696	-73721	26025	-63.51%	-746062	-516221	-229841	44.52%	-516221	-229841	44.52%	-885000	-885000
FIRST LEVEL CONTRIBUTION		149022	62059	86963	36.49%	428650	434559	-5909	-1.36%	434559	9261	2.13%	745000	745000
OTHER PRODUCT COSTS														
Repair Shop-L	568S	-2669	-171	-2498	-0.65%	-7633	-1196	-6437	538.21%	-3185	-4448	139.65%	-2051	-5461
Installation-L	568L	-18829	-11322	-7507	-13.08%	-153711	-98516	-55195	56.03%	-98516	-55195	56.03%	-161546	-161546
Installation-P	568X	-159	-121	-38	-0.19%	-2277	-850	-1427	167.88%	-850	-1427	167.88%	-1458	-1458
Maintenance-P	568J	-2725	-918	-1807	-0.91%	-10733	-6431	-4302	66.89%	-6431	-4302	66.89%	-11025	-11025
Maintenance-L	568R	-2249	-4681	2432	-1.60%	-18810	-32776	13966	-42.61%	-32776	13966	-42.61%	-56190	-56190
Material OH	89	-10804	-5184	-5620	-4.68%	-55017	-36299	-18718	51.57%	-36299	-18718	51.57%	-62330	-62330
Engineering	86			0	0.00%			0	0.00%			0.00%		
Revenue Tax		-1967	-1358	-609	-1.00%	-11747	-9508	-2239	23.55%	-9508	-2239	23.55%	-16300	-16300
Total Other Product Costs		-39402	-23755	-15647	-22.13%	-259928	-185576	-74352	40.07%	-187565	-72363	38.58%	-310900	-314310
SECOND LEVEL CONTRIBUTION		109620	38304	71316	14.36%	168722	248983	-80261	-32.24%	246994	-63102	-25.55%	434100	430690
ASSET RELATED COSTS														
Allocated Debt														
Depreciation		-1715	-421	-1294	-1.02%	-12011	-2947	-9064	307.57%	-12011	0	0.00%	-5052	-20592
Total Asset Related Costs		-1715	-421	-1294	-1.02%	-12011	-2947	-9064	307.57%	-12011	0	0.00%	-5052	-20592
CONTRIBUTION TO PRODUCT TYPE		107905	37883	70022	13.34%	156711	246036	-89325	-36.31%	234983	-63102	-26.85%	429048	410098
Contribution/$1000 Gross Sales		549	279	N/A		133	259	N/A	N/A	247	N/A	N/A	263	252

Exhibit 5

ED TEL NORSTAR KEY SYSTEMS—August Contribution for Modular Systems

Product Contribution Statement - Meridian Norstar Modular

	Object	MONTH August Actual	Budget	Variance	Actual	% Sale	Y.T.D. Budget	Variance	% Var	Project	Variance	% Var	ANNUAL Budget	Project
REVENUE														
Direct Sale	986	40190	36652	3538	217457	15.17%	293304	-75847	-25.86%	293304	-75847	-25.86%	440000	440000
DS - Discounts	98D	-35413	-4165	-31248	-93147	-6.50%	-33330	-59817	179.47%	-33330	-59817	179.47%	-50000	-50000
Trade Ins	98T	-1079		-1079	-11033	-0.77%		-11033	0.00%		-11033	0.00%		
Sale in Place	980	6517		6517	6517	0.45%		6517	0.00%		6517	0.00%		
Lease Purchase	987	231992	84966	147026	1037415	72.35%	679932	357483	52.58%	679932	357483	52.58%	1020000	1020000
Monthly Rental	989	1166	1666	-500	88684	6.18%	13332	75352	565.20%	13332	75352	565.20%	20000	20000
Revenue Adjustment	981	-11152		-11152	25176	1.76%		25176	0.00%		25176	0.00%		
Fractional Rental	98F	46		46	-41497	-2.89%		-41497	0.00%		-41497	0.00%		
Install - MRC	985	19536	13745	5791	177927	12.41%	109989	67938	61.77%	109989	67938	61.77%	165000	165000
Mtcs - Char Rep	98A	247	417	-170	1548	0.11%	3333	-1785	-53.56%	3333	-1785	-53.56%	5000	5000
Mtce Contract	98M	7132	2499	4633	24847	1.73%	19998	4849	24.25%	19998	4849	24.25%	30000	30000
Miscellaneous	988			0		0.00%		0	0.00%		0	0.00%		
Total Gross Revenue		259182	135780	123402	1433894	100.00%	1086558	347336	31.97%	1086558	368173	33.88%	1630000	1630000
COST OF GOODS SOLD (Material)														
Stock Issued-N	114	-158500	-77469	-81031	-943506	-65.80%	-619938	-323568	52.19%	-619938	-323568	52.19%	-930000	-930000
Stock Issued-R	115	-7455	-10413	2958	-56057	-3.91%	-83325	27268	-32.72%	-83325	27268	-32.72%	-125000	-125000
Stock Return-N	124	6585	9996	-3411	66800	4.66%	79992	-13192	-16.49%	79992	-13192	-16.49%	120000	120000
Stock Return-R	125	7381	4165	3216	34712	2.42%	33330	1382	4.15%	33330	1382	4.15%	50000	50000
Equipment Place	104			0		0.00%		0	0.00%		0	0.00%		
Total Cost of Goods Sold		-151989	-73721	-78268	-898051	-62.63%	-589941	-308110	52.23%	-589941	-308110	52.23%	-885000	-885000
FIRST LEVEL CONTRIBUTION		107193	62059	45134	535843	37.37%	496617	39226	7.90%	496617	60063	12.09%	745000	745000
OTHER PRODUCT COSTS														
Repair Shop-L	568S	-1118	-171	-947	-8878	-0.62%	-1367	-7511	549.45%	-3640	-5238	143.90%	-2051	-5461
Installation-L	568L	-31164	-11322	-19842	-184875	-12.89%	-109838	-75037	68.32%	-109838	-75037	68.32%	-161546	-161546
Installation-P	568X	-361	-121	-240	-2638	-0.18%	-972	-1666	171.40%	-972	-1666	171.40%	-1458	-1458
Maintenance-P	568J	-1360	-918	-442	-12093	-0.84%	-7349	-4744	64.55%	-7349	-4744	64.55%	-11025	-11025
Maintenance-L	568R	-3441	-4681	1240	-22252	-1.55%	-37456	15204	-40.59%	-37456	15204	-40.59%	-56190	-56190
Material OH	89	-12773	-5184	-7589	-67790	-4.73%	-41483	-26307	63.42%	-41483	-26307	63.42%	-62330	-62330
Engineering	86					0.00%								
Revenue Tax		-2592	-1358	-1234	-14339	-1.00%	-10866	-3473	31.96%	-10866	-3473	31.96%	-16300	-16300
Total Other Product Costs		-52809	-23755	-29054	-312865	-21.82%	-209331	-103534	49.46%	-211604	-101261	47.85%	-310900	-314310
SECOND LEVEL CONTRIBUTION		54384	38304	16080	222978	15.55%	287286	-64308	-22.38%	285013	-41198	-14.45%	434100	430690
ASSET RELATED COSTS														
Allocated Debt														
Depreciation		-1716	-421	-1295	-13727	-0.96%	-3368	-10359	307.57%	-13727	0	0.00%	-5052	-20592
Total Asset Related Costs		-1716	-421	-1295	-13727	-0.96%	-3368	-10359	307.57%	-13727	0	0.00%	-5052	-20592
CONTRIBUTION TO PRODUCT TYPE		52668	37883	14785	209251	14.59%	283918	-74667	-26.30%	271286	-41198	-15.19%	429048	410098
Contribution/$1000 Gross Sales		203	279	N/A	146		261	N/A	N/A	250	N/A	N/A	263	252

Exhibit 6

ED TEL NORSTAR KEY SYSTEMS—Compact DKS Contribution by Revenue Stream

Product Contribution Statement by Revenue Stream
Meridian Norstar Compact DKS

		Direct			Rental			YEAR TO DATE — Install			Maint		
	Object	Actual	Budget	Project	Actual	Budget	Project	Actual	Budget	Project	Actual	Budget	Project
REVENUE													
Direct Sale	986	159463	237310	127326									
Lease	987	445167	1053895	599940									
Rental	989				-5728								
Installation	985							108913	166650	103323			
Maintenance	98A 98M										78637	71993	71993
Miscellaneous	988												
Total Gross Revenue		604630	1291205	727266	-5728	0	0	108913	166650	103323	78637	71993	71993
COST OF GOODS SOLD (Material)													
Stock Issued-N	114	-375112	-666600	-433290									
Stock Issued-R	115	-75819	-86658	-73326									
Stock Return-N	124	35411	26664	26664									
Stock Return-R	125	83825	3333	79992									
Equipment Place													
Total Cost of Goods Sold		-331695	-723261	-399960	0	0	0	0	0	0	0	0	0
Adjustments:													
Internal Billing	978				2285	133	133						
Internal Equip Use													
Total Adjustments		0	0	0	2285	133	133	0	0	0	0	0	0
FIRST LEVEL CONTRIBUTION		272935	567944	327306	-3443	133	133	108913	166650	103323	78637	71993	71993
OTHER PRODUCT COSTS													
Repair Shop	408S							-86971	-161191	-161191	-14069	-5109	-14176
Installation-L	408L							-1521	-972	-972			
Installation-P	408X												
Maintenance-L	408R										-29505	-53843	-53843
Maintenance-P	408J										-14077	-3832	-3832
Material OH	89	-22377	44475	-29657									
Engineering	86	-437											
Norstar—Applic	418L	-7865	-15298	-9026									
Revenue Tax													
Depreciation—Rent					-12668	-6567	-12668						
Total Other Product Costs		-30679	29177	-38683	-12668	-6567	-12668	-88492	-162163	-162163	-57651	-62784	-71851
SECOND LEVEL CONTRIBUTION		242256	597121	288623	-16111	-6434	-12535	20421	4487	-58840	20986	9209	142
ASSET RELATED COSTS													
Allocated Debt													
Depreciation													
Total Asset Related Costs		0	0	0	0	0	0	0	0	0	0	0	0
CONTRIBUTION TO PRODUCT TYPE		242256	597121	288623	-16111	-6434	-12535	20421	4487	-58840	20986	9209	142
Contribution/$1000 Gross Rev		401	462	397	-71	0	0	187	27	-569	267	128	2

Exhibit 7

ED TEL NORSTAR KEY SYSTEMS—Modular Contribution by Revenue Stream

Product Contribution Statement by Revenue Stream
Meridian Norstar Modular

		YEAR TO DATE											
		Direct			Rental			Install			Maint		
	Object	Actual	Budget	Project	Actual	Budget	Project	Actual	Budget	Project	Actual	Budget	Project
REVENUE													
Direct Sale	986	119794	259974	259974									
Lease	987	1037415	679932	679932									
Rental	989				72363	13332	13332						
Installation	985							177927	109989	109989			
Maintenance	98A 98M										26395	23331	23331
Miscellaneous	988												
Total Gross Revenue		1157209	939906	939906	72363	13332	13332	177927	109989	109989	26395	23331	23331
COST OF GOODS SOLD (Material)													
Stock Issued-N	114	-943506	-619938	-619938									
Stock Issued-R	115	-56057	-83325	-83325									
Stock Return-N	124	66800	79992	79992									
Stock Return-R	125	34712	33330	33330									
Internal Equip Use					21228								
Total Cost of Goods Sold		-898051	-589941	-589941	21228								
Adjustments:													
Internal Billing	978												
Internal Equip Use													
Equipment Place													
Total Adjustments		0	0	0	0	0	0	0	0	0	0	0	0
FIRST LEVEL CONTRIBUTION		259158	349965	349965	93591	13332	13332	177927	109989	109989	26395	23331	23331
OTHER PRODUCT COSTS													
Repair Shop	568S										-8157	-1367	-3640
Installation-L	568L	-67790	-41483	-41483				-184875	-109838	-109838			
Installation-P	568X							-2638	-972	-972			
Maintenance-L	568R										-22252	-37456	-37456
Maintenance-P	568J										-12093	-7349	-7349
Material OH	89	-14339	-10866	-10866									
Engineering	86												
Revenue Tax													
Depreciation—Rent					-12668	-6567	-12668						
Total Other Product Costs		-82129	-52349	-52349	-12668	-6567	-12668	-187513	-110810	-110810	-42502	-46172	-48445
SECOND LEVEL CONTRIBUTION		177029	297616	297616	80923	6765	664	-9586	-821	-821	-16107	-22841	-25114
ASSET RELATED COSTS													
Allocated Debt													
Depreciation		0	0	0				0	0	0	0	0	0
Total Asset Related Costs		0	0	0				0	0	0	0	0	0
CONTRIBUTION TO PRODUCT TYPE		177029	297616	297616	80923	6765	664	-9586	-821	-821	-16107	-22841	-25114
Contribution/$1000 Gross Sales		153	317	317	1118	507	50	-54	-7	-7	-610	-979	-1076

EMCO SUPPLY—
TRANSFER PRICING

Rhonda English, Randolph Kudar, and John Graham*

The Central Regional Vice President of Emco Supply, Bob Johnston, was faced with a very difficult situation. A decision had to be made regarding what kind of transfer pricing procedure would be used for products between the Central Region Service Centre and the operating branches within that region. Since Mr. Johnston was evaluated on the region's overall return on net investment, it was important that he determine where the volume discounts obtained by the service centre would most benefit the company.

Should the volume discounts generated by the service centre be kept there to cover the operating costs of that facility? Or would the transfer price of the goods to the branches reduce their ability to compete agressively for business, thus reducing overall profits? It was these issues which Mr. Johnston had to address in order to both find an answer for his President, Mr. Ian Warburton, who had several regions under his jurisdiction, and to maximize his own as well as the company's profitability.

BACKGROUND

The Empire Manufacturing Company Limited began business in 1906. Located in London, Ontario, they operated a brass foundry and machine shop producing fittings for plumbing, farm implements, and small business. With the arrival of

World War I, the company experienced a business boom as it expanded into the production of military items. After the war, it reverted back to the manufacture of plumbing products. To secure an outlet for its factory products, the company purchased National Plumbing Supplies, a plumbing and heating wholesaler located in Toronto. This was the start of an aggressive acquisition pattern that characterized the growth of the company.

In 1920 the company's name changed to Empire Brass Manufacturing Limited. Business activities were extended into the western Canadian provinces as complementary companies were acquired. In 1957, Empire Brass became a public company, listed on the Toronto Stock Exchange. Business activities were subsequently expanded into the United Kingdom. In 1957 the name of the company was changed to EMCO Limited. By 1977, plants had been set up in the United States, Japan, West Germany, Australia, France, and Brazil.

Growth in EMCO has been strongly related to the aggressive acquisition strategy followed through the years. Today, EMCO has thirty-one (31) operating divisions, one hundred and thirty-six (136) distribution branches, and is active in over one hundred (100) countries. EMCO has become a diversified distribution and manufacturing organization. In 1988, EMCO generated sales of almost $1.2 billion and net earnings of approximately $12 million.

EMCO ORGANIZATION AND PRODUCTS

John Brant, CEO, had organized EMCO Ltd. into five separate operating groups. Each group had its own President and corporate staff. The groups were expected to operate independently and with an entrepreneurial spirit.

Petroleum Equipment

This group developed systems and manufactured products to handle petroleum and petrochemicals (e.g., gas pump nozzles), focusing on providing products which protected the environment. Petroleum Equipment contributed 9% of Emco's sales.

Home and Family Products

This manufacturing and marketing group was Canada's largest producer of faucets and stainless steel sinks. A wide range of kitchen, bathroom, and related products were provided, making up 12% of Emco's sales.

EML Distribution

This group distributed plumbing, heating, air conditioning, and industrial and related products across Canada, accounting for 49% of Emco's current annual sales.

Custom Products

Formed with the purchase of Waltec Enterprises in March 1984, this group produced engineered non-ferrous metal and plastic custom machine components, providing 6% of sales.

Building Products

Specially formed in 1987 with the purchase of Building Products of Canada Limited, the group produced high-quality roofing, fibreboard, insulation, and vinyl siding for residential and commercial buildings. The group accounted for 24% of Emco's annual sales.

EMCO SUPPLY

Within each operating group were a number of individual operating units. Emco Supply, a member of the largest operating group EML Distribution, was one such unit. Emco Supply was developed in 1960 as a major chain of wholesale plumbing and heating product branches, distributing approximately 60,000 different products. Other EML Distribution operating units included Western Supplies Limited, Westlund Industrial Supplies Limited, and Canadian Clyde Tube Forgings (CCTF). Western and Westlund were conventional plumbing and heating wholesalers operating in Western Canada. Members of EMCO Limited through acquistion, these two units actually competed with Emco Supply in the Western region. CCTF was a specialty wholesaler of welding fittings, flanges, and high alloy fittings.

Emco Supply was organized into four regions: Western, Central, Eastern, and Atlantic, each headed by a Regional Vice President. Reporting to each Regional V.P. was a Regional Operations Controller and Regional Credit Manager. Approximately 64 branches, functioning as autonomous profit centres, performed marketing and distribution activities across Canada for Emco Supply.

The Regional V.P. was in charge of all branches within his region, as well as the regional service centre. Because the branches had so much autonomy, the Regional V.P. did not have to make day-to-day operating decisions (e.g., setting bid prices, sourcing products). He was, however, responsible for overall supervision of his Branch Managers. He examined and monitored new product lines, inventory arrangements, general credit policy, and the efficient operation of his branches. He was also responsible for arranging special purchasing deals for branches from the regional service centre (i.e., one-time lower prices or extended payment terms on certain products), to enable branches to secure specific contracts and enhance margins. His most important function was usually considered to be the selection, training, and upgrading of all personnel under his jurisdiction.

The Regional V.P. was evaluated annually on the basis of return on net investment (RONI), where return was the pre-tax profit of the overall region and net investment was defined as total accounts receivable less allowance for doubtful accounts, plus total inventory less accounts payable. The extent to which the current year's profit and RONI surpassed the previous year's profit and RONI dictated the amount of bonus to be received by the V.P.

The Central region had 20 branches and five sub branches, comprising about 50% of Emco Supply business. Exhibit 1 outlines a partial organizational chart for EMCO Limited.

BRANCH OPERATIONS

The wholesale plumbing and heating industry was extremely competitive. Emco's major competitors included Westburne, Ideal Plumbing Group, Crane Company, and ITT Grinnel. Due to the lack of differentiation between competitive products and service, price was felt to be one of the biggest key success factors in the business. Sometimes special arrangements were made between the branch and a supplier to obtain a "deal" that the competition would not receive. However, suppliers would often give one purchaser a deal on one item and another purchaser a deal on a different item, thereby eliminating any overall competitive advantage. Established position within the industry and customer relations were other factors contributing to business success.

Approximately 80 to 85% of a branch's business was generated through a bid process, with the remainder made up of over-the-counter sales at the branch site. The initial process began when developers and financers decided to build a commercial complex. Once the building plans were developed and government approval received, the job was opened to bids by General Contractors, one of whom would become responsible for the completion of the building. The successful General Contractor then either requested bids from subcontractors on specific pieces of the construction project or, if an Engineering firm, undertook the construction itself. If opened for bid, one group of subcontractors, the mechanical contractors, normally performed about 25% of the total construction work, including such areas as: heating/air conditioning, piping, plumbing, and drainage. The mechanical contractors were one of Emco Supply's primary target markets. These contractors usually requested quotes from several alternative wholesalers, in most instances choosing a supplier based on lowest price.

A second, fairly large customer base was found in the residential construction housing market, where different types of mechanical contractors were pursued. A third, smaller market was in supplying replacement products for the renovation market.

Emco Supply branches were considered autonomous profit centres, with their own financial statements prepared monthly. Each branch was headed by a Branch Manager who had the authority to set prices, select suppliers, extend credit, pay suppliers, stock inventory, and select or dismiss personnel. The Branch Manager was typically a sales/marketing oriented person and had an Operations Manager reporting to him, who was more administratively oriented. Sub branches had a Sales Manager but no Branch Manager, since the subs were considered a part of the main branch under which they operated.

Similar to the Regional V.P., the Branch Manager was evaluated on the improvement in profit and RONI from one year to the next. Managers received base salaries with a high bonus system. In some cases, the bonus could be as much as 100% of the individual's salary or as little as nothing. The sales personnel at the branches were also on an incentive system, receiving a base salary plus commissions on gross profit. In fact, everyone in EML Distribution was on some sort of incentive plan, either salary plus commissions or salary plus profit sharing. EMCO relied heavily on the incentive system to motivate and thus increase individual remunerations.

INTERCOMPANY TRANSFERS

As previously stated, branches had a great deal of autonomy regarding the purchase of materials. Each branch inventoried on average 8,000 different wholesale products, catering to the specific needs of their particular geographic location. Branches were not required to purchase items only from Emco manufacturing units or from the regional service centre. They could purchase materials from wherever the best deal could be received — various manufacturers, other branches, or the regional service centre.

When branches purchased from one another, the transfer price was established by the branches involved. Traditionally the selling branch charged the buying branch net cost plus 3%, where the extra 3% represented a portion of the volume rebates and/or cash discounts received by the selling branch. Cash discount terms of 2%/20 E.O.M (20 days after end of month) were offered by many suppliers and most often taken by the wholesalers. The buying branch would be responsible for all freight costs on the goods transferred. Interbranch transfers were most common between main branches and sub branches but also took place between independent branches. Supplying other branches could be a very profitable business for some branches since larger individual orders could be placed by the supplying branch, thereby receiving larger volume discounts than would have been possible if the supplying branch had just been ordering for its own needs.

THE REGIONAL SERVICE CENTRE

Volume discounts and rebates played a significant role in the heating and plumbing wholesale business. As the volume of units purchased from a supplier increased, the magnitude of the rebate and discount to the purchaser could increase. Rebates were given by external suppliers at the end of the period, based on cumulative EML Distribution orders. An illustration of a cumulative rebate would be a supplier offering 1% on annual purchases up to $300,000, 2% on purchases up to $400,000, 3% up to $500,000, etc. Sometimes the highest rebate was effective back to the first purchase dollar, making the rebates even more significant. The rebates on cumulative purchases were distributed to specific purchasing units (branches or service centre) by Head Office accounting at the end of the given period.

Discounts were given by external suppliers based on volume purchased on individual orders. For example, Stelco, a major pipe supplier, might offer a 10% discount to a purchaser of 20 tons of one colour, one end finish pipe with one basic metal specification (one carload).

The regional service centres were originally set up solely as pipe warehouses, to take advantage of the large volume discounts and better freight terms available. As EML Distribution grew, use of the service centres expanded to include stocking such items as valves, fittings, and fixtures, in addition to pipe. Of total annual Emco Supply purchases from external suppliers of $300 million, approximately $42 million were purchased by the service centres (Western $10 million, Eastern $10 million, Central $22 million) and subsequently transferred to the branches. The branches benefitted by being able to obtain products at lower discounted costs than they would otherwise have been able to receive from an external supplier, as well as by not having to hold as much inventory at the branch location. A typical branch might purchase $500,000 worth of pipe in a year. If they bought from their Service Centre at maximum discounts rather than purchasing directly from the mill, their savings on average would be about 5%, or $25,000 on just one product line. The lower material costs were expected to have a significant impact on the successful bidding for contracts by the branches, or, if practical, enhance the margins on transactions.

The regional service centres were set up to act like separate businesses themselves. Handling and storage facilities and equipment were invested in, and full-time employees reported to a regional service centre Manager, who had control over all ordering and purchasing of products at the centre. Total annual expenses of operating the Central region service centre (which was the largest) were approximately $900,000. (See Exhibits 2 and 3.)

One approach to transfer pricing was for the service centres to charge the branches a 3 to 5% surcharge over discounted cost to cover operating expenses. If a small profit resulted at the centre, it would be distributed to the branches at year end, pro rata to purchases from the centre. Another option was to transfer product to the branches at discounted cost plus 1/2% to enable branches to be more competitive in their bidding in the market. For accounting purposes in the latter situation, the service centre would act as a cost centre, accumulating and retaining the overhead expenses it incurred. Transferring the product at net cost to the branch ran the risk of the extra margin being given away to the customers due to the extreme competitiveness of the industry.

Service was an important element in purchasing from any supplier. Branches would take their business elsewhere if the level of service (delivery, accuracy of orders, etc.) was not acceptable. In the past there had been numerous complaints about the regional centre mixing up orders and shipping the wrong goods. This could have negative impacts on a branch's business since often a branch worked under specific time deadlines with their customers. The branches themselves had to make a choice between lower costs from the service centre and level of service received.

CONCLUSION

As Mr. Johnston reviewed the situation, he realized that a prompt decision concerning transfer pricing was necessary. The basic issue was where the extra margins from volume discounts would best motivate people. Should the service centre hold the margin (by charging 3 to 5% above discounted cost) throughout the year or should the branches be given the opportunity to use the lower discounted cost (cost plus 1/2%) to become more competitive in the market? Also of importance were the objectives of minimizing Emco Supply's overall net cost of goods and inventory holding costs.

Exhibit 1

EMCO ORGANIZATION CHART

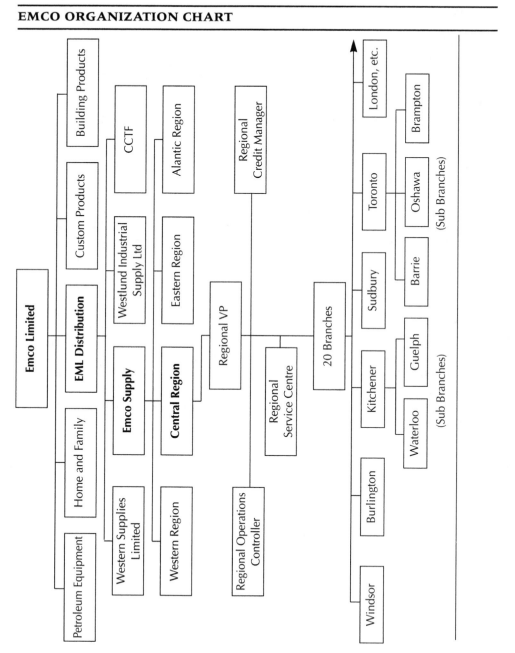

Exhibit 2

BRANCH OPERATING STATEMENT—Dec. 1988

C.S.C.   C.S.C.

CURRENT MONTH			ACCOUNT DESCRIPTION			YEAR TO DATE		
FORECAST	%	ACTUAL	%		FORECAST	%	ACTUAL	ACTUAL %
			SALES - FST INCL. FEDERAL SALES TAX					
			NET SALES*		20,000,000	100	22,000,000	100
			INV BEGINNING OF PERIOD				5,792,161	
			LONDON FACTORY					
			OTHER SUPPLIERS				22,532,847	
			PLASTICS					
			C.C.T.F.					
			PIPE WAREHOUSES					
			NTER-BR. TRANSFER IN					
			INTER-BR. TRANSFER OUT					
			DELTA					
							28,325,008	
			LESS INV. - END OF PERIOD				6,435,008	
			COST OF GOODS SOLD				21,890,000	99.5
			GROSS PROFIT				110,000	0.5
			OPERATING EXPENSES					
			VARIABLE				487,640	2.2
			SEMI-VARIABLE				104,695	.48
			FIXED				304,524	1.4
			H.O. AND DIV. SERVICES				197,219	.90
			TOTAL OPERATING EXPENSES				1,094,078	5.0
			OPERATING PROFIT				984,078–	4.5–
			CASH DISCOUNT EARNED				220,000	1.0
			PROFIT BEFORE D.A				764,078–	3.5–
			PROV FOR DOUBTFUL ACCTS					
			NET PROFIT BEFORE TAXES				764,078–	3.5–
			ACCOUNTS RECEIVABLE					
			BEGIN - RESERVE - END					
			SERVICE CHARGES					
			DEFERRED ACCTS PAYABLE					
			UNPAID ACCOUNTS PAYABLE					
			RONI 881– X 12					
			1,559 + 164 X 12					
			AVE. INV. AVE. REC					
			RATE OF TURNOVER					
			EMPLOYEE ANALYSIS					
			SUPERVISORY					
			CLERICAL					
			WAREHOUSE					
			TRUCK DRIVERS					
			SALESMEN					
			TRAINEES					
			HEATING					
			TOTAL					
			NET CLOSING INVENTORY					
			NET CLOSING RECEIVABLES					

NOTE: The numbers have been disguised to maintain confidentiality.
*Internal sales to Branches by the Service Centre.

Exhibit 3

BRANCH OPERATING EXPENSE STATEMENT—Dec. 1988

C.S.C.   663   C.S.C.

CURRENT MONTH			ACCOUNT DESCRIPTION			YEAR TO DATE	
FORECAST	%	ACTUAL	%	VARIABLE FORECAST	%	ACTUAL	%
			SALARIES-CLERICAL –			150,320	
			– WAREHOUSE			128,589	
			– TRUCK DRIVERS			7,472	
			OVERTIME-CLERICAL			3,767	
			– WAREHOUSE			15,152	
			– TRUCK DRIVERS			1,499	
			TEMP HELP-CLERICAL	3,217			
			– WAREHOUSE			9,573	
			– TRUCK DRIVERS				
			COMMISSIONS				
			PROFIT SHARING				
			TRAVEL – MANAGERS			1,719	
			– SALESMEN			537	
			– OTHERS			2,855	
			CAR OPERATING EXPENSES			786	
			LEASING – CARS,DEP'N ALLOW.			2,849	
			– TRUCKS			37,559	
			– FORK & YARD CRANE			13,555	
			FREIGHT OUT			88,798	
			TRUCK OPERATING EXPENSES			3,698	
			ADVERTISING & DONATIONS			2,665	
			ASSOC.DUES & SUBSCRIPTION			2,421	
			CREDIT COLLECTION & LEGAL			2,222	
			LONG DISTANCE TELEX & WAT			8,387	
			CASH DISCOUNT				
			*TOTAL *			487,640	2.2
			SEMI-VARIABLE				
			GENERAL OPERATING SUPPLY			34,623	
			STATIONERY			19,572	
			POSTAGE			3,709	
			BLDG. MTCE & ALTERATIONS			25,684	
			MTCE. – OFFICE MACHINES			2,800	
			– WAREHOUSE EQUIPMENT			18,060	
			INSURANCE- AUTOS & TRUCKS			247	
			COMPUTER EQUIPMENT LEASE				
			*TOTAL *			104,695	.48
			FIXED				
			SUPERVISION			25,176	
			FRINGE BENEFITS			30,738	
			SUPERANNUATION & PENSION			7,935	
			CLEANING & SNOW REMOVAL			13,308	
			COMMUNCAT EQUIP. RENTAL			12,596	
			UTILITIES			34,105	
			DEP'N – F. & F.			181	
			– M. & E.			7,711	
			RENT & LEASEHOLD			81,630	
			PROPERTY & BUSINESS TAXES			90,214	
			GENERAL INSURANCE			930	
			*TOTAL *			304,524	1.4
			***CONSOLIDATED ***			896,859	4.08

NOTE: The numbers have been disguised to maintain confidentiality.

NEWS & BOOKS UNLIMITED

Lori Beraznik, Steven Bloom, Jerome Horowitz, Lara Nadler,
Dina Silva, and Tony Dimnik

It was late March 1991, and Michelle Diamond, a third year Commerce student at the University of Toronto, was contemplating her father's offer to work in a management position at the family's chain of news and book stores after graduation. Diamond had worked at one of the stores for almost a year. She thought that the operation could be improved, but she didn't know exactly what should be done.

COMPANY BACKGROUND

News & Books Unlimited (NBU) was a chain of eight wholly owned bookstores in the Toronto area. Five of the stores were located in high traffic areas downtown, and the other three were located in popular suburban shopping malls. In addition to books, NBU carried the city's largest selection of magazines and newspapers, with over 4,000 titles from over 60 cities.

As avid and intellectual readers, NBU's customers were loyal patrons and frequent book purchasers who preferred to shop at NBU because of the selection, familiar environment, and convenient locations. The average NBU customer was over 25 years old and visited an NBU store two or three times a week.

Because of the different lifestyles of customers in different areas of Toronto, each NBU store manager was autonomous and had the freedom to choose the reading materials for their customers. For example, a manager located in a suburban mall might stock a large selection of books on cooking while a manager located in a business district might stock a large selection of business and computer books. This purchasing flexibility, combined with NBU's size, offered NBU the buying power of a large chain without the rigidity.

History

NBU had been founded by Saul Cohen in the 1920s. The first store was located just north of the downtown Toronto core, and was a confectionery store which carried some magazines and newspapers. In 1968, Joseph Diamond purchased the store and began importing newspapers from many cities across North America and Europe. In 1971, Joseph's son, Peter, entered the family business, and by 1973 began changing NBU's focus to books. He realized that books were money makers, with 40% margins, while magazines and newspapers generated traffic. Even though the newspapers and magazines had margins of only 20%, he continued to offer them in order to draw customers into the store to buy books.

By 1977, NBU consisted of three retail locations with a loyal clientele. To become more competitive, Diamond decided to focus on the "intellectual reader". Profits increased, and from 1982 to 1988, NBU expanded operations to eight stores.

Corporate Strategy

NBU's strategy of operating as a niche player and focusing on the intellectual reader had resulted in an annual sales growth of 5% to 10%. Current sales were approximately $11,000,000 per year. NBU management attributed success to the following factors:

- large, unique selection of inventory
- constantly stocked shelves
- high quality managers
- high traffic locations
- an excellent reputation
- word of mouth advertising.

THE BOOK INDUSTRY

By 1991, the book industry was in decline. Industry profits were slim because of the high costs of handling many titles. Maintaining many titles required extensive paperwork. As well, store overheads were high because book titles had to be exposed to customers, and shelf space in prime locations was expensive.

The book industry was losing customers. The younger generation was turning away from books and turning to videos and electronic games. NBU had been only slightly affected by this trend because of the average age of its regular customers and because of its focus on the intellectual reader.

The relationship between publishers and retailers was also changing. Big name authors were increasing their demands for royalties and publishers were often forced to lower their discounts to retailers. However, many large publishers had begun buying up their smaller competitors and these larger publishers had more leeway on discounts.

Competition

NBU's main competitors, Coles and W.H. Smith, were national chains that carried standard selections in all stores. The managers of these competing stores had limited autonomy and could only order books off a standardized checklist. They also did not stock as wide a variety of magazines and newspapers and did not have as focused a marketing strategy.

Other small independents and local chain stores were scattered throughout the Toronto area. Although the managers of these stores had greater flexibility in book selection, they were small operations and did not have much leverage with publishers.

ORGANIZATION OF NBU

Head Office

The NBU Head Office, which was located on the top floor of a small downtown building, was staffed by five people, two of whom were administrative employees. The organization chart, attached as Exhibit 1, shows the reporting structure.

Peter Diamond, the President and owner of NBU, was primarily involved in NBU's financial and strategic planning. Although he had previously been involved in the day-to-day management of operations, by 1991 he was spending a considerable amount of time with other business interests and with his family.

The day-to-day management of NBU was the responsibility of 61-year-old Keith Johnson, the General Manager, who had been a school teacher for 20 years before joining NBU in 1979. He was directly responsible for the operations of all eight stores and their managers, and handled the company's advertising and promotion. He was an extremely dedicated and efficient employee.

Linda Brock, the head book buyer, handled all purchasing activities and monitored the book returns. Because publishers guaranteed a 100% refund if books were returned within a specific time frame, careful monitoring of these returns was essential. Although Brock did have formal authority over store management, her ongoing relationship with the managers through the ordering and returning of books allowed her to join Johnson in the annual store evaluations to determine the managers' bonuses.

Store Managers and Staff

Store managers were usually promoted from within the company. Many of the managers had started off as part-time employees, then became full-time employees, assistant managers, and then finally managers. The Head Office staff believed successful NBU store managers possessed the following qualities: conscientiousness, ability, a sense of organization, and urgency. Internal promotion provided Johnson with the opportunity to select managers from a pool of employees who displayed these qualities. Johnson or Brock spent two six-week periods training new managers, who were always moved to different stores after their promotions.

Store managers were responsible for all management decisions at their locations, including all staffing decisions, training, local banking, purchasing and returning books, promotion and display, and customer service.

Staff

Store staff were expected to be avid readers in order to offer their customers more qualified assistance. Store managers determined the amount and content of staff training, as well as type and frequency of evaluation. New staff went through a three-month probationary term, and upon the successful completion of this term, were usually given a small raise. The cost of staff wages was kept low because of frequent staff turnover. New staff were paid at the lower base level.

EVALUATIONS OF THE MANAGERS

Store Visits

Johnson's weekly routine as General Manager involved visiting each store every Thursday. During these visits, he would spend about 20 minutes with each store manager. These informal meetings covered any problems that the manager had experienced during the past week. During these visits Johnson also performed minor store maintenance, and completed a routine check of the store operations (i.e., displays, cleanliness). The main reasons for these weekly visits were to stay close to the operations and to keep the managers on their toes.

Formal Evaluations

Evaluation of the managers occurred both informally and formally. Informal evaluations took place during the weekly visits. Formal evaluations, which determined each manager's yearly bonus, took place once a year. Exhibit 2 is a copy of the annual evaluation form. Each manager could score between 1 and 5 in each of ten evaluation categories. Particular emphasis was placed on returns, cash handling, and displays because Johnson and Diamond believed these were critical to store profitability. Theoretically, store managers could earn bonuses of 5% to 30% of their annual salaries. In actual fact, bonuses averaged between 12% and 15% on average evaluation scores of 30/50.

Every year, Brock, Johnson, and each store manager filled out individual evaluation forms. After reviewing the three evaluations of each manager, Brock and Johnson arrived at a final appraisal and bonus. A manager who was unhappy with the evaluation or bonus could meet with Johnson. The annual evaluation process had been implemented in 1988 to replace a more subjective evaluation system where Johnson had met with each managers and awarded bonuses based on what he thought was fair.

Other forms of evaluation were also done at Head Office. For mall locations, Johnson might compare a mall's sales growth per square foot with growth in the NBU store. Johnson would present the results of his statistical analyses to the appropriate store managers.

Johnson had once tried to make inter-store comparisons to create a competitive spirit amongst the stores but this effort had been short-lived because store managers had no control over factors such as mall or street construction which had significant impacts on sales.

OPERATIONS

Budgeting

There was no formal budgeting system at NBU. Managers could restock by ordering straight from publishers with no constraints on quantity. However, large expenditures required approval from Head Office. Budget analysis consisted of comparisons with the previous year's sales for the same month.

Computerization

NBU did not have a computer system. Although Diamond had been searching for a system that met NBU's needs, he had not yet found one with which he was satisfied. Consequently, all inventory control, purchases, and returns were still done manually. Since book returns were a key determinant of profitability, NBU management spent many hours each week on paperwork analyzing sales trends.

Theft Control and Security

One of the store manager's responsibilities was theft control. There was no measurement of theft although "shrinkage" was estimated to be between .5% and 2% of sales, an amount which was comparable to industry standards. Security measures consisted of bars at the exits, and checks from a security company. NBU used the services of a security company to make random checks of employees' bags as they left work. The security company had been hired six years ago when it had become evident that some of the employees and managers were stealing books. Head Office tried to relay the message that these security checks did not reflect personally on the honesty of the managers, but were necessary to ensure profits. On occasion, staff from the security company also posed as customers and reported to Head Office on the service and cleanliness of the stores.

Communications

Over and above the weekly visits and annual evaluations, there were several other forms of communication between the stores and Head Office. One of these was the weekly sales analysis, which consisted of a sheet of note paper with two columns. In the first column were several subject categories. In the second column were hash mark tallies of the number of books sold in each subject category during the week. This information was summarized from the daily receipts list, a handwritten list consisting of one entry for each sale. Each entry on the daily receipts list showed the title, price, ISBN code, and subject category of a sale. The weekly sales analysis was compiled monthly at Head Office and the results were returned to the managers about a week after the month end.

On rare occasions the Head Office would send a memo to a store manager indicating that a specific problem needed attention. A manager who received a memo knew that there was a serious problem.

Assessment of Operations

Johnson believed that the overall operating system worked well for the managers. He felt that they enjoyed their freedom to work independently, and that they liked the atmosphere in the bookstores. However, he thought that some managers became frustrated once they had been in the same position for several years because they saw no opportunity for promotion. Although he enjoyed his relationships with the managers, Johnson wanted to see better trained managers, a more sophisticated evaluation system, and a computer system to improve operations.

Johnson did not view himself as a "people person", but as one who got the job done as efficiently as possible. He stated, "They [the managers] probably think that I'm an old geezer and incompetent, and they are waiting for my retirement."

STORE MANAGERS' OPINIONS

Downtown Store Manager

Marcy McMillan, the manager of a high-traffic store located in the heart of the financial district of downtown Toronto, had been with NBU for many years. She had worked part-time at one of the suburban mall stores while attending Ryerson Polytechnical Institute. After finishing her studies-she took on a full-time position, and was later promoted to assistant manager, and then manager at two different stores.

McMillan described her store as business oriented, with a large selection of newspapers and magazines. Her clientele was fairly regular and had not grown much recently, but she saw an opportunity to go after the corporate market in a bigger way. She thought sales would greatly increase if she were able to offer volume discounts to corporations. She was concerned about the competition presented by an independent bookstore catering to business executives which had recently opened up on the same block.

Although she usually hired university students, she did not think that an interest in reading should necessarily be a criterion for hiring staff. She added that, "our location happens to be in a labour market that consists of university students, so we get educated employees."

McMillan was disturbed by the lack of networking amongst the eight store managers. There had once been monthly meetings of the eight managers and Head Office staff but these had stopped. McMillan thought that interacting with other managers would help to build more cooperative working relationships, resulting in increased customer service.

Suburban Mall Manager

Melissa McIntosh was the manager of a successful NBU store in an affluent suburban mall. She joined NBU in 1986 as a part-time cashier after graduating from the University of Toronto with a BA in Psychology and French. One year later she became assistant manager, and within six months she was promoted to store manager, a position she had held for the past three years. During this period she also worked at Head Office for a short time, but returned to her store for "personal and political" reasons. "It is the total responsibility coupled with almost complete independence that makes the job of managing a store so attractive."

Neither McIntosh nor her part-time staff of high school students read much. Her hiring decisions were based on responsibility: "It is a judgement call on who really wants the job and will best perform. I get suspicious when any applicant tells me that they like to read. I think they are trying to suck up."

The training of store staff consisted of three or four sessions dealing with the cash register, store layout, inventory, etc. McIntosh provided her staff with daily feedback but in accordance with the "family atmosphere" in the store, did not conduct formal evaluations of her staff.

McIntosh was concerned with the lack of management training, and the resulting necessity for managers to learn on the job. "There was a management training program several years ago but it lasted only three months and then was cancelled. A management training program would definitely be beneficial, especially to the new managers." She shared McMillan's concerns about the absence of networking amongst the store managers. She thought that the previous NBU practice of monthly meetings of the eight managers and Head Office staff at a local bar had been beneficial in keeping communication lines open. She wanted to see these meetings revived.

McIntosh thought that the evaluation system was unfair. One of her complaints was that the managers' bonuses were negatively affected by the delay in receiving evaluation feedback: by the time they were aware of problems, it was too late to correct them. And, although she knew the criteria for evaluations, she did not know how each category was weighted in determining her bonus. Therefore, she worked under the assumption that "higher sales and smooth operations will equal a high bonus." In addition, she wanted to receive the evaluation of her performance in writing.

McIntosh was also concerned about relationships with Head Office. Although she realized that Johnson's methods had improved considerably since she had started working at NBU, she still thought that he was a "troubleshooter" rather than a "people person" who could encourage the store managers. She knew that he was always available for help, but as she put it, "Keith is not a book person, and could not offer the help needed by most managers in the operation of the business." McIntosh also felt that the relationship between Head Office and the managers was not based on total trust as was evidenced by the use of security staff to check for theft and to evaluate the service provided to customers.

THE FUTURE

Given its market focus and its size, Peter Diamond had concluded that NBU expansion was not recommended in the Toronto area. "Perhaps one or two more stores in Metro Toronto, but we certainly won't have the growth that we saw in the 1980s."

Diamond was satisfied with his accomplishments at NBU and wanted to see expansion of the company outside Toronto. However, he was not interested in pursuing the venture himself. He hoped his daughter, Michelle, would carry on the business.

Exhibit 1

ORGANIZATION CHART

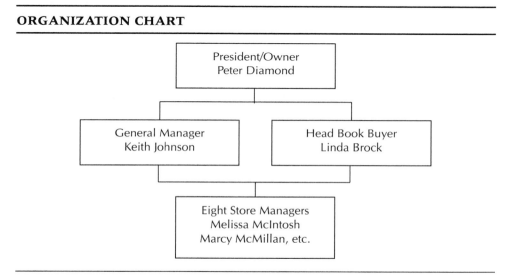

Exhibit 2

EVALUATION OF STORES AND MANAGERS

The purpose of this evaluation is to help managers to focus on areas of the store that need attention and to provide a more systematic basis for determining the amount of the manager's annual bonus. Managers are rated from 1 to 5 (1 - unsatisfactory, 2 - substandard, 3 -average, 4 - above average, 5 - outstanding) on each of the following areas. It is understood that the manager is ultimately responsible for seeing that the store operates efficiently in each of these areas.

AREAS OF CONCERN	RATING				
Sales - relative to monthly goals	1	2	3	4	5
Inventory - maintenance of adequate stock of newspapers, magazines, books, maps, tapes, etc.	1	2	3	4	5
Returns - regular processing of trade and mass market books, newspapers, and magazines	1	2	3	4	5
Housekeeping - clean floors, books straightened and dusted, no burned out lights, tidy magazines, clean shelves, carpets vacuumed, clean registers, aisles relatively free of boxes	1	2	3	4	5
Cash Handling - no serious overages or shortages, accurate charge-card transactions, trouble-free coin floats, error-free bank deposits, correct use of over-rings & refunds	1	2	3	4	5
Displays - effective window and store displays, good use of cash-out area, floor dumps, imaginative positioning of new releases, especially mass market titles	1	2	3	4	5
Customer Relations - develop customer loyalty by having knowledgeable staff, doing special orders, skilful handling of troublesome customers, judicious use of manager's discretion	1	2	3	4	5
Staff - develop and retain an effective staff, operate store within the designated number of staff hours	1	2	3	4	5
Security - train staff to be on guard for theft, see that a good selection of books contains security cards, care in the operation of alarm system, follow up with staff on security company reports	1	2	3	4	5
Paper Work - careful and prompt completion of payroll forms and cash-in reports, speedy sending of packing slips to the office, timely completion of sales report and stock checks	1	2	3	4	5

JONES BLACKWELL

Mark A. Heiz and Randolph Kudar

Early in the spring, Charles Griffith was preparing for another meeting to discuss the performance merit rating of an unhappy partner. Griffith was the Executive Partner of Jones Blackwell, a national firm of chartered accountants. The meeting, arranged at the request of the partner, was the eighth such meeting Griffith had conducted in the past few weeks. Griffith was very frustrated during these meetings and wondered whether the method of distributing the firm's income should be altered in order to address the concerns of many of the partners who had become disenchanted with the current profit sharing system.

THE PUBLIC ACCOUNTING INDUSTRY

Public accounting firms in Canada provided accounting and consulting services to businesses and individuals. The major activity of the firms was serving as external auditors to various organizations. Other allied services included tax return preparation, and non-accounting services such as insolvency work. Most of the services provided by the firm were carried out by chartered accountants or individuals working toward their C.A. qualification. The industry was dominated by several large national firms. They had offices in all major centres across Canada. These firms tended to attract many large organizations requiring auditing and other related services mainly through the breadth of services they offered and their reputation for being up-to-date on all relevant accounting problems. There also existed several smaller national chartered accounting firms and several firms with a strong regional base. These firms provided varying levels of depth and breadth of service depending upon their market niche. Finally, the industry had many small firms which operated predominantly in a fairly small geographical area and relied upon business contacts and specialized services to attract a client base.

All public accounting firms required chartered accountants recognized by the Canadian Institute of Chartered Accountants (C.I.C.A.) to perform or supervise the external auditing of an organization to which they provided that service. There were more than 30,000 chartered accountants in Canada, roughly half of whom were engaged in the practice of public accounting. Attainment of the C.A. designation required a university degree, several university level accounting and related courses, the passing of comprehensive final examinations, and two or three years of practical experience in public accounting. Prior to 1970, a university education was not a requirement for the attainment of the C.A. designation. Individuals could follow a long "apprentice" program and take accounting and related courses and pass the uniform final examination to be accredited. The change in the C.A. requirements had led to a significant shift in the people receiving the designation; they were younger, and had more formal education but much less practical experience.

In all provinces except Alberta, public accounting firms were precluded from incorporating and, therefore, all large firms were organized as partnerships. This form of organization ensured that all partners were jointly and severally responsible for all liabilities of the firm (even in Alberta, incorporation did not reduce partners' legal liability). Of most concern was the risk of liability resulting from deficiencies in the professional work done for clients. Admission to partnership was achieved through election by existing partners. The timing of admission depended primarily upon the needs of the firm and the individuals involved. In the large national firms, admission usually took place from eight to ten years after qualification as a chartered accountant.

Partners, as the owners and managers of the firm, were responsible for determining the firm's policies, marketing its services, ensuring the quality of the professional work, developing and managing employees, and finally sharing in the profits of the firm. Each partner had several employees whose work he or she reviewed and who reported to the partner. A typical organizational strategy had two managers reporting directly to the partner, and each manager would have a staff consisting of both C.A.s and C.A. students. The number of people reporting to each manager depended upon the particular requirements based on the work load assigned to the staff and upon the organization strategy of the firm.

Several firms used a pooling organization system rather than the staff system described previously. Under the pooling system, C.A.s and students were organized into pools upon which the various managers and partners drew depending upon their needs. The staff system was by far the more popular form of organization, particularly in the larger firms in Canada.

Each staff member (including the partners and managers) had an hourly billing rate which was based upon the experience of the staff member and expected number of chargeable hours. The rates were set to provide sufficient revenue to cover employee salaries and overhead costs and to provide adequate profits for the partners.

FIRM BACKGROUND

Jones Blackwell (JB) was formed in 1950, and had grown through internal expansion and purchase or merger to the point where the firm had 35 offices, of varying size, from coast to coast in Canada. While JB had offices in all major Canadian centres, most branches were located in smaller communities where typically JB would be the largest accounting practice in the community. Therefore, the firm had developed a stable client base consisting mainly of small and medium-sized businesses. Approximately 60% of JB's total fees was derived from audit services, while the remaining 40% was from allied services such as tax, bookkeeping, insolvency, and management advisory services.

The organization of JB was fairly straightforward, and much like that of the other national firms. The 35 practice offices were operated by the partners assigned to the offices. The number of partners in each office varied from one to ten depending upon the size of the particular practice. The branch partners were expected to expand their practices, generate profits, develop competent staff, maintain and improve their technical competence, and be prepared to "make sacrifices for the good of the firm" (this usually meant accepting transfers). The firm did not formally designate "partners in charge"; however, in most instances, the personalities were such that it was clear who was "in charge". Within the practice office, the partners had considerable discretion over how they organized and operated their branches. In most branches, the personnel were organized using a staff approach. Due to the nature of the client base of the firm, the staffs tended to be smaller than in other national firms. The firm also had three central specialty offices where specialists in the areas of taxation, insolvency, and management consulting provided services to clients referred by the practice offices. These specialists often assumed a supervisory role and utilized the branch office staff in carrying out their assignments.

The firm utilized an executive office, which essentially coordinated the day to day activities of the firm, and implemented the initiatives or policies approved by the Management Committee of the partnership. The executive office was functionally organized with partners and staff working in each of the following areas: Personnel, training, professional standards (quality control), financial control, and practice development (marketing). Within the executive office, these functions were integrated through two senior partners, the executive partner, Mr. Charles Griffith, and the administrative partner, Mr. John Thomas. These two partners were non-voting members of the management committee and, in addition to day to day administration, were responsible for purchase and merger negotiations and partner counselling.

The management committee consisted of six elected members of the partnership, each serving a three-year term. The committee met once each month, usually for two days. The major responsibilities of the committee involved:

1)   nomination of partners to replace retiring committee members.

2)   review of branch partner recommendations for admission to partnership and recommendation for admission of partners.

3)   approval of employee salary scales, partner evaluations, and profit sharing.

4)   approval of purchase and merger recommendations.

The ultimate authority in the firm was naturally with its owners, the partners. The partners met as a group once or twice a year. The meetings were a forum to discuss and establish firm policies, approve purchases and mergers, review performances, elect members to the management committee, admit new partners, and provide an opportunity to discuss issues facing the firm. In practice, there was relatively little discussion at the meetings, perhaps because individuals were reluctant to voice their views before a large group. Typically, however, there were numerous smaller informal meetings of partners in the evenings for discussion of contentious issues.

Jones Blackwell had approximately 100 partners, the majority of whom were employed in practice offices across the country. Due to expansion of the firm, the number of partners admitted to the partnership had grown considerably in the recent past. The magnitude of this trend was displayed in the following table.

Years as Partner	Number of Partners
0 – 5	45
6 – 10	35
over 10	20

Financially, JB's partners were thought to have earnings close to those of the partners of the larger national firms. In fact, since many JB partners lived in small communities, their housing and transportation costs were very low, and thus their discretionary income was particularly high.

MANAGEMENT PLANNING AND CONTROL SYSTEM

Due to the decentralized nature of JB's organizational structure, and the level of autonomy at the practice office level, each practice office was operated as a profit centre. Branch financial results were communicated to the executive office monthly and compared to budgeted performance. An income statement for a typical practice office is presented in Exhibit 1. In addition to financial budgets which were prepared each fall, practice offices prepared "staff budgets" two or three times a year. A sample staff budget is presented in Exhibit 2. The staff budget projected the level of professional fees for the following 12 months and the staff, both in terms of numbers and experience, required to generate the projected fees. The staff budget aided the personnel group in ensuring that the proper number of people with the required skills was hired. The staff budget also served as a control mechanism for personnel costs.

PROFIT SHARING SYSTEM

The profit sharing system used by Jones Blackwell had been in force since 1968. The system allocated the firm's net income to the partners as required by the *Income Tax Act*. A portion of the income was allocated to the retired partners based on the retirement provisions of the Partnership agreement which allowed that retired partners receive income based on their income for the past five active years in the partnership. The remaining income was allocated to active partners through three vehicles, a base share, a seniority share, and a merit pool. The base share for each partner was specified in the partnership agreement and ranged from $50,000 to $125,000. This base share represented a guaranteed minimum income for the partners, provided that the firm earnings were equal to the total base shares. Seniority shares essentially were allocated to bring the partners' income to the level of the previous year. Any remaining income was placed in a merit pool, and distributed based on partner merit units. The merit units were determined by the management committee. In essence, the merit pool contained the increase in net income for the firm over the previous year. However, the size of the pool was also impacted by the number of partners admitted to the partnership during the year, and the number and seniority of partners retiring during the year.

A significant feature of the profit sharing system was that it was an "open system" whereby each partner was aware of the income levels of all other partners. This practice was unusual in large partnerships and caused some concerns:

> Because of the open income sharing system here, everyone knows how everyone else has been rated. While this to some extent keeps management committee honest, it also places tremendous pressure on the evaluation system.

The distribution of the merit pool was of particular concern to many partners, and provided a source of constant frustration for Mr. Griffith.

DISTRIBUTION OF THE MERIT POOL

The merit ratings for each partner were determined by the management committee each fall. The committee requested a partner information report (PIR) from each partner. The partner completed the PIR which outlined such partner activities as professional and practice development, and office and partner performance detailing office profitability and partner productivity in terms of chargeable hours. A PIR questionnaire is presented in Exhibit 3. Each member of the management committee reviewed the partner's PIR, and using a Partner Evaluation Report, evaluated each partner. The Partner Evaluation Report required a ranking of the partner in nine areas including such quantifiable areas as office profitability, and partner chargeable hours and such non-quantifiable measures as client relations, practice development, and ability. A sample Partner Evaluation Report is shown in Exhibit 4. Each member of the management committee generated an evaluation for each partner. The highest and the lowest evaluations were eliminated. The remaining evaluations were averaged and converted to an overall ranking between 0 and 9 for each partner. The management committee then discussed the merit unit allocation and the atmosphere of the meetings was often described as heated and emotional. The process normally took two to three days of continuous meetings and was consistently described by members of the committee as the worst part of their job.

Upon completion of the assignment of merit units, all partners received a list of the assignable seniority share and merit units. The information was distributed by December 31, and the partners had one month to request formal reconsideration of merit ratings by the management committee.

PARTNER CONCERNS ABOUT
THE PROFIT SHARING SYSTEM

For the first ten years after adoption of the merit pool, the distribution of merit units over the partnership was quite even. Most partners received a rating of seven, while a few received six, and a small number received a rating of eight or nine. However, over the past five years, the distribution had changed significantly with unit awards between zero and five increasing and the average rating being reduced to six. The shift in award of merit allocation was thought to have been caused by pressure from younger partners who felt that the system did not adequately differentiate performance. The position of many younger partners was perhaps best voiced by a partner who had been in the partnership for five years:

> "I'm fed up with those fat cats at the top of the income sharing. While some of them earn their share, others are simply cruising on past efforts. Most of them are not prepared to move or take on challenges that are required to move the firm ahead. They expect us to make the sacrifices but they won't give us the merit in return".

Many other partners were concerned about various aspects of the merit system:

> "My biggest concern is that the system seems to be counter-productive. Most people seem to see themselves as being better than others see them. As a result, many people rate themselves as say a 7 and getting a 6 from the management committee turns them off. They spend a lot of time being upset rather than trying to improve."

> "My major concern is that it's a lot easier to lose units than it is to regain them. Two years ago, my rating dropped from an eight to a six. They never tell you why or give you any feedback. They just issue the units. Now I feel that the eight was too high but I think I should be a seven. I know it will take me a long time to recover. Once they mark you down, they keep you down for a while, sometimes for ever."

> "I've moved twice in the past six years for the firm. Although I don't formally have the title, I run one of the highest risk offices in the firm. The other partners in the office are weak, and as a result, the office is not doing as well as it should. Because of the high emphasis on financial results, I lost a merit unit last year. I have to ask, what's the point? I go through the agony of two moves, take on a high-risk assignment, put up with weak partners in the office, and still lose a point. I'd have been better off to turn down the transfer and play it safe. How do they expect to get other partners to accept transfers if this is the way they reward us?"

> "I only got a 6. They tell me that is strong performance in an average branch. If you look at our branch profits, they are excellent compared to most of the other branches. Oh I know I'm not the strongest technically in the firm, and I don't really bring in that many new accounts, but I sure know how to make money from a block of accounts. They say profits are important, why don't they show it with the merit units?"

> "...most members of the management committee only see most of the partners once or twice a year. How can they possibly do a proper job of evaluating the partners when they hardly know most of them and when they've never visited the branch offices?"

> "I have some real concerns about the method of calculation. I happened to get into the partnership in a year where the increase in net income was down, and when the net increase in the number of partners was high. As a result, the merit unit value that year was only $500. I got a seven, so my increase was $3,500. I know that the year before, the merit unit value was almost $2,000. If I had been admitted a year earlier, I would have made more than $10,000 extra.

And don't forget because of the system, that's not just $10,000 for one year, but that amount per year as long as I am a partner and it also affects the retirement arrangements."

The above concerns, voiced by some of the younger partners in the firm, led Mr. Griffith to ask the firm's long range planning committee to examine the profit sharing system and make recommendations for changes. The committee, composed of a representative group of partners, reviewed the system and found it to be conceptually sound. Therefore they did not make any significant recommendations. However the complaints continued and Griffith was spending more and more of his time meeting with disgruntled partners. He was having great difficulty holding his temper when dealing with partners whom he considered "average partners who were highly paid, and who apparently still wanted more".

While the younger partners voiced their concerns, the older partners also became upset. A partner of 21 years expressed the following concerns:

"I hear that some of the younger partners are complaining about the high incomes of the older partners. Those fellows should remember who built this practice. In the old days, we worked at least as hard and probably harder than the fellows work today, and for a lot less money. It's only been in the last few years that our incomes have grown quickly and much of that growth has come from our ability to keep ahead of inflation in our billing rates. Those young fellows should learn to be patient, they'll have their turn at the big money in time."

As Griffith sat down after his latest meeting with a disgruntled partner, he observed,

"this system that is supposed to motivate partners to act in the best interests of the firm is turning them off."

Griffith wondered how the income distribution system could be changed to address the concerns of the partners and coincidentally reduce the number of tension-filled meetings with unhappy partners.

Exhibit 1

JONES BLACKWELL
Statement of Branch Income for the Year Ended January 31

		Branch "A"
Gross Fees		$905,700
Billing Debits—Net		(45,100)
Other Income		6,300
Net Fees and Other Income		$866,900
Salaries		427,600
GROSS PROFIT		$439,300
Expenses:		
Employee Benefits	$27,500	
Office Operating Costs	35,700	
Office Occupancy	84,600	
Provision for Doubtful Accounts	34,000	
Interest Charges[1]	23,200	
Promotion and Miscellaneous	19,000	
Total Expenses		$224,000
NET INCOME		$215,300

[1] Executive Office Interest Charges

Exhibit 2

JONES BLACKWELL—Branch "A"

Staff Budget*
for the Twelve Months Ending April 30

Name	Classification	Salary	Hours	Rate	Potential Fees
Brown, A.B.	Partner	$48,000**	1,400	$72	$100,800
Jones, C.D.	Partner	48,000**	1,600	64	102,400
Black, E.F.	C.A.	32,000	1,600	53	84,800
LeBlanc, G.H.	C.A.	28,000	1,600	47	75,200
Smith, I.J.	C.A.	26,000	1,600	43	68,800
Green, K.L.	C.G.A.	25,000	1,600	42	67,200
White, M.N.	Student	19,200	1,400	32	44,800
Greene, O.O.	Student	19,200	1,400	32	44,800
Grey, P.R.	Student	16,200	1,500	27	40,500
MacDonald, S.T.	Student	13,200	1,500	22	33,000
Jacobson, I.V.	Student	13,200	1,500	22	33,000
Fraser, W.D.	Para-Professional	27,000	1,800	45	81,000
McNeil, R.R.	Para-Professional	22,000	1,700	37	62,900
Wright, I.M.	Accountant	16,500			
Martin, B.A.	Secretary	18,000	600	30	18,000
Forsythe, K.M.	Stenographer	13,200	800	22	17,600
Downey, A.F.	Stenographer	10,000	800	17	13,600
		$394,700	22,400		$888,400

Less — Estimated Billing Debits		48,400
Potential Net Professional Fees		$840,000
Prior Periods Actual		
12 Months to April 30, 19__	21,600	$780,000

* Salaries and rates have been altered; figures shown for illustration only.
** For internal financial reporting only.

Exhibit 3

JONES BLACKWELL—Partner Information Report

Prepared by:_____ Date: _____

This questionnaire is intended to provide information to Management Committee not already available in reports to the Executive Office.

Institute Activities
(Not Professional Development Courses)
Office held: _____
Committee memberships: _____
_____

Practice Development
Comment briefly on the nature of your practice development initiatives.
_____
_____
_____
_____
_____

List positions (board, executive, fund raising) held in the last twelve months in business associations, service clubs, charitable organization, church, sports clubs, hospitals, universities and similar community activities.
_____
_____
_____
_____

Professional Development
Excluding in-house training, list the courses you have taken or given.
_____
_____
_____

Personal Productivity
Comment on the number of your chargeable hours compared to the previous year (six months ended July 31).
_____
_____
_____
_____
_____
_____

Exhibit 3 (continued)

If your chargeable hours for the fiscal year ended January 31, 1983, were less than the average for all partners, please comment.

_____

_____

_____

_____

_____

Office Profitability

Comment on the profitability of your office for the fiscal year ended January 31, 19XX, in relation to other offices.

_____

_____

_____

_____

_____

_____

Billing and Collecting

Comment on the outstanding percentage of your office in relation to the firm average at January 31, 198X and at June 30, 198X .

_____

_____

_____

Other Information

Outline any other information not covered by this report or by financial and statistical information already submitted to the Executive Office which you feel may assist Management Committee in its partner evaluation process, including comments on your present position and location and your desires, objectives, goals, for other positions and/or locations in the firm.

_____

_____

_____

_____

_____

_____

_____

_____

_____

_____

_____

_____

_____

_____

Exhibit 4

JONES BLACKWELL—Partner Evaluation Report

Partner	Date

A. *Contribution to Branch Profitability* (Based on "office" results) _____
Firm average (net before purchase payments)

14 – 16	More than 10% above
11 – 13	More than 5% but less than 10% above
8 – 10	Firm average to 5% below
2 – 4	More than 5% but less than 10% below
0 – 1	More than 10% below

B. *Billing and Collection* (Based on "office" outstanding percentage) _____
Promptness in billing; effectiveness in collecting.
Firm average

11 – 12	More than 10% below
9 – 10	More than 5% but less than 10%
7 – 8	Between 5% below and 5% above
5 – 6	More than 5% but less than 10% above
3 – 4	More than 10% but less than 20% above
0 – 2	More than 20% above

C. *Personal Productivity* (Chargeable hours) _____
Partner average

11 – 12	Over 200 hours above
9 – 10	100 – 200 hours above
7 – 8	0 – 100 hours above
5 – 6	0 – 100 hours below
3 – 4	100 – 200 hours below
0 – 2	Over 200 hours below

D. *Staff Morale, Progress and Production* _____
Ability to effectively train staff; willingness to study and understand staff
problems, capacity to command the confidence and respect of staff; ability
to obtain effectiveness in staff productivity.

14 – 16	Very good
11 – 13	Good
7 – 10	Satisfactory
3 – 6	Reasonably satisfactory with some weaknesses
0 – 3	Weak

E. *Technical — Ability and Attitude* _____
Technical ability generally; interest in developing own knowledge; ability to
specialize in a chosen field; insistence on proper audit techniques; quality
of file review.

14 – 16	Very good
11 – 13	Good
7 – 10	Satisfactory
3 – 6	Reasonably satisfactory with some weaknesses
0 – 3	Weak

Exhibit 4 (continued)

F. *Client Relations* _____

Capacity to command the confidence and respect of clients; extent that services to present clients are expanded and upgraded; development and maintenance of dynamic continuing relationships with desirable clients; extent to which special services, management services and tax services (including use of specialists) are provided to clients; ability to impress clients in normal day-to-day handling of their affairs.

14 – 16	Very good
11 – 13	Good
7 – 10	Satisfactory
3 – 6	Reasonably satisfactory with some weaknesses
0 – 3	Weak

G. *Practice Development* _____

Attitude; initiative; participation in community activities; ability to attract new clientele; ability to develop contracts with media.

9 – 10	Very good
7 – 8	Good
5 – 6	Satisfactory
3 – 4	Reasonably satisfactory with some weaknesses
0 – 2	Weak

H. *Contribution to Firm Improvement and Development* _____

Capacity to command the confidence and respect of partners; ability to think of and implement improved methods; overall contribution to the firm; ability to think of and present new ideas for firm development; cooperation in the administrative problems of the firm.

11 – 12	Very good
9 – 10	Good
7 – 8	Satisfactory
5 – 6	Reasonably satisfactory with some weaknesses
0 – 4	Weak

I. *Ability*

Capacity for additional responsibility.

17 – 20	Capable of most assignments
13 – 16	Capable of leader role in present or other location
9 – 12	Capable of making a greater contribution in a similar assignment in another location
5 – 8	Making the best contribution in present position
0 – 4	Not performing well in present assignment and not capable of accepting new assignment.

TOTAL POINTS _____

Actual or perceived role as leader in present location does not *necessarily* mean points to be awarded as "capable of leader role in present or other location."

Unwilling to accept new assignment or leader role is a negative and should reduce the value assigned to that category.

Willingness to accept new assignment or increased responsibility but not considered capable is *not* a positive factor and should not increase the value assigned to a category.

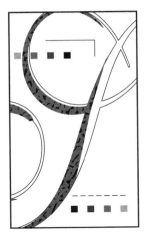

PART F

EMERGING ISSUES IN
MANAGEMENT

BRENTWOOD TRUCKING COMPANY

Sue Hanna, John Perry, and Randolph Kudar*

Mr. John Moser, Vice President of Training and Quality Development for Brentwood Trucking Company, was preparing a Cost of Quality report for presentation to Mr. G.K. Alexander, the president of Brentwood Trucking Ltd. Recently, the executive of Brentwood Trucking Ltd. had given approval for John to begin instilling "quality thinking" throughout the organization. Now, John was faced with the task of determining where these new concepts of quality might be applied within the activities of the firm. One part of the problem involved defining what was meant by a quality defect in various areas of the firm. A second problem included a determination of the cost associated with quality defects. A third task centred on the development of a strategy for addressing quality that would provide a competitive and sustainable advantage for the firm.

COMPANY BACKGROUND

Brentwood Trucking Ltd. is a holding company for one of the largest transportation groups in Canada. Brentwood Trucking Ltd. includes the following companies:

Brentwood Trucking Company

Speedivery

Speedpac / BrentAir

Brentwood International Express

Metro Towns Truck Lines (Canada) Inc.

Quikspress Services

Dominion Truck Lines Inc.

Regal Express and Multimessage Inc.

Prairie Express Inc.

Wheatfield Trucking Ltd.

Containfreight

Central Bulk Inc.

Buds Cartage Company

Brentwood Truckload International

The firm had its beginnings in central Ontario. The first transportation jobs involved the purchase of by-products in the chemical valley and transporting them to Toronto. In the early 1950s, the firm began direct service between Toronto and Winnipeg. In 1958, this service was extended east to include Montreal, and incorporated stops throughout Northwestern Ontario.

In 1962, the firm purchased Newbolt Truck Lines and expanded the service westward into Alberta. The name Newbolt was later changed to Brentwood Trucking (Western) Ltd. In 1967, the company moved into a new complex in Sheridan Park, Mississauga, and opened the head office there in 1968. In 1969, the firm purchased James Transport Ltd., which was later renamed Regal Express Ltd.

The over-the-road division, called Speedivery, was started in 1981. It offered two-day service from Toronto to Winnipeg, and three-day service for points further west in Canada. Speedpac was created in 1985. It offered small parcel road service throughout Canada. As well, BrentAir was set up to offer overnight air freight service across Canada as well as to 18,000 destinations in the United States.

Currently, Brentwood Trucking Company operates over 1,500 vehicles moving freight from thousands of shippers across Canada to their customers. The main business is transporting manufactured goods in less than truck load (LTL) quantities. Moving westbound, the vehicles often contain between 30 and 100 different shipments of various sizes and weights, coming from dozens of different shippers and going to many different receivers. Coming eastbound, the loads tend to be of truck load volume and often shipped by one supplier. Today, Brentwood Trucking Ltd. operates modern terminals in all major Canadian cities, as well as agencies in the smaller towns and more remote areas of the country. The firm also interlines with independent carriers outside of the regions served by the terminals and the agencies.

Brentwood Trucking Ltd. provides some fundamental services to all of its subsidiary companies. These include general accounting and financial controls, central banking, computer services and information, training and quality development, accounts payable and receivable, and human resources. In a manual issued to all new employees of the firm, the company philosophy is stated as follows:

> *We believe in providing good service and being completely honest with our customers. We believe work is more fun when we work hard, rather than when we just fill in time. We believe that good work should be recognized and that a steady job with a growing income, is in itself a fine reward for good work done. We believe that the people in our company are more important than the buildings or equipment and that we need to treat one another honestly, fairly, and with respect.*

THE STEERING COMMITTEE

During the 1980s, the transportation industry became intensely competitive. Firms, such as Brentwood, found themselves facing pressures from other carriers as well as from more demanding customers. In order to survive, the top executives believed that an "added advantage" had to be introduced in order to attract and keep customers at Brentwood. A steering committee was formed for the purpose of deciding how to differentiate Brentwood Trucking Company from its competition. The committee was made up of top executives of the firm, including Mr. John Moser.

Mr. Moser was born and educated in Canada. He began his career in the trucking industry upon completion of his schooling. He started his career by working overseas for transportation firms in England, Holland, and Germany. During this period, he was involved in the operations end of the business, primarily managing terminals. Eventually, he returned home to Canada and took a job with a transportation firm in Alberta. Subsequently, he joined Brentwood Trucking Company in the operations area.

While working in the terminals, John noticed problems that appeared to be common to the operations in any terminal, regardless of where it was located or who owned it. Moreover, these problems never seemed to be solved or eliminated. He became aware of the work of Dr. Edwards Deming, a consultant who advocated the use of statistical analysis to improve quality as a fundamental approach to business management. John felt that Deming's quality concepts had direct relevance to the problems that he had been dealing with in his years in the transportation industry.

The steering committee began their assignment by asking such questions as: "What do we want to do?", "Why?", and "What do we do with it once we have it?" Partly because of John's strong belief and interest in Deming's quality concepts, the committee agreed that quality of service would be Brentwood's primary area of concern. Based upon the report and recommendations of the steering committee, the executives of Brentwood Trucking Ltd. authorized John Moser to start a full scale quality development process within the Brentwood set of companies. As a starting point for the process and effort, the company developed a policy statement indicating its commitment to quality. It was stated as follows:

> TO PROVIDE ERROR-FREE SERVICES TO OUR CUSTOMERS BOTH INTERNAL AND EXTERNAL BY MEETING REQUIREMENTS AND PERFORMING OUR TASKS RIGHT THE FIRST TIME.

The intent of the quality development process was to involve every person in every department and in every location of the firm. John began the process by setting up Quality Management Teams (QMTs) at all locations for all people at the management and supervisory levels as a means of introducing them to the "quality way of thinking". It was felt that, as a first step, it was necessary to convince management about the critical importance of quality improvement before the concept could be successfully introduced to the rest of the employees.

In the steering committee John asked the executives to provide information regarding the concept of quality defects within their own functional activities, the cost associated with those quality defects, and any suggestions on how to address the quality issues. A summary of their comments is provided in the following paragraphs.

MANAGERIAL COMMENTS ON QUALITY

Terminals

Terminal operations involved the loading and unloading of shipments at central locations. These facilities included loading bays for the vehicles and storage areas for shipments that were awaiting transportation. There were a number of items that were raised by the manager of terminal operations regarding the errors and problems that affected his operations. Many of these were familiar to John.

On average, the terminals handled 28,000 deliveries a month. Of these, approximately 3% or 840 deliveries resulted in no charges being made to the customer because of company error, or redeliveries. The costs to handle these deliveries were estimated to be $50,000 per year to unload the delivery at the dock, and an additional $84,000 a year to deliver the shipment to the customer's site.

For each load that was brought into the terminal the dockmen were required to examine and complete tally sheets. On average, this amounted to 3,000 tally sheets a month. In a survey of tally sheet activities, it was found that there were four exceptions per sheet that required the time of the dockman to correct. An exception was defined as a checking or counting error on the tally sheet. If each exception took one minute of the dockman's time, this activity could cost $48,000 per year.

There were occasions when freight would arrive with no bills of lading, or bills of lading would arrive with no freight. The manager estimated that the supervisors at the terminals spent as much as two hours per day, in total, handling this type of issue. They also spent an additional two hours per day running counts to match up bills of lading with freight at the terminals. Based upon the average salary of supervisors, these activities were estimated to cost the company about $100,000 per year.

The manager estimated that at least one shipment per day was picked up in error. This meant that the firm not only incurred the cost of picking up the shipment, but had to redeliver the shipment to the site, as well as incur the cost of handling the documentation for the error. Often, there was a penalty cost for incurring this error. He estimated the cost of these errors to be $17,500 per year.

One of the tasks at the terminals was to load the trailers. It was estimated that improper loading of shipments was resulting in at least 500 lbs. of capacity per trailer being lost within the system daily. Assuming that this capacity travelled the average distance of all shipments, the equivalent capacity could have generated $300,000 of contribution in a year. The manager felt that the firm was almost 95% efficient in loading the shipments to cube capacity or weight capacity. Given that the firm travelled approximately 30 million miles per year, at an average cost of $1.00 per mile, this translated into an additional cost of $1,500,000 incurred in extra travel because the loads were not full.

One of the elements of service provided by Brentwood was guaranteed service of Speedivery deliveries. Scheduling problems created occasions when the deliveries would be late. As a result, extra time costs were incurred as people had to wait at the docks to receive the shipments. The manager estimated that the company was incurring over 40 hours per working day of extra time. In addition, the productivity at some of the terminals where the overnight deliveries were late was being reduced. He felt this cost to be in the range of $325,000 per year.

The manager also indicated that there were costs associated with the location and layout of some of the docks at the terminals. Under the current conditions, he felt that he was incurring up to 10% additional labour time to handle the same volume of work that could be done with improvements to the location and layout of the docks. The cost for this situation was calculated at $1,000,000 per year.

The manager felt that there was insufficient capacity at some of the terminals in Western Canada to accommodate the volume of business available. He estimated that five loads of temperature-controlled product had to be turned down each working day due to lack of space. On average, each load generated about $3,000 of revenue and the normal margin on this business was in the order of 5% of sales.

Given the complexity and volume of shipments that were handled by the terminals across the country, the manager required 12 people to spend their full time tracing orders and shipments within the system. The salary and benefits of these people were estimated to be $250,000 a year.

In some instances, where problems arose, it had been necessary to hire external cartage to deliver or pick up the shipment. Last year, this cost had been $375,000. The phone bill for this department was budgeted at $245,000 p.a.

Finally, there were various accidents that occurred within the terminals. The damages and costs associated with these had been $140,000 for the past year.

Transportation Department

The transportation department handled the highway operations of Brentwood Trucking Company to carry shipments from customers to their destinations. Here John found out several facts. As with any complex operation, it was not uncommon for activities to go contrary to plan. The manager of the department identified several errors and problems that affected his operations.

The manager indicated that there were instances where the trailers were loaded too heavily and the firm incurred fines for overweight loads. There was also the issue of accidents. Driving vehicles back and forth across the country inevitably meant accidents. Currently, he thought that the firm was paying in the order of $400,000 a year for accident costs and fines.

The manager reported that there were instances where loads would not be ready to leave even though the vehicle was waiting to pick them up. Considering the cost of the drivers, their benefits, and the frequency of occurrence, the manager thought this could cost as much as $60,000 a year. There were also occasions where the load would be ready, but no tractor was available. People were then required to stand around and wait for the trailer to be moved before they could begin filling another trailer. Similarly, there were occasions when the tractor would be ready, but the trailer would not be available. Again, people would be forced to wait on the docks until the trailer was ready. Finally, there were instances where the driver was late in picking up an order and thus blocked the dock. The manager felt that these cases could cost up to $7,500 a year.

At the receiving end of the delivery, the driver was sometimes required to lay over for an unscheduled stop because of time requirements, or loading/unloading requirements. In some cases, the driver would be required to obtain accommodations for overnight while the load was attended to. These cases were thought to cost as much as $100,000 in expenses, salaries, and fringe benefits.

Given the scale of operations, and the problems indicated previously, the manager felt that it was necessary for the firm to carry excess trailers. There were instances where the trailers were in the wrong location when they were needed. The manager estimated that the total cost to the firm of this excess capacity was up to $325,000 in the year.

The final issue raised by the manager of transportation involved driver turnover. During the previous year the firm had experienced a turnover of 102 drivers. This meant that there would be registration costs associated with ensuring that the new driver was qualified to operate the vehicles. He estimated the cost of this turnover at $20,500 for the year.

Maintenance Department

The maintenance department was responsible for the repair and servicing of all equipment for the firm. In addition to scheduling maintenance and repairs, the department also carried spare parts inventory. The maintenance manager reported on several common problems that existed.

On occasion, vehicles would experience premature failure of parts that would put the vehicles out of service at times other than when they were scheduled for maintenance and repairs. There had been instances of incorrect diagnoses by mechanics regarding problems with the vehicles. The manager talked about repair orders that were almost totally illegible and others where the coding for the work orders had been completed improperly. He mentioned how some of the trip sheets filled out by the drivers indicating problems contained unclear or incomplete information, resulting in additional time and effort by maintenance personnel to find and repair the problem. Analysis of activities had revealed that there was some excessive lubrication on the fifth wheels of the vehicles (the link pin connecting the trailer to the highway tractor). Of course, there were the common maintenance issues of tool misuse and housekeeping problems. The manager had indicated that the cost to Brentwood of accommodating these issues was approximately $87,400.

In the parts department the problems centred around excess and obsolete inventory. Often, as the equipment changed, parts purchased for some pieces of equipment became obsolete. In other instances, efforts to get quantity price discounts had resulted in the firm holding excess levels of inventory. Audits of the inventory stores revealed that there had been some losses caused by inadequate control of the stores areas. As well, the audit had revealed that some of the parts were not the correct ones needed for the equipment and some were actually defective in stores. Lastly, there had been some instances where the vendor had issued an incorrect billing to the firm and time had been spent checking the packing slips and receipt cards to correct the billing. These items were estimated to cost $90,500.

One issue raised by the maintenance manager involved the wash bays. It was here that the vehicles were cleaned up regularly after use. Unfortunately, the expansion of the firm had outstripped the capability of the wash bay to handle the load. It was the opinion of the manager that this lack of capacity was requiring increased vehicle maintenance to avoid corrosion. He thought that the cost of the additional maintenance could be as high as $116,000 a year.

Quality Department

The quality department consisted of one and one half people full time. The task of this group was to act as consultants for the various units within the firm. This involved travel and materials to discuss quality issues with the people in the locations where Brentwood operated. The wage and benefit cost of this department was listed as $70,000 per year. The budget for this operation had been set at $170,000 for the year. The department intended to develop materials that would bring the issue of quality to the attention of the employees of the firm. The manager proposed the publication of a newsletter, manuals, posters, booklets, and other communication devices to keep people focused on quality. This was expected to cost $10,000. The other part of his plan included a series of quality system seminars to be conducted with the employees of the firm across the country. Travel expense for the training work was budgeted at $20,000. The supervisors, after training, would begin the quality development process with the people at their own location.

Training Department

The training department consisted of two and a half people who were responsible for the development of training programs within the firm. The wage and benefits cost of the department was approximately $80,000 a year. The department had an array of television and video equipment available at the head office to assist them in the presentation of education programs for the firm. These were valued at $11,000. It was the responsibility of the department to produce, develop, distribute, and conduct management development and employee training programs for the firm. The manager had received a budget of $45,000 to cover the production costs of the programs that he planned on presenting during the year.

Sales and Marketing Department

The sales and marketing department was charged with the responsibility of quoting rates for services to customers, getting new business, retaining established accounts, dealing with issues arising from late deliveries of goods, and of meeting and dealing with customer complaints about the services offered by Brentwood. The marketing manager indicated that one of the most common problems facing his area was errors in the quotation rates. It was estimated that the department made over 2,000 rate quotes a year. Each quote took approximately 20 minutes to complete by a secretary. He felt that about 10% of all the quotes had some error in them that required the quote to be redone. He thought that this could cost up to $12,000 a year.

As part of their service, Brentwood offered customers a guarantee on the delivery of their shipments on time. As a result of late deliveries, the marketing manager indicated that the company had been required to reduce rates on those shipments by $30,000 in the past year. In the same vein, when shipments were not on time, it was necessary for someone from the department to spend time tracking down the shipment and dealing with the concerns of the customer. He felt that each of his sales representatives spent almost one hour each working day dealing with the complaints of customers in the office. He costed this at $303,000 per year. In addition to dealing with the issues in the office, some of the sales representatives found it necessary to travel to the customer's site to address the issues. This was estimated to cost $37,000 for the year.

It was necessary to cope with turnover among the sales representatives in the department. The hiring process involved advertising the position, reviewing the resumes of applicants, interviews, and reference checks. Once a hire was made, it was necessary to train the individual, including some on-the-job training in the field with an experienced sales representative. Last year, the department had hired nine people. The manager felt that each new representative took the equivalent of almost two full months to become fully active in the job. Generally, this was spread out over the first six months of their employment in the business. Based upon the initial salary levels for new sales representatives, the marketing manager thought that this effort would cost the firm $156,000 a year.

Claims Department

The claims department was responsible for settling all claims from customers that resulted from errors made by the company in handling the customers' shipments. The manager reported that, in the past year, the firm had paid out almost $1,800,000 in claims to customers for damages sustained during shipment by Brentwood. The department consisted of three people and the manager. The salary and benefits cost of the department was almost $138,000 a year. In addition, the department had a travel budget of almost $5,000 for the year. The manager indicated that almost 35% of the time of the people in his department was spent dealing with administrative rework due to wrong information being submitted to the claims office from the field. This was estimated to cost in the order of $70,000.

Administration Department

The accounts receivable department consisted of the accountant and a staff of people who were charged with the responsibility of providing credit to customers and of collecting the revenues from customers. The salaries and wages for this department were listed as $401,000.

The controller in the accounting department indicated that the firm would likely experience bad debts in the order of $36,000 to $37,000 over the coming year. In addition, he was budgeting approximately $35,500 to cover legal fees and credit company checks on customers seeking credit from the firm. Currently, there were some problems collecting receivables from customers. The accountant suggested that the interest value on those receivables that were not being paid on time was as high as $300,000.

During an internal audit of his department, the accountant determined that, in the space of one month, 2,830 bills issued to customers had to be reprocessed because of adjustments to the amounts. The cost of this reprocessing was in the order of $88,000, if extended for a full year.

THE ASSESSMENT

Now that he had some data about errors and problems within the different operations of the firm, John wondered how he should use this information to assess the current situation. He felt that it was necessary to be able to tell the executive committee of Brentwood Trucking Ltd. what the impact of quality thinking could be upon the firm. Finally, he wanted to develop some type of strategy to guide the implementation of the quality development process that he was about to commence within the firm.

INTERFIRM COMPARISON—CELLMITE CORPORATION

Rob Ceshan, Randolph Kudar, and Robert Britney

Charles Halston, President of the Cellmite Corporation headquartered in Prince Rupert, British Columbia, was curious as to the findings of the report he received from the Department of Regional Industrial Expansion under the Interfirm Comparison Program. He was aware that the report contained productivity measures on his company which were compared against other firms within the softwood lumber finishing industry.

In anticipation of a meeting the following week with the consultant who prepared the report, he studied the report to make sure he clearly understood the measurement data and findings contained therein.

PROCESS OF THE INTERFIRM COMPARISON PROGRAM

The interfirm comparison program, which is sponsored and implemented by the federal Department of Regional Industrial Expansion (DRIE), allows a business within an industry to compare its productivity and profitability to the competition. It can be used as a tool for measuring a firm's performance and therefore for management planning and control purposes.

The process of the program begins with the decision by DRIE to undertake a comparison of a particular industrial sector. Firms within that industry are identified and invited to participate in the program.

Should a sufficient number of firms be interested, a set of performance ratios are developed with the cooperation of senior management of the firms. Only those ratios deemed to be of most significance to the success of firms within the industry, are calculated. Return on assets invested, which is a measure of operating profits as a percent of operating assets, is the key ratio calculated since it reflects a firm's profit-making capacity. This ratio, along with a series of other ratios, indicates a firm's efficiency in utilizing available resources. The hierarchy of ratios used to establish the relative success of each firm in this sector of the softwood lumber finishing industry is shown in Exhibit 1.

To gather the data necessary to calculate the ratios, each participating firm is visited by a representative of DRIE. The required financial, statistical, physical, and other background information is collected directly from senior management of the firm and from the firm's records. This visit by the DRIE representative also includes a tour of the production facilities to understand the process used by the firm and identify any significant differences between the participating companies that might have an impact on the comparability of the ratios.

The data is gathered in a standardized format. Each item has an operational definition that allows the DRIE consultant to properly classify cost items in a consistent manner across the firms in the industry sector to provide comparability. This process is discussed in Appendix 1.

The gathered accounting data is reconciled with the accounting records of the firm to ensure that no items are omitted or double counted. A "Statement of Data Used" is forwarded to the participating firm to allow them to reconcile their accounting and other data with the data used in the interfirm comparison. Following an appropriate response time, each company's data is analyzed using the interfirm comparison methodology before the required performance ratios are calculated.

A confidential report is prepared for each participating company. The report outlines the purpose, method, and results of the comparison and provides an analysis of the company's performance based on the various measures calculated. The essence of the report is a table similar to Exhibit 4 which gives the performance ratios of all the firms that participated in the comparison.

The participating company can expect a return visit from the consultant who gathered the data within one to two weeks of receipt of the report. The purpose of this return visit is to help management interpret their report, understand the implications of the results to their operations, and plan appropriate corrective actions.

For a more detailed discussion of the interfirm comparison program, the ratios generated and the process refer to Appendix 1. Definitions for each factor used in the make-up of the developed ratios used in Exhibit 1 are given in Appendix 2.

THE SOFTWOOD LUMBER FINISHING INDUSTRY

The finishing industry primarily concerns itself with the appearance of softwood lumber which is slated for high-quality uses such as door stock and frames, and window sills and frames. Such products require smoother surfaces than that found in dimension lumber such as wood studs and 2×4s, to name a few. It is estimated that three-quarters of the lumber produced in Canada undergoes some additional processing. Planer mills are used to dress the rough lumber surfaces and thereby produce a uniformly smooth product. This more valuable lumber includes the following categories: appearance framing, clears, factory, and/or shop lumber.

As shown in Exhibit 2, British Columbia is the largest producer of softwood lumber in Canada. Of this production, over 70% is exported. A breakdown of the quantity and value of softwood lumber exported by major importing country is given in Exhibit 3. Besides worldwide economic growth, other economic factors which have swayed the competitive position of the industry are: 1) fluctuations in exchange rates, e.g., devaluation of the Canadian dollar improves the industry's worldwide competitive position; 2) interest rates, e.g., rising mortgage rates decreases housing demand; and 3) increasing popularity of alternate construction materials such as concrete, steel, and plastic, and other lumber products such as plywood and waferboard.

This particular interfirm comparison study dealt with a sector within the softwood finishing industry in British Columbia that almost exclusively worked with spruce. Only 6.5% of the wood used as a raw material involved pine. The program covered a year's operation of 12 British Columbia firms which were closely tied to the softwood finishing industry. Total sales of these firms exceeded $44 million. The program was unable to estimate total sales in this sector because of a high turnover of firms within the industry. A $250,000 investment in equipment and working capital can result in a sizeable operation that would support $2.5 million in annual sales.

The low entry investment was a major contributor to the industry's problems. Capacity utilization for the 12 firms studied within the industry averaged 56.3%. Capacity is defined as two shifts of eight hours operating five days a week and fifty weeks a year. The lowest utilization rate was 23.3%, two others were in the mid 30% range, and a fourth was below 45%. Two firms had better than an 80% capacity utilization rate and operated in areas where the other firms' capacity utilization rates were very low.

The mills in this industrial sector were run by the owners who spent most of their time on market related activities. Production managers generally ran the plants.

The accounting and control functions within this sector received less than adequate attention. Only a few of the people interviewed during the comparison understood their potential for cost control. Eight of the firms used computers for accounting functions. Two other mill owners indicated that a one-write system was adequate for their fairly simple business and they had no intention of using computers. Computers were not used for production control by most firms.

A fairly standard production process was used throughout the industry. The first step was to bring the lumber into the shop from outside storage followed by cutting to the required lengths. The cutting job was identified in several firms as the bottleneck in the plant.

The industry used one of two types of cut-off saws. The more prevalent was an enclosed automatic saw with a feeder belt on which the operator placed the lengths of wood. It had four saw blades and could perform four different cuts on one pass. Most companies that used this saw required a second operator to stack the cut lengths of wood on hand-trucks as they came off the saw. Those companies often cited the stackers as an area in which production methods could be improved. The other companies had automatic stackers that replaced this operator.

A few of the smaller companies used hand-operated radial arm saws. For those companies an automatic saw was often cited as the best production improvement opportunity available. The larger companies only used radial arm saws for short runs when the set-up of the automatic saws could not be justified.

Other equipment found within the mills included planers, sanders, and joiners.

The workforce within the industry appeared to be satisfied with their working conditions. Four of the firms had unionized workforces of which three had hourly labour costs that were almost double the industry median as shown by Ratio #25 in Exhibit 4. Despite their relatively higher productivity, those firms encountered sales problems because of the higher prices that had to be asked.

The interfirm comparison report revealed that nine of the twelve firms paid their employees on an hourly rate. Of the three remaining firms, one added a piecework bonus to the hourly rate, another added a bonus based on the sales value of the daily output, and the other paid wages based entirely on piecework.

The pricing strategy of the firms across this sector was consistent; that being double raw materials costs. Eleven of the twelve firms sold FOB. Half of the firms regularly charged for delivery which was consequently subtracted from sales for purposes of the interfirm comparison study. Several other firms charged for delivery to customers outside a free delivery zone.

Most firms maintained their own delivery vehicles because of the need to deliver on a timely basis. Two of the firms relied mostly on outside trucking. A third firm had 30% of its deliveries made in this manner.

Overall, the report indicated that 20% of sales were picked up by the customers. However, this figure was distorted by one firm that delivered all of its production and another that delivered 75% of its production in this manner.

Most of the firms studied delivered 78.8% of their production within their immediate regions, and 3.8% outside their provinces.

THE CELLMITE CORPORATION — PRELIMINARY OBSERVATIONS

Headquartered in Prince Rupert, the Cellmite Corporation had several plants scattered across British Columbia. Raw materials were purchased in bulk for all plants in the Corporation. Charles indicated that the strategy of the corporation was to custom finish softwood lumber and therefore command higher prices. The smaller market for these products, however, necessitated that an expanded market be served.

Exhibit 4 shows the performance calculated for the corporation; these are highlighted. He noted that as you proceeded from left to right, the order of desirability of the ratio decreased. For example, Cellmite's return on assets (#1) was third worst in the industry. However, its sales increase (#23) was better than the industry median.

Over the past few years, management had invested a great amount of money in modernizing and rationalizing the production process at their plants. This resulted in one of the more modern and best organized and laid out plants in the industry. A sophisticated microcomputer-based production control system and several specialty-built material handling devices further characterized these plants.

Although production volume had increased significantly over the past year, the plants were designed in such a manner that no strains were imposed upon their production resources. Activity on the floor was very calm and sedate. Furthermore, the firm operated at less than one full shift per day.

To produce the specialized products made by the Corporation, the labour force was highly skilled and well paid. Like many of the other firms in the industry, the workforce was unionized.

The Corporation's current marketing strategy had necessitated increased investment in vehicles to deliver the finished products to the customers who were widely spread across the province. It was thought that this additional service contributed to the ability of the firm to ask for premium prices on its product.

THE SITUATION

As Charles neared his review of the interfirm comparison report, in which he paid particular attention to Exhibits 1 and 4, he was alarmed at the corporation's poor performance within the industry. The company's increased sales had translated into a net loss as indicated by #2 of Exhibit 4.

Charles wondered how representative the ratios were of the corporation's productivity and if some of the standardizations made to the data by the interfirm comparisons program were valid. A meeting with senior management was in order so that the report could be discussed prior to his meeting with the consultant who produced the report.

Exhibit 1

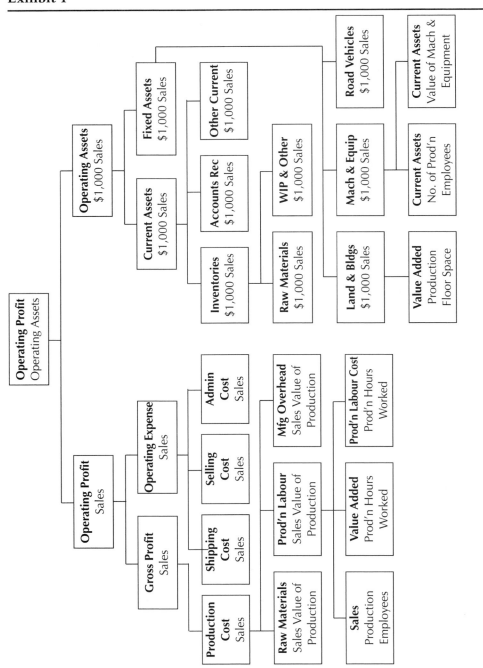

Exhibit 2

SOFTWOOD LUMBER PRODUCTION—(× 1,000,000m³) by Region

	1982	*Year* *1983*	*1984*
Canada	35.7	47.7	48.0
By Region:			
British Columbia	22.5	30.1	30.2
Quebec	6.0	8.6	8.7
Ontario	3.6	3.8	4.8
Prairie Provinces	2.5	3.3	2.9
Atlantic Provinces	1.1	1.9	1.4

Source: Selected Forestry Statistics Canada 1985, April 1986, *Information Report EX-37*, p.V

Exhibit 3

SOFTWOOD LUMBER EXPORTS IN 1984

	Quantity (× 1,000m³)		*Value ($000)*	
Importing Nation:	*Canada*	*B.C.*	*Canada*	*B.C.*
United States	31,153	17,960	3,271,129	1,822,584
Europe	1,973	1,612	277,437	224,783
United Kingdom	1,391	1,132	171,705	133,064
Other EEC	560	459	99,911	86,250
Japan	2,174	2,170	351,127	350,233

Source: Selected Forestry Statistics Canada 1985, April 1986, *Information Report EX-37*, pp.60-63.

Exhibit 4

PERFORMANCE RATIOS IN ORDER OF MAGNITUDE	Interfirm Comparison of Two Companies in the Same Industry										COMPANY 10 HIGHLIGHTED		
	1	2	3	4	5	6	Median	7	8	9	10	11	12
Return of Assets													
1. Operating profit/Operating assets	28.1%	27.7%	17.5%	10.0%	7.8%	6.9%	6.8%	6.6%	4.1%	2.8%	–1.8%	–6.2%	–8.2%
Profit Margin, Turnover of Assets													
2. Operating profit/Sales	12.9%	12.1%	9.8%	8.7%	8.4%	6.3%	5.5%	4.7%	3.0%	2.0%	–1.6%	–7.6%	–8.9%
3. Sales/Operating assets (times)	2.33	2.16	1.79	1.47	1.39	1.35	1.30	1.25	1.19	1.12	0.92	0.81	0.75
Gross Profit Margins													
4. Gross Profit/Sales	32.5%	28.9%	27.6%	26.8%	25.5%	25.3%	25.1%	25.0%	24.1%	18.4%	12.9%	11.0%	9.9%
Production Cost / Sales Value of Prod'n													
5. Production cost of sales	67.5%	71.1%	72.4%	73.2%	74.5%	74.7%	74.9%	75.0%	75.9%	81.6%	87.1%	89.0%	90.1%
6. Raw materials & components	46.8%	47.1%	47.4%	50.2%	51.6%	53.5%	53.9%	54.3%	55.1%	56.0%	57.9%	58.7%	63.4%
7. Total production labour cost	13.0%	13.3%	14.4%	14.6%	16.5%	17.3%	17.5%	17.7%	17.9%	19.1%	20.2%	23.3%	23.9%
8. Manufacturing overhead	3.0%	3.9%	4.6%	5.0%	5.4%	5.5%	5.5%	5.5%	6.7%	7.2%	7.5%	8.9%	15.7%
Operating Expenses													
9. Total Operating expenses/Sales	4.7%	12.6%	15.4%	16.6%	18.8%	19.1%	19.2%	19.2%	20.3%	20.4%	20.5%	22.1%	28.4%
10. Warehouse & shipping exp./Sales	0.0%	2.8%	4.0%	5.6%	6.0%	6.7%	6.9%	7.0%	7.0%	8.1%	8.2%	10.3%	15.8%
11. Selling & promotion exp./Sales	1.9%	2.9%	4.7%	4.7%	5.3%	5.7%	5.8%	5.8%	5.9%	6.2%	6.3%	7.8%	9.0%
12. Administration/Sales	2.8%	3.8%	4.8%	5.1%	5.5%	6.2%	6.3%	6.4%	6.5%	6.6%	6.9%	7.4%	8.4%
Asset Utilization (per $1,000 sales)													
3a. Total operating assets	$430	$463	$560	$695	$722	$739	$770	$801	$842	$893	$1,981	$1,228	$1,330
13. Current assets	$156	$173	$211	$212	$223	$229	$240	$251	$254	$259	$271	$280	$348
14. Fixed assets	$274	$290	$349	$426	$463	$488	$505	$521	$571	$670	$733	$999	$1,118
Current Asset (per $1,000 sales)													
15. Raw material inventory	$46	$48	$59	$63	$67	$80	$81	$82	$86	$117	$133	$151	$206
16. Other inventories	$0	$0	$0	$0	$0	$3	$7	$10	$18	$22	$22	$23	$27
17. Total inventory	$46	$48	$73	$80	$86	$89	$97	$104	$109	$133	$135	$154	$206
18. Accounts receivable	$84	$94	$106	$126	$126	$136	$136	$137	$142	$145	$146	$154	$160
19. Other current assets	$0	$0	$0	$0	$0	$0	$1	$1	$4	$9	$9	$11	$15
Fixed Assets (per $1,000 sales)													
20. Land & building	$146	$162	$181	$212	$226	$274	$294	$313	$331	$357	$371	$505	$691
21. Machinery & equipment	$65	$90	$125	$151	$154	$164	$169	$173	$211	$218	$326	$351	$386
22. Road vehicles	$0	$19	$27	$28	$36	$46	$49	$51	$78	$79	$101	$108	$146
Productivity & Related Ratios													
23. Sales incr. (decr.) over preced. yr.	47.8%	39.3%	24.6%	24.3%	17.5%	16.5%	13.4%	10.3%	4.6%	4.2%	2.3%	1.6%	0.0%
24. Sales per production employee	$150,645	$130,833	$123,194	$121,231	$111,259	$107,984	$103,201	$98,417	$92,720	$88,475	$88,235	$86,207	$78,316
25. Prod. labour cost/Prod. labour hrs.	$5.80	$7.32	$7.49	$8.15	$8.18	$8.30	$8.37	$8.43	$10.76	$10.92	$15.41	$15.64	$16.69
26. Value added/Prod. labour hrs. worked	$39.68	$33.81	$30.40	$26.62	$24.02	$23.58	$23.13	$22.67	$22.08	$21.21	$21.01	$18.45	$17.53
27. Mach. & equip.& prod'n employees	$5,052	$6,897	$11,600	$11,765	$16,167	$16,635	$18,995	$21,355	$24,296	$27,051	$31,742	$42,615	$50,500
28. Value added/Production floor area	$114.24	$97.85	$97.25	$94.43	$88.09	$49.00	$45.82	$42.63	$39.42	$38.72	$34.43	$31.44	$25.92
29. Value added/Value of mach. & equip.	$8.10	$7.14	$3.38	$3.37	$2.96	$2.69	$2.52	$2.34	$2.11	$2.02	$1.55	$1.11	$1.02

Source: Canada Department of Regional Industrial Expansion, Interfirm Comparison Sample Analysis of Two Firms in the Same Industry, Ottawa, p. 3.

Appendix 1

OBJECTIVES OF
THE INTERFIRM COMPARISON PROGRAM

The interfirm comparison program is sponsored and implemented by the federal Department of Regional Industrial Expansion. Firms included in a comparison are taken from the same industry sector.

The program has two main objectives:
1) to enable individual firms to compare their own productivity and profitability with those of their competitors or other firms in their industry; and
2) to provide the Department of Regional Industrial Expansion with a unique source of information as to the performance, needs, weaknesses, and potential for improvement and development within an industry sector.

These objectives are accomplished through the use of critical operating ratios within a sector. The ratios are decided upon in consultation with firms in the industry sector. The ratios selected provide a fair measurement of the participants' performance in those operating areas having the most influence on the firms' profitability. This also assures that the program will give each participant a quantitative analytical tool for better understanding the strengths and weaknesses of its operations, and to identify the critical areas that need productivity improvements.

Each productivity measure ratio expresses an output of the firm relative to a related input. Where necessary, results are subgrouped on the basis of types of operations within the industry and thus provide a higher degree of usefulness to the resulting conclusions.

Scope of the Comparisons
Firms are invited by the Department of Regional Industrial Expansion, in consultation with industry associations or industry leaders, to participate in an interfirm comparison. Every attempt is made to include all of the significant firms within the industry. Firms that meet the response deadline are included initially but subsequently excluded if they are unable to provide adequate data as described below.

A comparison usually covers a year's operations of firms within an industrial sector and therefore covers peak sales months, such as May through October, of a cyclical industry. Since participating firms may have varied year-end dates, the gathered data may cover parts of two fiscal years. It was sometimes necessary to create accounting cut-off information out of the participants' statements. In instances where creating a satisfactory cut-off was not possible, the firms were dropped from the comparison. The most common cut-off date, after adjustments, was October 31. In cases where a firm's accounting period ends more than a month from this date, special care was taken to make sure the data is comparable.

Data Sources
The data was collected in the field by members of a firm of management consultants under the direction of Interfirm Comparison program staff. Interviews were conducted with one or more officers of each participating company. The outline of

two working documents prepared by the Department of Regional Industrial Expansion was followed after an investigation of the industry.

During these interviews a considerable amount of general information was gathered in addition to the financial and other quantitative results required for the comparisons. This data was normally obtained in the course of a single interview lasting from four to seven hours. The level of company officers that attended the interviews typically included the president, treasurer, and/or general manager.

Financial data was obtained from the company's financial statements, general ledger, monthly statements, production reports, appraisal reports, payroll records, and other documents considered necessary for purposes of the comparison. In addition, tours were made of each participant's production facilities to physically observe and compare the procedures in use and identify significant differences between companies that might have an impact on the ratio results.

Basis of Comparison

The ratio structure adapted to a comparison has been developed over several years using sound financial and economic principles and forms the basic methodology for a project. To ensure no misunderstanding as to their meanings, clear definitions of each factor in the make-up of the ratios have been developed and are presented in Appendix 2.

The ratios form a hierarchy of interrelated results called the Structure of Management Ratios as shown in Exhibit 1. It establishes the relative success of each firm with respect to the key Ratio 1, a measure of operating profits as a percent of operating assets (Return on assets). This ratio is of prime importance because it reflects the firm's profit-making capacity. In combination with other ratio results, an indication of the relative efficiency in the use of available resources is provided. Activities which are not homogeneous are excluded.

Since significant differences between participating companies in many operating areas can exist which decreases their comparability, adjustments are made to render the data more comparable. For example, resale of purchased items should be eliminated because their inclusion could distort key cost to sales ratios. Another example is that the comparison measure of operating profit to operating assets excludes income from sources not directly related to the participants' main activity. Furthermore, the comparison should not examine the financing aspect of the operations and thus excludes interest costs. Profit is therefore defined as total earnings from the operating assets used in the normal operations of the business, less the related expenses and before income tax and interest expense.

Additionally, many of the ratios are related to production output rather than sales for a year. This ensures that production costs are properly matched to sales activity and is stated in terms of its equivalent sales value. This eliminates the impact of differences between production volume and sales volume, as reflected by changes in work-in-process and finished goods inventories. This production output measure is called the Sales Value of Production.

Except for land, fixed assets are also restated on a uniform basis to enhance comparability between participants. Inflation indices are applied to the costs of each asset class by year of acquisition, so that the total values are restated in inflation adjusted current dollar equivalents. Land is shown at cost with no indexing.

To ensure uniform depreciation rates, a standard depreciation schedule is used to provide depreciation expenses which replaces those recorded by the participants. For example, the following annual rates are used for the softwood lumber finishing industry:

Buildings	2.5%
Machinery & Equipment	10.0%
Road Vehicles	30.0%
Furniture & Fixtures	10.0%

Leased assets are treated as if they were owned, and are valued in inflation adjusted current equivalent dollars. Lease payments, therefore, are excluded from expenses.

Classifications that are used for manufacturing costs and operating expenses are selected to conform to those in general use throughout an industry. Nevertheless, for each individual company a reclassification may be necessary in order to make the results comparable.

Production labour costs used in a comparison include wages of direct and indirect workers which include those responsible for any repairs and maintenance, salaries of production supervisors and managers, overtime premiums and production bonuses paid to these people, and their fringe benefits. As a result, Ratio 21, production labour costs per production labour hour can be expected to be higher than the average production floor rate for each company.

The net result of the above adjustments is a compilation of data that is reasonably comparable and valid for purposes of the study. By standardizing the data, the relative strengths and weaknesses of individual companies within an industry can be deduced.

The interfirm comparison program introduces a concept of Value Added in relationship to several asset base and operating activity measures to provide a measure of relative productivity in their use. Value added is the difference between the physical resources contributed by the firm into the production process and the sales value of the outputs.

Ratio 2 results are linked to Ratio 1 results by Ratio 3, which measures the asset turnover rate by comparing net sales to asset levels. A satisfactory rate of return on operating assets as measured by Ratio 1 is the product of good profit margins (Ratio 2) and a reasonable level of asset turnover (Ratio 3). The levels of operating profit reflected by Ratio 2 are the direct result of sufficient gross profit (Ratio 4) to more than meet the total operating expenses (Ratio 9).

Reporting to Participants

The data taken from each firm is reconciled to their financial statements or reports to ensure that no mechanical errors were made. The data is then incorporated into a form called a Statement of Data Used which is forwarded to the participants along with the reconciliation. This gives a firm's management the opportunity to question any aspect they do not understand or agree with. After an appropriate interval for response, the Statements of Data Used serves as the basis for the calculations of the ratios used in the comparison.

Each participating company receives a report that outlines the purpose, method, and results of a comparison which contains an analysis of a firm's performance based on the various measures calculated. This is followed by a visit from the consultant who gathered the data. The purpose of this visit is to help management interpret their report, understand the implications of the results to their operations, and plan appropriate corrective action. Even the better performing firms had areas where improvements could be made.

Since the individual participant's managers do not see the other company's operations, it is possible to improve their understanding of their own results during this interview by placing the results in a broader perspective. It also provides an opportunity for the consultants to correct unwarranted inferences that may be made by some of the participants. A typical example is as follows — a manager may read a below median labour productivity as being bad without relating the fact to a below median investment in machinery and equipment per production employee. In the follow-up interview the manager can be made aware of the nature of the trade-off that was made.

Appendix 2

INCOME STATEMENT

Sales:
Stated on a net basis, after discounts, allowances, and returns, and excluding sales taxes. Packaging and delivery expenses charged to customers are excluded unless such exclusion would impair comparability. Shipping and promotion charges paid by the manufacturer are part of sales and reported under operating expenses. Non-manufacturing revenue, such as investment and rental income, is excluded. Sales of goods purchased and sold in the same condition are broken out and offset against the cost of their purchase. Revenue for purchased and resold materials or components which are part of the finished product package is included.

Resale Sales:
Sales of goods purchased for resale in the same condition.

Note:
In special cases where resale is a significant part of the normal business activity in the industry sector, "Sales" includes sales of goods purchased for resale in the same condition (i.e., "Resale Sales") as well as "Sales of Manufactured Goods."

Production Costs:
Includes the cost of materials, labour, and production overhead, i.e., all costs up to the point where the product is finally inspected and approved for transfer to storage or for shipment.

1. *Materials and Components* — includes all materials used in the manufacturing process, inward transportation costs, and consumable stores used in production. The cost of goods purchased and sold in the same condition is broken out and netted against corresponding sales proceeds. Excludes supplies and parts used in the maintenance of buildings and machinery.

   The purchases and the opening inventory of materials and components are added and the closing inventory subtracted to arrive at total cost of materials and components used in production.

2a. *Production Labour Costs* — includes wages, salaries, and fringe benefits of all employees that are directly and indirectly involved in the production process, including production managers dedicated to the production process, those engaged in supervision, quality control, production planning, material handling, machinery set-up, rework, maintenance, etc.

2b. *Average Hourly Production Labour Cost* — hourly cost of production labour as defined in 2a. It is usually higher than the average floor rate because of the broad definition.

3. *Production Overhead* — consists of maintenance and repair costs (excluding related wages and salaries), and items generally recognized as production

overhead, except indirect production labour fringe benefits classified under the previous heading. Indirect labour engaged in sales processing and functions of a clerical or administrative nature is included under administration costs.

The following items may be broken out and shown separately: (i) cost of energy (fuel, electricity, steam) consumed in the production process; (ii) I.F.C. calculated depreciation and amortization charges; (iii) work sub-contracted to other firms; (iv) repairs and maintenance of equipment and/or buildings; (v) any other significant factor specific to an industry.

A depreciation charge computed at standardized rates for all participating companies on the present dollar value of assets is substituted for the depreciation recorded in company accounts (see definition of fixed assets on page 355). Although these rates may vary somewhat between industries, the most frequently used are: 10% on machinery, equipment, and office furniture; $2^{1}/_{2}$% on buildings; and 30% on road vehicles. Heavy highway vehicles may have a lower depreciation rate to reflect their longer operating lives.

Inventories:

Includes all materials and components utilized in the manufacturing process, work in process, and finished goods manufactured by the firm. Opening inventories of work in process are added to Production Costs and closing inventories are deducted, to obtain Cost of Goods Manufactured.

The further addition of opening inventories and subtraction of closing inventories of finished goods results in Cost of Goods Sold.

Resale Goods Inventories:

Goods purchased for resale in the same condition.

Note:

In special cases where resale is a significant part of the normal business activity and is included in sales, "Inventories" includes inventories of goods purchased for resale in the same condition (i.e., Resale Goods Inventories) as well as "Manufacturing Inventories."

Gross Margin:

Calculated by subtracting from sales the cost of production of the goods sold. This margin differs from that reported by the firm since certain expenses have been reclassified and depreciation has been recalculated.

Gross Profit:

Is obtained by deducting Cost of Goods Sold from Sales. This is likely to differ from the corresponding figure in the company's accounts owing to reclassification and recalculation, for comparability reasons, of cost and sales items.

Operating Expenses - Comprises:

1. *Warehousing and Shipping Costs* — costs incurred by the participating company and directly associated with warehousing, packing finished products, and the cost of transportation to the point of delivery. Depreciation on buildings and owned or rented warehouses are calculated and charged to this category based on the estimated floorspace used.

2. *Marketing and Selling Costs* — costs directly associated with marketing and selling of products (salaries, fringe benefits and sales commissions, advertising expenses, travel and entertainment, etc.), but not clerical functions such as invoicing and credit management which have been classified as administrative functions. This classification of costs assures uniformity of treatment among companies, since those firms that do not employ staff exclusively or primarily to process sales-related documents typically report such costs under administrative expenses.

3. *Administration Costs* — includes salaries and fringe benefits of management, accounting and clerical employees, and the remuneration of administrative employees that may be classified by a firm as indirect production labour or as sales clerical labour. Also included are bad debts, general office expenses, research and development costs, and rental charges for rented equipment. A standardized depreciation charge for owned office equipment and the building space occupied are included in administration costs. Management fees paid to related corporations are included if they relate to tangible services rendered by that corporation.

In cases where extra management bonuses are paid in lieu of management salaries for tax planning purposes, an adjustment is made to management salaries to put these companies on a comparable basis with other participants.

The following items are broken out and excluded for purposes of the comparisons: (i) depreciation and amortization included in the company's accounts; (ii) interest payments; (iii) interest and sundry income credited; (iv) non-comparable business activities, wherever the impact is significant. A computed depreciation charge is substituted for the charge included in the accounts.

Any operating expense category may be broken into two or more sub-categories if this is useful in a particular industry sector.

Cost of Sales:
Is obtained by adding Operating Expenses to Cost of Goods Sold.

Operating Profit (Before Tax and Extraordinary Items):
Is obtained by deducting Cost of Sales from Sales; or by deducting Operating Expenses from Gross Profit.

BALANCE SHEET ITEMS

Operating Assets:
Includes current and fixed assets that were available to carry on the business during the year; excludes assets that were not held for the purpose of operating the business subject to the comparison. Other assets that are excluded from the comparison are direct and portfolio investments and certain excess assets, for instance, land held for long-term development or excess cash above that needed to support the business.

Note:
In special cases where resale is a significant part of the normal business activity, "Operating Assets" includes goods purchased for resale and sold in the same condition, if the resale items were included in sales.

1. *Current Assets* — represents average levels of these assets held during the year: *Accounts Receivable:* preferably computed from 12 monthly balances. Uncollectible accounts are excluded. Where only part of the operations of a firm is considered for the purposes of the comparison, the receivables corresponding to that part only are taken into account.

   Values of Inventories: often the best estimate of company officials; broken down between:

   - Inventory of raw materials;
   - Inventory of work in process;
   - Other Inventory, including components purchased for assembly into a finished product, and inventories of finished products manufactured by the company. (Finished goods purchased for resale are included if specified.) Resale sales are included in sales.

   Other Current Assets: includes a company's average prepaid expenses. Non-operating receivables owed by shareholders or employees are excluded for purposes of comparisons.

   All Current Assets: includes resale assets, if resales are included in sales.

2. *Fixed Operating Assets:*

   Land — usually carried at cost. In most cases this value is a relatively minor part of a company's operating assets.

   Buildings — the value of buildings is expressed in inflation-adjusted, i.e., present (today's) dollars, obtained by applying an appropriate Interfirm Comparison index to the purchase cost. Alternatively, market values or insurance appraisal may be used if detailed fixed asset acquisition information is not readily available. Where a company rents a building, its present value is added to the assets owned by the company. This value may be obtained by multiplying the annual rent by an appropriate capitalization factor. To this cost is added the present dollar value of leasehold improvements. Another approach is to determine market value by comparison to other buildings or by indexing municipal tax assessments.

   In cases where the majority of the firms in a comparison rent their premises, the value of land and buildings owned may be excluded from the pool of operating assets and replaced by an imputed rental value. The imputed rental represents the estimated cost of renting equivalent premises for the period under review on a "net" lease basis. This imputed value is generally established by multiplying the annual rental by a factor of ten times (10 x) or by determining an appropriate market value of the production or warehouse space in question if rents are artificially low due to long-term party leasing arrangements.

   Machinery and Equipment — the value of machinery and equipment is the present dollar value of the company's investment in these assets, which is obtained by applying an appropriate price index to the purchase cost of each owned asset.

Office Equipment — the treatment is the same as for machinery and equipment.

Furniture and Fixtures — the treatment is the same as for machinery and equipment.

Road Vehicles — the treatment is the same as for machinery and equipment.

OTHER ITEMS

Floor Areas:
The number or square feet or square metres devoted to (i) production and (ii) other functions.

Employment:
The average number of employees during the year engaged in (i) production (direct and indirect) in accordance with the definition of production labour costs, and in (ii) other functions.

Production Labour Hours:
The number of labour hours worked by the direct and indirect production employees above. Salaried workers are imputed at an annual hours equivalent, often, 2,080 hours.

The number of production employees, labour hours, and labour costs must correspond.

Value Added:
A measure of the value added to the materials that are taken into the plant (an economic indicator of the firm's output performance). It is computed by subtracting from sales the cost of externally purchased inputs comprising raw materials, production and shipping, supplies, energy, outside repairs and maintenance, and subcontract costs, and by adjusting for changes in inventory levels (by adding or subtracting the net of the opening less the closing inventories of work-in-process and finished goods).

Note:
In special cases where resale is a significant part of the normal business activity and is included in sales, "Value Added" is an all-inclusive figure (i.e., value added to production materials and to goods for resale).

Sales Value of Production:
Expresses the value of the year's production in terms of sales dollars. It is obtained by multiplying Production Costs by the ratio of Sales to Cost of Goods Sold. It is an actual figure, adjusted by the sales value of the change in finished goods and work-in-process inventories. Sales Value of Production equals Sales if Production Costs equal Cost of Goods Sold, i.e., when there is no change in inventories.

Average Collection Period:
Average number of days to collect the amount due by customers.

Rejected Production/Total Production:
Calculated by dividing scrap and remnants by the total material used.

GIFFELS ASSOCIATES LIMITED

Wendy Osborne and Randolph Kudar

Despite having one of the highest labour productivity rates in the world in 1990, the Canadian construction industry had reported very low productivity growth over most of the last decade. Don Caswell, a Senior Project Manager at the Giffels Group, one of Canada's largest consulting engineering and architectural firms, believed that companies, such as Giffels, could have a positive effect on construction labour productivity growth in Canada.

THE CANADIAN CONSTRUCTION INDUSTRY

People in the industry defined construction broadly as the economic sector which supplied all materials, products, and equipment to build structures such as buildings, tunnels, highways, and dams. In 1991, the Canadian construction industry directly employed approximately 700,000 workers (5% of the total employed workforce). Expenditures on construction amounted to $96 billion, about 14% of total Gross Domestic Product (GDP). Because it was closely linked to the rest of the economy, investment in construction had a ripple effect on other sectors. A dollar spent in the purchase of construction output generated a multiplier effect worth about $1.83 in the whole economy. Canada, unlike many industrialized countries, had not developed integrated construction companies with the size and resources required to compete effectively with top international firms.

The construction industry included four key participants — owners, professionals, material suppliers, and contractors. Exhibit 1 shows Giffels' view of the traditional general contract approach to a construction project. Professionals were primarily architects and consulting engineers. The architectural services industry consisted of private firms owned and operated by architects licensed under provincial legislation to provide independent architectural design and consulting services. Architects also carried out non-design functions such as feasibility studies, heritage restoration, urban planning and design, project management, and functional programming.

The Canadian consulting engineering industry, which commanded worldwide respect, was aggressive and dynamic. Services provided included feasibility studies, planning, detailed design, and project, construction, and operational management. Consulting engineering projects covered many categories, from infrastructural[1] facilities and buildings to industrial and resource projects. Services to other fields included traffic flow analyses and environmental assessments.

An evolving technological innovation was Computer Aided Drafting and Design (CADD), a new medium for design drawings. CADD allowed drawing on a computer screen, a change from traditional drafting using pencil and eraser. Software provided templates for common design elements such as doors or windows. In addition, draftsmen could draw customized symbols and store them for later use. Professional CADD packages could create multi-layer drawings just as a draftsman would create several overlays on paper. A major benefit of CADD was the ease with which designers could update and reformat drawings.

Although the Canadian construction industry had one of the world's highest labour productivity rates, its growth rate was among the lowest (Exhibit 2). This was partially due to a general levelling of the construction community on a worldwide basis. In Canada, the construction labour productivity rate was about 80% of the manufacturing rate. The Canadian construction industry was notorious for underspending on research and development (R&D), allocating about $100 million annually (0.1% of revenue) during the peak revenue years in the late 1980s.

THE JAPANESE CONSTRUCTION INDUSTRY

The Japanese construction industry was huge, with more than 515,000 licensed construction enterprises which employed about 5.4 million people (9.4% of the total working population) in 1986. The industry structure was fairly similar to Canada's with the following important differences:

— the government supported the growth of six very large general contractors[2] (the Big Six) while the rest competed in a free market

---

[1] Infrastructure facilities provided support services such as highways, airport runways, streets, tunnels, subways, bridges, water treatment and distribution systems, and sewage systems.

— there was less emphasis on cost, and more on efficient use of materials

— contractors usually acted as project managers

— lawyers were rarely involved in drawing up contracts.

Japan's Ministry of Construction provided ongoing support, in the form of continuing contracts, to enable the Big Six companies to develop the expertise required to win large foreign contracts. These companies provided a comprehensive range of construction services. They located construction sites for clients; helped find financing; and designed, constructed, and maintained high quality structures. The Big Six emphasized market development, invested heavily in research, and provided good site-based construction management. These companies scheduled on-site construction activities one day at a time and every party involved in the project considered it extremely important to complete their tasks on time. The Big Six had financial muscle from their own retained profits and from banks within their business groups.

Prefabricated parts used by the Japanese construction industry included tile-covered cladding panels, bathrooms and toilets, sanitary fittings complete with plumbing, and steel staircases. Building site protection and provisions for access to work places were of paramount importance. Japanese builders generally fully enclosed sites vertically with a strong sheet steel fence at ground level and with reinforced plastic sheeting on scaffolding at the higher storeys. Access through the sheet steel fencing was via steel shutters or large reinforced canvas or plastic sliding folding gates. This resulted in an enclosed, controlled, reasonably predictable environment, ideal for orderly building.

The use of alternate building materials was common in Japan for several reasons. The Big Six spent as much as 10% of revenues on R&D to encourage the development of alternate materials. Contractors frequently had close relationships with material suppliers and sometimes embarked on joint ventures. Fewer lawyers being involved in the industry reduced fears of lawsuits over using a new material.

Japanese construction professionals were generally engineers. Most architects trained as architectural engineers. Professionals usually worked for contractors rather than operate separate companies. The Big Six used computer-aided scheduling and design extensively. The Japanese emphasis on high quality and meeting schedules came at the expense of cost and resulted in one of the lowest construction labour productivity rates in the world (Exhibit 2). The overheads associated with larger in-house design and management staff also contributed to the lower productivity rate. The Japanese companies approached this cost disadvantage as a long-term problem. They invested heavily in R&D to find new, high-tech products and more efficient construction methods that would provide a competitive edge.

---

2 Kajima Corp., Kumagai Gumi Co. Ltd., Ohbayashi Corp., Shimizu Corp., Taisei Corp., Takenaka Corp.

GIFFELS ASSOCIATES LIMITED

The Giffels Group was an integrated group of companies providing comprehensive engineering, architectural, and management services to the construction industry. A Canadian company incorporated in 1949, in 1992 it had 300 employees in Rexdale (head office) and Ottawa, plus people on construction sites all over southern Ontario. The Group (employee-owned with ownership extending throughout the company) consisted of three companies (Exhibit 3).

Giffels Enterprises Inc. focused on the management of capital projects and provided design/build services. Giffels Associates Limited (Giffels) was an architectural and engineering company which applied state-of-the-art technology to the design of buildings, and civil engineering projects. Since the early 1980s, Giffels had used CADD which allowed the company to make design changes to projects quickly and easily. In-house systems experts developed software packages which Giffels used internally and marketed to other companies.

In the early 1980s, the Ontario Government set up several Centres of Excellence with different areas of expertise — for example, microelectronics in Ottawa, robotics in Peterborough, and CADD in Cambridge (OCAM — Ontario Centre for Advanced Manufacturing). The government hoped these Centres would provide the impetus for developing new technologies which could then be privatized. Giffels acquired OCAM because management believed that its area of expertise would dovetail with the work being done by the industrial engineering group. Giffels recognized the OCAM personnel's proficiency in high performance manufacturing technology. OCAM also specialized in industrial process design, control systems engineering, and applied information technology.

Giffels had civil, electrical, industrial, mechanical, and structural engineers on staff as well as architects and architectural technologists. In-house industrial engineers provided Giffels with unique expertise in warehousing and materials handling. Giffels specialized in constructing industrial buildings such as warehouses. Its package of services included the design and lay-out of the building (including the specification of the materials-handling equipment and the production equipment lay-out), construction (including project management, scheduling, cost control, procurement, on-site field staff, and occasionally work as the general contractor), and training the owner's staff in using the equipment.

Maximizing Productivity

When Giffels worked on a construction contract, the project team used their experience to consider the entire project including the construction process, the scheduling of activities, and the end use of the building. Giffels' clients could be assured of compliance with all necessary regulations and codes. For example, if the building required firewalls, Giffels included them in the plans. Major cost overruns could occur if the designer overlooked a detail like this in the initial design of the building. Also, underwriters could refuse to provide insurance for buildings that did not comply with all regulations.

Alternative Construction Methods

Giffels' teams used their experience to arrive at alternative construction solutions. For example, contractors usually built firewalls using masonry which required scaffolding. The process was slow and labour intensive as tradespeople placed the blocks one by one. Using pre-cast concrete was an alternative which cost more, but could be put in place quickly.

One reason construction productivity was lower than manufacturing productivity was because construction took place outdoors in an uncontrolled environment. Giffels tried to overcome this obstacle in two ways — using prefabricated parts and controlling the construction environment. For example, manufacturers could assemble heating and air conditioning units off-site thus eliminating construction labour. Prefabrication also had disadvantages. Prefabricated units could be difficult to locate on large buildings. Sometimes helicopters lifted units into place in the middle of a large roof which was inaccessible by crane.

Instead of using prefabricated heating and air conditioning units, Giffels sometimes designed buildings with galleries within the structure of the building. Tradespeople could then install (and later maintain) these services in a controlled environment. The decision to use this solution depended on costs, type of building, amount of equipment to be housed, etc.

Alternate Building Materials

Roofing materials offered one area where a number of alternatives for materials existed. Traditionally, industrial roofing used labour intensive built-up roofing (BUR): build the structure, add a metal roof deck, add insulation, cover with asphalt and felt, then cover with gravel. Three types of felt were available — organic (e.g., cotton), asbestos, and glass fibre (in order of cost). The more expensive materials required fewer layers.

An alternative solution considered by Giffels was replacing the asphalt and felt with single ply membranes of man-made material (such as polyvinyl chloride (PVC)) on rolls which could simply be rolled out. It was much faster (more roof covered per unit of labour) and, therefore, resulted in significant savings. Rolled goods worked better in diverse working conditions (it was very difficult to do an asphalt roof in the winter) and had a more consistent quality.

Don Caswell believed Giffels' integrated approach to construction helped improve its productivity. The company had been quite successful in introducing new ideas and many of its customers came back for new projects and recommended the company to others.

Exhibit 1

THE KEY PARTICIPANTS IN THE CONSTRUCTION INDUSTRY

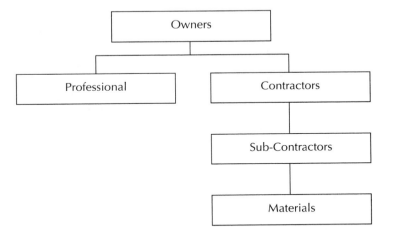

Exhibit 2

LABOUR PRODUCTIVITY IN THE CONSTRUCTION SECTOR

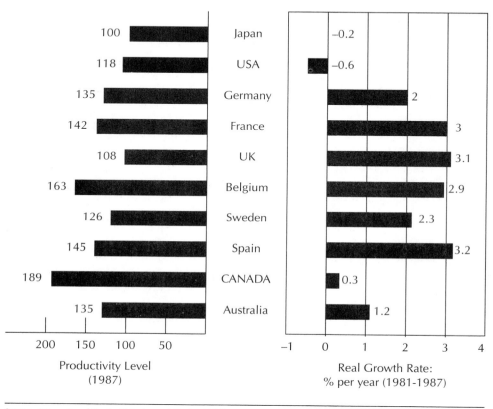

Productivity Level (1987)		Real Growth Rate: % per year (1981-1987)
100	Japan	−0.2
118	USA	−0.6
135	Germany	2
142	France	3
108	UK	3.1
163	Belgium	2.9
126	Sweden	2.3
145	Spain	3.2
189	CANADA	0.3
135	Australia	1.2

Source: *International Productivity Journal* (Spring 1990), pp. 74,83.

Exhibit 3

GIFFELS GROUP— Corporate Structure

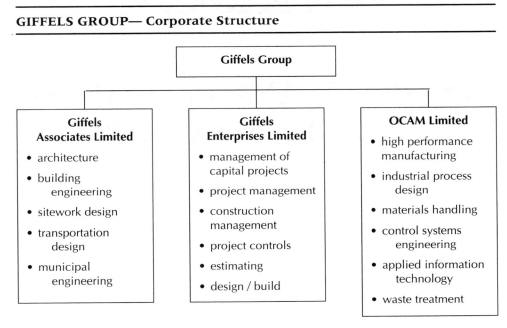

Giffels Group

Giffels Associates Limited

- architecture
- building engineering
- sitework design
- transportation design
- municipal engineering

Giffels Enterprises Limited

- management of capital projects
- project management
- construction management
- project controls
- estimating
- design / build

OCAM Limited

- high performance manufacturing
- industrial process design
- materials handling
- control systems engineering
- applied information technology
- waste treatment

SYNCRUDE CANADA LIMITED— THE NEW MANDATE

Sue Hanna and Randolph Kudar*

Dr. Ken Nickerson, Chief Medical Officer of Syncrude Canada Limited, sat at his downtown office desk in Fort McMurray, Alberta. It was a cool October day in 1985. The President of the company, Mr. Ralph Shepherd, had just issued a new mandate for the firm that had the capability to fundamentally change the way in which the business operated. The mandate was expressed as follows:

> Safety and Reliability are Number 1.
> Production will follow.

Dr. Nickerson felt that his department would play an important role in fulfilling this mandate. He realized that it would take time for this new way of thinking to sink into the organization. He wondered what action his department should take to encourage employee commitment to the mandate. He was aware that such a mandate would require a cost-effective program of health care if it were to be successful.

BACKGROUND

Syncrude Canada Limited (SCL) was in the business of extracting bitumen (a heavy molasses-like substance) from the Athabasca Oil Sands, and upgrading it into synthetic crude oil. The company was incorporated on December 18, 1964, and was authorized to build a plant capable of producing 80,000 barrels per day.

Site preparations commenced in December 1973. The plant commenced production in July 1976. By the fall of 1978, the capacity agreement had been amended several times, with a final approved capacity of 129,000 barrels per day. Since then, SCL had increased to over 165,000 barrels per day and had developed into the world's largest producer of synthetic crude oil and supplied Canada with 10% of its national crude oil needs.

SCL's production site was located at Mildred Lake, about 40 kilometres north of Fort McMurray, Alberta, a small town 440 kilometres north of Edmonton (Exhibit 1). In 1977, Fort McMurray's total population was approximately 11,000 people. Syncrude needed a highly trained work force. However, due to the remoteness of the location of the production facility, it was difficult to attract and retain these people. Nevertheless, people from all over the world were attracted to the site. The birth of SCL created prosperity in this small town. In a short period of time, the population level doubled.

Opportunities also became available for many of the natives in this northern part of Alberta. Those natives with proper qualifications were hired as part of the production team. For others, employment opportunities developed with many native-owned businesses including a transportation contract to provide transportation for SCL employees travelling from Fort McMurray to the plant site during the day and also between the different production areas located on the plant site. This contract provided the native community of Fort McKay with over one million dollars in revenue annually.

Ownership of SCL was spread among eight different Canadian resource companies (Exhibit 1) who took the end product of synthetic crude oil in proportion to their ownership holdings.

The original project's cost was approximately 2.3 billion dollars, and by 1982, Syncrude had already produced its 100 millionth barrel of synthetic crude oil. The company's goal for 1985 was to produce its 200 millionth barrel.

PRODUCTION PROCESS

Unlike conventional oil operations, Syncrude did not explore for and locate oil under the ground, sink a well, and pump the oil out. Instead, it had to convert the oil from one form, bitumen in sand, into the final form of crude oil (Exhibit 2). This process was relatively more expensive per barrel than the conventional approach of pumping crude oil.

Mining

In order to remove the oil sands from the ground, a layer of overburden (earth and muskeg) approximately 22 metres thick had to be removed. Removal of the overburden was accomplished using electric shovels. The overburden was taken away by giant 170 and 200 tonne trucks. Selected portions of the overburden were used during reclamation of the mined land.

Once the overburden was removed, it was possible for the oil sands to be mined from the open pit. Excavation was performed utilizing SCL's four huge draglines. Each dragline, which was originally purchased and assembled in 1978 at a unit cost of $30 million, had a boom that was 25 storeys high and a bucket as large as a two-car garage. The excavated oil sands were piled in windrows along the sides of the mine pit and were later transferred to conveyor belts via one of four bucketwheel reclaimers, machines each the length of a football field. The conveyors then transported the oil sands to the Extraction plant.

Extraction

Bitumen was separated from the sand by mixing steam, hot water, and caustic soda with the oil sands inside huge rotating tumblers to produce a slurry. The slurry was discharged into huge settling vessels where the sand and clays would settle out as tailings which were removed from the mixture. The remaining bitumen froth would be combined with naphtha, then centrifuged to remove the fine solids, contaminants, and excess water. The naphtha was then removed from the product by distillation and recovered for reuse. The result was pure bitumen. Over 90% of the bitumen orginally present in the mined ore was recovered from this process.

The sand and clay mixture that remained after bitumen extraction was pumped into a tailings pond. This pond was 17 square kilometres and designed to prevent contaminated water from discharging into the environment. Each year, an average of half a million barrels of bitumen were reclaimed from this tailings pond, as the remaining bitumen separated from the discharged water after extraction.

Upgrading

The upgrading process converted the bitumen into synthetic crude oil through a number of highly specialized process units. Primary upgrading involved feeding the bitumen into fluid cokers operating at a temperature of 530°C to break down the molasses-like bitumen in a process known as cracking. The resulting products were primarily naphtha and gas oil which were the main ingredients in synthetic crude oil. These were further processed in secondary upgrading. By products included fuel gas, and coke.

Secondary upgrading involved removing the nitrogen, sulphur, and metals from the naphtha and gas oil. Stabilizing the product by saturating the unsaturated hydrocarbons was accomplished by reacting the gas and naphtha with hydrogen at a controlled pressure and temperature in the presence of a catalyst.

Hydrogen sulphide was removed and later converted into elemental sulphur. The upgraded oil gas and naphtha were then combined into synthetic crude oil.

The resulting synthetic crude oil was sent to Edmonton, via underground pipelines. Some of the product was further processed in refineries near Edmonton while the remainder was sent to various refineries located from Montreal to Vancouver.

Utilities

Due to the immense power requirements of SCL, the company operated a utilities plant on site. The energy was supplied to the operation in a variety of forms including steam, electricity, compressed air, and nitrogen. The facilities provided SCL with enough energy to supply a city of 250,000 people per day. The Utilities Plant consisted of numerous energy-generating devices, including: five main boilers, along with a variety of associated facilities including four steam-driven and two gas turbine-driven generators, a demineralizing plant, seven water pumping stations, two forced draft cooling towers, and a potable water treatment plant. Operations within this plant were monitored from a state-of-the-art control room.

OPERATIONS OVERVIEW

During the early years of operations, each of these four different operating area groups was managed and run semi-independently. For example, the chemicals required in Upgrading were purchased independently of the chemicals bought in Extraction. It was common for each operating department to utilize different suppliers. Managers in Upgrading felt that there was no reason to know where or how the manager in Extraction was carrying out that end of the business. Another example of this operational unit independence was the fact that many of the same jobs existed across departments but were performed quite differently. For example, a work order written up in Mining was not the same in terms of format or process as a work order written up in Extraction. As a result of this operational independence, the firm did not always share a common focus. Goals were set by the individual operating units, and were not always coordinated with all the operating units.

Production costs per barrel of synthetic crude oil had varied over the past few years (Exhibit 3) as the production levels continued to increase (Exhibit 4). Last year, 1984, had been a poor year for SCL, partially due to a large plant-site fire. The fire caused an extensive shut-down within areas of the plant, resulting in higher production costs and lower production levels. By 1985, operations were back on track, and it appeared that the upcoming year would be the best since production start-up in 1978.

SYNCRUDE'S HEALTH CENTRE

Due to the nature and location of Syncrude's business, it was essential for the company to supply many of its own services. SCL had an emergency response department located on the plant site to ensure speedy reaction to accidents and fire. For similar reasons, the company set up its own on-site health centre, staffed with nurses, a doctor, and the facilities to deal with minor injuries. Most major injuries which occurred on the site were transferred to the Fort McMurray Hospital.

The SCL Health Centre was viewed as a necessary facility within the firm, as injuries were seen as "part of the job". The facility was used reactively, indicating that employees utilized the service usually only when they were injured or sick.

The mining department experienced the highest number of injured personnel among the operating units. These injuries included cuts, sprains, and bruises. Various severities of back sprains were the most common injuries experienced by the miners, due to the constant bending and lifting motions performed in the task. The cuts and bruises were usually received on fingers, arms, and heads.

The injuries experienced by employees within the extraction department were very similar to those experienced within the Mining department, with the exception of a higher frequency of burns to the arms. The most common injury within this operating unit was sprains to the back. Similar injury patterns were reported among workers in the Upgrading operations. Cut fingers and burned hands were also common injuries in this area.

The Utilities plant experienced the lowest frequency rate of employee injuries among the four operating units. The most common injuries reported were back sprains and burns to the hands.

Injury frequency rates were declining within SCL (Exhibit 5). It was believed that much of the decline was the result of the company progressing from a construction phase into the production phase in terms of operations. The firm felt that it was moving up the learning curve. The company was beginning to operate according to employee experience rather than from production theories or texts. Employees were learning how to perform their jobs more efficiently and effectively, thus leading to increased production rates, decreased injury rates, and decreased production costs.

The local medical community within Fort McMurray had over time developed ambivalent feelings toward the Syncrude plant. This was the result of seeing so many SCL employees pass through their facilities who had been injured on the job. The company was blamed by the medical community for these injuries. It was not clear how many of these injuries were the result of careless employees and how many were the result of company neglect. SCL had tried to create a friendly and co-operative working relationship within the medical community; however, reactions were cool and detached. Many doctors and nurses did not believe that SCL was a safe working environment for its employees.

EXISTING PROGRAMS

The existing programs at Syncrude looked at absenteeism and safety focusing on issues related to occupational injuries. The programs concentrated on how to treat problems when they occurred. The Syncrude approach included the following programs:

Emergency Responses

This consisted of fire and medical teams that were trained and equipped in first aid and trauma care as well as being capable of containing and dealing with fire, explosion, release of toxic chemicals, and evacuation type emergencies. The remote location of the production facility made these teams a necessity.

Disaster Plans

This program included plans to deal with major disasters in the area. As well, the personnel of Syncrude participated in simulation exercises for disasters, competed in provincial mine rescue competitions, and contributed to plans for mutual aid with local government emergency service units.

Disability Programs

The firm offered assistance to anyone who was disabled due to injury or illness. Over time, the insurance cost for disability was becoming greater.

Employee Assistance Program (EAP)

This program involved primarily assessment of the situation, using in-house staff who then referred the employee to the various government agencies that were involved in the type of problem. This program also offered a family advisor service primarily to welcome new people to the community and to inform them of the various activities and services available. The third aspect of this program was a critical stress briefing unit to provide counselling to personnel following a traumatic event on the job.

Attendance Management Program (AMP)

This element tracked the level of overall absenteeism as a percentage. When the level of absenteeism became too great, it was the task of the particular manager to admonish the employee for being absent.

Benefits

The firm supplied the usual array of benefits to cover disability periods, and pay medical and drug bills.

It was estimated that the cost of absenteeism and the attendant benefits package were costing the firm in the region of 36 million dollars a year.

Dr. Nickerson, the company's Chief Medical Officer, worked directly with the Vice President of Human Resources, Mr. Phil Lachambre. These two individuals were aware that the new mandate emphasizing safety was going to have an important impact upon their day-to-day operations. Their first priority was to develop some type of company-wide approach to increasing employee awareness and commitment to the new mandate. If safety and reliability were to be considered before production, employees had to be shown that management meant exactly this. Creating a new corporate culture within SCL would take much time and effort from all employees, from the President right down to the front-line worker.

Dr. Nickerson was certain that the implementation of a program to improve safety and health care would consequently result in new cost savings and production advantages. By determining the potential areas of significant cost savings, it would be possible to determine the most beneficial areas in which to direct company resources. Dr. Nickerson felt that it would be useful to lay out all of the areas of current cost incurrence, and the areas of potential cost savings.

Exhibit 1

SYNCRUDE CANADA LIMITED OWNERSHIP

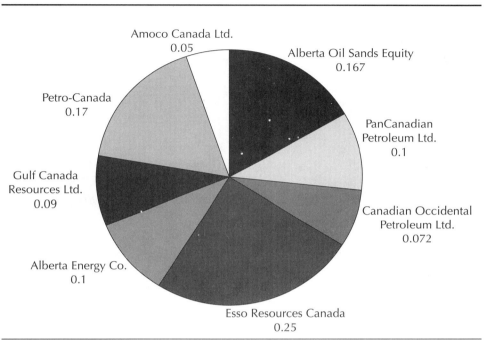

Exhibit 3

PRODUCTS PER BARREL OF BITUMEN

Products per barrel bitumen:

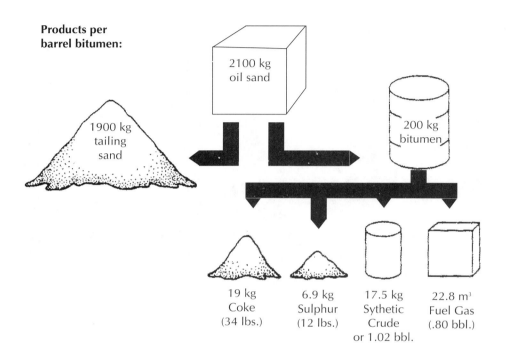

Exhibit 3

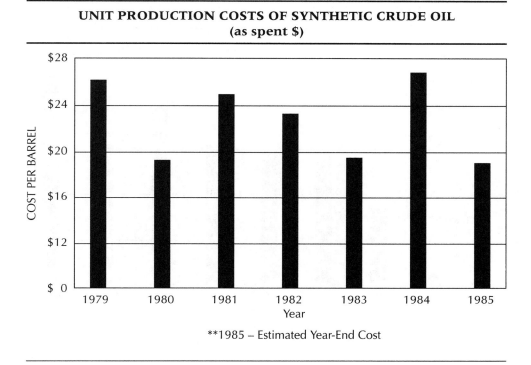

UNIT PRODUCTION COSTS OF SYNTHETIC CRUDE OIL
(as spent $)

**1985 – Estimated Year-End Cost

Exhibit 4

PRODUCTION LEVELS OF SYNTHETIC CRUDE OIL

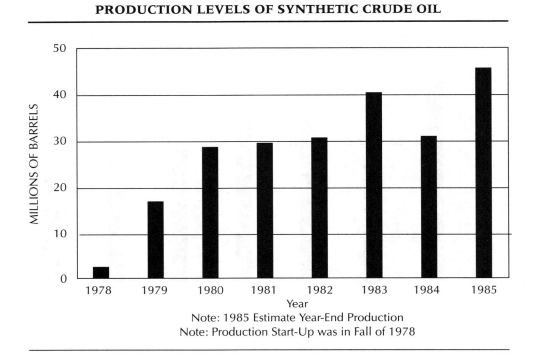

Note: 1985 Estimate Year-End Production
Note: Production Start-Up was in Fall of 1978

Exhibit 5

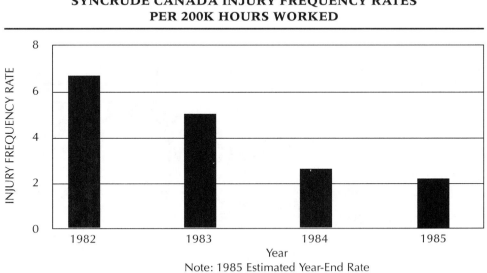

SYNCRUDE CANADA INJURY FREQUENCY RATES
PER 200K HOURS WORKED

Note: 1985 Estimated Year-End Rate

SYNCRUDE CANADA LIMITED— THE LOSS MANAGEMENT PROGRAM

Randolph Kudar*

Five years ago, Mr. Ralph Shepherd, the President and Chief Executive Officer of Syncrude Canada Limited (SCL) had proclaimed that

> Safety and Reliability are Number 1.
> Production will follow.

would be the operating mandate for the firm. During this period, several programs and activities had been undertaken to implement the mandate. It seemed a suitable time to assess what had been achieved and what other steps, if any, needed to be taken.

BACKGROUND

Syncrude Canada Limited was in the business of extracting bitumen (a heavy molasses-like substance) from the Athabasca Oil Sands, and upgrading it into synthetic crude oil. The company was incorporated on December 18, 1964, and was authorized to build a plant capable of producing 80,000 barrels of oil per day. Site preparations commenced in December 1973. The plant commenced production in July 1976. By the fall of 1978, the capacity agreement had been amended several times, with a final approved capacity of 129,000 barrels per day. Since this time, SCL had increased to over 165,000 barrels per day and had developed into the world's largest producer of synthetic crude oil and supplied Canada with over 11% of its national crude oil requirements.

SCL's production site was located at Mildred Lake, about 40 kilometres north of Fort McMurray, Alberta, a small town that was 440 kilometres north of Edmonton. In 1977, Fort McMurray's total population was approximately 11,000 people. The birth of SCL created prosperity in this small town. The population level doubled as people from all over the world were attracted to the site.

Opportunities also became available for many of the natives in this northern part of Alberta. Those natives with proper qualifications were hired as part of the production team. For others, employment opportunities developed with many native-owned businesses including a transportation contract to provide transportation for SCL employees travelling from Fort McMurray to the plant site during the day and also between the different production areas located on the plant site. This contract provided the native community of Fort McKay with over one million dollars in revenue annually.

Ownership of SCL was spread among eight different Canadian resource companies (Exhibit 1), who took the end product of synthetic crude oil in proportion to their ownership holdings.

At this time, Syncrude employed about 4,400 people and another 1,000 contractors at the plant site. As the largest private sector employer in Alberta, SCL also generated about 16,000 other jobs annually in Canada.

LOSS MANAGEMENT SYSTEM

An analysis of the absentee data for Syncrude revealed that only 5.5% of all the absenteeism was linked to occupational injuries. Further analysis revealed that 80% of these injuries occurred because individuals did not comply with established procedures for operations. An additional 8.7% of the absenteeism was linked to non-occupational injuries. These included sports injuries, home injuries, and vehicle injuries. The remaining 85.3% of the absentees were associated with things other than injuries. The original systems used by the company focused totally upon absenteeism related to occupational injuries.

The decision to develop and implement a Loss Management System involved recognition that Syncrude needed a competitive weapon to survive in the crude oil business. Unlike their competitors who simply pumped crude oil from the ground, Syncrude had to transform bitumen into crude oil. This was a more expensive process. It was also felt that focusing on safety and reliability would help the company attract and retain the highly trained people that were needed.

The operations at SCL integrated a mine, a refinery, an extraction plant, and a utilities plant. From the open pit mine area which was about 31 square kilometres in size, the mining operation, using 170 tonne trucks, and draglines longer than a football field extracted the oil sand. This oil sand was transferred to the extraction plant where the bitumen was extracted. The resulting bitumen was upgraded into synthetic crude oil.

If the working conditions were unsafe, the results would include injuries, disabilities, and possibly death. If the processes and the equipment were unreliable, the results would be asset losses, and business interruptions. In all cases, the cost of a barrel of crude would be higher. However, if the efforts in Loss Management could reduce accidents and maintenance needs, the productivity of the firm would increase. With the increase in productivity, the profits would follow.

Goal

The Loss Management System was placed under the direction of the President. It was the intent of the system to create a safe and reliable workplace. Safety would mean that all the risks had been identified and evaluated. The employees could feel confident that precautions had been taken to minimize all potential losses. Reliability meant that there would be dependable equipment and efficient day-to-day operations on the site.

The goal of the system was stated as follows:

> *Identify, reduce, eliminate all potential incidents that adversely affect safety of individuals and reliability of production.*

Process

The development of the long-term plan for the Loss Management System was based upon a set of nine principles (see Exhibit 2). The process to implement the system involved four distinct phases.

The first phase was Risk Assessment. This phase utilized the knowledge of everyone in the workplace. Each unit undertook an analysis of how the process within its area functioned and what elements of that process could go wrong. Each potential problem or defect was then assessed in terms of the probability of the problem occurring and the possible impact that the problem would have on individuals and the operations. These problems were then ranked in order of importance. The personnel in each unit then made a commitment to address each of these problems that had been identified.

The second phase was the development of Standardized Procedures. It was recognized that there was a critical need to develop explicit operating procedures within each unit. This proved to be a very time-consuming and paper-intensive process. A major problem involved the risk of creating a highly bureaucratic approach to the development of these standards. The mandate for writing the standards was to "visualize it big — but keep it small". This phase sought simple but comprehensive statements of the procedures. The intent was to capture the proper and best practice but not to make the practice inflexible. The procedures were intended to present current practice.

The third phase was the introduction of training for all employees. The purpose of this phase was to ensure that every employee was provided with the proper tools to identify, reduce, and eliminate injury and loss on the job. The training involved how to operate the equipment properly, with specific emphasis on the operator's own safety and the reliability of the equipment.

The final phase of the process was Compliance. It was critical that compliance with safe operating procedures be enforced. This proved to be the most difficult step. The objective was to have every employee buy into the concept of safety and reliability first. The key was good communications. One approach involved the extensive use of videos. A second involved the assignment of responsibility for compliance to the appropriate levels within the unit. A third involved recognition for successful performance. Efforts were made to obtain top-notch data that would assist in establishing benchmarks for complying with the set procedures. A fourth element was the use of regular audits to identify problems and develop actions to correct deficiencies.

The overall intent of the process was to communicate the message of the system that the firm's actions and statements affirmed that a safe and reliable operation was its number one concern. This demanded hard work on the part of everyone to implement the process within each unit. It demanded vision and leadership and, to some extent, faith. The process took time to implement and become operational. It took perseverance in the face of other pressures to operate the business. Finally, it required consistency of purpose to keep it on track through the formative stages.

Programs

The Loss Management System included a number of different programs. Some of these programs previously existed within the firm. Others were new. Some of the programs involved in the system are described in the following section.

Pre-Employment

This program involved two elements. The first was a medical examination required of every new employee. The second element was a Job Advisement Record. This document listed the general and specific working conditions for each individual position. It described the physical skills, the medical condition, and the educational knowledge or certifications required for the position. It also listed the specific health standards that would be required by a doctor of an applicant for the position.

Health Hazard Assessment (HHA)

This program involved the systematic examination of the work environment and its operations. It identified and evaluated potential and existing hazards associated with the employee's work environment and the work practices. This assessment was carried out in each unit and each function of the entire operations of the firm including offices. It included assessments of lighting, air quality, and noise levels. Health surveillance activities were tied to areas where potential health hazards existed, and had not yet been eliminated. The standards to be met included those legislated by government, as well as those set by internal initiatives.

Chemical Management Information System (CMIS)

This program operated in all areas of Syncrude. It was the company method of compliance to the workplace hazardous materials identification legislation set by the government. It involved a team approach. At this time, over 2,200 different chemicals and materials were used at Syncrude. The program focused on worker education associated with these materials. In addition to requirements for labelling of materials, the program also centered on efforts to find suitable replacements for unsafe chemicals, and to simplify and reduce the number of chemicals purchased for similar applications. This program also included Industrial Hygiene Investigations. These efforts looked at heating and ventilating problems, workplace ergonomics, and odour concerns.

Health Promotion

This program relied heavily upon the findings of the HHA program. The program concentrated on initiating medical surveillance on the greatest opportunities for affecting absenteeism within the firm. A major thrust of the program was to concentrate on prevention rather than treatment. It looked at off-the-job safety efforts. It emphasized the promotion of early returns to work and the use of rehabilitation work. The medical monitoring of employees attempted to identify changes in individual health, to initiate treatment before the change became serious, and to foster rehabilitation from injuries.

Employee Assistance Program (EAP)

This program had existed within the firm prior to the establishment of the Loss Management System. Now it involved both self-referral and company-intiated referral for employees. A new step in the program required that all employees referred for performance reasons would be screened in a medical fashion to eliminate any possibility that the problem was caused by a medical condition that was not known to the firm. The program employed a counsellor and nurses. It included a personal support network office in Fort McMurray. This facility, supported by a regular grant from the firm, was staffed by non-employees. The program also included Family Advisor Support, which consisted of a social worker-type of role. The activities ranged from babysitting to funeral arrangements for deaths in the family. Other activities included new family visits and hospital visiting if requested. The intent of the program was to address employee problems at the beginning rather than when they became too complicated or too large. The efforts sought to try to prevent problems. Counselling was offered in the areas of stress awareness, substance abuse, and economics.

Rehabilitation Management Program

This program emphasized an early return to work for any employee. The objective was to restore employees either to their original, primary employment or to train them for a different job which would accommodate their disability. This program required the firm to identify rehabilitative work opportunities. The mandate was for the rehabilitation to be undertaken regardless of any budget limitations. It also emphasized the fact that disabled employees had a responsibility to undertake rehabilitation efforts. The proper handling of disability cases was included as a performance review item for managers in the same way that safety statistics were included. A Rehab Management Committee of Senior managers was created to oversee the program.

Attendance Management Program (AMP)

This was another program that had existed before the introduction of the Loss Management System. The focus of this program became one of identifying and assessing potential health problems before they became chronic problems. The tracking system for absenteeism converted from totalling the number of days missed to assessing the illness occasions of the employee. Thus, someone who missed 40 days with one illness was not of as much concern as the person who missed 2 days on 20 different occasions. The expectation of this program was that the monitoring would seek early recognition of issues such as harmful stress and substance abuse. It would also attempt to address absenteeism problems through a case control process.

Blue Cross Benefits

This program involved a tie-in with Blue Cross and its health statistics. It allowed Syncrude to track the pattern of its health costs with respect to drug costs and medical costs. Blue Cross provided health promotion literature for distribution within the firm.

RESULTS

With the implementation of the Loss Management System during the previous five years, efforts had been undertaken by Syncrude to measure and track changes in selected indicators regarding safety, reliability, and the possible consequences of achieving changes in these areas. During the past several years, management noted some of the following results.

Maintenance costs had been lowered, and production throughput had increased. In fact, production rates had increased annually, and by this time, the rate was almost 50% greater than in 1983. The unit cost per barrel and the maintenance cost per barrel of crude had dropped to the point where the synthetic crude oil from the oil sands was fast becoming Canada's most competitive and reliable source of new crude to replace conventional crude oil supplies. The equipment downtime had been reduced. Equipment throughput had increased.

There had been a substantial drop in human suffering at the firm in this period. Recordable injuries had declined steadily to 15% of the rate six years earlier. The rate of growth of Blue Cross drug claims had declined from 24% a year prior to the start of the Loss Management system to 5% per year for the latest period. Almost half of the visits to the medical centre were now for preventative purposes. Of these types of visits, blood pressure checks accounted for 40%. Management found that the employees were now extending the training in safety and personal health care to their treatment and care of the equipment.

Some data related to absenteeism (Exhibit 3) indicated several interesting trends. The number of employees at Syncrude had remained stable during the past five years. In this time, the turnover rate had declined by almost half from 9% to 5%. However, absenteeism as a percentage was higher by almost a full percentage point. It had increased from 3.1% in 1985 to 3.9% in 1990. First-aid injuries had declined from 548 in 1985 to 394 in 1990. Medical-aid injuries had also declined. Disabling injuries had significantly dropped from 59 in 1985 to 23 in 1990. The number of days lost due to injury was down from 816 in 1985 to 561 in the current year. There had never been any fatalities to Syncrude Employees.

It was felt that the role of management in the firm was changing. Now management was more involved in setting objectives. The managers were expected to spend more time measuring, analyzing, and stewarding performance. They spent more time and involvement in the review of work practices. They had more time to spend on the shop floor and to participate with other team members in addressing issues.

Exhibit 1

SYNCUDE CANADA LIMITED OWNERSHIP

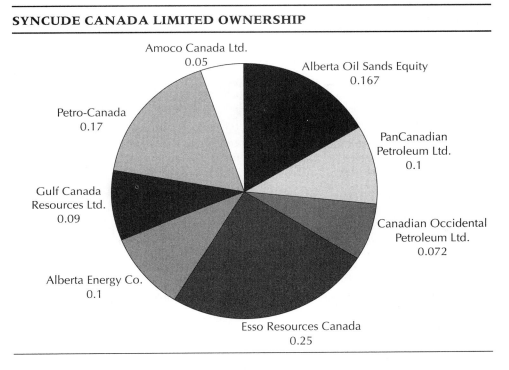

Exhibit 2

LOSS MANAGEMENT SYSTEM PRINCIPLES

1. Management is responsible for implementation of the program. Each unit must have a Loss Management Plan. The results will be part of the performance appraisal of management.

2. Compliance with policies, procedures, and practices is mandatory. Management and supervisors are responsible for setting the standards, communicating these standards, and measuring compliance with the standards.

3. All operating exposures and risks can be controlled. This risk management allows solutions to be found before an incident occurs, not afterwards. This applies to all contractors as well as employees.

4. All employees and contractors must be thoroughly trained to work safely, regardless of what area they operate in.

5. All objectives must be clear, measurable, and attainable. They must be understood by all involved. This allows evaluation of the efforts and determination of the changes that are needed.

6. Safe work practices must be implemented.

7. Workplace audits will be conducted to assess compliance with loss management standards.

8. All injuries and occupational illnesses can be prevented by using this approach to assess risk and to prevent occurrence of the problem.

9. Loss management will be part of the way we conduct our business. The corporate objectives and activities will reflect overall loss management goals.

Exhibit 3

SELECTED DATA

	1985	1986	1987	YEAR 1988	1989	1990	1991
Shipment Crude (m bbls)	46.9	47.4	50.0	54.9	54.0	57.1	60.3
Op cost per barrel	17.74	14.98	14.77	14.82	17.17	17.41	16.48
Injury Freq. (per 200k hr)	2.37	1.87	1.51	1.20	1.03	1.12	0.80
Number of Empl.	4,520	4,219	4,467	4,671	4,621	4,546	4,435
Turnover Rate %		9.1	7.8	7	8	6	5
Absenteeism %	3.1	3.2	3.4	3.5	4.1	3.9	3.2
Workforce/m bbl prod.	96	89	89	85	86	80	74
First Aid Inj	548	440	420	445	446	394	303
Medic Aid Inj	44	50	40	30	27	27	19
Disabling Inj.	59	25	24	23	20	23	15
Days Lost Inj.	816	531	553	468	688	561	531
Fatalities	0	0	0	0	0	0	0

FALCONBRIDGE LIMITED — REDUCING SO₂ EMISSIONS

Nola Buhr and Randolph Kudar*

Richard Laine, Director of Public Affairs for the Sudbury operations of Falconbridge Limited, was reviewing a press release (Exhibit 1) that had been prepared by the head office in Toronto. The press release, dated January 30, 1991, announced that Falconbridge had already met the 1994 government-mandated levels for sulphur dioxide (SO_2) emissions. However, Richard noticed that the press release didn't say anything about the costs and benefits of having reached these levels ahead of schedule.

Richard had formerly been the Superintendent of Technology for the smelter in Sudbury. He knew that the current success enjoyed by Falconbridge was the result of decades of research and development directed at reducing sulphur dioxide emissions. The need to reduce emissions had presented the Company with a great deal of uncertainty, some costly failures and some profitable successes.

Richard sat back and thought about the uncertainty, the failures and the successes. He wondered if there was a common thread in the management processes over the years that had ensured that success won out over uncertainty and failure.

THE COMPANY

Falconbridge was an international resource company engaged in the exploration, development, mining, processing and marketing of metals and minerals.

The Falconbridge group of companies had operations in Canada, Norway, the Dominican Republic, and Zimbabwe; marketing and sales offices in Toronto, Brussels, Pittsburgh, Tokyo, and Barbados; research laboratories in Canada and Norway; and exploration offices in Canada and abroad. Its products included nickel, ferronickel, copper, zinc, cobalt, cadmium, silver, gold, platinum group metals, various metal concentrates, and sulphuric acid. In September 1989, Noranda and Trelleborg AB became joint owners of Falconbridge, making Falconbridge a privately held company. Consolidated revenue for Falconbridge in 1990 was $2.03 billion dollars (Canadian).

Sudbury Operations

Falconbridge started as a company in Sudbury in 1928. Since then, the Sudbury operations (which actually take place in Falconbridge, Ontario, just outside of Sudbury) have focused on the mining, milling, and smelting of nickel-copper ores. In 1990, 2.8 million tonnes of ore were hoisted out of the ground which resulted in the production of 33,600 tonnes of nickel.

The ore in the Sudbury basin is mined not only for its nickel and copper but also for the valuable amounts of cobalt, gold, silver, and platinum that it contains. The ore-bearing minerals are pentlandite (which contains nickel), chalcopyrite (which contains copper) and pyrrhotite (which contains iron and sulphur). Sulfur is a significant component of all three minerals, but it is the sulphur in the pyrrhotite that is responsible for sulphur dioxide emissions. For the most part, the ore mined in Sudbury contains 7 times more sulphur than nickel. The challenge throughout the milling and smelting process is to reject the sulphur but retain the nickel, copper, and other valuable minerals.

The ore from underground is hoisted from five mines and then processed further in one of two mills. The first step is crushing. The ore is put through three stages of gyratory and cone crushers. The final stage of crushing reduces the ore to pass 13 mm.

Then the ore goes to a concentrator for grinding, flotation, and magnetic separation. The concentrators have three purposes: (1) to make concentrates containing the highest recoveries of nickel; (2) to make concentrates high in copper but low in nickel; and (3) to make further recoveries of nickel from the pyrrhotite.

The grinding is done in two stages. At the end of the first stage, the product is 60% minus 200 mesh. Then the product is re-ground to a size of 80% minus 325 mesh in order to release fine pentlandite.

The product is then concentrated by flotation techniques. During this process reagents are used in roughing, cleaning, and scavenging stages. The scavenger concentrates are passed through magnetic separators to collect the low nickel grade pyrrhotite for re-grinding and another stage of flotation. There is also a magnetic separation circuit which separates the magnetic pyrrhotite part and the non-magnetic part which contains particles of pentlandite and chalcopyrite. The pyrrhotite portion is re-ground and put through the flotation process again. The flotation concentrate from this process is added to the main stream of nickel-copper concentrate and loaded into rail tank cars in slurry form for delivery to the smelter.

The pyrrhotite tailings from the flotation process are rejected into tailings ponds where they are carefully controlled to avoid acidic effluent generation.

There are several stages of processing in the smelter. First, the slurry is filtered and then fed into a fluid bed roaster along with sand flux to reduce the thermal burden on the electric furnace. The concentrate is partially roasted at this stage for the oxidation of iron and sulphur. About 50% of the sulphur is removed.

This material is then subject to gas cleaning. A sulphur dioxide gas is released and transferred to the acid plant to be turned into sulphuric acid. The end product from the roaster is conveyed to two electric furnaces for smelting to produce a waste slag and furnace matte. The slag goes to the disposal area and furnace matte containing the metal values is processed in the converters for further removal of iron and sulphur. During the whole process the goal is to minimize the loss of nickel, copper, and cobalt to slag.

The final product of the smelter is nickel matte which is about 75 percent nickel plus copper. This matte is shipped to a Falconbridge company in Norway for refining.

EFFORTS TO REDUCE SO₂ EMISSIONS

There were several nickel mining companies in operation in Sudbury before Falconbridge started up in 1928. (The most notable of them, and the only one remaining, is INCO.) As a result, sulphur fumes had been a problem in Sudbury for a long time. A Sudbury area farmer quoted in the *Sudbury Star* in 1916 gave an indication of how the Sudbury community felt about smelter emissions:

"Some apologists say (cutting down sulphur emissions) can't be done. Nor it won't be done, as long as we fellows grin and bear it — as long as we keep spitting and coughing. These companies should be indicted tomorrow for maintaining a public nuisance."

Falconbridge made its first efforts to reduce sulphur dioxide emissions in the early 1950s. Over the years there have been three main approaches taken by Falconbridge to reducing SO₂ emissions: (1) increased pyrrhotite rejection in the mill; (2) increased degrees of roasting in the fluid bed roasters in the smelter; and (3) converter slag cleaning. Exhibit 2 illustrates, over time, how the sulphur content in the ore has been distributed during the milling and smelting process.

Pyrrhotite Rejection

The first efforts at reducing sulphur dioxide emissions began in 1953 with research on the pyrrhotite process and the development of a pyrrhotite treatment plant. The goal of these efforts was to reject the high sulphur and low nickel pyrrhotite in the mill before sending the feed to the smelter. At this time there was no government regulation controlling SO_2 emissions. Therefore, the motivation behind this research and development was economic: to maintain overall metal recoveries at a reduced cost per pound.

The pyrrhotite plant opened in 1955. However, due to a number of problems, it did not become fully operational until 1956. The technology at the plant involved a roasting process to burn the sulphur and separate the nickel and the iron.

Falconbridge undertook many additional research and development efforts throughout the 1950s and 1960s in order to increase the grade of material smelted and remove more waste in the concentrating process. For example, in 1961 and 1962, re-grind and magnetic separation equipment was installed in the milling plants. The installation of this equipment resulted in continued improvement in metal recoveries. By upgrading the quality of the smelter feed, Falconbridge could increase the nickel produced per tonne smelted.

The nickel-iron refinery and sulphur recovery plant commissioned in 1968 constituted one of the more significant failures. The refinery and plant were designed to recover increasing amounts of sulphur from the pyrrhotite and the mill concentrate so that the resulting elemental sulphur could be sold as a product. However, the refinery turned out not to be viable as a result of several technical and economic factors. The plant only worked well at half capacity. At the same time, the price of coal which was used to fire the process doubled. The plant was closed in early 1973 and Falconbridge walked away from a $65 million investment (measured in 1973 dollars which was equal to $235 million in 1988 dollars).

In November 1969, the Ontario government issued its first control order regarding SO_2 emissions. The control order required a 50% reduction in SO_2 emission from the current (1969) rate of 1,028 tonnes per day to 465 tonnes per day by December 31, 1975. This order focused on ambient air quality only and was motivated by a public desire to improve the local air quality around Sudbury.

At this time the super stack approach to pollution control was acceptable because it improved local air quality (by dispersing the pollution to a location outside of Sudbury). However, the super stack concept was not an option for Falconbridge. The Falconbridge site was located about 20 kilometres outside of Sudbury, three to four kilometres away from the airport. Therefore, any super stack would be extremely hazardous for air travel. So, rather than disperse the pollution, Falconbridge had to take a process approach to reducing sulphur dioxide emissions.

In response to the control order, Falconbridge commissioned the Smelter Environmental Improvement Project (SEIP) in 1969. It was recognized that the current technological limits had been reached on the rejection of pyrrhotite. It would now be necessary to focus on the smelting process which would be more costly than pyrrhotite rejection in the mill.

Falconbridge also had other motivation to develop new smelter technology: (i) the internal working environment was very dusty and working conditions needed to be improved; (ii) the current process was labour intensive and, therefore, very costly — the economic performance of the smelter was not satisfactory; (iii) there was a desire for improved metallurgical performance (a desire to recover more nickel in an economically efficient manner); and (iv) the old blast furnace which was put into use in 1930 had a limited capacity. Therefore, with a multi-faceted motivation Falconbridge began to develop the technology to meet the mandated level of emissions.

In 1971, the pyrrhotite plant operation was reduced to 80% of capacity throughout the year in order to meet government regulations. In 1972, after 17 years of operation, the pyrrhotite plant was closed permanently in order to comply with the requirements of the Air Management Branch of the Ontario Government. The pyrrhotite plant had reduced the sulphur in the concentrate going to the smelter but the process resulted in a red plume of smoke being dispersed in the area.

Because of the failure of the nickel-iron refinery and the shut-down of the pyrrhotite treatment plant, Falconbridge knew that it would have serious problems in meeting the government deadlines for reduced sulphur dioxide emissions. After many meetings with government officials, the 1975 government deadlines for the control order were extended to 1979.

However, despite the failures, during the 20-year period from 1950 to 1970, sulphur dioxide emissions were almost halved (Exhibit 3). Emissions were reduced from the 1950 levels of 15.6 tonnes of sulphur dioxide emitted per tonne of nickel produced to the 1970 levels of 8.1 tonnes of sulphur dioxide emitted per tonne of nickel produced.

Increased Degrees of Roast

The Smelter Environmental Improvement Project resulted in a new fluid bed roaster, electric furnace smelter, and a sulphuric acid plant commissioned in 1978. The research and development for SEIP was carried out from 1969 to 1975. During the process most of the nickel and copper smelters of the world were visited to transfer the latest technology.

The new smelter was designed on the basis of 50% sulphur elimination in roasting. There were several problems associated with raising the roasting temperature higher to eliminate more sulphur. These problems were: increased metal losses in the slag; increased reduction burdens in the electric furnace; high electric furnace off-gas temperatures; high matte and slag temperatures causing high-risk of refractory failure; and electric furnace hearth build-up.

From 1970 to 1979 Falconbridge spent 98 million dollars (equivalent to 215 million 1988 dollars) on research and development, plus capital costs, to reduce emissions by process revisions which resulted in fixation of sulphur dioxide into sulphuric acid.

The new smelter was deemed an excellent commercial success. It allowed the Company to meet the 1979 Ontario Ministry of Environment Control Order limiting SO_2 emissions to 154 kilotonnes per year. This resulted in a production capacity of 88 million pounds of nickel per year with a 50% sulphur elimination roast.

Mineral prices in the early 1980s were so low that mining companies were unable to recover their costs. The work force at Falconbridge in Sudbury was slashed from 4,000 at the end of 1981 to 2,650 at the end of 1982. The massive lay-offs could not have been done without the new technology that resulted from the Smelter Environmental Improvement Project. These lay-offs were seen as essential for the survival of the Company.

Other positive financial outcomes from the Smelter Environmental Improvement Project have been the acid plant and the custom feed operations.

The development of an acid plant in 1978 produced a commercial product, sulphuric acid. Unfortunately, because of the ongoing low prices for sulphuric acid, the project has only been recovering operating costs and not capital costs.

When the new smelter came on-line in 1978, it was built with additional capacity. As a result, Falconbridge started a custom feed operation in 1982. This was essentially a recycling operation. Custom feed was defined as anything that was processed by the smelter that did not originate in Falconbridge's Sudbury mines. The custom feed operations recycled three types of material: (i) distressed material that would otherwise go to landfill, (ii) marginal material such as miscast pieces; and (iii) because of Falconbridge's unique world position, material containing cobalt. Falconbridge became the largest recycler of cobalt in the world.

Materials put through the custom feed operations provided revenue (in excess of cost) to Falconbridge for performing the service and returned the value of the recovered metal to the customer. Even in the case of material that would otherwise go to landfill, customers ended up paying significantly less for recycling than they would for landfill fees.

Despite several years of financial losses in the early 1980s, funding for research and development to reduce sulphur dioxide emissions continued to be provided. Exploration and mine development are two areas of capital expenditure that are critical for the long-term viability of a mining company. However, rather than abandon efforts to reduce SO_2 emissions, research and development efforts continued throughout the 1980s and focused on attempting to overcome the constraints to higher roasting temperatures. The major means to reduce SO_2 emissions further was to increase the degree of sulphur elimination in the fluid-bed roasters to 65% to fix more sulphur as acid.

From 1980 to 1988 Falconbridge spent $20 million dollars on research and development and process improvements in the mill and the smelter.

Converter Slag Cleaning

The key reason for developing a new process for converter slag cleaning was the need to counteract high metal losses caused by increased degrees of roast. A patentable converter slag cleaning operation was developed and implemented in 1986.

By cleaning the slag before recycling it to the electric furnace, Falconbridge had decreased the reduction burning of smelting by 20% and increased the recovery of cobalt by 15% and nickel by 0.3%.

This development resulted in the following capabilities to reduce sulphur dioxide emissions:

(1) Higher degrees of roast were possible. The build-up formation in the hearth of the electric furnace was controllable and the slag losses of metal were acceptable.

(2) Secondary recycle material containing nickel, copper and cobalt could be fed to the smelter economically because of the higher cobalt recoveries. This recycle material combined with sulphur on producing the final matte which reduced the emissions of sulphur dioxide.

The Countdown Acid Rain Program

As a result of an ongoing commitment to reduce sulphur dioxide emissions, Falconbridge undertook a number of feasibility studies in 1985 in order to develop a strategy and an action plan to reduce smelter emissions further. Therefore, Falconbridge was already well on its way to developing a plan to meet the reduced emissions levels when the next set of government regulations were introduced.

The Countdown Acid Rain program was announced by the Ontario Ministry of the Environment in December 1985 and was addressed to four companies. Falconbridge was one of the four companies that combined contributed about 80% of the SO_2 emission produced in Ontario. The new government regulations required Falconbridge to reduce its Sudbury SO₂ emissions level from 154 kilotonnes per year to 100 kilotonnes per year by 1994. All four companies were given until December 31, 1988 to report to the ministry on the best available technology and design needed to meet the new required limits.

In its December 31, 1988, report Falconbridge detailed its plans and indicated that capital expenditure of $38 million would be required to meet the government mandated emission levels.

In its January 1991 report to the Ontario government, Falconbridge announced that it had achieved the operational capability in the Sudbury smelter to not exceed 100 kilotonnes per year of sulphur dioxide emissions. In the same report Falconbridge made a public commitment to voluntarily reduce sulphur dioxide emissions to 75 kilotonnes per year by 1998.

RICHARD'S THOUGHTS

As Richard reflected on the press release he thought about the successes and failures throughout the years. The reduction of sulphur dioxide emissions was a victim of the law of diminishing returns. It was costing the Company more and more to eliminate the same amounts of sulphur dioxide emissions. Over the years it had been successful at meeting government regulations (Exhibit 4) and right now it was ahead of schedule. The Company had already publicly stated that it would go beyond government limits. But how much farther should the Company go to lower sulphur dioxide emissions on a voluntary basis? Or, would there come a day when the government would demand zero emissions?

Exhibit 1

FALCONBRIDGE

Falconbridge Limited
Box 40, Commerce Court West
Toronto, Canada M5L 1B4
Telephone 416/863-7000
Telex 065-24211 Rapifax 364-8986

FOR IMMEDIATE RELEASE

January 30, 1991, TORONTO, Ontario — Falconbridge Limited announced today that it is able to meet the Ontario government's 1994 "Countdown Acid Rain" goal three years ahead of schedule. The government limit for sulphur dioxide emissions from the company's Sudbury smelter is 100 kilotonnes per year by 1994.

Since 1970, Falconbridge has been operating under increasingly stringent Ontario government control orders which cap its allowable levels of emissions. Falconbridge has consistently operated well under these limits. For example, while producing 34 kilotonnes of nickel in 1990, the company released 70 kilotonnes of sulphur dioxide, less than half of the government's current allowable limit of 154 kilotonnes.

Some of this was achieved by reduced output from the Sudbury smelter. The major challenge has been to meet the Ontario government's target while operating at full production. According to Mike Amsden, Falconbridge's Vice-President of Environmental Services, this is now possible: "Even operating at 40 kilotonnes of nickel per year, we are now confident that we can keep sulphur dioxide emissions under 100 kilotonnes per year."

This is due to a number of technical and operational improvements which have been developed and implemented over the years. The installation of a new smelter and acid plant in 1978, along with significant additional process improvements through the 1980s, contributed to reducing the tonnes of sulphur dioxide emitted per tonne of nickel produced from 6.5 in 1975 to 1.9 in 1990.

During the next three years the company will continue to invest capital in both the mill and smelter and will conduct ongoing research and development to find ways to further reduce sulphur dioxide emissions and to do so as quickly as possible. Said Mike Amsden, "Some time ago, we had set a voluntary target of 75 kilotonnes of sulphur dioxide per year at full smelter capacity, to be achieved by 1998. We want to reach that before 1998."

-30-

For further information:
Michael Amsden, Vice-President of Environmental Services (416) 863-7214
Richard Laine, Director of Public Affairs, Sudbury (705) 693-2761
Colleen Wilkinson, Director of Public Affairs, Toronto (416) 863-7066

Exhibit 2[1]

SULPHUR DISTRIBUTION

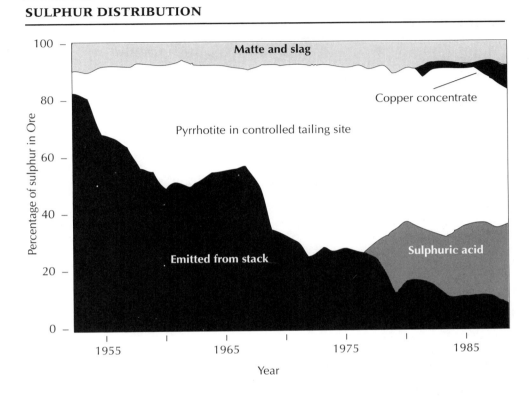

[1] From *Report Required by 31st Day of December 1988 Under Ontario Regulation 661/85 of the Environmental Protection Act for The Falconbridge Smelter Complex – 1994*, Toronto: Falconbridge Limited, 22 December 1988, p. 3.

Exhibit 3[2]

HISTORY OF SULPHUR DIOXIDE EMISSIONS PER TONNE OF NICKEL PRODUCED AT THE SMELTER IN FALCONBRIDGE, ONTARIO

Year	Tonnes of Sulphur Dioxide Emitted per Tonne of Nickel Produced
1950	15.6
1955	14.2
1960	9.8
1965	9.1
1970	8.1
1975	6.5
1980	4.1
1985	2.4
1987	2.2
1988	2.1

---

[2] From Report required by 31st Day of December 1988 under Ontario Regulation 661/85 of the Environmental Protection Act for the Falconbridge Smelter Complex—1994, Toronto: Falconbridge Limited, 22 December 1988, p.4

Exhibit 4[3]

FALCONBRIDGE ANNUAL SO₂ EMISSIONS

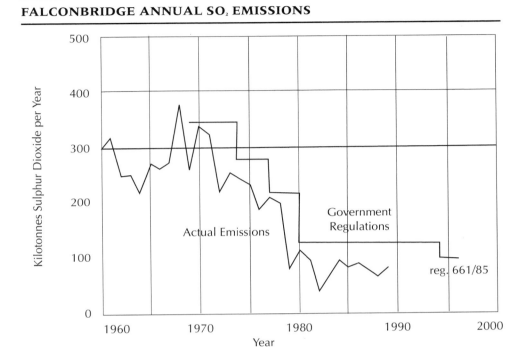

[3] (From *SO₂ Abatement Program Progress Report No. 4, July – December 1990*, Toronto: Falconbridge, Limited 30 January 1991).